Encounters with Nineteenth-Century Continental Philosophy

New Research in the History of Western Philosophy

VOLUME 4

The titles published in this series are listed at *brill.com/nrhw*

Encounters with Nineteenth-Century Continental Philosophy

Discussions and Debates

Edited by

Jon Stewart
Patricia C. Dip

BRILL

LEIDEN | BOSTON

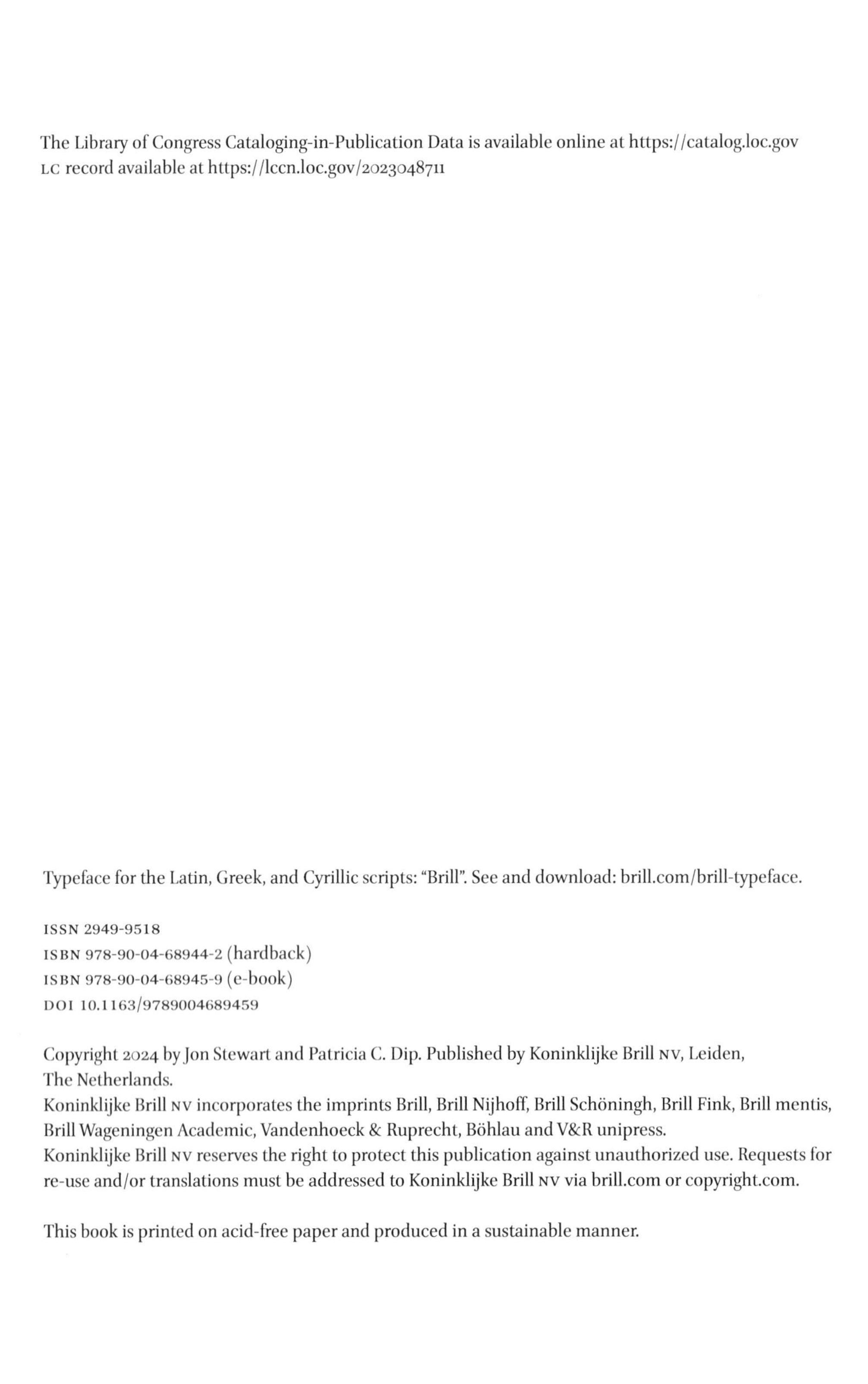

The Library of Congress Cataloging-in-Publication Data is available online at https://catalog.loc.gov
LC record available at https://lccn.loc.gov/2023048711

Typeface for the Latin, Greek, and Cyrillic scripts: "Brill". See and download: brill.com/brill-typeface.

ISSN 2949-9518
ISBN 978-90-04-68944-2 (hardback)
ISBN 978-90-04-68945-9 (e-book)
DOI 10.1163/9789004689459

This book is printed on acid-free paper and produced in a sustainable manner.

Contents

PART 3
Philosophical Anthropology and Social Sciences

PART 4
Politics and Social Criticism

Acknowledgments

This volume was produced in the context of a joint international project entitled "Research in Post-Hegelian Philosophy." The institutional participants in the project were the "Programa de Investigación en Filosofía Poshegeliana" at the Instituto de Ciencias at the Universidad Nacional de General Sarmiento and the Department of Social Philosophy and Philosophical Anthropology at the Institute of Philosophy, Slovak Academy of Sciences. We would like to thank all the contributing authors for their cooperation in realizing this work.

In Argentina we would like to thank National Council for Scientific and Technical Research (CONICET) and the Universidad Nacional de General Sarmiento for supporting the research we have made for years, and which has prepared the way for the publication of this volume. In Slovakia we are thankful to the Slovak Research and Development Agency for its support of the project "Philosophical Anthropology in the Context of Current Crises of Symbolic Structures" (APVV-20-0137).

Abbreviations

Feuerbach's Writings

EC	*The Essence of Christianity*, trans. by George Elliot, New York: Prometheus Books 1989.
EF	*The Essence of Faith according to Luther*, trans. by Melvin Cherno, New York: Harper & Row 1967.
FPD	"Fragments Concerning the Characteristics of My Philosophical Development," in *The Fiery Brook: Selected Writings*, trans. and ed. by Zawar Hafi, London: Verso 2012, pp. 265–296.
LER	*Lectures on the Essence of Religion*, trans. by Ralph Manheim, New York: Harper & Row 1967.
NR	"Necessity of a Reform of Philosophy," in *The Fiery Brook: Selected Writings*, trans. and ed. by Zawar Hafi, London: Verso 2012, pp. 145–152.
PPF	"Principles of the Philosophy of the Future," in *The Fiery Brook: Selected Writings*, trans. and ed. by Zawar Hafi, London: Verso 2012, pp. 175–244.
SW	*Sämtliche Werke*, vols. 1–12, ed. by Wilhelm Bolin and Friedrich Jodl, Stuttgart-Bad Cannstatt: Fromman Verlag-Gunther Holzboog 1959–1964.
WC	*Das Wesen des Christenthums*, vol. 5, in *Gesammelte Werke*, vols. 1–21, ed. by Werner Schuffenhauer, Berlin: Akademie Verlag 2000–2022.

Freud's Writings

SE	*The Standard Edition of the Complete Works of Sigmund Freud*, vols. 1–24, trans. from the German under the General Editorship of James Strachey, in Collaboration with Anna Freud, assisted by Alix Starchey and Alan Tyson, London: The Hogarth Press 1953–74.

Hegel's Writings

Aesthetics I-II	*Hegel's Aesthetics: Lectures on Fine Art*, vols. 1–2, trans. by T.M. Knox, Oxford: Clarendon Press 1975, 1998.

Jub — *Sämtliche Werke. Jubiläumsausgabe in 20 Bänden*, ed. by Hermann Glockner, Stuttgart: Friedrich Frommann Verlag 1928–41.

LPR — *Lectures on the Philosophy of Religion*, vols. 1–3, ed. by Peter C. Hodgson, trans. by Robert F. Brown, P.C. Hodgson and J.M. Stewart with the assistance of H.S. Harris, Berkeley: University of California Press 1984–87.

VPR — *Vorlesungen* über *die Philosophie der Religion*, Parts 1–3, ed. by Walter Jaeschke, Hamburg: Felix Meiner 1983–85, 1993–95. (This corresponds to vols. 3–5 in the edition, Hegel, *Vorlesungen. Ausgewählte Nachschriften und Manuskripte*, vols. 1–17, Hamburg: Meiner 1983–2008. Part 1, *Einleitung. Der Begriff der Religion* = vol. 3. Part 2, *Die Bestimmte Religion. a: Text* = vol. 4a. Part 2, *Die Bestimmte Religion. b: Anhang* = vol. 4b. Part 3, *Die vollendete Religion* = vol. 5.)

Kierkegaard's Writings

CA — *The Concept of Anxiety*, trans. by Reidar Thomte in collaboration with Albert B. Anderson, Princeton: Princeton University Press 1980. (*KW*, vol. 8.)

CI — *The Concept of Irony; Schelling Lecture Notes*, trans. by Howard V. Hong and Edna H. Hong, Princeton: Princeton University Press 1989. (*KW*, vol. 2.)

CUP1 — *Concluding Unscientific Postscript*, vols. 1–2, trans. by Howard V. Hong and Edna H. Hong, Princeton: Princeton University Press 1992, vol. 1. (*KW*, vol. 12.1.)

EO1 — *Either/Or 1*, trans. by Howard V. Hong and Edna H. Hong, Princeton: Princeton University Press 1987. (*KW*, vol. 3.)

EO2 — *Either/Or 2*, trans. by Howard V. Hong and Edna H. Hong, Princeton: Princeton University Press 1987. (*KW*, vol. 4.)

EPW — *Early Polemical Writings: From the Papers of One Still Living; Articles from Student Days; The Battle between the Old and the New Soap-Cellars*, trans. by Julia Watkin, Princeton: Princeton University Press 1990. (*KW*, vol. 1.)

FT — *Fear and Trembling; Repetition*, trans. by Howard V. Hong and Edna H. Hong, Princeton: Princeton University Press 1983. (*KW*, vol. 6.)

KJN — *Kierkegaard's Journals and Notebooks*, vols. 1–11, ed. by Niels Jørgen Cappelørn, Alastair Hannay, David Kangas, Bruce H. Kirmmse, George Pattison, Vanessa Rumble and K. Brian Söderquist, Princeton and Oxford: Princeton University Press 2007–2020.

KW	*Kierkegaard's Writings*, vols. 1–26, trans. by Howard V. Hong and Edna H. Hong, Princeton: Princeton University Press 1978–2000.
P	*Prefaces*, trans. by Todd W. Nichol, Princeton: Princeton University Press 1998. (*KW*, vol. 9.)
PC	*Practice in Christianity*, trans. by Howard V. Hong and Edna H. Hong, Princeton: Princeton University Press 1991. (*KW*, vol. 20.)
PV	*The Point of View*, trans. by Howard V. Hong and Edna H. Hong, Princeton: Princeton University Press 1998. (*KW*, vol. 22.)
SKS	*Søren Kierkegaards Skrifter*, vols. 1–28, K1–K28, ed. by Niels Jørgen Cappelørn, Joakim Garff, Johnny Kondrup, et al., Copenhagen: Gad Publishers 1997–2012.
SLW	*Stages on Life's Way*, trans. by Howard V. Hong and Edna H. Hong, Princeton: Princeton University Press 1988. (*KW*, vol. 11.)
SUD	*The Sickness unto Death*, trans. by Howard V. Hong and Edna H. Hong, Princeton: Princeton University Press 1980. (*KW*, vol. 19.)
TA	*Two Ages: The Age of Revolution and the Present Age, A Literary Review*, trans. by Howard V. Hong and Edna H. Hong, Princeton: Princeton University Press 1978. (*KW*, vol. 14.)
WL	*Works of Love*, trans. by Howard V. Hong and Edna H. Hong, Princeton: Princeton University Press 1995. (*KW*, vol. 16.)

Marx's Writings

Capital	*Capital: A Critique of Political Economy*, trans. by Ben Fowkes, London and New York: Penguin Books in association with New Left Review 1982.
Critique	*Critique of Hegel's Philosophy of Right*, trans. by Annette Jolin and Joseph O'Malley, New York: Cambridge University Press 1982.

Nietzsche's Writings

BGE	*Beyond Good and Evil: Prelude to a Philosophy of the Future* and *On the Genealogy of Morality*, trans. by Adrian Del Caro in *The Complete Works of Friedrich Nietzsche*, vol. 8, Stanford: Stanford University Press 2014.
EH	*Ecce Homo*, in *The Case of Wagner, Twilight of the Idols, The Antichrist, Ecce Homo, Dionysus Dithyrambs,* and *Nietzsche Contra Wagner*, translated (in various configurations) by Adrian Del Caro, Carol Diethe, Duncan Large, George H. Leiner, Paul S. Loeb, Alan D.

	Schrift, David F. Tinsley, and Mirko Wittwar, with an afterword by Andreas Urs Sommer, in *The Complete Works of Friedrich Nietzsche*, vol. 9, Stanford, CA: Stanford University Press 2021.
GM	*On the Genealogy of Morality*, in *Beyond Good and Evil: Prelude to a Philosophy of the Future* and *On the Genealogy of Morality*, trans. by Adrian Del Caro in *The Complete Works of Friedrich Nietzsche*, vol. 8, Stanford: Stanford University Press 2014.
GS	*The Gay Science*, trans. by Walter Kaufmann, New York: Vintage Books 1974.
TI	*Twilight of the Idols* in *The Case of Wagner*, *Twilight of the Idols*, *The Antichrist*, *Ecce Homo*, *Dionysus Dithyrambs*, and *Nietzsche Contra Wagner*, translated (in various configurations) by Adrian Del Caro, Carol Diethe, Duncan Large, George H. Leiner, Paul S. Loeb, Alan D. Schrift, David F. Tinsley, and Mirko Wittwar, with an afterword by Andreas Urs Sommer, in *The Complete Works of Friedrich Nietzsche*, vol. 9, Stanford, CA: Stanford University Press 2021.

Notes on Contributors

Alejandro Peña Arroyave
is a graduate from Antioquia University (Colombia), with a thesis about Søren Kierkegaard and the aesthetics of German Romanticism. He earned his doctorate in Philosophy at Salvador University (Argentina) with a thesis about the dialectics of melancholy in Søren Kierkegaard's thought. He currently teaches at the School of Philosophy, Letters and Oriental Studies of the University of El Salvador, at the National University of La Matanza and at ADEN International Business School (Argentina). He is a member of several research groups linked to post-Hegelian philosophy. He was a Doctoral Fellow at National Council for Scientific and Technical Research (CONICET). He is part of the Editorial Committee of the journal *El arco y la lira Tensiones y debates* and of the journal *Nuevo Pensamiento*. He has published articles in academic journals and book chapters as well as participated in conferences and congresses.

Kristína Bosáková
is an Associate Professor at the Department of Philosophy at the Pavol Josef Šafárik University in Košice, Slovakia and a collaborator of the Arbeitsstelle Internationale Feuerbachforschung am Institut für Erziehungswissenschaft, Westfälische Wilhelms Universität in Münster, Germany. She works in the field of nineteenth- and twentieth-century Continental philosophy with a specialization in German philosophy, above all Hegel, Feuerbach and Gadamer. She co-edited a special issue of the *Studies in East European Thought* dedicated to the Czech philosopher and dissident, Jan Patočka. She has participated in research projects sponsored by the Fulbright Commission and the Slovak Research and Development Agency. Her recent works include, *Gadamer a nemecká filozofia*, Košice: UPJŠ 2021; "Against the Self-Sufficiency of Reason: The Concept of Corporeity in Feuerbach and Patočka," in *Studies in East European Thought*, vol. 73, no. 3, 2021, pp. 327–345; "Hegel and Niethammer on the Educational Practice in Civil Society" (co-authored with M. Bykova), in *Journal of Philosophy of Education*, vol. 55, no. 1, 2021, pp. 1–27; "Friedrich Feuerbach und G.W.F. Hegel. Hegel und Friedrich Feuerbach im Gespräch über Religion, Christentum und Liebe," in *Philosophie und Pädagogik der Zukunft. Ludwig und Friedrich Feuerbach im Dialog*, ed. by Stephan Schlüter, Thassilo Polcik, and Jan Thumann, Münster: Waxmann Verlag 2018, pp. 153–169; "El concepto de armonía en la recepción hermenéutica gadameriana de la filosofía kantiana," in *Bajo Palabra*, no. 18, 2018, pp. 43–59.

Nassim Bravo
is a Research Fellow and Associate Professor at the Institute of Humanities, Universidad Panamericana. He is the head of the line of research on philosophy of religion at the same university. He is one of the editors of the journal *Estudios Kierkegaardianos. Revista de Filosofía*. He has translated several works by Søren Kierkegaard into Spanish such as *Para un examen de conciencia* (2008), *Postscriptum no científico y definitivo a las Migajas filosóficas* (2009), and *Prefacios* (2011). He worked as the head translator of the Spanish translation of Kierkegaard's journals and papers (2011–2021). He has published a number of articles and chapters in the field of Kierkegaard studies and Golden Age Denmark, including, more recently, "Heiberg's 'A Soul after Death': A Comedic Wake-Up Call for the Age" (2020), "The Faust Project in Kierkegaard's Early Journals" (2020), "In Search of 'That Archimedean Point': The Development of Selfhood in Kierkegaard's Journal of Gilleleje" (2021), and "Johan Ludvig Heiberg y su diagnóstico de la crisis de la época en la Edad de Oro de Dinamarca" (2022). He co-edited (with Gustavo Esparza) *The Bounds of Myth. The Logical Path from Action to Knowledge* (Brill, 2021), and (with Jon Stewart) *The Modern Experience of the Religious* (Brill, 2023).

Ramiro Cardenes
graduated with honors in Philosophy at Buenos Aires University. Currently, he is studying for a master's degree in Political Philosophy at the Faculty of Philosophy and Letters (Buenos Aires University). His field of research is political philosophy, and especially the work of Karl Marx, Antonio Gramsci, and the discussions about the Marxist theory of the state. He has presented papers at conferences on Marx and the State (2019) and the concept of democracy in Aristotle (2019). He has published texts in Spanish on Marx and the production of theory (2011), the teaching of philosophy (2016), and has collaborated in collective editions on democracy and the theory of the state (2021).

Daniel Conway
is Professor of Philosophy and Humanities, Affiliate Professor of Film Studies and Religious Studies, and Courtesy Professor in the TAMU School of Law and the George Bush School of Government and Public Service at Texas A&M University (USA). He has lectured and published widely on topics in post-Kantian European philosophy, American philosophy, political theory, aesthetics (especially film and literature), religion, and genocide studies. In addition to his leadership positions in the Space Governance Research Group and the Philosophy for Children Initiative (P4C Texas), Conway serves as Convener of

the Working Group in Social, Cultural, and Political Theory, Liaison to the International Consortium of Critical Theory Programs, Liaison to the *Fédération Internationale des Sociétés de Philosophie,* and as a member of the Executive Committee of the local chapter of Phi Beta Kappa.

Patricia C. Dip
is a Research Fellow at National Council for Scientific and Technical Research (CONICET) and Associate Professor at National University of General Sarmiento, where she is responsible for teaching Metaphysics. She is the director of the Research Program in Post-Hegelian Philosophy (Institute of Sciences, National University of General Sarmiento, UNGS) and the director of the research project: "Kierkegaard and psychoanalysis: discussions on modern subjectivity," UNGS, 2020–2023. She is also the director of the postgraduate curriculum "Updating Program in Contemporary Philosophical Problems" (Buenos Aires University, UBA). She has served as dean of the Institute of Sciences, UNGS, (2018–2022). Her publications include the following: *Teoría y praxis en Las obras del amor. Un recorrido por la erótica kierkegaardiana*, Buenos Aires: Gorla 2010 and *Kierkegaard*, Buenos Aires: Galerna 2018. She has translated into Spanish Kierkegaard's *Johannes Climacus eller the omnibus dubitandum est*, Buenos Aires: Gorla 2007 and Antonio Gramsci, *Escritos de juventud* (1914–1917), Buenos Aires: Gorla 2014–2016. Her fields of interest include the history of psychology and Marxism. She is responsible for the journal *El arco y la lira. Tensiones y debates.* She has published articles and books on Kierkegaard's philosophy and articles about Freud, Wittgenstein, and Gramsci.

František Novosád
is a Research Fellow at the Institute of Philosophy of the Slovak Academy of Sciences. His field of interest includes the history of post-classical philosophy (Marxism, neoKantianism, Heidegger) and philosophical anthropology. He has translated books of Ludwig Wittgenstein, Nicolai Hartmann, and Michail Bachtin into Slovak. From 1990–2007 he was the editor of journal *Filozofia*, published by the Slovak Academy of Sciences. In the Slovak language, he has published monographs on Austromarxism (1988), Martin Heidegger (1995), Max Weber (1997/2016), Karl Marx (2018), theory of culture (2016) and philosophical anthropology (2020).

Pablo Uriel Rodríguez
is an Assistant Researcher at the National Council for Scientific and Technical Research (CONICET) and a member of the Post-Hegelian Philosophy Research Program (Institute of Sciences, National University of General Sarmiento). He teaches at the University of Morón and at Buenos Aires University in the

postgraduate program "Updating Program in Contemporary Philosophical Problems." He specializes in post-Hegelian philosophy of the 19th century, its sources in German idealism and its influence on various contemporary philosophical currents. He has published articles on the work of Kierkegaard and has translated into Spanish several writings of Ludwig Feuerbach. He is a member of the editorial board of the journal *El arco y la lira. Tensiones y debates.*

Yésica Rodríguez
is a National Council for Scientific and Technical Research (CONICET) Postdoctoral Fellow and a University Professor at the National University of General Sarmiento (UNGS). She is also a member of the Post-Hegelian Philosophy Research Program (Institute of Sciences, National University of General Sarmiento). Her field of interest is the thought of the Danish philosopher Kierkegaard and ethical philosophy. She is a member of the editorial committee of the journal *El arco y la lira. Tensiones y debates.* She published the book *Las éticas de Kierkegaard. Apropiación y abandono de Kant* (2022). She has also published the chapters "The Kantian Antecedent of the Concept of Personality Choice in Kierkegaard's Thought" in the book *Kierkegaard através do tempo* (2021); "Time as Subjectivity. Kant, Thinker of Time as a Condition for the Possibility of the Self," in *The Challenge of Interdisciplinarity in Research. Science and Time* (2018) and "Kierkegaard and Kant: An Interpretation of the Self from the Second Kantian Ethics" in the *Origin and Meaning of Post-Hegelian Philosophy* (2017).

Jorge Schulz
is Professor of Philosophy and Theology at the International Baptist Theological Seminary (SITB). He holds a degree in Philosophy from the Universidad Nacional de San Martín (UNSAM) and is a PhD candidate in Philosophy at the same University. He is a doctoral fellow of the National Council for Scientific and Technical Research (CONICET) and an associate researcher at the Center for Philosophical Research (CIF). He currently teaches philosophy and theology at the International Baptist Theological Seminary. His field of research is contemporary philosophy and Protestant theology. He has published articles on the theology of Paul in the Letter to the Romans, the thought of Martin Luther, and Søren Kierkegaard.

Jon Stewart
is a Research Fellow at the Institute of Philosophy of the Slovak Academy of Sciences. He has worked for many years in the field of nineteenth-century Continental philosophy with a specialization in Hegel and Kierkegaard. He edited the now complete series, *Kierkegaard Research: Sources, Reception and Resources*. He is currently the editor of *Danish Golden Age Studies* and *Texts from*

Golden Age Denmark (Brill) as well as the co-editor of the *Kierkegaard Studies Yearbook* and *Monograph Series* (De Gruyter). He has led large research projects sponsored by the Danish Research Council for the Humanities, Nordforsk, and the Slovak Research and Development Agency. His recent works include *A History of Nihilism in the Nineteenth Century: Confrontations with Nothingness* (Cambridge University Press 2023); *An Introduction to Hegel's Lectures on the Philosophy of Religion: The Issue of Religious Content in the Enlightenment and Romanticism* (Oxford University Press 2022); *Hegel's Century: Alienation and Recognition in a Time of Revolution* (Cambridge University Press 2021); *The Emergence of Subjectivity in the Ancient and Medieval World: An Interpretation of Western Civilization* (Oxford University Press 2020); *Faust, Romantic Irony, and System: German Culture in the Thought of Søren Kierkegaard* (Museum Tusculanum Press 2019); and *Hegel's Interpretation of the Religions of the World: The Logic of the Gods* (Oxford University Press 2018).

Peter Šajda
is a senior researcher at the Institute of Philosophy at the Slovak Academy of Sciences. His research focuses on anthropological, social-political, and religious issues, which he examines against the background of the philosophies of Kierkegaard, Buber, Schmitt, and Jünger. He collaborates with the Søren Kierkegaard Research Center in Copenhagen, where he is an editor of the *Kierkegaard Studies Yearbook* and the *Kierkegaard Studies Monograph Series*. He is the author of the monographs *Buber's Polemic with Kierkegaard: On the Relation of Religion to Ethics and Politics* (in Slovak, 2013); *The Kierkegaard Renaissance: Philosophy, Religion, Politics* (in Slovak, 2016); and *Existence between Conflict and Humanity: Philosophy of Existence and the Conservative Revolution* (in Slovak, 2021). He is the editor of the anthologies *Modern and Postmodern Crises of Symbolic Structures: Essays in Philosophical Anthropology* (Brill, 2021) and *Affectivity, Agency and Intersubjectivity* (L'Harmattan, 2012).

Introduction

Patricia C. Dip and Jon Stewart

With seminal thinkers such as Fichte, Hegel, Marx, Feuerbach, Kierkegaard, and Nietzsche, the nineteenth century was a dynamic period which made lasting contributions to every field of philosophy. In addition, it prepared the way for the development of the social sciences at the turn of the twentieth century. This volume is dedicated to exploring the rich tradition of nineteenth-century Continental philosophy in its different areas with the main purpose of highlighting the importance of this tradition for the development of the leading streams of thought of the twentieth and twenty-first century. During the nineteenth century both practical and theoretical debates began which paved the way for the philosophical, political, and religious discussions that subsequently defined Western culture up to our own time.

The philosophical research that took place in nineteenth-century Europe generated the conditions for the development of four schools of thought that shaped the conceptual horizon of the early twentieth century: Marxism, phenomenology, existentialism, and psychoanalysis. Discussions on orthodoxies and heterodoxies in each of these schools continue up to the present day, highlighting the power of their explanatory principles.

Philosophy in the nineteenth and the twentieth century was produced in step with a series of social and political transformations that originated with the French Revolution of 1789. Today our existence is determined by new crises in a global context. We have selected a series of nineteenth-century authors who approached their work from psychological, historical, sociological, and religious perspectives, which we believe to be relevant to illuminate the permanent state of "crisis" that runs through our present history. We hope that taking up again the path of thinkers who contributed their theoretical proposals to an emancipatory theory will allow us not only to think about the present, but also to make a contribution to its possible transformation.

The present collection is divided into four key rubrics: 1. Ethics, 2. Philosophy of Religion, 3. Philosophical Anthropology and the Social Sciences, and 4. Politics and Social Criticism. Articles in each category identify and explore the works of key figures from the nineteenth century, who had an important impact on subsequent philosophy.

The first article under the rubric "Ethics" is Daniel Conway's "Nietzsche's Philosophical and Rhetorical Aims in *Beyond Good and Evil*." Conway uses as his point of departure the idea that Nietzsche's surprising evaluation of the

 | DOI:10.1163/9789004689459_002

title that he assigned to the book *Beyond Good and Evil* (1886) may be understood to motivate a re-appraisal of the words that he extends to those readers whom he intends to include within the circle of his "we." Acknowledging that the title of *Beyond Good and Evil* essays a "dangerous slogan," which he elsewhere describes as "malicious," Nietzsche signals to his friends and readers that the business of emigrating "beyond good and evil" is far more complicated than they initially might have realized. This article demonstrates that the "danger" and "malice" in question arise from the precise nature of the relationship to morality that Nietzsche's target readership is encouraged to cultivate. Rather than emigrate cleanly beyond the jurisdiction of the morality of good and evil, his best readers are invited (and dared) to find support in the morality they have pledged to retire from service. In their capacity as "immoralists," Nietzsche and his best readers will tell the truth about the morality of good and evil and thereby expose the lies, fictions, and calumnies on which it continues to trade. They will do so, it is argued, by aligning themselves with the recently ascendant disciplinary regime of "Christian truthfulness," the authority of which they will channel (and eventually exhaust) in their truth-intensive assault on the fading disciplinary regime of "Christian morality."

Alejandro Peña Arroyave's article "Evasion? Profession? Writing and the Dominion of Melancholy in Søren Kierkegaard" concentrates on Kierkegaard's analysis of his own writing, understood as a profession and a task, within the framework of a more general concern for the way of communicating. The article's hypothesis is that writing is the domain of melancholy, not only as a field for its development, but also as work, creation, and transformative praxis. In this context, Arroyave describes a gradual progression from writing understood as an escape to writing understood as a profession.

The final article in the "Ethics" section is Pablo Uriel Rodríguez's "God as 'intermediate determinant': The Debate between Feuerbach and Kierkegaard on Christian Love." This article tries to show that the positions of Kierkegaard and Feuerbach on love are not as dissimilar as it might seem at first sight. To do so, he starts from the analysis of the common point of view of these authors regarding Christian charity as a mode of love that questions the intersubjective relations of a temporal character.

The second section, dedicated to the philosophy of religion, begins with Kristína Bosáková's article, "*Ich und Du ist Gott*. The Impact of Ludwig Feuerbach's Philosophy of Dialogical Communication on Modern Intersubjectivity and Recognition Theory." This work examines Feuerbach's philosophy of dialogical communication based on the relationship between a concrete, corporal I and a concrete, corporal Thou, and its impact on contemporary thinking about communication and intersubjective relations. Reflections on the relationship between the I and Thou can be traced back to the times of the Old Testament, but it was only in the modern era that the issue began to be examined systematically when Hegel developed the lord-bondsman dialectic to focus philosophical thinking on the problem of the mutual recognition of two different subjects. Feuerbach's efforts to discover and rehabilitate the emotional side of the human being represented a significant innovation in the philosophical reception of interpersonal relations, but it is open to question whether Feuerbach's philosophy of dialogical communication can be perceived as a specific theory of intersubjectivity. It is argued that regardless of whether we consider Feuerbach a precursor to modern intersubjectivity, the influence of his philosophy of the I and Thou is apparent in the writings of Husserl, Buber, Levinas, Honneth, and Taylor.

Jorge Schulz's article, "The Humorist in the Face of Religious Existence," investigates the role of humor in existential transitions to the religious sphere based on the analysis developed by Johannes Climacus in the *Concluding Unscientific Postscript*. The humorist dwells in the proximity of the religious, which through imagination provides him with a vision of life that allows him a sort of "humorous transvaluation" of the poles of joking and seriousness.

The final paper in this section is Jon Stewart's "Hegel's Philosophy of Religion and Durkheim's Sociology of Religion: A Comparative Study." It is usually thought that Hegel's philosophy of religion did not have much of an impact on the twentieth and twenty-first centuries. Stewart claims that, while this is generally true with regard to the field of philosophy, the influence of Hegel can be detected in the social sciences. This paper offers a comparison of Hegel's *Lectures on the Philosophy of Religion* and Durkheim's *The Elementary Forms of Religious Life*. Points of commonality are explored in the two thinkers' respective accounts of (1) the scientific methodology for the study of religion, (2) the need to establish the origin of religion and its history, (3) the understanding of the truth of religion, (4) the role of symbolism, (5) and the social basis of religion.

The third section of the present collection is dedicated to philosophical anthropology and the social sciences. In her article Yésica Rodríguez argues that *The Concept of Anxiety* and *The Sickness unto Death* are psychological works that presuppose a theory of subjectivity based on the concept of sin, as opposed to the philosophical ideas about subjectivity that unfold in modernity, according to which a human being can be self-founded.

The next article is František Novosád's "*Encore* Cassirer: Meta-worlds of Symbolic Forms." The work explains that the philosophical conceptions elaborated by the representatives of the Marburg School of Neo-Kantianism, namely, Herman Cohen, Paul Natorp, and Ernst Cassirer, admit of characterization as an endeavor to give a contemporary answer to Kant's principal problem—the quandary of the possibility of the mutual coexistence of science (causality), ethics (norms), and aesthetics (purposefulness). The neo-Kantians were conscious of the fact that the fundamental forms of our being-in-the-world—which Cassirer dubs "symbolic forms"—obey distinct and irreducible principles. The response to Kant's question of the "harmony in contrariety" existing among science, ethics, and art is just a theory of culture as a concurrence of diverse forms—equally valid and legitimate—of humans' bestowing of sense and world-building. Through the power of symbolic thought, as a coping mechanism for survival in the indifferent materiality of the cosmos, human beings build up, Cassirer proposes, a spiritual cosmos, an "ideal" world of their own.

In her article, "Anxiety and Sexuality in Kierkegaard and Freud: From the Psychology of Spirit to *Neurosenpsychologie*," Patricia C. Dip argues that the central themes of Kierkegaard's *The Concept of Anxiety* constitute a thematic and conceptual anticipation of Freud's early writings, in which the Viennese writer attempts to find the etiology of neurosis. Hence, there would be a thematic continuity between the psychology of spirit of Haufniensis (Kierkegaard's pseudonym) and *Neurosenpsychology*, prior to the actual formulation of psychoanalysis, once the concept of the unconscious had been discovered.

The final section of the collection is "Politics and Social Criticism," which begins with Nassim Bravo's article "Morning and Noon Political Observations: Kierkegaard on Liberalism and the Issue of Press Freedom." Despite living in one of the most politically turbulent times in European history, the age of revolutions, Kierkegaard, as is well known, showed little interest in politics, either national or international. An exception to this was the debate he engaged in with Johannes Ostermann in late 1835, in which Kierkegaard developed his position regarding contemporary political issues such as the role of the press and the monarchy, the transition to liberalism, the nature of revolutions, etc. This article argues that these political considerations were not disconnected from Kierkegaard's early philosophical reflections, especially with his interest in the existential question on the development of selfhood.

Peter Šajda's article, "Jaspers' Diagnosis of the Spiritual Condition of the Age as a Continuation of Kierkegaard's Critique of *the Present Age*," explores the thematic continuity between Kierkegaard's and Jaspers' social criticism. In *The Spiritual Condition of the Age* (1931) Jaspers draws substantial inspiration from Kierkegaard's *A Literary Review* (1846), claiming that Kierkegaard identified a social development which at his time was still not as disquieting as in the twentieth century when it intensified substantially. Kierkegaard's diagnosis is thus even more relevant in the first half of the twentieth century than it was at the time of its origin. Jaspers complements, develops, and updates Kierkegaard's diagnosis of the age. The article discusses key concepts in Kierkegaard's and Jaspers' critiques of the age, primarily *the public* and *the mass*, as well as the related concepts of *excellence, envy, leveling* and *the modern press*. Both authors provide original and insightful analyses of the self-contradictions and degenerative tendencies of modern society.

Ramiro Cardenes' article "The Notion of Political Abstraction and the Concept of the Modern State in Marx" starts from the analysis of the concept of political abstraction with the aim of demonstrating that it is possible to connect it with the analysis of modern sociability made by Marx in works subsequent to the *Critique of Hegel's Philosophy of Right*. In this work, Marx critically treats the notion of the abstraction of the state and identifies specific aspects of the modern state, which allows him to argue that both the political sphere and the state constitute an autonomous field of Marxian reflection. Cardenes establishes a relationship between the young Marx and the mature Marx from the analysis of the political and state spheres.

The articles in the present collection establish a number of important links between the philosophy of the nineteenth century and that of the twentieth century. In this way they help to ensure the rich legacy on nineteenth-century philosophical thought. The key thinkers treated here—Hegel, Feuerbach, Marx, Kierkegaard, Nietzsche, Cassirer—continue to be sources of inspiration today.

PART 1

Ethics

CHAPTER 1

Nietzsche's Philosophical and Rhetorical Aims in *Beyond Good and Evil*

Daniel Conway

Abstract

Friedrich Nietzsche's surprising evaluation of the title he assigned to the book *Beyond Good and Evil* (1886) may be understood to motivate a re-appraisal of the brief he extends to those readers whom he intends to include within the circle of his "we." Acknowledging that the title of *Beyond Good and Evil* essays a "dangerous slogan," which he elsewhere describes as "malicious," Nietzsche signals to his friends and readers that the business of emigrating "beyond good and evil" is far more complicated than they initially might have realized. In this chapter, I demonstrate that the "danger" and "malice" in question arise from the precise nature of the relationship to morality that his target readership is encouraged to cultivate. Rather than emigrate cleanly beyond the jurisdiction of the morality of good and evil, his best readers are invited (and dared) to lean into the morality they have pledged to retire from service. In their capacity as "immoralists," Nietzsche and his best readers will tell the truth about the morality of good and evil and thereby expose the lies, fictions, and calumnies on which it continues to trade. They will do so, I offer, by aligning themselves with the recently ascendant disciplinary regime of "Christian truthfulness," whose authority they will channel (and eventually exhaust) in their truth-intensive assault on the fading disciplinary regime of "Christian morality."

In the year following the publication of *Beyond Good and Evil*, Nietzsche openly acknowledged that the title of the work essays a "dangerous slogan."[1] Although this acknowledgment no doubt alludes to the perils incident to the "task" he has reserved for his best readers, in whom he intends to cultivate an appetite

1 Friedrich Nietzsche, *On the Genealogy of Morality* (hereafter GM), in *Beyond Good and Evil: Prelude to a Philosophy of the Future* and *On the Genealogy of Morality*, trans. by Adrian Del Caro in *The Complete Works of Friedrich Nietzsche*, vol. 8, Stanford: Stanford University Press 2014, p. 244.

 | DOI:10.1163/9789004689459_003

for risky innovation,[2] it also may be understood to confirm the snares he has laid for his readers in the rhetorical-dramatic case he builds in *Beyond Good and Evil* itself. Inasmuch as the title delivers a "slogan," after all, it is evidently meant to mislead (or manipulate) his readers to some extent, creating in them expectations that he will be obliged in due course to lower, prune, or tame. Indeed, this (admittedly speculative) interpretation may help to account for his warning, on a separate occasion, that the title of *Beyond Good and Evil* is in fact "malicious."[3]

Especially at risk are those among Nietzsche's readers whose interest has been piqued by his apparent invitation to join him in a daring excursion beyond the precincts and jurisdiction of morality. As they learn soon enough, the excursion referenced in the title of *Beyond Good and Evil* will be made available, if at all, only to the audiences of a distant posterity, who, owing in large part to the preliminary labours performed by Nietzsche and his best readers, may face the future free of the distractions, doubts, and estrangements that were introduced and/or exacerbated by the morality of good and evil. Moreover, what Nietzsche *does* offer his contemporary and late modern readers—namely, the *experience* of having ventured beyond good and evil—will oblige them to intensify their investments in a morality whose fetters they are understandably eager to shed. Simply put, the *feeling* that one resides beyond good and evil will be most consistently enjoyed by those among Nietzsche's readers who resolutely lean into the morality they have pledged to retire.[4] As we shall see, in fact, complaints of a bait-and-switch scheme are not altogether without merit.

The grand expectations raised by the title of *Beyond Good and Evil* are partially deflated by the book's comparatively sober subtitle. Nietzsche presents *Beyond Good and Evil* as preliminary to the as-yet-provisional "philosophy of the future," with which it should not be confused, even if Nietzsche himself

2 Robert Gooding-Williams thus characterizes *Beyond Good and Evil* as "a school for the modernist innovator," who "attempts to realize what is possible by transforming what is actual" (Robert Gooding-Williams, *Zarathustra's Dionysian Modernism*, Stanford: Stanford University Press 2011, pp. 306–308).

3 See Nietzsche's letter to Irene von Seydlitz on 7 May 1886, in Friedrich Nietzsche, *Sämtliche Briefe: Kritische Studienausgabe in 8 Bänden*, ed. by Giorgio Colli and Mazzino Montinari, Berlin: dtv/de Gruyter 1986, vol. 7, p. 189.

4 I am indebted here to the "fatalistic" interpretations developed by Brian Leiter, *Nietzsche and Morality*, London: Routledge 2002, pp. 81–88; Donovan Miyasaki, "Feeling, not Freedom: Nietzsche Against Agency," *Journal of Nietzsche Studies*, vol. 47, no. 2, 2016, pp. 256–274: pp. 257–261, pp. 270–271; and Brian Leiter, *Moral Psychology with Nietzsche*, Oxford: Oxford University Press 2019, pp. 147–157.

occasionally promotes this very confusion. As the subtitle of *Beyond Good and Evil* confirms, in fact, his readers should neither form nor retain any expectation of completing the emigration suggested by the book's title. The takeaway that awaits his best readers involves their positive (albeit limited) contribution to the timely demise of what we might call the "philosophy of the present," i.e., a philosophy hopelessly entangled in moral prejudices and popular convictions that cannot be reconciled with the most thrilling of the recent advances in the natural and social sciences. As parties to the designated "prelude," Nietzsche's best readers will learn that the optimal experience of freedom and agency that is available to them actually presupposes their ongoing placement *within* a regime of morality that is predicated on the (increasingly untenable) polar opposition between the values of "good" and "evil."[5] Persuading them to accept this placement, and to affirm it in due course, is perhaps the most daunting rhetorical challenge he faces in *Beyond Good and Evil*.[6]

1 Taking a Stand Beyond Good and Evil

With respect to the "dangerous slogan" embedded in the title of *Beyond Good and Evil*, Nietzsche provides additional clarity in *Twilight of the Idols*, where he elaborates on the role of philosophers in exposing the illusions on which contemporary morality trades:

> People know my demand [*Forderung*] for philosophers to place themselves *beyond* good and evil—to have the illusion of moral judgment *beneath* them. This demand results from an insight first formulated by myself: that *there are no moral facts at all*. Moral judgment has this in common with religious judgment, that it believes in non-existent realities.[7]

5 I develop this feature of my interpretation in Daniel Conway, *Nietzsche's* On the Genealogy of Morals: *A Critical Guide*, London: Continuum 2008, pp. 142–147; and in Daniel Conway, "We Who Are Different, We Immoralists," in *Nietzsche's Political Theory*, ed. by Manuel Knoll and Barry Stocker, Berlin: Walter de Gruyter 2014, pp. 287–311; 287–92.

6 Here I follow Robert Pippin, "Figurative Philosophy in Nietzsche's *Beyond Good and Evil*," in *The New Cambridge Companion to Nietzsche*, ed. by Tom Stern, Cambridge: Cambridge University Press 2019, pp. 195–221; pp. 197–198.

7 Friedrich Nietzsche, *Twilight of the Idols*, (hereafter *TI*) in *The Case of Wagner*, *Twilight of the Idols*, *The Antichrist*, *Ecce Homo*, *Dionysus Dithyrambs*, and *Nietzsche Contra Wagner*, translated (in various configurations) by Adrian Del Caro, Carol Diethe, Duncan Large, George H. Leiner, Paul S. Loeb, Alan D. Schrift, David F. Tinsley, and Mirko Wittwar, with an afterword by Andreas Urs Sommer, in *The Complete Works of Friedrich Nietzsche*, vol. 9, Stanford, CA: Stanford University Press 2021, p. 77.

This rich passage is instructive in several respects. First, Nietzsche objects not to the practice of morality itself, the value of which will (or should) be determined in the context of its particular applications, but to the "illusion of moral judgment" on which the cultural authority of morality invariably depends. Apparently, moreover, the "illusion" in question arises from a misguided appeal to the "moral facts" on which the judgment in question is said to rest. If there are no moral facts, as Nietzsche insists, then any judgment that is said to emerge from a careful consideration of the relevant moral facts must be dismissed as illusory. He furthermore implies that the prescription and enforcement of any moral judgment are likely to involve a relatively uncomplicated exercise of power, which the "illusion of moral judgment" serves to disguise. That the "illusion" in question is deemed necessary, either to justify the exercise of power or to palliate those to whom the morality is prescribed, is not sufficient to make it true.[8]

Nietzsche elaborates on this point in his letter of 29 July 1888 to Carl Fuchs. Complaining there that he has not yet been properly "*characterized*"—viz. neither as a "*Psychologist,*" a "*writer* (including *poet*)," the "inventor of a new kind of pessimism," nor as "an *Immoralist*"—Nietzsche explains to Fuchs that the "intellectual rectitude" he has cultivated "permit[s him] to treat morality as illusion, having itself become [in him] *instinct* and *inevitability.*"[9] His account here of the genesis of his "immoralism" is especially noteworthy. He explicitly traces his prerogative to "treat morality as illusion" to his acquired capacity for "intellectual rectitude," which, as we shall see, allows him to appeal to the crescent authority of the most recently ascendant disciplinary regime of morality. Rather than endure any longer the indignity of not being properly "characterized," Nietzsche introduces himself in *Ecce Homo* as the "first *immoralist,*" i.e., the "*destroyer* par excellence."[10] He also identifies the two "fundamental

8 He proceeds to discuss the ersatz "moral fact" that practitioners of morality can and should aim at the "improvement" of those to whom they prescribe. Efforts at "improvement" may aim at "the *taming* of the human beast," or at "the *breeding* of a certain category of human being," but they do not produce genuine, verifiable improvements (Nietzsche, *TI*, pp. 77–78).

9 Nietzsche, *Sämtliche Briefe*, vol. 8, pp. 374–76. See also Christopher Middleton, *Selected Letters of Friedrich Nietzsche*, Chicago: University of Chicago Press 1969, p. 305.

10 Friedrich Nietzsche, *Ecce Homo* (hereafter *EH*), in *The Case of Wagner, Twilight of the Idols, The Antichrist, Ecce Homo, Dionysus Dithyrambs,* and *Nietzsche Contra Wagner*, translated (in various configurations) by Adrian Del Caro, Carol Diethe, Duncan Large, George H. Leiner, Paul S. Loeb, Alan D. Schrift, David F. Tinsley, and Mirko Wittwar, with an afterword by Andreas Urs Sommer, in *The Complete Works of Friedrich Nietzsche*, vol. 9, Stanford, CA: Stanford University Press 2021, p. 306.

negations" required of any practicing "immoralist," both of which involve broadsides against the fading disciplinary regime of Christian morality.[11]

In taking care to "characterize" himself, Nietzsche provides his readers with a shorthand formula for achieving what he has in mind for them in *Beyond Good and Evil*. Like him, they will "place themselves beyond good and evil" by optimizing their "intellectual rectitude" and becoming "immoralists" in their own right. Following his lead, they will align themselves with the recently ascendant, truth-friendly regime of moral authority—known to them as "Christian truthfulness"—and expose the illusions on which the fading regime of Christian morality is now known to trade.[12] They will do so, as we also know from *Beyond Good and Evil*, with a frolicsome ferocity that is likely to elicit charges of *cruelty*—hence Nietzsche's stated preference for the euphemism "extravagant honesty"[13]—from those whose lives depend on the illusions the "immoralists" so gleefully explode.[14]

Before we proceed, we would do well to determine what might remain of Christian morality when its sustaining "illusions" are finally exposed and its judgments discredited. Once Christian morality is obliged to disavow the "moral facts" that have authorized its signature "moral judgments," it will be revealed to be what it has been all along—namely, an anthropogenic tool of discipline and control. In and of itself, of course, this revelation need not be considered sufficient to motivate a serious philosophical objection. According to Nietzsche (and Zarathustra), after all, *every* morality is anthropogenic, irrespective of what its adherents have been led to believe. The philosophical objection arises when we consider the merit of the *ends* served by Christian

11 Nietzsche, *EH*, pp. 307–308.

12 See Nietzsche, *GM*, pp. 346–348. See also Daniel Conway: "Nietzsche's Immoralism and the Advent of 'Great Politics,'" in *Nietzsche and Political Thought*, ed. by Keith Ansell-Pearson, London: Bloomsbury 2014, pp. 197–217; pp. 200–206.

13 Nietzsche, *BGE*, p. 135.

14 As Lampert observes, "*Beyond Good and Evil* attains one of its greatest summits when the argument of 'Our Virtues' climaxes as a case for cruelty ... " (Laurence Lampert, *Nietzsche's Task: An Interpretation of* Beyond Good and Evil, New Haven: Yale University Press 2001, p. 208). See also Leo Strauss, "Note on the Plan of Nietzsche's *Beyond Good and Evil*," in *Nietzsche: Critical Assessments of Leading Philosophers*, vols. 1–4, ed. by Daniel Conway, London: Routledge 1998, vol. 4, pp. 174–191; pp. 188–190. According to Alexander Nehamas, Nietzsche finds the "risk" of "physical cruelty of the worst sort" to be "desirable," even though he "does not in any way think that [the "physical cruelty" in question] is desirable" (Alexander Nehamas, *Nietzsche: Life as Literature*, Cambridge: Harvard University Press 1985, pp. 218–219). See also Douglas Burnham, *Reading Nietzsche: An Analysis of* Beyond Good and Evil, Montreal: McGill-Queen's University Press 2007, pp. 165–67; and Rainer Schäfer, "Die Wandlungen des Dionysischen bei Nietzsche," *Nietzsche-Studien*, vol. 40, 2011, pp. 178–202; pp. 198–202.

morality, especially with respect to its sustaining ideal of human flourishing. It is on this score that Nietzsche objects most vehemently to Christian morality:

> Finally—what is worst of all—the concept of the *good* human joining forces with everything weak, sick, malformed, suffering from itself, everything *that ought to perish*—the law of *selection* crossed through, an ideal constructed from the opposite of the proud, well-formed, Yes-saying human, certain of the future, guarantor of the future—who from now on is called *the evil one* ... And all that was believed in *as morality*![15]

Inasmuch as the "illusion of moral judgment" is largely responsible for supporting the robust cultural authority of Christian morality, it stands to reason that the philosophers whom Nietzsche summons eventually will succeed in reducing Christian morality to its core commitments to resentment and nihilism. The abiding resentment of Christian morality will be made evident, as it already is to Nietzsche and his "we," in its campaign to vilify and level those human being who defy its normalizing strictures as they aspire to unknown heights of human achievement. Similarly, the potent nihilism of Christian morality will be rendered manifest, as it already is to Nietzsche and his "we," in its campaign to ease its adherents into the "will to nothingness" that finally will relieve them of their suffering.[16] With respect to both of its core commitments, Christian morality will be identified as having conducted a power play designed to stifle—and, eventually, to cripple—the will for the future of humankind.

According to Nietzsche's sketch of the endgame scenario he anticipates, the disciplinary regime of Christian morality will be vanquished by its successor regime, known to us as "Christian truthfulness," whose brief reign will culminate in the "self-sublation" of the morality of good and evil.[17] Consequent upon its victory over Christian morality, or so we apparently are meant to understand, the disciplinary regime of Christian truthfulness will render its summary judgment against the morality of good and evil. Encouraged, as we have seen, by the "immoral" exploits of Nietzsche's best readers, the disciplinary regime of

15 Nietzsche, *EH*, p. 313.

16 Nietzsche, *GM*, pp. 348–349.

17 See Nietzsche, *GM*, p. 347. I am indebted here to Randall Havas, *Nietzsche's Genealogy: Nihilism and the Will to Knowledge*, Ithaca: Cornell University Press 1995, pp. 164–173; and Maudemarie Clark and David Dudrick, *The Soul of Nietzsche's* Beyond Good and Evil, Cambridge: Cambridge University Press 2012, pp. 37–48.

Christian truthfulness will determine that the morality of good and evil poses an existential threat to humanity.

2 Philosophy Beyond Good and Evil

Second, Nietzsche directs his "demand" to the *philosophers* among his readers, those whom he has determined to be particularly inclined (and uniquely empowered) to seek and tell the truth. Whereas the guardians and practitioners of contemporary morality may be expected to adhere, slavishly, to the "illusion of moral judgment," Nietzsche intends to hold philosophers to a higher standard: They are both permitted and obliged to resist (and in fact expose) any such adherence. In doing so, as we have seen, they will "place themselves beyond good and evil"—*not* by liberating themselves from the claims of morality, which is not an option available to them in any event, but by building a truth-infused moral case against the morality of good and evil. (As we have seen, the "immoralists" among Nietzsche's readers will prosecute the case against Christian morality from their recently attained position of authority within the successor regime of Christian truthfulness.[18]) What is "beneath" them, he thus indicates, is not morality itself, some elements of which they will be powerless to renounce, but the "illusion of moral judgment," which arises, as we have seen, from a misplaced confidence in the "moral facts" in question.[19]

The placement that Nietzsche "demands" of philosophers involves both an insight, i.e., a cognitive achievement, and a corresponding experience of emancipation, i.e., a conative surge. Let us consider these elements in turn. In order to appreciate the illusory nature of a moral judgment, philosophers must be able to discern that the proffered "moral facts" do not pass scientific (or scholarly) muster. Those philosophers who succeed in doing so will see and understand what their contemporaries do not, which is likely to incur the resentment

18 While I am heedful of Sommer's caution that the "we" of Part Seven of *Beyond Good and Evil* may not be identical to the "we" of Part Six, my sense of Nietzsche's practice in *Beyond Good and Evil* is that the progression of his first person plural modes of address is meant to reflect the education of his best readers as they gradually acquire the self-knowledge they will need in order to join him in performing the task reserved for them (Andreas Urs Sommer, *Kommentar zu Nietzsches* Jenseits von Gut und Böse, Berlin: Walter De Gruyter 2016, pp. 605–606).

19 See Simon May, *Nietzsche's Ethics and his War on "Morality,"* Oxford: Oxford University Press 1999, pp. 107–126; Brian Leiter, *Nietzsche and Morality*, London: Routledge 2002, pp. 115–125, pp. 156–163; and Christopher Janaway, *Beyond Selflessness: Reading Nietzsche's* Genealogy, Oxford: Oxford University Press 2007, pp. 252–254.

(or wrath) of those among their contemporaries—identified by Nietzsche as "oafs"[20]—who derive meaning and direction from the now-disputed "moral facts." Nietzsche's "demand" thus presupposes an understanding of philosophy that is unique to late modernity and the aftermath of the "death of God." Whereas philosophers in previous epochs and ages may (but need not) be excused for failing to take the prescribed stand, no such special pleading is available to the late modern philosophers whom Nietzsche addresses in this passage. As we have seen, the willing truth-seekers and truth-tellers whom he recruits in *Beyond Good and Evil* finally have history on their side.[21] Owing to the rise of the disciplinary regime of Christian truthfulness, morality itself now encourages them to tell the truth, including the truth about the morality of good and evil.[22]

In exposing the "illusions" on which moral judgments invariably trade, philosophers may expect to partake of an enhanced experience of freedom and power—hence his recourse in this passage to the kinetic imagery of philosophers lifting themselves above the miasma of moral judgments. The imperative to "place themselves beyond good and evil" thus connotes an audacity of self-assertion in which familiar constraints are suspended, including, at the limit, the constraints associated with self-preservation.[23] Having seen through the "illusions" supporting Christian morality, the emboldened philosophers will press their case against it, thereby placing at risk their health, wellbeing, reputation, and social standing. As we know, Nietzsche promises a similar experience of freedom and power to the readers of *Beyond Good and Evil*, whom he invites to join him in exposing the untruths on which contemporary morality trades. Baiting the hook for the intrepid readers whom he seeks as comrades and fellow travellers, Nietzsche concludes Part One of *Beyond Good and Evil* with a stirring (but ominous) image: "[W]e're sailing straight over and *away* from morality, we're smashing, maybe we're crushing our own remnant of morality by daring to travel there—but what do *we* matter!"[24]

20 Nietzsche, BGE, pp. 129–30.

21 See Karl Jaspers, *Nietzsche: Einführung in das Verständnis seines Philosophierens*, Berlin: Walter de Gruyter 1950, pp. 201–211.

22 I am indebted here to Sommer, *Kommentar zu Nietzsches Jenseits von Gut und Böse*, pp. 632–34.

23 Solomon notes that "truthfulness is not primarily service to others. It is first of all self-overflowing" (Robert Solomon, *Living with Nietzsche: What the Great "Immoralist" Has to Teach Us*, Oxford: Oxford University Press 2003, p. 153). For a similar interpretation of the excessive character of *Redlichkeit*, see Vanessa Lemm, *Homo Natura: Nietzsche, Philosophical Anthropology and Biopolitics*, Edinburgh: Edinburgh University Press 2020, pp. 36–37.

24 Nietzsche, *BGE*, p. 26.

To be sure, the "illusion of moral judgment" would be objectionable, and Nietzsche's "demand" compelling, only if the philosophers whom he addresses remain bound by the claims of morality. While it may be tempting here to catch Nietzsche in an inconsistency, or to suppose that truth-telling and illusion-busting are deemed valuable in some as-yet-unspecified "extra-moral" sense, the larger argument of *Beyond Good and Evil* indicates that the stand demanded and described in this passage is the product of a recognizably *moral* claim and evaluation.[25] In the aftermath of the "death of God," placing oneself beyond good and evil will oblige philosophers to exploit the most recently ascendant disciplinary regime of the morality in which they are both involuntarily practiced and presently immersed. If the practice of contemporary morality is demonstrated to rest on a hive of illusions, for example, the philosophers whom Nietzsche addresses must judge it to be immoral by virtue of being untruthful.

For additional context, let us consider another section of *TI*. The rise of the disciplinary regime of Christian truthfulness and the heyday of Nietzsche's "immoralists" are not mentioned by name, but they may be understood to occur in (what he designates as) Stage 5 in his pithy account of "The History of an Error," over the course of which the so-called "true world" gradually became recognizable as nothing more than a "fable."[26] Having liberated themselves from the "obligations" associated, unpersuasively, with a "true world" that eludes attainment (Stage 4), the post-Kantian philosophers whom Nietzsche describes here declare the "true world" to be "superfluous" and, on that basis, a "refuted idea" (Stage 5).

Nietzsche proceeds to treat this refutation as a landmark achievement in the history of Western philosophy: "Broad daylight; breakfast; return of *bon sens* and cheerfulness; Plato's blush of shame; devilish noise from all free spirits" (Stage 5).[27] Indeed, he believes this achievement may yet yield a Stage 6 in the progression, which, he predicts, will mark the "high point of humanity," as confirmed by the world-historical moment at which "Zarathustra begins."[28]

---

25 I am indebted here to the related interpretations developed by Aaron Ridley, *Nietzsche's Conscience: Six Character Studies from the* Genealogy, Ithaca: Cornell University Press 1998, pp. 115–126; May, *Nietzsche's Ethics*, pp. 137–138, pp. 177–180; and Lawrence J. Hatab, *Nietzsche's* Genealogy of Morality*: An Introduction*, Cambridge: Cambridge University Press 2008, pp. 164–171. See also Daniel Conway, "Nietzsche's Immoralism," pp. 207–213.

26 Nietzsche, *TI*, pp. 62–63.

27 Nietzsche, *TI*, p. 63.

28 Nietzsche, *TI*, p. 63. Nietzsche's reprise here of "INCIPIT ZARATHUSTA" is likely meant to put us in mind of Section 342 of *The Gay Science*, where the "beginning" of Zarathustra's journey is introduced by way of the title "*Incipit tragoedia*" ["The tragedy begins."]. In the

As we know from *Beyond Good and Evil*, however, the desired "abolition" of the "apparent world" will not immediately follow the achieved "abolition" of the "true world." In order to transit from Stage 5 to Stage 6 in the conjectured progression, the discredited morality of good and evil will need to be retired and its remnants cleared from view. Indeed, this is the task—both preparatory and remedial in nature—that falls to Nietzsche and his best readers.

As it turns out, in fact, those philosophers who place themselves beyond good and evil will do so while remaining very much in the thrall of morality, even as they oppose and contest its continued legitimacy.[29] In doing so, they may expect to become subjects (or authors) of history, which is what they understandably wish to accomplish, but only if they first acknowledge the extent to which they are, and must remain, objects (or creatures) of history.[30] As we know from *Beyond Good and Evil*, the optimal experience of freedom and power that is available to them will be predicated on a creative re-appropriation of their status as ineluctably moral (i.e., honest, truth-directed) creatures. Although his readers will not emigrate cleanly "beyond good and evil," they nevertheless may expect to revel in the experience of having done so, even as they continue to labor within the environs of the morality they have pledged to retire.[31] In other words: So long as they are immersed in the performance of the task Nietzsche has reserved for them, they will feel themselves to be emancipated from the constraints of the morality of good and evil, even as they channel the authority and currency of this morality in its final, fading form.[32] For the first time in their lives, they will want and wish to be moral, and

Preface he attaches to the 1887 edition of *The Gay Science*, Nietzsche further complicates matters by cautioning his readers: "'*Incipit tragoedia*' we read at the end of this awesomely aweless book. Beware! Something downright wicked and malicious is announced here: *incipit parodia* [the parody begins], no doubt" (Friedrich Nietzsche, *The Gay Science* (hereafter *GS*), trans. by Walter Kaufmann, New York: Vintage Books 1974, p. 33).

29 Alternative Nietzsche-inspired strategies for repurposing morality are explored by Richard Schacht, "Nietzschean Normativity," in *Nietzsche's Postmoralism: Essays on Nietzsche's Prelude to Philosophy's Future*, ed. by Richard Schacht, Cambridge: Cambridge University Press 2001, pp. 149–80: pp. 156–173; Janaway, *Beyond Selflessness*, 252–260; Paul S. Loeb, *The Death of Nietzsche's Zarathustra*, Cambridge: Cambridge University Press 2010, pp. 234–240; and Christa Davis Acampora, *Contesting Nietzsche*, Chicago: University of Chicago Press 2013, pp. 131–139.

30 Here I follow Donovan Miyasaki, "Feeling, not Freedom," pp. 257–261.

31 See Janaway, *Beyond Selflessness*, pp. 236–39.

32 See John Richardson, *Nietzsche's System*, Oxford: Oxford University Press 1996, pp. 26–27; and Lemm, *Homo Natura*, pp. 32–35.

they will revere themselves for participating wholeheartedly in the irreducibly moral task assigned to them.[33]

Finally, the slogan "beyond good and evil" both calls to mind and designates the strongly affirmative outlook and stance that Nietzsche more generally recommends to his readers. To stand beyond good and evil in this sense, such that one places the illusions of moral judgment *beneath* oneself, involves projecting oneself imaginatively into a future whose residents know (and feel) themselves to have outgrown the morality of good and evil.[34] The key to this exercise in affirmation—and, for that matter, to Nietzsche's post-Zarathustran philosophy more generally—lies in the *gratitude* his readers will feel and express when they preview a future in which they understand themselves to have survived the morality of good and evil. Having glimpsed this future, they will acquire a will for its fruition and a desire to contribute to its production. But what exactly will they glimpse in the future they envision?

According to Nietzsche, the enduring value of the morality of good and evil lies neither in the validity of its guiding distinction, nor in its imagined replication of a cosmic battle waged between opposing forces or deities, but in the discipline and spiritual growth it has compelled its adherents to undergo.[35] When one projects oneself imaginatively into an "extra-moral" future, in other words, one's hope for this future is likely to be restored, and one's will for the future of humanity is likely to be renewed. A notable example of the gratefully affirmative stance that Nietzsche recommends appears in his breath-taking profile of the unnamed "pessimist" who responds to the death of God not by expressing resignation or disappointment, but by demanding an immediate reprise of his life *in its entirety*, without a single revision, subtraction, or addition.[36] By shouting *da capo* to himself (and to the conjectured spectators of his mortal existence), the unnamed "pessimist" declares his gratitude for everything that has shaped his life, *including* the morality he has decisively outgrown.[37]

Looking back on *Beyond Good and Evil*, we may find evidence to support this understanding of the book's "malicious" title. The goal of the book is to prepare Nietzsche's best readers to lean into the morality of good and evil, thereby availing themselves of the moral authority vested in the disciplinary regime of Christian truthfulness, and to revel in the experience of freedom and power

33 See Janaway, *Beyond Selflessness*, pp. 249–254; and David Owen, *Nietzsche's Genealogy*, Stocksfield: Acumen 2007, pp. 63–65, pp. 126–129.

34 Nietzsche, *BGE*, pp. 1–3.

35 Nietzsche, *BGE*, pp. 2–3; and *GM*, pp. 213–214. See also Lampert, *Nietzsche's Task*, pp. 102–103.

36 Nietzsche, *BGE*, p. 55.

37 Nietzsche, *BGE*, p. 55.

that attends their "extravagantly honest" assault on Christian morality. They will not emigrate cleanly beyond good and evil, but they will make it possible for future generations to outgrow and outlive the morality of good and evil. The education and training on offer in *Beyond Good and Evil* are thus meant to prepare them to host the "self-overcoming of morality" and to immunize themselves against the pity and disgust they are certain to experience in the process.[38]

3 The Morality of Good and Evil

Nietzsche traces the historical emergence of the morality of good and evil to the teachings of Zoroaster, the influential Persian prophet who lived and taught in the 5th or 6th century BCE. As Nietzsche explains, he holds Zoroaster responsible for identifying "the battle of good and evil" as "the actual wheel that drives things."[39] According to Nietzsche, the most significant outcome of this teaching was Zoroaster's success in accomplishing "the translation of morality into the metaphysical [realm], as force, cause, purpose in itself."[40] Here Nietzsche apparently means to assert two claims: first, that Zoroaster understood "good" and "evil" to be related as strictly opposing (rather than diverse or complementary) forces; and second, that Zoroaster located the source or cause of this opposition in the very fabric of the cosmos. Although Nietzsche does not say so explicitly, this second claim suggests that he holds Zoroaster to account for introducing the idea that moral judgments are (and should be) grounded in "moral facts" pertaining to the cosmic order. As we have seen, of course, Nietzsche insists that "there are no moral facts."

Although Zoroaster is not named in Nietzsche's fanciful "History of an Error," it is likely that he belongs, alongside Plato, in Stage One, wherein "the true world [is known to be] attainable for one who is wise, devout, virtuous."[41] As Nietzsche explains, Stage One is home to the "oldest form of the idea [of the true world]," which is "relatively clever, simple, convincing."[42] Rather than characterize truth as external to himself, subject to pursuit, discovery, possession, and dispossession, he who is "wise, devout, [and] virtuous ... lives in it,

38 Here I follow Jaspers, *Nietzsche*, pp. 211–13; Ridley, *Nietzsche's Conscience*, pp. 124–126; May, *Nietzsche's Morality*, pp. 90–92; and Owen, *Nietzsche's Genealogy*, pp. 126–129.

39 Nietzsche, *EH*, pp. 306–307.

40 Nietzsche, *EH*, p. 307.

41 Nietzsche, *TI*, p. 62.

42 Nietzsche, *TI*, p. 62.

he is it."[43] Presumably, that is, we may assign to Zoroaster something akin to the immodest "proposition" that Nietzsche attributes to Plato: "'I, Plato, *am* the truth'."[44] Knowing (and feeling) himself to be a vessel of truth, Zoroaster confidently established in the microcosm a morality that would accurately reflect the enduring truth of the macrocosm. In this morality, the values of "good" and "evil" are posited (and subsequently fixed) as polar opposites, such that the morality of mere mortals is perfectly aligned with the natural (and supernatural) order of the cosmos.

That "good" and "evil" are to be understood as diametric opposites, Zoroaster taught, is not simply a supposition that may prove beneficial for a particular nation or people or tribe to adopt at a specific stage in its development, but a non-negotiable truth of the cosmos and, so, of its human inhabitants. According to Nietzsche, that is, Zoroaster elevated the morality of good and evil from the status of an anthropogenic construct, which might have been evaluated and/or embraced in its various historical and geopolitical contexts, to a faithful reflection of the natural (and supernatural) order of things. As a result, what might have been an optional (e.g., initiatory, temporary, or stabilizing) feature of morality—viz. its insistence on the polar opposition of good and evil—became a permanent (and in fact defining) feature of morality.

While it may be the case that the founding of a morality requires the clarity and simplicity associated with binary oppositions (e.g., good vs. evil)—indeed, Nietzsche would hardly object in principle to this or any other *pia fraus*—the ongoing development of a thriving tribe, people, or nation is likely to depend upon the eventual relaxation of these oppositions. When considered from the broadly anthropological perspective favoured by Nietzsche, a tribe, people, or nation will flourish only if its defining morality adapts in response to changing circumstances and improved prosperity. As we know from the title of *Beyond Good and Evil*, after all, Nietzsche believes that it is high time for humanity (or European civilization as its proxy) to begin (or to accelerate) the process of outgrowing (and subsequently abjuring) the binary oppositions on which it has grown so stubbornly reliant. Indeed, although Zoroaster placed the morality of good and evil on a firm metaphysical foundation, which secured for humanity a hopeful short-term future, he achieved his success at the expense of the long-term future of humanity. Despite the undeniably positive role the morality of good and evil has played in promoting the survival and development of the human species, Nietzsche insists, it has very nearly exhausted its value for those whom it is supposed to serve.

43 Nietzsche, *TI*, p. 62.

44 Nietzsche, *TI*, p. 62.

According to Nietzsche, the metaphysical-cosmological warrant that is claimed for the morality of good and evil is ultimately responsible for replacing a vibrant (if noisy) polyculture with a uniform, increasingly homogenous monoculture. If the pitched battle between good and evil is understood to be a fixed and universal feature of the natural order, we should not expect the founders and guardians of morality to insist on fashioning tables of value that reflect the specific circumstances—e.g., historical epoch, geo-political setting, climate, geography, mode of production, etc.—of the tribes, peoples, or nations they lead. Instead of treating the morality of good and evil as simply a starter morality, destined to be revised and reformed as conditions permit, the founders and guardians of morality acquired an incentive to content themselves with the order and stability the morality of good and evil afforded them. Indeed, when the morality of good and evil was situated against the metaphysical backdrop of an enduring cosmic struggle, the comparative advantages that formerly accrued to bespoke moralities were rendered null and void. Owing to the metaphysical-cosmological innovation attributed by Nietzsche to Zoroaster, the versatility of morality as a tool of "breeding" and acculturation was artificially limited and constrained.

As formerly diverse moralities either adjusted or succumbed to Zoroaster's dominant account of the natural (and supernatural) order of the cosmos, they became increasingly similar to one another and increasingly hostile to those "higher" human beings who dared to defy their overly restrictive norms. The devolution of a vibrant polyculture into a stultifying monoculture reached its nadir with the emergence of Christian morality, which, according to Nietzsche, preaches the virtues of "selflessness" to a universal clientele.[45] Nietzsche thus holds Zoroaster to account for having "*created* this most disastrous of errors, morality" and for having advanced the oft-refuted "proposition of [the] so-called moral world order."[46] What Nietzsche means to claim here is not that Zoroaster created morality itself, but that he created a metaphysically-reinforced version of morality, which, over the course of centuries, has successfully outbid all of its former and upstart rivals.

The task of undoing Zoroaster's establishment of the morality of good and evil initially fell to Zarathustra, whose name, a modern variant of "Zoroaster," reflects this calling. Having surveyed "many lands and many peoples," and having "discovered the good and evil of many peoples," Zarathustra declared that

---

45 Nietzsche, *EH*, pp. 312–313.

46 Nietzsche, *EH*, p. 307.

he "found no greater power on earth than good and evil."[47] After commenting with apparent approval on the diversity of the various determinations of good and evil he encountered on his travels, Zarathustra takes direct aim at the contributions of his predecessor and namesake: "Verily, men gave themselves all their good and evil. Verily, they did not take it, they did not find it, nor did it come to them as a voice from heaven. Only man placed value in things to preserve himself—he alone created a meaning for things, a human meaning."[48] As this disclosure confirms, Zarathustra has no quarrel with those bespoke determinations of good and evil that reflect the unique conditions of the tribes, peoples, and nations responsible for their creation. He treats the resulting polyculture of diverse valuations as both natural and desirable, in part because he regards the friction between and among them as potentially conducive to cultural elevation and potentially productive of novel feats of self-overcoming.

When placed in regular contact (and eventual conflict) with other bespoke moralities, any single determination of good and evil will be obliged to grow, adapt, and develop in response to the challenges posed to its authority by these other moralities. As a result of the conflict that defines the polyculture, some bespoke moralities will be fortified while others will stagnate or shrivel. Ideally, in Zarathustra's view, a noisy polyculture of bespoke moralities will naturally lead to the emergence in (at least) some of these moralities of a progressively greater degree of nuance and variegation. In particular, he believes, those bespoke moralities that successfully promote the health and prosperity of a particular tribe, people, or nation eventually will outgrow the polar oppositions on which they were reliant throughout their respective periods of incubation and maturation. Anticipating the "dangerous slogan" that Nietzsche chooses as the title of *Beyond Good and Evil*, Zarathustra gestures in the direction of a morality that has managed to vault itself "beyond good and evil."

Although he does not say so explicitly, Zarathustra apparently believes that the problem with determinations of good and evil arises only when the polyculture of bespoke moralities yields to a monoculture dominated by a universal morality that no longer requires its clientele to persevere in the pursuit of ongoing spiritual growth. Indeed, the monoculture dominated by European Christianity is defined in large part by the success of its twin campaigns to: (1) squelch all bespoke challenges to its preponderance; and (2) to eliminate (or emasculate) those rare exemplary types whose immoral exploits prompt the elevation of humanity itself. According to Zarathustra and Nietzsche, the

47 Friedrich Nietzsche, *Thus Spoke Zarathustra*, in *The Portable Nietzsche*, ed. and trans. by Walter Kaufmann, New York: Viking Penguin 1982, p. 170.

48 Nietzsche, *Thus Spoke Zarathustra*, p. 171.

triumph of European Christianity reflects its success in waging (and winning) a war of attrition.

Zarathustra's speech conveys an additional point of contention with Zoroaster's role in determining the current character and shape of the morality of good and evil. According to Zarathustra, the metaphysical-cosmological warrant that is claimed for the morality of good and evil is ultimately responsible for alienating human beings from the meaning-conferring process and experience of creating values. Convinced that mere mortals are ill suited to the task of creating values and determining good and evil for themselves, the self-appointed guardians of the morality of good and evil, most notably Zoroaster, have persuasively (but mistakenly) insisted that only a divine (or supernatural) source of authority is entitled to create and enforce a credible morality. That "men gave themselves all their good and evil," as Zarathustra avers, is a truth that has been expressly (and effectively) denied by Zoroaster and his priestly followers.

Owing to this artificially imposed condition of protracted alienation, contemporary human beings are not yet optimally positioned to reclaim their prerogative to "give themselves" a morality that suits *their* needs and aspirations.[49] Indeed, even those among Nietzsche's readers who side with Zarathustra will know themselves to be un- or underprepared to participate meaningfully in the creation (or revaluation) of moral values. If they wish to remedy their alienation, as we shall see, they would do well to join Nietzsche in destroying the remnants of the morality of good and evil. In doing so, they may expect to begin the process of unlearning the catechism of self-contempt that the (universal) morality of good and evil has obliged them to internalize.[50]

In keeping with his "No-saying, *'No-doing'*" campaign to cultivate an audience sympathetic to the as-yet-underappreciated teachings of Zarathustra,[51] Nietzsche addresses these (and other) concerns in *Beyond Good and Evil*.[52] First, he anticipates (and urges his readers to prepare for) the arrival of those "new"

49 Here I follow a general line of interpretation pursued, variously, by Leiter, *Nietzsche on Morality*, pp. 79–281; Tracy B. Strong, "Where Are We When We Are Beyond Good and Evil?" *Cardozo Law Review*, vol. 24, no. 2, 2003, pp. 535–562: pp. 544–45; Janaway, *Beyond Selflessness*, pp. 236–239; Owen, *Nietzsche's Genealogy*, pp. 128–129; Loeb, *The Death of Nietzsche's Zarathustra*, pp. 234–237; and Acampora, *Contesting Nietzsche*, pp. 192–197.

50 Here I follow Sommer, *Kommentar zu Nietzsches* Jenseits von Gut und Böse, pp. 618–620.

51 Nietzsche, *EH*, p. 291.

52 Leiter, *Nietzsche and Morality*, pp. 74–77. See also Christa Davis Acampora and Keith Ansell Pearson, *Nietzsche's* Beyond Good and Evil: *A Reader's Guide*, London: Continuum, 2011, pp. 154–165. For a characterization of the task as both subtractive (or destructive) *and* creative (or constructive), see Lemm, *Homo Natura*, pp. 31–37; pp. 42–43.

philosophers who will repurpose the current monoculture as the raw material from which a new, improved polyculture might be raised. Toward this end, he assigns his best readers a "task" that is intended to accelerate the destruction of the morality of good and evil in its current (and final) incarnation.[53] Second, he alerts his readers to the opportunity to contribute to the inauguration of an "extra-moral" period in human history, wherein the aforementioned "new" philosophers will install a new ideal of human flourishing and create the new values that will support the twin goals of human advancement and cultural elevation.[54] Nietzsche thus invites his readers to envision—and, subsequently, to produce—a future in which humanity finally assumes full, executive control of its own destiny. In such a future, humankind may finally dispense with the supernatural banisters conjured by Zoroaster and peddled by his priestly brethren and successors.

Although Nietzsche often adopts a strongly critical tone when assessing the morality of good and evil, his actual position—as elaborated in *Beyond Good and Evil*, for example—is more complex. What we learn in *Beyond Good and Evil* is that the morality of good and evil has contributed decisively to the survival thus far of the human species. When regarded as a (crude) tool of discipline and control, which is the approach Nietzsche recommends in *Beyond Good and Evil*, the morality of good and evil may be appreciated for its various successes in remaking human beings as the memorial, obedient, self-monitoring, pro-social, and imperfectly responsible creatures they (and we) have become.[55] At the same time, however, Nietzsche insists that the morality of good and evil has (largely) exhausted its value as a tool of discipline and control. As evidenced by the toxic homogeneity of the emergent monoculture, and by the efforts of Christian morality to extinguish those rare and higher human beings whose immoral exploits refresh humanity's will for the future, the discipline and control imparted by the morality of good and evil no longer yield a net positive outcome.[56] Inasmuch as the morality of good and evil

53 On the proposed use of morality to unseat itself, see Janaway, *Beyond Selflessness*, pp. 234–239; and Paul van Tongeren, "Nietzsches 'Redlichkeit'. Das siebte Hauptstück: 'unsere Tugenden,'" in *Texturen des Denkens. Nietzsches Inszenierung der Philosophie in "Jenseits von Gut und Böse,"* ed. by Marcus Andreas Born and Axel Pitcher, Berlin: Walter De Gruyter 2013, pp. 147–165; pp. 155–157.

54 Establishing a heretofore unremarked order of rank among free spirits, Nietzsche elaborates: "These philosophers of the future ... will not be merely [*bloss*] free spirits but something more, something higher, greater, and thoroughly different that does not want to be misunderstood and mistaken for something else" (Nietzsche, *BGE*, p. 44).

55 Nietzsche, *GM*, pp. 225–226.

56 Nietzsche, *BGE*, pp. 82–84.

has become ruinous to the health and welfare of contemporary humanity,[57] it must be retired from service.

Nietzsche's well-known animus against Christian morality is directed against its role in accelerating and normalizing the transition to the stultifying monoculture on which it depends for its authority. Building on (and in fact perfecting) the anti-natural inversion strategy that is the hallmark of "the slave revolt in morality,"[58] Christian morality has prevailed in the West not by introducing a more sustainable regime of discipline and control, but by crowding out other, rival moralities.[59] Having initially gained currency among the downtrodden and victimized, whose non-negotiable suffering it (creatively) re-branded as an index of their native "goodness," Christian morality has steadily remade itself as a morality "for all," i.e., as universal in its scope and application. What this means, according to Nietzsche, is that Christian morality has triumphed in late modern Europe not by establishing an improved, choice-worthy, future-oriented standard of good and evil, but by poisoning the good conscience of anyone who dares to resist its obsessive emphasis on the virtues and practices associated with *selflessness*.[60] No longer one morality among several or many, Christian morality now presents itself as the one, true morality: "I am morality itself, and nothing besides is morality!"[61]

According to Nietzsche, Christian morality now poses a mortal threat to humanity.[62] Its wildly successful campaign against the rise of upstart rivals and the emergence of higher, i.e., "immoral," human beings has effectively deflated humanity's will for its own future. Rather than continue to take the risks and accept the burdens that Nietzsche claims are instrumental to the advancement of humanity and the elevation of culture, contemporary Europeans have become increasingly (and alarmingly) content with the validation they receive for cultivating the virtues of selflessness. Hence the urgency that he attaches to the task of exposing Christian morality as the single greatest impediment to the positive reception of Zarathustra's teachings: "Whoever uncovers morality has uncovered at the same time the worthlessness of all values that people believe in or have believed in; he sees in the most exalted types of human, even those pronounced *holy*, nothing venerable anymore, he sees in them the most doom-laden form of monstrosities, doom-laden *because they were fascinating*."[63]

57 Nietzsche, BGE, pp. 61–63.
58 Nietzsche, BGE, pp. 61–63.
59 See Strong, "Where Are We ... ?," pp. 538–539.
60 Nietzsche, EH, pp. 312–313.
61 Nietzsche, BGE, p. 97.
62 Nietzsche, EH, pp. 307–309.
63 Nietzsche, EH, p. 312.

Nietzsche's decision to write and publish *Beyond Good and Evil* confirms his recognition that Zarathustra has not yet succeeded, as planned, in correcting for the mistakes of his predecessor and namesake. As we learn in *Beyond Good and Evil,* it now falls to Nietzsche and his best readers to retire the morality of good and evil once and for all, and to do so by speaking and acting with the authority of the recently ascendant disciplinary regime of Christian truthfulness.[64] By way of performing the "task" reserved for them, he and his best readers will tell the truth about the morality of good and evil. On its diminished behalf, and speaking with its expiring authority, they will judge the morality of good and evil to be immoral and declare it to be bankrupt. In so doing, he and they will complete the destructive task bequeathed to them by Zarathustra: "Have I been understood? ... The self-overcoming of morality through truthfulness, the self-overcoming of the moralist into his antithesis—into *myself*—that is what the name Zarathustra means in my mouth."[65] As we know, Nietzsche invites the readers of *Beyond Good and Evil* not only to participate in the "self-overcoming of morality,"[66] but also to host it. As he subsequently explains, they will do so most effectively, as the extracted passage confirms, by leaning into their vocation as "extravagantly honest" (and occasionally cruel) merchants of truthfulness [*Redlichkeit*].[67] As the extracted passage also confirms, they may look to the example he has set for them in hosting the "self-overcoming of the moralist" and emerging thereby as the "antithesis" of "the moralist."

---

64 As Born notes, "*Beyond Good and Evil* does not give an explicit answer to the question of how far it is possible to exceed a criticized morality if the philosopher who tries to do so stands in this moral tradition himself. Quite the contrary seems to be the case: the text seems to irritate its readers in an almost programmatic way" (Marcus Andreas Born, "Perspectives on a Philosophy of the Future in Nietzsche's *Beyond Good and Evil,*" in *Nietzsche's Free Spirit Philosophy*, ed. by Rebecca Bamford, New York: Rowman and Littlefield 2015, pp. 157–168: p. 160.

65 Nietzsche, *EH*, p. 307.

66 Nietzsche, *BGE*, p. 36.

67 Nietzsche, *BGE*, p. 135. For my understanding of Nietzsche's emphasis on the virtue of *Redlichkeit,* I am indebted to Alan White, "The Youngest Virtue," in *Nietzsche's Postmoralism: Essays on Nietzsche's Prelude to Philosophy's Future,* ed. by Richard Schacht, Cambridge: Cambridge University Press 2001, pp. 63–66; Lampert, *Nietzsche's Task,* pp. 219–223; Paul Franco, *Nietzsche's Enlightenment: The Free-Spirit Trilogy of the Middle Period,* Chicago: University of Chicago Press 2011, pp. 184–187; and Marco Brusotti, " 'der schreckliche Grundtext homo natura'. Texturen des Natürlichen im Aphorism 230 von Jenseits von Gut und Böse," in *Texturen des Denkens. Nietzsches Inszenierung der Philosophie in "Jenseits von Gut und Böse,"* ed. by Marcus Andreas Born and Axel Pichler, Berlin: Walter De Gruyter, 2013, pp. 259–278; pp. 272–275. See also Conway, "Nietzsche's Immoralism," pp. 207–209.

As we know from *Beyond Good and Evil*, the "antithesis" of "the moralist" is none other than what Nietzsche calls an "immoralist."[68]

Hence the interpretive payoff of the extracted passage: "What the name Zarathustra means in [Nietzsche's] mouth" is that Nietzsche and his best readers will pave the way for the eventual actualization of the (merely notional) triumph of Zarathustra over his namesake. They will do so, moreover, as "immoralists," which is the *nom de guerre* he recommends for anyone who turns the authority of morality against its generative source.[69] Although their oafish contemporaries are likely to judge them to be *simply* "immoral," as lacking a sense of "duty,"[70] Nietzsche and his best readers will consecrate themselves to the ascendant disciplinary regime of Christian truthfulness and deliver a rousing moral indictment of Christian morality.[71] By dint of their risk-seeking experiments in truth-telling, Nietzsche and his best readers will inaugurate (and in fact host) the "self-overcoming of morality." Fulfilling their pledge to the "No-Saying, '*No-Doing*'" agenda of Nietzsche's post-Zarathustran philosophical project,[72] they will hasten the collapse of the morality of good and evil and clear away any remnants of the wreckage they have caused. Owing to their efforts, the aforementioned "new" philosophers will be free to inaugurate the "extra-moral" period in human history, to complete the awaited revaluation of values, and to install a new ideal of worldly human flourishing.

4 What Nietzsche Wants

Will the future that Nietzsche envisions be altogether free of morality? Despite acknowledging that this question should (and will) be answered only by the "new" philosophers whose arrival he heralds, Nietzsche cannot resist the temptation to weigh in on a matter of such importance for the future of humanity. He indulges himself in this case not only to model to his best readers the potentially productive effects of artful transgression, but also to buoy their spirits with an uplifting image of the future they may yet produce. As he steers Essay 1 of *On the Genealogy of Morality* toward its conclusion, he reminds his readers of the "dangerous slogan" that serves as the title of *Beyond Good and*

68 Nietzsche, *BGE*, pp. 129–130.

69 Nietzsche, *BGE*, pp. 129–130. Here I follow Lampert, *Nietzsche's Task*, p. 219.

70 Nietzsche, *BGE*, pp. 129–130.

71 Here I follow Solomon, *Living with Nietzsche*, p. 50. See also Daniel Conway, "We Who Are Different," in *Nietzsche's Political Theory*, ed. by Manuel Knoll and Barry Stocker, Berlin: Walter De Gruyter 2014, pp. 287–311: pp. 287–292.

72 Nietzsche, *EH*, p. 291.

Evil: "[W]hat I want, what I want precisely with that dangerous slogan worn so well by my last book: 'Beyond Good and Evil' … This at least does not mean 'Beyond Good and Bad.'"[73]

The context of this timely reminder bears noting. Having identified the "*opposing* values" that have presided in alternation over the development of European history, he has observed that one of these "*opposing* values"—viz. "good and evil"—has scored a resounding (and apparently final) victory over its rival—viz. "good and bad."[74] Designating these "*opposing* values" as representative, respectively, of "Judea" and "Rome," he concedes that "there is simply no doubt" that the forces of "Judea" have triumphed over the forces of "Rome."[75] After reminding his readers of several relatively recent instances of the recrudescence of "Rome," he asks (rhetorically) if the "opposition" between these values has in fact ended, implying thereby that the staccato development of European culture may have ceased as well.[76] He indirectly answers this crucial question by clarifying what he "*wants*," at which point he refers, approvingly, to the "dangerous slogan" embedded in the title of *Beyond Good and Evil*.

What Nietzsche "*wants*," apparently, would involve "an even more terrible flaring up of the old fire, one much longer in the making," such that we would realize that "the greatest of all oppositions of ideals" has *not* concluded after all, despite all appearances to the contrary.[77] The "old fire" is an allusion to what he identifies, in the previous section, as a resurgence of the galvanizing, form-giving forces of "Rome," wherein we might glimpse yet again the resurgence of the noble "ideal of antiquity," which was embodied most recently by none other than Napoleon.[78] If we collect these assorted references and allusions under the canopy of the "dangerous slogan worn so well by [his] last book, *Beyond Good and Evil*,"[79] we will see that what he "*wants*" is consistent with the return of a morality of "good and bad," which, as we know, is the evaluative basis on which the *noble* (or *masterly*) type of morality is said to rest.[80] Such a morality, we also know, would be seasoned and hardened by its contact (and conflict) with other moralities within the vibrant polyculture that sustains them. If Nietzsche has any say in the matter, the aforementioned "new"

73 Nietzsche, *GM*, p. 244.
74 Nietzsche, *GM*, p. 242.
75 Nietzsche, *GM*, p. 243.
76 Nietzsche, *GM*, p. 244.
77 Nietzsche, *GM*, p. 244.
78 Nietzsche, *GM*, p. 244.
79 Nietzsche, *GM*, p. 244.
80 Nietzsche, *GM*, pp. 220–223.

philosophers will not only restore (something like) the noisy polyculture of yore, but also protect this polyculture from invasive incursions by any potential recrudescence of the morality of good and evil.[81]

Bibliography

Acampora, Christa Davis, *Contesting Nietzsche*, Chicago: University of Chicago Press 2013.

Acampora, Christa Davis, and Ansell Pearson, Keith, *Nietzsche's* Beyond Good and Evil: *A Reader's Guide*, London: Continuum 2011.

Born, Marcus Andreas, "Perspectives on a Philosophy of the Future in Nietzsche's *Beyond Good and Evil*," in *Nietzsche's Free Spirit Philosophy*, ed. by Rebecca Bamford, London: Rowman & Littlefield International 2015, pp. 157–168.

Burnham, Douglas, *Reading Nietzsche: An Analysis of* Beyond Good and Evil, Montreal: McGill-Queen's University Press 2007.

Brusotti, Marco, " 'der schreckliche Grundtext homo natura'. Texturen des Natürlichen im Aphorism 230 von *Jenseits von Gut und Böse*," in *Texturen des Denkens. Nietzsches Inszenierung der Philosophie in "Jenseits von Gut und Böse,"* ed. by Marcus Andreas and Axel Pichler, Berlin: Walter De Gruyter 2013, pp. 259–278.

Clark, Maudemarie and Dudrick, David, *The Soul of Nietzsche's* Beyond Good and Evil, Cambridge: Cambridge University Press 2012.

Conway, Daniel, *Nietzsche's* On the Genealogy of Morals: *A Critical Guide*, London: Continuum 2008.

Conway, Daniel, "We Who Are Different, We Immoralists," in *Nietzsche's Political Theory*, ed. by Manuel Knoll and Barry Stocker, Berlin: Walter de Gruyter 2014, pp. 287–311.

Conway, Daniel, "Nietzsche's Immoralism and the Advent of 'Great Politics,'" in *Nietzsche and Political Thought*, ed. by Keith Ansell-Pearson, London: Bloomsbury 2014, pp. 197–217.

Franco, Paul. *Nietzsche's Enlightenment: The Free-Spirit Trilogy of the Middle Period*, Chicago: University of Chicago Press 2011.

Gooding-Williams, Robert, *Zarathustra's Dionysian Modernism*, Stanford: Stanford University Press 2011.

Hatab, Lawrence J., *Nietzsche's* Genealogy of Morality*: An Introduction*, Cambridge: Cambridge University Press 2008.

81 I am grateful to the Editors for their instructive comments on an earlier version of this chapter.

Havas, Randall, *Nietzsche's Genealogy: Nihilism and the Will to Knowledge*, Ithaca: Cornell University Press 1995.

Janaway, Christopher, *Beyond Selflessness: Reading Nietzsche's* Genealogy, Oxford: Oxford University Press 2007.

Jaspers, Karl, *Nietzsche: Einführung in das Verständnis seines Philosophierens*, Berlin: Walter de Gruyter 1950.

Lampert, Laurence, *Nietzsche's Task: An Interpretation of* Beyond Good and Evil, New Haven: Yale University Press 2001.

Leiter, Brian, *Nietzsche on Morality*, London: Routledge 2002.

Leiter, Brian, *Moral Psychology with Nietzsche*, Oxford: Oxford University Press 2019.

Lemm, Vanessa, *Homo Natura: Nietzsche, Philosophical Anthropology and Biopolitics*, Edinburgh: Edinburgh University Press 2020.

Loeb, Paul S., *The Death of Nietzsche's Zarathustra*, Cambridge: Cambridge University Press 2010.

May, Simon, *Nietzsche's Ethics and his War on "Morality,"* Oxford: Oxford University Press 1999.

Middleton, Christopher, *Selected Letters of Friedrich Nietzsche*, Chicago: University of Chicago Press 1969.

Miyasaki, Donovan, "Feeling, not Freedom: Nietzsche Against Agency," *Journal of Nietzsche Studies*, vol. 47, no. 2, 2016, pp. 256–274.

Nehamas, Alexander, *Nietzsche: Life as Literature*, Cambridge: Harvard University Press 1985.

Nietzsche, Friedrich, *Sämtliche Werke: Kritische Studienausgabe in 15 Bänden*, ed. by Giorgio Colli and Mazzino Montinari, Berlin: dtv/de Gruyter 1980.

Nietzsche, Friedrich, *Sämtliche Briefe: Kritische Studienausgabe in 8 Bänden*, ed. by Giorgio Colli and Mazzino Montinari, Berlin: dtv/de Gruyter 1986.

Nietzsche, Friedrich, *The Gay Science*, trans. by Walter Kaufmann, New York: Vintage Books 1974.

Nietzsche, Friedrich, *Thus Spoke Zarathustra*, in *The Portable Nietzsche*, ed. and trans. by Walter Kaufmann, New York: Viking Penguin 1982.

Nietzsche, Friedrich, *Beyond Good and Evil: Prelude to a Philosophy of the Future* and *On the Genealogy of Morality*, trans. by Adrian Del Caro in *The Complete Works of Friedrich Nietzsche*, vol. 8, Stanford, CA: Stanford University Press 2014.

Nietzsche, Friedrich, *The Case of Wagner*, *Twilight of the Idols*, *The Antichrist*, *Ecce Homo*, *Dionysus Dithyrambs*, and *Nietzsche Contra Wagner*, translated (in various configurations) by Adrian Del Caro, Carol Diethe, Duncan Large, George H. Leiner, Paul S. Loeb, Alan D. Schrift, David F. Tinsley, and Mirko Wittwar, with an afterword by Andreas Urs Sommer, in *The Complete Works of Friedrich Nietzsche*, vol. 9, Stanford, CA: Stanford University Press 2021.

Owen, David, *Nietzsche's Genealogy*, Stocksfield: Acumen 2007.
Pippin, Robert, "Figurative Philosophy in Nietzsche's *Beyond Good and Evil*," in *The New Cambridge Companion to Nietzsche*, ed. by Tom Stern, Cambridge: Cambridge University Press 2019, pp. 195–221.
Richardson, John, *Nietzsche's System*, Oxford: Oxford University Press 1996.
Ridley, Aaron, *Nietzsche's Conscience: Six Character Studies from the* Genealogy, Ithaca: Cornell University Press 1998.
Schacht, Richard, "Nietzschean Normativity," in *Nietzsche's Postmoralism*, ed. by Richard Schacht. Cambridge: Cambridge University Press 2001, pp. 149–180.
Solomon, Robert C., *Living with Nietzsche: What the Great "Immoralist" Has to Teach Us*, Oxford: Oxford University Press 2003.
Sommer, Andreas Urs, *Kommentar zu Nietzsches* Jenseits von Gut und Böse, Berlin: Walter de Gruyter 2016.
Strauss, Leo, "Note on the Plan of Nietzsche's *Beyond Good and Evil*," in *Nietzsche: Critical Assessments of Leading Philosophers*, vol. 4, ed. by Daniel Conway, London: Routledge 1998, pp. 323–339.
Strong, Tracy B. "Where Are We When We Are Beyond Good and Evil?" *Cardozo Law Review*, vol. 24, no. 2, 2003, pp. 535–562.
van Tongeren, Paul, "Nietzsches 'Redlichkeit'. Das siebte Hauptstück: 'unsere Tugenden,'" in *Texturen des Denkens. Nietzsches Inszenierung der Philosophie in "Jenseits von Gut und Böse,"* ed. by Marcus Andreas Born and Axel Pichler, Berlin: Walter De Gruyter 2013, pp. 147–165.
White, Alan, "The Youngest Virtue," in *Nietzsche's Postmoralism: Essays on Nietzsche's Prelude to Philosophy's Future*, ed. by Richard Schacht, Cambridge: Cambridge University Press 2001, pp. 63–78.

CHAPTER 2

Evasion? Profession? Writing and the Dominion of Melancholy in Søren Kierkegaard

Alejandro Peña Arroyave

Abstract

Søren Kierkegaard's work presents a special concern for the way of communication. In this context, the Danish philosopher develops deep thoughts, not only about the concepts or existential positions to be communicated, but also about writing itself. This constant reflection makes it possible to appreciate his gradual appropriation of writing as a profession. After thinking of giving up writing several times and retiring to the life of a rural pastor, Kierkegaard commits himself more and more to writing by assuming it as his profession and task. The melancholy that pushed him to write is the same thorn in the flesh that leads him to assume writing as his sacred task in existence. The hypothesis of this chapter is that, in Kierkegaard, writing is the dominion of melancholy both as a particular field for its development, but also as work, creation and transformative praxis. From writing as an escape, Kierkegaard passes to writing as a profession without leaving the dominion of melancholy.

1 The Dominion of Melancholy

Mit ausgebeulten Gedanken
fuhrwerkt der Schmerz.
...
Der Schwermut, aufs neue geduldet,
pendelt sich ein.
Paul Celan.[1]

In the *Concluding Unscientific Postscript to Philosophical Fragments* Johannes Climacus says that *Either/Or* is a work the central concept of which is

1 Paul Celan, "Fadensonnen," in *Obras completas*, trans. by José Luis Reina Palazón, bilingual edition, Madrid: Trotta 2000, p. 289.

 | DOI:10.1163/9789004689459_004

melancholy. According to Climacus, the first part of the work consists in explaining melancholy in its different forms, while the second part represents an attempt to overcome melancholy through the ethical life.[2] This reading of Climacus is, then, thought-provoking in its suggestion that what is presented in *Either/Or* has to do with the exposition of existential positions in the face of a constitutive phenomenon of human existence: melancholy. Such positions are clearly located, at least in principle, in terms of the aesthetic and the ethical. Given that it is impossible to deny melancholy, since it becomes the background to existence, the question around which the two positions expounded in *Either/Or* revolve is: What is to be done in the face of melancholy? The hypothesis of this work is that, while the aesthetic is the dominion of melancholy as a fertile soil for becoming melancholic, the ethical position is—at least in its assumptions—the dominion of melancholy conceived in terms of an elaboration or overcoming—in Hegelian terms—of melancholy, as Climacus has suggested.

In one of the *Diapsalmata* of the first part of *Either/Or*, the aesthetic pseudonym says: "I seem destined to have to suffer through all possible moods, to be required to have experiences of all kinds."[3] Following Climacus' thesis, according to which melancholy determines the entire movement of *Either/Or*, it is clear that when referring to states of mind, the aesthetic pseudonym refers to those that are within the orbit of melancholy. In his specific case, he will take up tedium as the main state of mind in his existence.[4] But for esthete A, taking up tedium implies a game: the game of possibilities. Indeed, the tedium that makes the esthete A aware of the paralysis of his existence and with it the futility of reality is accompanied by an overflowing fantasy that allows him precisely to play with that reality that for him becomes inaccessible. The aesthetic pseudonym takes up overflowing fantasy as the just balance in the face of the pain of melancholy. And it is under this conception that he takes up his own state as a terrain on which to experiment, since, strictly speaking, his only relationship with reality is in terms of experimentation.

On the basis of this premise, the aesthetic pseudonym creates a method with which to dominate melancholy with a view to experimentation. His method focuses on the calculation and mastery of states of mind. That is why he writes in "Rotation of Crops," "Just as an experienced sailor always scans the sea and

2 See *SKS* 7, 213 / *CUP1*, 253.

3 *SKS* 2, 40 / *EO1*, 31.

4 It will be B who best specifies that what A calls tedium or boredom is a previous moment of melancholy.

detects a squall far in advance, so one should always detect a mood a little in advance."[5] But what is the purpose of such a method? Its end is conscious distancing from reality, distraction, and subjectivity's enjoyment of itself in the possibilities offered by his fantasy. This purpose, therefore, drives the aesthetic position increasingly into confinement and seclusion in its own interiority.[6] This can be seen clearly in Johannes' strategy against Cordelia in "The Seducer's Diary." There, in an imagined dialogue, Johannes tells Cordelia: "but you have no inkling of the kind of kingdom I have dominion over. It is over the tempests of moods. Like Aeolus, I keep them shut up in the mountain of my personality."[7] Indeed, here we see the two moments of the aesthetic position face to face with the game with the states of mind: the struggle to dominate them, and the resulting confinement to which such domination leads. For the aesthetic pseudonym, this confinement is the final distinguishing feature of his own genius in the face of an anodyne reality. In this way, heading towards a consequent confinement, melancholy increases and the esthete has to make his mechanisms of control increasingly strict or, in his terms, increase his capacity for self-limitation. But where does his method lead? It leads to the death of the inner life. This is how the esthete himself makes it clear when he affirms that death dies and describes his existence as an experience of emptiness:

> I lie prostrate, inert; the only thing I see is emptiness, the only thing I live on is emptiness, the only thing I move in is emptiness. I do not even suffer pain.... My soul is like the Dead Sea, over which no bird is able to fly; when it has come midway, it sinks down, exhausted, to death and destruction.[8]

That emptiness is the nothingness of interiority in which melancholy grows. It is the fertile field for a negative passion that leads to a distancing from reality, the impossibility of precision and of the free play of the imagination. The esthete A has become a melancholic. For this reason, he will find in laughter

---

5 *SKS* 2, 287 / *EO1*, 298–299.

6 This is an interiority that will show itself to be illusory and empty, as B points out. In this sense, it is necessary to take into account Hegel's criticism of romanticism in general and of irony in particular. See Jon Stewart, *An Introduction to Hegel's Lectures on the Philosophy of Religion: The Issue of Religious Content in the Enlightenment and Romanticism*, Oxford: Oxford University Press 2022, pp. 105–114.

7 *SKS* 2, 388 / *EO1*, 400.

8 *SKS* 2, 46 / *EO1*, 37.

and irony mechanisms that will help him to bear the emptiness of his own interiority but that distances him more and more from himself.

In letters to his friend A, B, or Wilhelm seems to have a clearer awareness of his friend's condition than A himself. In effect, Wilhelm asserts that the confinement into which A falls is due to his being melancholic. However, unlike A, the ethical pseudonym does not see melancholy as a trait that defines exceptionality, but affirms that melancholy is innate to human beings. In this sense, according to B, every man, even the most calm and peaceful, "will still always retain a little depression."[9] This conception of the problem refers not only to what Climacus says later about the centrality of the concept—at least in this work—but also to an anthropological dimension not taken into account by esthete A. From his ethical position, and in accordance with his intention of encouraging his esthete friend to transform himself, Wilhelm speaks of a mastery of melancholy. But now it is a question of a task, an elaboration that must move in the direction of concrete reality and not seclusion.

B exhorts the esthete with this apparently ambiguous formula: "In order that you will be able to live, you must see to mastering your innate depression.... This depression has been your misfortune, but you will see that a time will come when you yourself will admit that it has been your good fortune."[10] On the one hand, as we saw in A's own words, his method of dominating melancholy through fantasy leads him to an inner death, which is why B emphasizes that it is a question of being able to live. And, on the other hand, it is not a question of denying or eliminating melancholy but of dominating it, not doing experiments; instead, it is a question of taking up another relationship with reality that B sums up in the concept of vocation.[11] Indeed, for B it is the vocation that limits us, and in that limitation, not through fantasy but rather through the incorporation of human ordinariness, there would be a true overcoming of melancholy through the transformation of its strength into vocation. What is the strength of melancholy and why does B affirm of A that it will become his happiness? Its strength lies in the fact that it is a category of the spirit, and therefore its appearance is a call to a transformation. That is why it is not a question of denying melancholy but of taking responsibility for it insofar as it is a category of human existence. For this reason, B exhorts the esthete A not to use his strength to hide his melancholy by masking it, but rather to cope with it, to take responsibility for it.

---

9 *SKS* 3, 184 / *EO2*, 190.

10 *SKS* 3, 274 / *EO2*, 289.

11 See *SKS* 3, 277 / *EO2*, 292.

B has stated that if his friend A falls into confinement, it is because he is a melancholic, but at the same time he affirms not only that melancholy is natural to human beings but that it is also for that reason a phenomenon of spiritual activity and therefore a condition that can represent his happiness. In this apparent ambiguity into which B's argument falls, it seems that there is a subtle but great difference between suffering melancholy and becoming melancholic. In the fragile passage from the one to the other, the idea of dominance postulated by B is played out. As stated by Wilhelm, melancholy is a disease of the spirit.[12] It is a disease of spiritual development. The ethical work on melancholy implies that a human being suffers melancholy, but that he should not become melancholic because in that case his spiritual development stops. That is, awakening melancholy has in itself the power of transformation.[13] The mastery of melancholy consists in renewing over and over again or rather in persisting constantly since melancholy is always present, but it must be mastered over and over again with a positive relationship with time, as B affirms of himself.[14] For this reason Wilhelm adopts vocation as a frame of reference for the limitation of his melancholy, that is, for the concretion of the personality, since in vocation man finds not only the expression of his nature, but, as Hegel says, his limitation in objectivity.[15] In this limitation, time and continuity are crucial.

If the question of ethics is ultimately the question of a successful, fulfilled life, it follows that, from Wilhelm's point of view, the question is not how to represent or how to understand phenomena, that is, it is not about the carrying out of experiments, but about how to become oneself. Experimentation is the carelessness and self-forgetfulness that ends in reification and self-reification. Remaining at the stage of vulnerability indicated above, implies taking responsibility for the fact of suffering melancholy, that is, spirit. Melancholy then shows itself to be a sign of responsibility. For this reason, B affirms that man is not to blame for suffering melancholy, but he is to blame for becoming a melancholic. In this sense, the true strength of melancholy is not played out in the field of creative exceptionality, but in how, as a category of the spirit, it can lead to a life fulfilled in ordinary existence where the great work of the melancholic would be, or to put it more precisely, the work of the man who suffers

12 See *SKS* 3, 184 / *EO2*, 190.

13 *SKS* 3, 183 / *EO2*, 188–189.

14 See *SKS* 3, 290 / *EO2*, 307.

15 See G.W.F. Hegel, *Philosophischen Propädeutik*, in *Werke*, vols. 1–20, ed. by Eva Moldenhauer and Karl Markus Michel, Frankfurt am Main: Suhrkamp 1986, vol. 4, *Nürnberger und Heidelberger Schriften 1808–1817*, § 45, pp. 262–263.

melancholy but does not become melancholic. Is ethical life enough to sustain that fragile balance?

In an entry in the journals Kierkegaard states the following:

> For many years my depression has prevented me from saying "Du" to myself in the profoundest sense. Between my "Du" and my depression lay a whole world of imagination. This is what I partially discharged in the pseudonyms. Just as a person who does not have a happy home goes out as much as possible and would rather not be encumbered with it, so my depression has kept me outside myself while I have been discovering and poetically experiencing a whole world of imagination.[16]

This entry that could well be one of the *Diapsalmata* of A or one of the annotations of Quidam in *Stages on Life's Way*, such as: "What is my sickness? Depression. Where does this sickness have its seat? In the power of the imagination, and possibility is its nourishment."[17] As we have said, this affirmation made by Kierkegaard clearly shows the intrinsic relationship between, on the one hand, the melancholic temperament that Kierkegaard attributes to himself and, on the other, writing. Indeed, the overabundance of fantasy is what, according to Kierkegaard, would have led him to the creation of a great work but also to a distancing of himself from himself. As in the case of the esthete A expounded above, the author, Kierkegaard, would have mastered melancholy with his own lure, that is, the imagination. Therefore, it would be a false dominion and in that sense a falling into increasingly closed circles.

However, Kierkegaard's own discourse on writing undergoes a transformation as expressed in *The Point of View for My Work as an Author*, where he seems to turn towards the other sense of dominating melancholy that we have outlined above. There Kierkegaard argues that his profession of writing has been watched over by God, that is, by religious duty. Indeed, according to Kierkegaard, fantasy is poetic impatience, which wards off the real task. For this reason, in his consciousness of his work as a writer, fantasy must be dominated: "And if that poet passion awakens in me again for a moment, I seem to hear a voice speak to me as a teacher speaks to a boy: Now, just hold the pen properly and write each letter exactly. Then I can do it, then I dare not do anything else."[18] According to Kierkegaard, in this religious duty, there is the imposition of a

16 *SKS* 20, 97, NB:141 / *KJN* 4, 96–97.

17 *SKS* 6, 363 / *SLW*, 391.

18 *SKS* 16, 53 / *PV*, 73.

limit to the imagination and creative fantasy.[19] Religious duty forms writing. That is why the work, says Kierkegaard, "it is not the work of the poet passion or of the thinker passion, but of devotion to God, and for me a divine worship."[20] Under this idea of limitation, writing is then conceived of as the mission or vocation to stay obedient in what one does.[21] The very melancholy that would have conditioned and provoked writing would thus become obedient to a superior power. Such obedience occurs, according to Kierkegaard, by recognizing that excess imagination and fantasy can become destructive: "I have needed God every day to defend myself against the abundance of thoughts."[22] Or put another way, "Without God I am too strong for myself."[23] In this sense, writing is conditioned by melancholy but the limitation imposed by the task would maintain it in the fragile balance of seeking in or introducing into the creative game of writing and the construction of fictions, meaning, the idea of communicating something of human ordinariness, the search to communicate, even in its impossibility, interiority.

2 Evasion? Profession? Melancholy and Writing in Søren Kierkegaard

As is common among post-Hegelian thinkers, Kierkegaard presents a special concern not only because of the content of his philosophical work, but also for the way in which it should be presented.[24] On the one hand, this has to do with the fact that he "has a lucid epochal consciousness,"[25] and, on the other, because, in reaction to the philosophy of idealism and specifically inspired by his reading of Hegel (in which the German thinker appears especially systematic and speculative), Kierkegaard attempts a new form of communication. Indeed, while Hegelian philosophy would be characterized by a form of objective expression in which interiority would disappear in favor of universality,

19 See *SKS* 16, 51–52 / *PV*, 71–72. The idea of the limitation of talent by vocation coincides with the limitation that, from the point of view of the writing profession, religious duty imposes on fantasy. In this sense, religious duty establishes a formation or an education on writing.

20 *SKS* 16, 53 / *PV*, 73.

21 From the point of view of Protestant ethics.

22 *SKS* 16, 53 / *PV*, 73–74.

23 *SKS* 16, 54 / *PV*, 74–75.

24 See Jon Stewart, "Kierkegaard's Use of Genre in the Struggle with German Philosophy," in his *The Unity of Content and Form in Philosophical Writing: The Perils of Conformity*, London: Bloomsbury 2013, pp. 81–95.

25 Arsenio Ginzo Fernández, *Protestantismo y filosofía. La recepción de la Reforma en la filosofía alemana*, Madrid: Universidad de Alcalá 2000, p. 256.

the pressing need for philosophy would be, from Kierkegaard's point of view, to dwell precisely on interiority or, to put it in a Hegelian way, on the subjective spirit. In this sense, it is consistent that Kierkegaard seeks a form of communication in accordance with the requirement to respect the freedom and interiority of the person with whom one speaks, since that person is also an individual, an interiority. How to communicate without imposing? How to communicate interiority in the face of another interiority? As Adorno has said, this concern of Kierkegaard's is another way of interpreting and taking up the problem common to the thinkers of the epoch: the alienation between subject and object.[26] Kierkegaard would attribute this separation to modern philosophy, and his interest in interiority would consist in recovering the validity of individuality that the Reformation would have forgotten "in its process of secularization."[27] For this reason, the category that he presents in opposition to what he calls "the system" is that of the individual, that is, that of irreducible interiority in general. In this way, the concern for writing consists in designing a strategy of communication that makes it possible to maintain the independence of the reader and which expresses, at the same time, the position or existential categories of the person who speaks. If we refer to the exposition of the spheres or of the different stages of existence, then insofar as certain categories correspond to each moment, a mode of expression corresponds to itself and, consequently, a conception of writing.

The first of the *Diapsalmata* of *Either/Or* says:

> What is a poet? An unhappy person who conceals profound anguish in his heart but whose lips are so formed that as sighs and cries pass over them they sound like beautiful music. It is with him as with the poor wretches in Phalaris's bronze bull, who were slowly tortured over a slow fire; their screams could not reach the tyrant's ears to terrify him; to him they sounded like sweet music. And people crowd around the poet and say to him, "Sing again soon"—in other words, may new sufferings torture your soul, and may your lips continue to be formed as before, because your screams would only alarm us, but the music is charming.[28]

26 Theodor Adorno, *Kierkegaard. Konstruktion des Ästhetischen*, Frankfurt am Main: Suhrkamp 1966, p. 51.

27 Ginzo Fernández, *Protestantismo y filosofía. La recepción de la Reforma en la filosofía alemana*, p. 258.

28 *SKS* 2, 27 / *EO1*, 19.

Right at the beginning of the work, a double characterization of writing embodied in the figure of the poet is already problematized. On the one hand, his work represents, mere entertainment for the reader, and, on the other, it presents the problem of the very impossibility of communicating interiority, in this case pain, such as it is. In other words, it problematizes the issue of masking and the double distance that poetic creation implies. That writing is just fun means, then, that the reader is distracted from his own task and avoids it. And, from the poet's point of view, its expression is the catharsis of pain by means of a power of masking that uses pain to create a beautiful form.[29]

The figure of the poet set forth here by the esthete A is inspired by the problem of the romantic genius and the tragedy of the work of art that fails time and again in its attempt to communicate the interiority of genius. Writing in this case is presented as the cipher of a misunderstanding between the author and the reader: the painful spectacle of pain turned into entertainment and the alienation of those who are entertained or seek only fun. The esthete A is himself aware of this impossibility to the point at which he becomes illegible to himself precisely because of the impossibility of communicating: "I am as timorous as a *sheva*, as weak and muted as a *daghesch lene*; I feel like a letter printed backward in the line, and yet as uncontrollable as a pasha with three horse tails, as solicitous for myself and my thoughts as a bank for its banknotes."[30] Taking refuge in interiority and the zeal before the world on the part of the esthete A then expresses the insufficiency of poetic communication and the increasing impossibility of communicating interiority. Seen in this way, writing becomes a game and the world becomes the spectacle that nourishes it. The pain that constitutes interiority becomes incommunicable:

> My sorrow is my baronial castle, which lies like an eagle's nest high up on the mountain peak among the clouds. No one can take it by storm. From it I swoop down into actuality and snatch my prey, but I do not stay down there. I bring my booty home, and this booty is a picture I weave into the tapestries at my castle.[31]

Communication is truncated, and the message or expression of interiority bounces off the walls of an interiority that increasingly close in on itself and

29 The position of the esthete A is similar to that of Kierkegaard himself. Cf. Karl Löwith, *Von Hegel zu Nietzsche. Der revolutionäre Bruch im Denken des neunzehnten Jahrhunderts*, Stuttgart: S. Fischer 1969, p. 311; Adorno, *Kierkegaard. Konstruktion des Ästhetischen*, p. 51.

30 *SKS* 2, 30 / *EO1*, 22.

31 *SKS* 2, 30 / *EO1*, 42.

thus becomes empty. Communication is brought to a close and, with it, the growth of interiority evaporates.

In his letters to the esthete A, the ethical pseudonym says that he only takes up the pen with the motivation of writing to his friend to expound to him the superiority of the ethical life. B emphasizes that the philosophical digressions into which he sometimes enters are not due to a real interest in philosophy, but rather consist of, as he says to the esthete A: "to address you, to make you feel in every way that you are the one addressed."[32] This direct and exhortatory communication makes B consider ethics as a closed and complete sphere, as the final objective.[33] Writing itself is posed as a means of exhortation or instruction, but it ceases to be an end in itself as happens in the aesthetic moment. In this sense, from the point of view of B, it seems that writing cannot become a valid profession in which the expression of the general can be undertaken. According to B, the expression of the general occurs within the vocation, since it is the vocation that makes us human.[34] In this, B coincides with what Hegel stated in *The Philosophical Propaedeutic*: "When a man has a Vocation, he enters into cooperation and participation with the Whole. Through this he becomes objective.... If a man is *to become something he must know how to limit himself*, that is, make some specialty his Vocation."[35] Even more radically, B affirms that the greatest sin of all consists in being unfaithful to one's vocation. Like Hegel, B points out that talent must be limited by vocation. Indeed, the vocation allows the work to be perfected insofar as it has continuity. Talent, for its part and through its association with the instant, requires that everything be done "*uno tenore*."[36] Despite the fact that B postulates that talent can become a vocation, writing seems to be left out of that validation, and instead

32 *SKS* 3, 18; *EO2*, 172–173.

33 On this subject, see Wilfried Greve, "El dudoso eticista. *O lo uno o lo otro II*, de Kierkegaard," trans. by Daniel Gamper Sachse, *Enrahonar*, vol. 29, 1998, p. 25. See Harvie Ferguson, *Melancholy and the Critique of Modernity: Søren Kierkegaard's Religious Psychology of Melancholy*, London and New York: Routledge 1995, p. 119. See Patricia C. Dip, "Judge William: The Limits of the Ethical," in *Kierkegaard's Pseudonyms*, ed. by Katalin Nun and Jon Stewart, Farnham and Burlington: Ashgate 2015 (*Kierkegaard Research: Sources, Reception and Resources*, vol. 17), p. 190.

34 See *SKS* 3, 277 / *EO2*, 292.

35 G.W.F. Hegel, *The Philosophical Propaedeutic*, trans. by A. V. Miller, New York: Basil Blackwell 1986, § 45, p. 45. See Hegel, *Philosophischen Propädeutik*, in *Werke*, vol. 4, *Nürnberger und Heidelberger Schriften 1808–1817*, § 45, p. 263.

36 *SKS* 3, 278 / *EO2*, 294.

he exhorts the esthete A to find a vocation that allows him to overcome his melancholy.[37]

These negative ideas about writing are further emphasized in the introduction to *Prefaces*. There, Nicolaus Notabene raises from the outset the question of the relationship between ethics and aesthetics, taking for granted the superiority of ethics. In this sense, he considers it natural to move away from writing, calling it something clandestine.[38] Assuming, as B does, that marriage is the expression of ethical life, the demand that his wife makes to Notabene when she disregards his literary occupations is the claim of ethics over aesthetics.[39] At that point ethics literally makes writing burn. Notabene tries to seduce ethics with writing, but ethics argues that writing is something worse than a vice because it is socially validated. It is worse than a vice above all because the writer is snatched from the present, that is, from the place where he has to fulfill his duty. Beyond Notabene's ruse and the interest that he may arouse, for example, from the point of view of genres, the work calls into question the validity of the profession of a writer.[40]

In his famous book on the ethics of Protestantism, Max Weber points out, following what Luther said in the Augsburg Confession, that it is the legitimacy of the profession that marks its value before God.[41] Therefore, the problem of writing is to show what validity it has as a profession. As we have already seen, ethics condemns it, while aesthetics exalts it but makes it lose itself in an empty interiority. What about the religious sphere? In *The Point of View for My Work as an Author*, an ambiguous work in which, after much hesitation, Kierkegaard tries to explain the intention of his work as a writer, and which he conceives as "attestation,"[42] he reaffirms the idea that the whole of his work is that of a religious writer. However, Kierkegaard introduces an idea that seems paradoxical by stating that what corresponds to the religious sphere is silence. What relationship is there then between the plan of the work, writing and

37 In this sense, it seems that writing is a profession that must move away from melancholy, that is, that can encourage it rather than dominate it.

38 See *SKS* 4, 471–472 / *P*, 8–9.

39 See *SKS* 4, 472–473 / *P*, 9–10.

40 The question is how to maintain writing as an aesthetic expression in the ethical-religious task. That is how to make it or how to manage to make it the voice of ourselves. The voice of ourselves is not accepted because it requires a transparency that the individual cannot have.

41 Max Weber, *Die protestantische Ethik und der Geist des Kapitalismus/Die protestantischen Sekten und der Geist des Kapitalismus. Schriften 1904–1920*, Tübingen: Mohr Siebeck 2019, p. 231.

42 *SKS* 16, 12 / *PV*, 24.

silence? Beyond the apparent contradiction into which Kierkegaard's argument falls, the paradox consists in the following: that the awareness of the "the authorship" seems to imply that writing is taken up as an attempt to communicate religious silence,[43] in other words, to communicate the incommunicable. This impossibility also occurs in *The Point of View for My Work as an Author* itself, because Kierkegaard points out that he cannot fully explain his work as its writer since, he says, "I cannot make my God relationship public."[44] It is, as Kierkegaard adds, the very impossibility of explaining "the universally human inwardness, which every human being can have."[45] The dominant idea in relation to writing resides in the fact that it is in it that Kierkegaard assumes that he expresses his relationship with God, but for this to be the case, then the profession, writing, must be validated by religion itself.

Thus, Kierkegaard affirms that as a writer he has been educated by God. According to Kierkegaard, what he has written is not pleasant to write because he does it out of duty since he is—like Socrates—at the service of God.[46] In that duty of the religious, there is the imposition of a limit to the imagination and creative fantasy.[47] Religious duty forms writing. That is why the work, says Kierkegaard, does not arise from poetic passion but from the fear of God.[48] Under this idea of limitation, writing is then conceived as the mission or vocation to remain obedient in what each person does. Indeed, in a note in his journals, Kierkegaard recounts that after the publication of each of his works—up to the *Postscript*—he considered giving up writing and becoming a rural pastor.[49] However, after that date he no longer mentions the idea of giving up writing but rather constructs or writes a public justification, such as *The Point of View for My Work as an Author*, in which the confession about giving up writing in favor of a valid profession is not present. Beyond the cloak of doubt that may cover the truth of what Kierkegaard himself said about the plan of his work designed from the beginning with a clear linearity, what is important

43 *SKS* 16, 12 / *PV*, 23.
44 *SKS* 16, 13 / *PV*, 25.
45 *SKS* 16, 13 / *PV*, 25–26.
46 See *SKS* 16, 50 / *PV*, 71.
47 See *SKS* 16, 52–53 / *PV*, 72–73. The idea of the limitation of talent by a vocation coincides with the limitation that, from the point of view of the profession of writing, religious duty imposes on fantasy. In this sense, religious duty establishes a formation or an education in writing.
48 See *SKS* 16, 53 / *PV*, 73.
49 See *SKS* 25, 259, NB28: 54 / *KJN* 9, 261.

here is to see the sense of appropriation of the profession in relation to validating an aesthetic occupation for religious purposes.[50]

As Weber rightly points out, from the point of view of Lutheranism—and this is clear in what B states—the professions do not form a hierarchy. This is what Climacus does when he points out that there would be no differences in principle between a pastor and a poet, and even a poet can do his job better than a pastor if he has religious pathos. In this sense, Climacus affirms: "to become a poet requires a call; to become a religious speaker requires only three examinations."[51] The poet borders on the religious, but his mistake is that he seeks to avoid suffering, or, in other words, he seeks to use writing as a catharsis to sublimate suffering, while religious seriousness does not reflect on suffering in order to evade it but rather is reflected *within* suffering.[52] In the journals, Kierkegaard states, in connection with what is presented in *The Point of View for My Work as an Author*, that he has remained faithful to the task by renouncing the applause and the achievements of the interesting.[53] He concludes that he is two things at once: a poet and a Christian thinker. The effort of the writer's work would then have been to reconcile these two things. The key to the problem of the profession of writing lies in how to make a religious *use* of an aesthetic medium and maintain in that aesthetic medium the freedom of the person to whom it is communicated. There is a moment of appropriation of writing and acceptance as a destiny, as a vocation. Aesthetic writing and religious writing meet, while ethics seems to be left out. The meeting between the aesthetic and the religious is given by the impossibility of communicating interiority, in the esthete by default and in the religious because, as Kierkegaard points out, it is impossible to communicate the relationship with God and also because respect for the freedom of the reader is required. The ethical sphere is left out precisely because it requires transparency.

The religious aspect of writing as the impossibility of explaining existence is also pointed out by Climacus in the *Postscript* when he states: "Even if someone gave me ten rix-dollars, I would not take it upon myself to explain the riddle of existence."[54] Writing and its inability to communicate interiority, as

50 Perhaps one can see a relationship between, on the one hand, B's idea that every man has a vocation and that in it he expresses the general-human and, on the other, the idea that takes shape in Kierkegaard—from the autobiographical point of view—about writing as a profession.

51 *SKS* 7, 395 / *CUP1*, 435.

52 *SKS* 21, 249, NB9:78 / *KJN* 5, 259: "The fact that I cannot present myself fully means that I am, after all, essentially a poet."

53 See *SKS* 22, 23, NB11:27 / *KJN* 6, 19.

54 *SKS* 7, 392 / *CUP1*, 451.

Adorno has rightly said, becomes a cipher, an allegory, which would lead to an intermediate dominion that in Kierkegaard would be presented as the treatment of the affects.[55] In other words, writing is the expression of reading in the blurred writing that is existence itself. An existence becomes blurred precisely because it is determined by melancholy. In relationship with this, it is striking, on the other hand, that, even in the last years of his life, Kierkegaard refers to melancholy using aesthetic-religious categories, showing himself to have taken a step back with respect to what was pointed out by some of his pseudonyms. This can be seen, for example, in the fact that he speaks of melancholy as something that does not affect the spirit and as something that the spirit cannot eradicate.[56] For Alastair Hannay, commenting on Gordon Marino's essay, "Despair and Depression," the fact that melancholy remains alien to the spirit would show that it is precisely thanks to that distance that Kierkegaard was able to build a body of work, but on the other hand, it would show that without melancholy such a body of work would not have been possible.[57] This detail is not of minor importance. That Kierkegaard takes a step backwards in his theoretical understanding of melancholy and, above all, with respect to the possibility of overcoming it, means that the phenomenon can be understood theoretically but not overcome existentially. In other words, although the pseudonyms are created as a strategy of approaching and distancing at the same time, (approaching the reader by showing existential figures; distancing themselves from the author as authority), they are the discourse's forms of existence, that is, they are thoughts. In this sense, some of the pseudonyms can capture what the problem is in theoretical terms, but they cannot effectively specify the form in which it can be overcome. In this sense, think of what was said repeatedly by Johannes de Silentio regarding his understanding of the leap into the absurd but his inability to execute it. Kierkegaard's reference to melancholy in a primary sense, so to speak, would indicate that man can know but not overcome it. Redoubling the effort would not be possible in any case. Or it would be so in the sense of aesthetic transformation. On the other hand, the fact that Kierkegaard affirms that his melancholy does not affect the spirit, may mean either that Kierkegaard understands his own melancholy as a state of mind or that he did not understand it in the sense of a spiritual metamorphosis and therefore it did not in itself lead him to an ethical-religious existence.

---

55 Theodor Adorno, *Kierkegaard. Konstruktion des Ästhetischen*, p. 49.

56 See *SKS* 20, 35, NB:34 / *KJN* 4, 34.

57 See Alastair Hannay, "Kierkegaard on Melancholy and Despair," in *Ethics, Love, and Faith in Kierkegaard: Philosophical Engagements*, ed. by Edward F. Mooney, Bloomington: Indiana University Press 2008, p. 147. Marino's article appears in this same collection.

In Kierkegaard the ethical-religious existence is writing itself. Perhaps in that sense it is possible to say that it is an aesthetic form but taken to another level. In this respect, what Starobinski points out about the relationship between fiction and melancholy is valuable.[58] By taking responsibility for himself as a writer, Kierkegaard is for that very reason assuming that the essence of his existence is melancholy.

When we keep with the idea of the validity of the profession in the Protestant context, the impossibility of explaining writing has to do with the very impossibility of confession,[59] that is, with the impossibility of the ethical demand for transparency. The fundamental question that betrays itself here consists in knowing whether writing, that is to say, the relationship with God, can only be explained by means of writing itself. If the answer is affirmative, then the validity—and the impossibility—of writing are already given in its origin by a religious interest as a search to make interiority known, or, in other words, to make the relationship with God known. The relationship with God is expressed only in the profession. In this sense, and if we believe the uniqueness of Kierkegaard's work with respect to the religious sphere, then the exposition of the spheres or stages would have the same intention: to show that there is only one sphere, the religious one, and that what happens in its exposition is in reality its unfolding.

Interiority is elevated to mystery, to the level of a secret, which seeks to communicate itself through vocation. In other words, there is a vocation to communicate the secret that is interiority, no longer intentionally hiding it as in an aesthetic game, nor demanding its transparent manifestation as in ethics, but rather manifesting it in the figure of writing itself. In this respect, Maurice Blanchot points out: "that is the calling that Kierkegaard recognizes, and it expresses the torment of the man who, enclosed in himself, wants to announce his secret to others and can only do so by abolishing it."[60] But the abolition of secrecy is, in terms of indirect communication, the gesture towards the interiority of the reader himself. More strictly, what is abolished is not the secret but the person who communicates it. In the appendix to the *Postscript* signed by Kierkegaard himself, and where he indicates that he is thus saying goodbye to the pseudonyms, he makes an important gesture in this regard:

---

58 See Jean Starobinski, *L'Encre de la mélancholie*, Paris: Éditions du Seuil 2012, pp. 402–405.

59 Volker Rühle, *En los laberintos del autoconocimiento. El* Sturm und Drang *y la Ilustración alemana*, Madrid: Akal 1997, pp. 31–32.

60 Maurice Blanchot, *Faux Pas*, trans. by Charlotte Mandell, Stanford: Stanford University Press 2001, p. 20.

> What I in one way or another know about the pseudonymous authors of course does not entitle me to any opinion, but not to any doubt, either, of their assent, since their importance (whatever that may become *actually*) unconditionally does not consist in making any new proposal, some unheard-of discovery, or in founding a new party and wanting to go further, but precisely in the opposite, in wanting to have no importance, in wanting, at a remove that is the distance of double-reflection, once again to read through solo, if possible in a more inward way, the original text of individual human existence-relationships, the old familiar text handed down from the fathers.[61]

As writing consists of the reading of human existence and its transmission, it must, therefore, refer the reader to those human categories. This making reference through writing to one's own interiority is what is characteristic of religious writing. In the words of Climacus, what is edifying consists properly in that reference to interiority. Indeed, as expressed by Climacus in the *Postscript*, and by Kierkegaard himself in *The Point of View for My Work as an Author*, writing from a religious point of view implies taking up suffering as religious pathos.[62] With this we return to the beginning, since the conception of possession as catharsis expressed by A in the *Diapsalmata* quoted at the beginning of this work is also based on suffering as a fundamental category. But unlike the religious position, the poetic position seeks to escape from suffering. Uplifting communication reflects on suffering and tries "*uplifting through suffering*."[63] The work of the appropriation of writing as a profession leads us to consider that it is precisely this appropriation that marks the passage from escape or entertainment to edification. In taking up writing as a profession, Kierkegaard redefines the idea of the poetic life as a form of cowardice,[64] and instead he begins to understand poetry itself as another way of being a Christian. Being a poet in the service of Christianity thus implies understanding the transformation of talent into vocation. The imagination and the theatrical game of pseudonyms driven by melancholy are redirected by the voice of God. Writing then appears as the expression of the ethical-religious task. Proper writing as a profession is not the testimony of the relationship with God, but it is itself the relationship with God.

---

61 *SKS* 7, 572–573 / *CUP1*, 629–630.
62 See *SKS* 7, 395 / *CUP1*, 435.
63 *SKS* 7, 396 / *CUP1*, 436.
64 See *SKS* 1, 332 / *CI*, 298.

Bibliography

Adorno, Theodor, *Kierkegaard. Konstruktion des Ästhetischen*, Frankfurt am Main: Suhrkamp 1966.

Blanchot, Maurice, *Faux Pas*, trans. by Charlotte Mandell, Stanford: Stanford University Press 2001.

Celan, Paul, "Fadensonnen," in *Obras completas*, trans. by José Luis Reina Palazón, bilingual edition, Madrid: Trotta 2000.

Dip, Patricia C., "Judge William: The Limits of the Ethical," in *Kierkegaard's Pseudonyms*, ed. by Katalin Nun and Jon Stewart, Farnham and Burlington: Ashgate 2015 (*Kierkegaard Research: Sources, Reception and Resources*, vol. 17), pp. 177–192.

Ferguson, Harvie, *Melancholy and the Critique of Modernity: Søren Kierkegaard's Religious Psychology of Melancholy*, London and New York: Routledge 1995.

Ginzo Fernández, Arsenio, *Protestantismo y filosofía. La recepción de la Reforma en la filosofía alemana*, Madrid: Universidad de Alcalá 2000.

Greve, Wilfried, "El dudoso eticista. *O lo uno, o lo otro II*, de Kierkegaard," trans. by Daniel Gamper Sachse, *Enrahonar*, vol. 29, 1998, pp. 19–33.

Hannay, Alastair, "Kierkegaard on Melancholy and Despair," in *Ethics, Love, and Faith in Kierkegaard: Philosophical Engagements*, ed. by Edward F. Mooney, Bloomington: Indiana University Press 2008, pp. 147–152.

Hegel, G.W.F., *Werke*, vols. 1–20, ed. by Eva Moldenhauer and Karl Markus Michel, Frankfurt am Main: Suhrkamp 1986.

Hegel, G.W.F. *The Philosophical Propaedeutic*, trans. by A.V. Miller, New York: Basil Blackwell 1986.

[Kierkegaard, Søren] *Søren Kierkegaards Skrifter*, vols. 1–28, K1-K28, ed. by Niels Jørgen Cappelørn, Joakim Garff, Jette Knudsen, Johnny Kondrup and Alastair McKinnon, Copenhagen: Gad Publishers 1997–2012.

Kierkegaard, Søren, *The Concept of Irony*, trans. by Howard and Edna Hong, Princeton: Princeton University Press 1992 (*Kierkegaard's Writings*, vol. 2).

Kierkegaard, Søren, *Either/Or, Part 1*, trans. by Howard and Edna Hong, Princeton: Princeton University Press 1988 (*Kierkegaard's Writings*, vol. 3, Part 1).

Kierkegaard, Søren, *Either/Or, Part 2*, trans. by Howard and Edna Hong, Princeton: Princeton University Press 1988 (*Kierkegaard's Writings*, vol. 3, Part 2).

Kierkegaard, Søren, *Concluding Unscientific Postscript to* Philosophical Fragments, vol. 1, trans. by Howard and Edna Hong, Princeton: Princeton University Press 1992 (*Kierkegaard's Writings*, vol. 11, Part 1).

Kierkegaard, Søren, *Stages on Life's Way*, trans. by Howard and Edna Hong, Princeton: Princeton University Press 1989 (*Kierkegaard's Writings*, vol. 11).

Kierkegaard, Søren, *Kierkegaard's Journals and Notebooks*, vols. 1–11, ed. by Niels Jørgen Cappelørn, Alastair Hannay, David Kangas, Bruce H. Kirmmse, George Pattison,

Vanessa Rumble and K. Brian Söderquist, Princeton and Oxford: Princeton University Press 2007–2020.

Kierkegaard, Søren, *Prefaces. Writing Sampler*, trans. by Todd W. Nichol, Princeton: Princeton University Press 2009 (*Kierkegaard's Writings*, vol. 9).

Kierkegaard, Søren, *The Point of View*, trans. by Howard and Edna Hong, Princeton: Princeton University Press 2009 (*Kierkegaard's Writings*, vol. [illegible])

Löwith, Karl, *Von Hegel zu Nietzsche. Der revolutionäre Bruch im Denken des neunzehnten Jahrhunderts*, Stuttgart: S. Fischer 1969.

Rühle, Volker, *En los laberintos del autoconocimiento. El* Sturm und Drang *y la Ilustración alemana*, Madrid: Akal 1997.

Starobinski, Jean, *L'Encre de la mélancholie*, Paris: Éditions du Seuil 2012.

Stewart, Jon, *An Introduction to Hegel's Lectures on the Philosophy of Religion: The Issue of Religious Content in the Enlightenment and Romanticism*, Oxford: Oxford University Press 2022.

Stewart, Jon, *The Unity of Content and Form in Philosophical Writing: The Perils of Conformity*, London: Bloomsbury 2013.

Weber, Max, *Die protestantische Ethik und der Geist des Kapitalismus/Die protestantischen Sekten und der Geist des Kapitalismus. Schriften 1904–1920*, Tübingen: Mohr Siebeck 2019.

CHAPTER 3

God as "Intermediate Determinant": The Debate between Feuerbach and Kierkegaard on Christian Love

Pablo Uriel Rodríguez

Abstract

Feuerbach and Kierkegaard share the thesis that Christian charity strains temporal intersubjective bonds. However, they draw opposite conclusions from this premise. Feuerbach thinks that Christian love ultimately hinders true contact and cooperation among men. Kierkegaard, by contrast, considers that only the religious transfiguration of worldly love grounds the actual realization of what natural love merely promises but never fulfills: the authentic encounter of two free personalities. I shall defend the idea that both thinkers are not as far apart as a first reading might lead us to assume.

After Kant's critique of metaphysics and despite Hegel's effort to rehabilitate a rational inquiry into the nature of God, 19th-century philosophy of religion moved away from the question of the existence of a Supreme Being to the question of how the notion of such a being affects and conditions the earthly life of human beings. The field opened up by this new question is the space in which Feuerbach's anthropological reflections and Kierkegaard's psychological analysis develop. And it is also the horizon of the discussion in which both philosophers apparently confront each other as antagonists. Feuerbach's critique of theology means to show the contradictory character of the essence and existence of the Christian God because the affirmation of these inconsistencies amounts to a direct denial of the human being. According to Feuerbach, the strongest proof against God is the pathological and alienated existence in which the concrete individuals who inhabit Christian culture are submerged.[1] Kierkegaard, for his part, considered intellectually sterile and ethically

1 See *SW* II, 410–411. I use *SW* as the abbreviation for Ludwig Feuerbach, *Sämtliche Werke*, vols. 1–12, ed. by Wilhelm Bolin and Friedrich Jodl, Stuttgart-Bad Cannstatt, Fromman Verlag-Gunther Holzboog 1959–1964.

 | DOI:10.1163/9789004689459_005

reprehensible both the attempt to argue theoretically in favor of the existence of God and the project of rationally determining his essence.[2] Kierkegaard does not want to weigh up the reasons for the reality or the unreality of God. His concern is to place before the concrete individual an exclusive alternative (*aut-aut*). *Either* the inconsistency of the self that, consciously or unconsciously, chooses *being-in-the world without God*, *or* the fullness achieved by the self that chooses *being-in-the-world-from and before God*.

Researchers into the relationship between Kierkegaard and Feuerbach have followed two main strategies. On the one hand, some scholars analyze the explicit references to Feuerbach in Kierkegaard's *corpus*.[3] This approach underscores the fact that Feuerbach's critique of the sweetened and hypocritical Christianity of modern civilization is regarded positively by Kierkegaard. Unlike most human beings who construct themselves as Christians, Feuerbach's rejection of Christian dogma constitutes an authentic (negative) link with Christian truth. Up to a point, Kierkegaard shares Feuerbach's attack upon Christianity because its target is the religion of the aesthetic or ethical stages. Other scholars, however, suggest that Kierkegaard's thought reacts against the modern anthropologization of theology, the central figure of which is perhaps Feuerbach himself.[4] The latter aims to make human beings recognize the identity between the human essence and the divine essence. Kierkegaard's intention, by contrast, is to show that there is an absolute difference between the human being and the true God (religiousness B), so that the well-known identity of God and man (Feuerbach's fundamental thesis) is nothing other than the identity of human essence and the human representation of the divine essence (religiousness A). Feuerbach overturns the traditional Christian doctrine: religion fantastically claims that God creates man, but, in truth, it is man who invents God. Kierkegaard, however, "turns Feuerbach's theory of projection back on Feuerbach himself in order to emphasize that a religion of

2 See *SKS* 18, 204, JJ:202 / *KJN* 2, 188; *SKS* 18, 271, JJ:393 / *KJN* 2, 251; and *SKS* 25, 239, NB28:31 / *KJN* 9, 241.

3 See István Czakó, "Feuerbach: A Malicious Demon in the Service of Christianity," in *Kierkegaard and his German Contemporaries*, Tome I, *Philosophy*, ed. by Jon Stewart, Aldershot and Burlington: Ashgate 2007; Abingdon and New York: Routledge 2016 (*Kierkegaard Research: Sources, Reception and Resources*, vol. 6), p. 41. See also George Arbaugh, "Kierkegaard and Feuerbach," *Kierkegaardiana*, vol. 11, 1980, pp. 9–10.

4 See Nelly Viallaneix, *Kierkegaard. El único ante Dios,* trans. by Juan Llopis, Barcelona: Herder 1977, pp. 55–56 and pp. 70–71. See also Jean Brun, "Feuerbach et Kierkegaard," *Cahiers de Sud*, vol. 50, no. 371, 1963, p. 39.

transcendence necessarily offends the understanding ... [he] suggests that the immanentist critic itself, and not the Christian, is the victim of an illusion."[5]

I am interested in contrasting these philosophers' thinking, using a strategy different from previous ones. Both Kierkegaard and, to a greater extent, Feuerbach, emphasize the co-existential nature of man. "Being-in-the-world" implies "being-with-others." Both philosophers produce a kind of *decentering* of the modern subject. Descartes' "*Ego cogito*," the fundamental assumption from which modern philosophy begins to think, is replaced by Kierkegaard's "*Du skal* [*elske-troe*]" (You shall [love-believe])[6] and by Feuerbach's "*Ego sentio*" (I feel), in which the self understands and experiences itself as the *You* of an other.[7] Both philosophers maintain that human beings feel and know themselves to be intimately pierced by an opening to the other. In *The Concept of Anxiety*, Kierkegaard's pseudonym explains that through modesty the individual experiences himself as a sexually determined being and, at the same time, foreshadows an impulse towards the other.[8] In *The Essence of Christianity*, Feuerbach argues that sexuality is an essential determination that penetrates the whole being of men,[9] and he later states that thanks to the erotic drive, the individual becomes aware of the limits of his being and longs to be fulfilled by a third-party.[10] On the other hand, whereas Kierkegaard, through Vigilius Haufniensis, holds that the *individuum* is himself and the race and that human freedom is essentially communicative,[11] through Anti-Climacus, he affirms that, in relating itself to itself, the self relates to another and, also, that this other is the *criterion* and *goal* of the self's selfhood.[12] Feuerbach's philosophical development begins in his dissertation *De Ratione* (1828) where he asserts that the individual separated from his fellows is a *res ficta*.[13] Four decades later, in his unfinished *Zur Ethik: Der Eudämonismus* (1867–68), he writes: "I am only

---

5 Jonathan Malesic, "Illusion and Offense in *Philosophical Fragments*: Kierkegaard's Inversion of Feuerbach's Critique of Christianity," *International Journal for Philosophy of Religion*, vol. 62, no. 1, 2007, p. 45.

6 See *SKS* 9, 95 / *WL*, 90 and *SKS* 11, 234 / *SUD*, 122.

7 See *SW* II, 296–297 / *PPF* pp. 224–225. (I use *PPF* as an abbreviation for "Principles of the Philosophy of the Future," in *The Fiery Brook: Selected Writings*, trans. and ed. by Zawar Hafi, London: Verso 2012, pp. 175–244.)

8 See *SKS* 4, 372–373 / *CA*, 68–69.

9 *SW* VI, 110 / *EC*, p. 92. (I use *EC* to abbreviate Ludwig Feuerbach, *The Essence of Christianity*, trans. by George Elliot, New York: Prometheus Books 1989.)

10 See *SW* VI, 188–189 and 203 / *EC*, p. 156 and p. 167.

11 See *SKS* 4, 335 and 425 / *CA*, 28 and 123–124.

12 *SKS* 11, 130 and 193 / *SUD*, 13–14 and 79–80.

13 See *SW* XI, 65.

I through You and with You. I am aware of myself only because you are facing my consciousness as a visible and tangible me, as another human being."[14]

Logically, if Kierkegaard and Feuerbach give intersubjectivity a preponderant role in their respective analyses of human existence, then the influence of the notion of God on interpersonal bonds must have been a central concern for both of them. This paper aims to show how Kierkegaard and Feuerbach assess the impact of the Christian commandment of neighbor-love on human relationships. Does God as "intermediate-determinant" (*mellembestemmelse*) break the "I-You" relationship, or does He make possible an authentic bond between the self and its neighbor?[15] Feuerbach and Kierkegaard share the thesis that Christian charity strains temporal intersubjective bonds. However, they draw opposite conclusions from this premise. Feuerbach thinks that Christian love ultimately hinders true contact and cooperation among men. Kierkegaard, by contrast, considers that only the religious transfiguration of worldly love grounds the actual realization of what natural love merely promises but never fulfills: the authentic encounter of two free personalities. I shall defend the idea that the two thinkers are not as far apart as a first reading might lead us to assume.

1 Feuerbach's Attack upon Christian Love in *The Essence of Christianity*

In *Works of Love*, Kierkegaard argues that, from a rigorously Christian perspective, intersubjective relations have a triadic character: self - God - other. Feuerbach agrees with him and, in the final chapter of *The Essence of Christianity*, writes:

> Love should be *immediate*, undetermined by anything else than its object.... But if I interpose between my fellow man and myself the idea of an individuality, in whom the idea of the species is supposed to be already realized, I annihilate the very soul of love, I disturb the unity by the idea of a third external to us.[16]

Love is the active confirmation of our identity: love gives us the awareness that our existence is worthy. "Whoever loves me," writes Feuerbach in *The Essence of Faith According to Luther*, "calls to me: 'Love yourself, for I love you; I only

14 *SW* X, 269.

15 This paper further expands on a suggestion made by M. Jamie Ferreira (see M. Jamie Ferreira, *Love's Grateful Striving: A Commentary on Kierkegaard's* Works of Love, New York: Oxford University Press 2001, p. 71).

16 *SW* VI, 323–324 / *EC*, p. 268.

show you and make clear to you what you are and must do. My love justifies and, indeed, obligates you to love yourself.'"[17] The word "love" means the core affection that carries a proper and successful relationship with another human being, when I recognize this other as my "You," and I place myself as the "You" of this other "I." This recognition is not a mere inner feeling but needs to be, and should be, manifested: "you cannot love without confessing, expressing, and practicing your love, for love is something that you have not for yourself but the other."[18] Love then is *authentic love* when it is materialized through concrete practices of solidarity (economic assistance and psychological care), whose main objective is the other's integral well-being (physical and mental). To be true, this recognition cannot be conditioned by any particular determination of its object: it must be a universal recognition. As Feuerbach points out at the beginning of his *History of Modern Philosophy from Bacon to Spinoza*, the men of the pagan world attributed true humanity only to the members of their race, culture, or country: "man was not man as such, but the nationally defined man."[19] Pagan philosophy, by contrast, rises to a cosmopolitan perspective and transcends the limits of the narrow and local vision of pagan religions: rational reflection demands the breaking down of ethnic or ideological walls. The Greek or the Latin philosopher knows that Athens or Rome does not exhaust humanity, but such knowledge is, however, purely theoretical. The *head* (philosophy) does not have the necessary power to bring about historical change; only the *heart* (religion) does. Christian religion is a more intense and concrete manifestation of pagan philosophical internationalism. The great historical merit of the New Testament was the translation of the philosophical concept of humanity into a popular language, which made it possible to overcome the ethnic and cultural barriers of paganism. Christ symbolizes the popular consciousness of the unity of the species: "he wished to bless and unite them all without distinction of sex, age, rank, or nationality."[20] Christianity leaves behind all particularism and commands a universal love: *Man is to be loved for man's sake*. The difficulty lies in the fact that Christian theology can only express this duty in its mystical language and thus distorts and offends this *law of intelligence*. The others are not an object worthy of love for their singularity but only because they are *children of God*, who created them in His image and likeness. Christianity gives with one hand and takes away with the

17 SW VII, 362–363 / EF, p. 100. (I use EF to abbreviate Ludwig Feuerbach, *The Essence of Faith according to Luther*, trans. by Melvin Cherno, New York: Harper & Row 1967.

18 SW II, 372 / FPD, p. 278. (I use FPD to abbreviate Ludwig Feuerbach, "Fragments Concerning the Characteristics of My Philosophical Development," in *The Fiery Brook*, pp. 265–296.)

19 SW III, 1.

20 SW VI, 324 / EC, p. 268.

other: it announces *universal love* but in reality practices *particular love*. The Christian believer is allowed to love only another Christian believer or, at best, a potential Christian believer. However, in this way, the Christian lover loses his neighbor: "religious love gives itself to man only for God's sake, so that it is given only in appearance to man, but in reality to God."[21] Feuerbach rejects the indirect love of man because the love of man that depends on the will of God is not real love. The mediation of a third party, who comes *between* the partners in their relationships, destroys the essence of love. Feuerbach returns to the words of the New Testament (1 John 4:20–21) and inquires: How strongly will the individual, who devoutly fulfills the commandment to love God with all his heart, love his neighbor? If one truly loves the man who one sees, there is no strength left for loving God, and conversely.[22] The restriction that the Christian faith imposes on love suspends the ties and obligations between human beings. Feuerbach thinks that Christian neighbor-love denaturalizes the mere "living together" that characterizes man's earthly existence and undermines social cohesion (horizontal relationships) which allow for individuation. That is, neighbor-love, paradoxically, requires and at the same time realizes the "isolation" of the individual, a mode of isolation that is the condition of the higher vertical relationship between the Creator and the creature. Faith reconnects (*re-ligare*) human beings with God and disconnects men from each other. For this reason, the attempt to derive an order of the state from Christian premises is a supreme contradiction. If we want to think about the emergence of political institutions from the perspective of the concrete human being, says Feuerbach in his unpublished essay, "Necessity of a Reform of Philosophy," we have to admit that "the reason why men come together is precisely that they do not believe in any god, that they negate their religious belief unconsciously, involuntarily, and in practice. Not the belief in God, but rather the doubt concerning him is the actual cause underlying the foundation of states."[23] Therefore, the suppression of the theological illusion allows men to focus on their temporal existence.

In the first part of Feuerbach's book, we find the basic assumptions of this radical critique of Christian love. At the beginning of *The Essence of Christianity*, the German philosopher wonders what man is. He answers: the unity of reason, will, and love. *Reason* makes us able to think, imagine and calculate. *Will* makes us able to overcome our instincts and become free. And *Love* makes

21 *SW* VI, 331 / *EC*, p. 274.

22 See *SW* II, 383–384 / *FPD*, p. 288.

23 *SW* II, 220 / *NR*, pp. 149–150. (I use the abbreviation *NR* for Ludwig Feuerbach, "Necessity of a Reform of Philosophy," in *The Fiery Brook*, pp. 145–152.)

us able to be emotionally affected by others and the things around us. Reason, will, and love are perfections of the essence of man, of the species (*Gattung*).[24] What does this mean? These absolute properties "are not powers which [individual] man possesses, for he is nothing without them, he is what he is only by them; they are the constituent elements of his nature, which he neither has nor makes the animating, determining, governing powers—divine, absolute powers—to which he can oppose no resistance."[25] When the eternal flame of passion burns in his soul, the individual goes beyond his limits and is driven to the most beautiful and heroic actions by his beloved. In this sense, the tension between finite (individual existence) and infinite (species essence), which defines the conscious life of the self and makes possible the delusion of a Supreme Being, has the following meaning: the self experiences its being as not coincident with its foundation. Therefore, the self feels supported by a power beyond its total control: the activity of the self is, at some point and to some degree, a passive one.

If the essence of God is nothing more than human nature, then the essence of God is also the unity of reason, will, and love, but *purified*, not limited by the boundaries of the individual human self. What follows from this *purification*? Reason, will, and love are powers that God possesses. God rules over them. Let's look at the case of love. The starting point is the statement "God is love." It is composed of a subject and a predicate, two different things: God and love. This is how Christian dogmatics presents the matter. The same theological construction of this affirmation suggests, with total coherence, that the subject (God) must be something distinct from the predicate (love). According to Feuerbach, the theological approach transforms the statement "God is love" into the statement "God has love." Thus, Christian theology places God *above* love, and dogmatics understands God as a being who can choose to love or not to love.[26] The theological assertion "God is love" weakens the power of feeling and contradicts the human experience of love. The concrete individual, the flesh and blood human being, has no sovereignty over love. He can neither choose to love nor not to love nor, much less, whom to love. God, on the contrary, makes his love dependent on his will. But, when it becomes the property of an absolute and infinite self, love is denied: it no longer acts in conformity

---

24 *SW* VI, 3 / *EC*, p. 3.

25 *SW* VI, 3–4 / *EC*, p. 3.

26 See *SW* VI, 64 / *EC*, pp. 52–53: "God appears to me in another form besides that of love; in the form of omnipotence, of a severe power not bound by love ... so long there lurks in the background of love a subject who *even without love* is *something by himself*, an unloving monster, a diabolical being, whose *personality*, separable and *actually separated from love*, delights in the *blood* of heretics and unbelievers,—the *phantom of religious fanaticism*."

with its law and submits to the law of that self. Theology transforms God's love into grace.[27]

Here, it must be remembered what Feuerbach says toward the end of Part One: "[God] is what individuals *ought to be* and *will be*."[28] Therefore, the particular bond that theology establishes between God and love is the goal to be achieved by the Christian individual in his relation with love. Establishing this aspiration, the Christian believer already demonstrates that he is mentally above and beyond the proper determinations of his finitude. And this aspiration follows logically from the fact that the believer conceives himself as the image and likeness of a God, who is above and beyond the determinations of nature. Thus, for Christianity, the self possesses an ontological consistency that is *prior to* and ultimately *independent* of all its intersubjective relationships. The natural man needs his fellow man for the realization of his being; the Christian "does not need of any other 'I'… 'he possesses the total fullness of his perfection in God,' that is, in himself."[29] For the Christian, love is not a necessity of the heart but an act of the will.

The results of this section can be summarized as follows: (1) When theology speaks about God, the predicate is what determines, and the subject is what is determined: the predicate (the power of love) is the real object of devotion in religion and not the subject (God) who possesses this predicate. Thus, the actual (human) meaning of the theological phrase "God is love" is "Love is divine" or, to put it in a natural and secular way, "the true social relations (*sittlichen Verhältnisse*) are sacred *as such*."[30]

(2) Christianity preaches *peace*—the unity of humankind—but brings the *sword* on earth. God demands what is God's; He also claims what belongs to Caesar. Faith not only undermines respect for moral and legal order but brings the believer into confrontation with the unbeliever: "Faith recognizes man

27 See *WC*, 576 / *EC*, p. 320 (note that this text is missing in *SW*): "The highest worship of God as a *personal* being is therefore the worship of God as an absolutely unlimited, arbitrary being. Personality, as such, is indifferent to all substantial determinations, which lie in the nature of things.… The love of God, as the predicate of a personal being, has here the significance of grace, favour.… Grace is arbitrary love,—love which does not act from an inward necessity of the nature, but which is equally capable of *not* doing what it does, which could, if it would, condemn its object; thus it is a groundless, unessential, arbitrary, absolutely subjective, merely personal love." I use *WC* as the abbreviation for Ludwig Feuerbach, *Das Wesen des Christenthums*, vol. 5 in *Gesammelte Werke*, vols. 1–21, ed. by Werner Schuffenhauer, Berlin: Akademie Verlag 2000–2022.

28 *SW* VI, 222 / *EC*, p. 184.

29 *SW* VI, 183 (this text appears in a footnote of the third edition which is missing in the English version).

30 *SW* VI, 329 / *EC*, p. 273.

only on condition that he recognizes God, i.e., faith itself.... The unbeliever is thus an outlaw—a man worthy of extermination."[31]

(3) Christian dogma substitutes the horizontal socio-political relationship "I - You" for the vertical theological relationship "I - God." Christians are required to love their neighbor only because in doing so they love God. This indirect form of love breaks up social links by making them derivative, accidental, and ultimately superfluous. The Christian community is the association of individuals who relate to each other without really relating to each other. The Christian believer lives in isolation from others and, therefore, stands above his own *factual being*.

2 Kierkegaard's Critique of the (Feuerbachian) Preferential Love

Kierkegaard's program in *Works of Love* is the careful and patient elucidation of Christian love (*Kjerlighed*). The cornerstone upon which this doctrine of love is constructed is the distinction between *preferential love* (*Forkjerlighed*) and *non-preferential love*. The fundamental thesis underlying this distinction is set out in the following statement: preferential love is *self-love* (*Selvkjerlighed*). This assertion remains hidden in the earthly (pagan) conception of love and is only established when approached from the Christian perspective. However, Kierkegaard also claims that paganism glorifies erotic love and friendship and condemns egoism. Therefore, Kierkegaard is perfectly aware that paganism differentiates between erotic love and friendship, on the one hand, and self-love, on the other. It is obvious that paganism is able to identify the selfishness that underlies false love: the earthly conception of love strongly rejects any kind of instrumentalization of the other for the sake of individual benefit. Paganism, then, succeeds in detecting the self-assertion that is present in erotic love (*Elskov - eros*) and friendship (*Venskab - philia*), that is, the presence of self-love in relationships in which both partners genuinely seek the personal benefit of the other. So, why does Kierkegaard observe that it is necessary to overcome the pagan conception of love? In answering this question, it is helpful first to take a detour through Feuerbach and then return to Kierkegaard.

In *The Essence of Christianity*, Feuerbach argues that "every being loves itself, its existence," so that to exist consciously means "self-verification, self-affirmation, self-love, joy in one's own perfection."[32] A few years later, in 1848, Feuerbach takes up these thoughts again and elaborates on them in his *Lectures on the Essence of Religion*. At the beginning of the Seventh Lecture, he explains the metaphysical (not moral or ethical) meaning of the word "egoism"

31 WC, 578–579 / EC, p. 321 (note that this text is missing in SW).

32 SW VI, 7–8 / EC, pp. 6–7. See also SW VI, 77–78 / EC, p. 63.

(*Egoismus*). Metaphysical egoism implies that a finite being can exist only if it is related to itself, that is, a finite being can preserve its life only if it cares for itself. Therefore, the human being, qua finite being, is (even without his knowledge and will) a self-centered being and cannot help but be so. By egoism, Feuerbach understands men's love of themselves: "the love that spurs him on to satisfy and develop all the impulses and tendencies without whose satisfaction and development he neither is nor can be a true, complete human being."[33] Udo Kern explains that metaphysical egoism also means self-defense against artificial and inhuman demands arising from theological hypocrisy, speculative fantasy, and political despotism.[34] What is most relevant in this context is, however, that Feuerbach points out that egoism includes the individual's love of the *human essence,* and, precisely for this reason, it also includes his love for other human beings because without this passion, without other selves, the self would lose its identity: "every love of an object or being is an indirect self-love."[35] Feuerbach goes a step further. The individual who does not care for himself is also unable to care for those around him. Consider an individual who does not love himself, who does nothing for the attainment of his purposes, or who is devoid of personal interests; such an individual would not appreciate others either, because he would be unable to determine what is beneficial and convenient for him: "unless I first love and worship myself, how can I love and worship what is useful and beneficial to me? How can I love a physician unless I love health? Or a teacher unless I am eager to acquire knowledge?"[36]

Does Feuerbach fail to see that *preferential love is self-love*? According to Kierkegaard, Feuerbach still misses something fundamental. Kierkegaard finds Feuerbach's dualistic distinction between positive self-love (*metaphysical egoism*) and selfish self-love (*vulgar egoism*) insufficient and proposes a triadic classification: (1) *negative self-love,* (2) *positive temporal or earthly self-love* and (3) *positive eternal or Christian self-love.*[37]

33 SW VI, 64 / LER, p. 50. (I use LER to abbreviate Ludwig Feuerbach, *Lectures on the Essence of Religion,* trans. by Ralph Manheim, New York: Harper & Row 1967.)

34 See Udo Kern, "'Nur der *ist etwas,* der *etwas liebt*' Zu Ludwig Feuerbachs dialogisch-ontologischer Philosophie der Liebe," in *Liebe in Zeiten pädagogischer Professionalisierung,* ed. by Elmar Driescher and Detlef Gaus, Heidelberg: VS Verlag für Sozialwissenschaften 2011, p. 256.

35 SW VI, 64 / LER, p. 50. Feuerbach considers self-love to be essentially social. As he explains in his late writing *Zur Ethik: Der Eudämonismus:* human beings benefit themselves by benefiting others (see SW X, 277). The metaphysical egoism feels happy only in unison with the happiness of others (see SW X, 287–288).

36 SW VIII, 65–66 / LER, p. 52.

37 I take and reformulate this distinction between three kinds of self-love from Sharon Krishek: *selfish self-love, proper unqualified self-love,* and *proper qualified self-love*

(1) The self seeks its private happiness without concern for the goals and needs of the other. In the extreme case, the selfishly self-loving individual is capable of even injuring the other so as to succeed. This kind of self-love is at odds with the good of the other.

(2) The self acts to achieve its well-being, its temporal happiness, which includes the fulfillment of its drives, desires, social commitments, duties, and preferences, with a lingering and unselfish concern for the well-being of the other. Both Kierkegaard and Feuerbach firmly believe that this kind of self-love would go as far as self-denial for the sake of the *beloved*, the *friend*, or the *compatriot*. In his *Lectures on the Essence of Religion*, Feuerbach says that "self-abnegation is only a form, a means, of self-affirmation, of self-love."[38] For example, when I sacrifice myself for the benefit of my compatriots their interest is mine: "it is my own desire that my country be saved. Thus, I am not sacrificing my life to any alien, theological being distinct from myself."[39] Kierkegaard, for his part, claims that earthly self-love is ready to sacrifice its own life and, therefore, could become a noble, abnegated, and generous self-love: a pure *human* love which the calculating mentality calls *reckless* and *foolish*, but which is still not Christian love, that is, it is not an *absolutely* pure love.

(3) The self respects and wishes for its own well-being, in a restricted sense of well-being: the eternal or Christian happiness of the self. It is this kind of qualified self-love that Christianity commands. This self-love demands from the human being an absolute relationship with the Absolute and a relative relationship with the relative. Since this kind of self-lover must tirelessly seek the eternal well-being of the others, more often than not he is at odds with the others' earthly understanding of their own happiness. For this reason, both the love of the other and the self-love of this self-lover are regarded by *worldly wisdom* as if they were not loving; even more, they are regarded as if they were *hate*, and *rewarded* as such.

Feuerbach seems to remain unaware of the risk inherent in self-assertion because, for him, the presence of self-love in the love of the other does not compromise the goal of love, namely the genuine recognition of the other's selfhood. Kierkegaard, on the other hand, evaluates the self-love that Feuerbach advocates against vulgar selfishness as a potential obstacle to the attainment of authentic love. In the words of *Works of Love*, Feuerbachian love still

(see Sharon Krishek, *Kierkegaard on Faith and Love*, New York: Cambridge University Press 2009, pp. 115–118).

38 *SW* VIII, 84 / *LER*, p. 67.

39 *SW* VIII, 96 / *LER*, p. 77.

seeks its own and therefore cannot recognize *what is the other's own.*[40] The problem with Feuerbachian love is that its source is a sensibly defined self. Its starting point is summed up in the expression "*I love.*" For Kierkegaard, this beginning is problematic because if one starts from the "I," one will remain within the horizon of the "I." The negative consequences of this failed starting point are twofold: *exclusivity* and *dissolution of otherness.*

The first danger of preferential (natural) love is the danger of restricting ourselves to building up relationships only with those we are sensually or psychologically inclined to relate to. Feuerbach says that when "I feel love," I'm the "You" of another "I," and so I'm determined by the object.[41] Kierkegaard agrees: *erotic love and friendship are determined by the object*,[42] i.e., by certain features and qualities of the other. However, this determination does not decenter the subject:

> When the lover or friend is able to love *only this one single person* in the whole world (which is a delight to the poet's ears), there is an enormous self-willfulness in this enormous devotion, and in his impetuous, unlimited devotion the lover is actually relating himself to himself in self-love.[43]

The "I" is affected by the other, but it is not completely passive in this very affection because such affection is pre-defined by the peculiarities of the "I." As the young esthete A from *Either/Or* explains in his essay on the emergence of erotic love, in its earliest stages, as a natural human force, desire *glimpses* and *exceeds* its object. The *dreaming desire* (the First Stage) is an unaccountable inner emotion, that is, a longing without motion, altogether vague about its goal. The *searching desire* (the Second Stage) awakens from its repose in itself and starts to move. In this stage, desire is already object-oriented, but its object is fragmented into a plurality. This desire does not turn toward a determinate goal but turns toward *all* possible goals. "Perhaps the most suggestive predicate for it is: it discovers."[44] However, this desire enjoys its journey of discovery more than the possession of what it has discovered. It is important to note that the searching desire is not absolutely undetermined: the young esthete A points out that in that journey of discovery a *deeper desire* is glimpsed. Therefore, it may be said that the searching desire *foreshadows* its object. We have seen that

40 See *SKS* 9, 268 / *WL*, 269.
41 See *SW* II, 296–297 / *PPF*, pp. 224–225 (§ 32).
42 See *SKS* 9, 73 / *WL*, 66.
43 *SKS* 9, 62 / *WL*, 55 (the emphasis is mine)
44 *SKS* 2, 86 / *EO1*, 80.

desire is understood as a natural power that is not yet able to determine its object, and thus has no fixed orientation. But what is the reason for this lack of orientation? Desire does not yet have any specific orientation because it does not yet possess a concrete and formed identity. With the emergence of an individualized self, desire becomes the desire of an individualized self. Therefore, desire turns into a specific desire, and its object becomes specific and individualized. The precedence and surplus of desire over its object become the determination of the object by the desiring individual self. Sensual and psychological love is preferential because the lover is an individual being. And the particular character of this individualized subject ultimately defines his preferences, obligations, commitments, and inclinations. In short, the subject determines his object of love.

In our everyday life, preferential love appears to us as something imposed, as a necessity: *the beloved (and in a certain sense the friend) is given to us, not chosen by us*. At the same time, when a person preferentially loves another specific person, her works of love live as *free works,* as if she had chosen them. This is completely understandable because, in this case, *operari sequitur esse* (action follows being): the lovers feel in agreement with themselves.[45] How can the paradox of this unity of necessity and freedom be explained? Superficially, it can be said that the lover does not choose his beloved, as a choice, at least in an immanent sense of the word, implying that one consciously establishes some criteria upon which one will choose. The Young Man, the first speaker of "In Vino Veritas," and Judge Wilhelm, the married man of "Some Reflections on Marriage in Answer to Objections," are in agreement: for the lovers, the unfathomable ground of their passion is hidden in darkness. The lovers, comments Wilhelm, prefer not to choose because their passion chooses better than they do. The lovers know that they have no communicable and unquestionable reason to love their beloved. The lovers refuse to found the whole substance of their erotic love, that which underlies the mutual feeling, on something trivial or circumstantial: the lovers cannot say that they love their beloved because he/she has green eyes and a beautiful smile. From these very same thoughts, the first speaker of "In Vino Veritas" concludes that the loving passion cannot be justified at all, and one lover is just as ludicrous as another. Therefore, the inexperienced Young Man refrains from love.[46]

However, according to the approach of *Works of Love*, although there is no *conscious choice*, this does not mean that there is no *choice*: the object of preferential love is found "by choosing, yes, by unconditionally selecting one single

45 See *SKS* 3, 50 / *EO2*, 43.

46 See *SKS* 6, 38–41 / *SLW*, 34 -37.

individual."[47] In this work, as Patricia Dip states, choosing an object of love means that what makes the beloved or the friend lovable always comes from the lover's identity.[48] Although the choice of the object of love is indeed an action that itself has a relative admixture of passivity (it is, to some extent, a tragic action), it still is an *action of the self.* And because of this, the limits, contingency, and peculiarities of the lovers are reflected in their object of love. The psychological and sensitive receptivity of the "I" is not universal: there are objects that remain outside its field of attention. Neighbor-love, says Feuerbach in his celebrated book, is arbitrary and absolutely subjective: based on faith: Christian love "has the significance of an act of grace, of a love in itself *superfluous*, of a love *without neediness* (*bedürfnislosen*)."[49] Kierkegaard takes Feuerbach's side: if love makes distinctions between men (if love is not universal), it is arbitrary. But this is just what love grounded on sensual passion, preferential love, Feuerbachian love, does! Thus, Kierkegaard takes Feuerbach's accusation and throws it in his face: love-need expresses a human richness. The greater this need is, the greater the richness. If someone loves one single person or a certain group of persons, he only needs that person or group. His love and richness are finite. We must say that this human being does not need loving, but he needs that person or group. In contrast, if someone needs to love without preferences, if someone needs to love everyone, which is what it means to love one's neighbor, then his need and richness are infinite. In the first case, the emphasis is on the particularity of the lover and his beloved. In the second case, the focus is on the universal essence of love and the deepness of the need. Only in this latter case is need a sign of richness. Preferential love can fail to find, can mistake, or can even lose its object; neighbor-love always finds its proper object and never loses it.[50] Kierkegaard's warning against preferential love, then, is the warning against the unavoidably excluding nature of this kind of love: *the lovers or the friends love each other by virtue of the similarity by which they are like each other and different from other people.*[51]

47 *SKS* 9, 62 / *WL*, 55.

48 See Patricia Dip, *Teoría y Praxis en* Las obras del amor. *Un recorrido por la erótica kierkegaardiana*, Buenos Aires: Editorial Gorla 2010, p. 100.

49 *WC*, 578 / *EC*, p. 321 (note that this text is missing in *SW* and the word "*bedürfnislosen*" is missing in English translation).

50 See *SKS* 9, 73–74 / *WL*, 67. Kierkegaard transfers the responsibility for the absence of the preferential love's object to the preferential lover: it is the absence of weakness of love in the lover.

51 See *SKS* 9, 63 / *WL*, 56. For Kierkegaard, the problem is not that the lovers or friends have identical wishes, thoughts, and lifestyle, but that their joining together separates them from others.

Now, it is necessary to deal with the problem of the *dissolution of otherness*. Let us review, once again, what Feuerbach says at the end of *The Essence of Christianity*. Feuerbach makes the following assertions: (1) the essence of religion is the *identity* of God with the human being; (2) the conscious form of religion is the *distinction* between God and the human being; and (3) love reveals the essence of religion, and faith manifests its conscious form. Therefore, he concludes that faith produces in the human individual an *inward division* (between himself and his essence) and an *outward division* (between himself and the others). Love, on the contrary, reunites man with his nature and his fellows, or, in Feuerbach's poetic words, "love heals the wounds which are made by faith in the heart of man."[52]

This notion of love clearly implies a movement of return to oneself from alienation. With love, man moves through the other to himself, and he finds himself again in the other. In the chapter on "The Distinction between Christianity and Heathenism," Feuerbach defines the other as (1) "the deputy of mankind," (2) "my *alter ego*," and (3) "the revelation of my own nature."[53] Thus, love does not relate the self to otherness but to its authentic identity. The other cannot escape the fate of every object given to the human individual: in the worst case, to be a reflection of that individual's particular finitude, and in the best case, to be a reflection of the universal infinitude of human nature. Christian believers, explains Feuerbach in the final chapter of *The Essence of Christianity*, hold that a fellow man is an object of love only on account of his resemblance to God. According to the true law of love, argues Feuerbach, the fellow man is an object of love *for his own sake*, i.e., *for the sake of his essence.*[54] However, the essence of the other is nothing more than the essence of the human race. Thus, if the "I" loves the "You" for the sake of its essence, the "I" does not love this particular "You" but human nature in general in the "You."[55] Even more since the essence of the "I" and the essence of the human race are the same, then the "I" loves himself in his fellow man. The *other of the* "I," at least in *The Essence of Christianity*, is not a "You." It is just an "other I" or a "second I."

Kierkegaard is suspicious of such an understanding because it makes love a "being-for-itself," or, in other words, it turns the "being-for-other" into a

---

52 See *SW* VI, 298 / *EC*, p. 247.

53 *SW* VI, 191 / *EC*, p. 158.

54 *SW* VI, 323–324 / *EC*, p. 268 (Here the English translation is incomplete.)

55 After all, the relation between the lover and the beloved is the human race's self-relation (see *SW* VI, 188 and 324 / *EC*, p. 156 and pp. 268–269). When the self loves, when it feels the need of the other, the self feels in him the will of the species to preserve and grow itself. The real lover and the real beloved are not individuals but humankind.

means for self-affirmation and self-esteem.[56] The most profound doubt of the self is practical and existential and not theoretical and metaphysical. The self does not look for an ontological certainty ("I am") but for the reassurance of its worth ("I am beloved"). The self does not struggle for self-preservation but rather for self-respect. The direct earthly love of self cannot give us this reassurance. As Kierkegaard argues, people may not have the strength to be alone by themselves and love themselves. Therefore, preferential love enhances a person's self-esteem through the mediation of another's gaze, or in Kierkegaard's words, "[self-affirmation] does not really manifest itself until the other *I* is found and the one *I* and the *other I* in this alliance find the strength for the self-esteem of self-love."[57]

In *The Essence of Christianity,* the others are estimated by virtue of their human faculties and nature. The others are respected because they are ends in themselves, they are rational (*Reason*) and sensible (*Heart*) practical agents (*Will*).[58] The Feuerbachian "I," seeks and recognizes *Man* in men. Therefore, his recognition is not unconditional. According to Kierkegaard, *seeing* Man turns the concrete human being into an *unseen* one. Feuerbach replaces the concrete person with his own ideal conception of the human being, that is, with his imaginary idea of how people should be.[59] This doctrine of love entails risks for both partners in the relationship. For the self, loving humankind or the human race means the self-deception of relating to a *specter* and being deprived of a genuine bond with a concrete being.[60] For the other, it involves a latent external critique that may become an explicit internal one. Between the two partners, the "I" posits the picture he has imagined of the "You." The self and the other are not alone: a *measure* separates them. On the one hand, this measure is the *criterion* by which the "I" *tests* and *judges* the "You." On the other hand, this measure stands before the "You" as an *ethical task imposed* by the "I."[61] This ethical task consists in the realization of certain qualities and perfections of the "You" considered as a *representative and member* of humankind. Thus, this task is not addressed to the "You" *qua* individual self. This ethical task presupposes that the "You" has the power and the capacities to fulfil it, that is, it assumes that the "You" has the strength to become "the true and the whole man, the man κατ' εξοχην (in an eminent sense)."[62]

56 See *SKS* 9, 225 / *WL*, 223.

57 *SKS* 9, 63 / *WL*, 57.

58 See *SW* VI, 323 / *EC*, p. 368.

59 See *SKS* 9, 164 / *WL*, 164.

60 Kierkegaard states that "humankind" or the "human race" are abstractions. See *SKS* 11, 197 / *SUD*, 83.

61 See *SKS* 9, 166 / *WL*, 165–166.

62 *SKS* 4, 325 / *CA*, 18.

3 God's Function in Human Relationships

One of Feuerbach's most relevant insights is that the theological explanation of the believer's faith betrays the anthropological truth that inhabits the Christian religion. In the mystery of the Incarnation, Christianity shows that love is a mightier force than God because it obliges God to the sacrifice of His majesty for the redemption of humankind. Therefore, our love for God is nothing other than the indirect manifestation of the holiest, namely our love for men.[63] However, Christian dogmatics sanctions the exclusive love of man for God and makes the fellow man a mere occasion for human worship of God. At first glance, it would seem that Kierkegaard holds the precise view that Feuerbach is criticizing: love for one's neighbor has God as its true motive. One can easily quote certain passages from *Works of Love* to support this impression.[64] But is it possible to find in Kierkegaard's Christian deliberations an understanding of neighbor-love that is reconcilable with the anthropological truth of the religion, of which Feuerbach speaks in *The Essence of Christianity*?

In the fourth deliberation of the Second Series of *Works of Love* ("Love Does Not Seek Its Own"), Kierkegaard writes the following formula: "[1] without *You* and *I* there is no love, and [2] with *mine* and *yours* there is no love."[65] This formula stipulates that an intersubjective relationship is positive for both partners if and only if it satisfies two conditions. First, [1], the relationship demands *two separated selves*. Therefore, it must ensure that both participants preserve and assert their independence vis-à-vis the other. Authentic love can leap the gap between the self and the other, but it never eliminates it. Nobody should alienate himself to the point of fusing with the other or becoming the property of the other. Second, [2], this self-affirmation before the other must not become the self's mastery over the other. The other should not be conceived of and treated as a simple tool at the service of the private projects of the self. Briefly stated, the love relationship is an interpersonal attachment of mutual recognition. According to Kierkegaard, the merely worldly view conceives mutual recognition as a *simultaneous and egalitarian reciprocity*. A and B must love each other at the same time and with the same intensity. The relationship between A and B is like a marketplace transaction, and they only are content with this relationship to the extent to which what they're giving is in line with what they're getting: "as others do unto you, by all means take care that you also do likewise unto them."[66] For Kierkegaard, this is a pagan

63 See *SW* VI, 70–71 / *EC*, pp. 58–59.

64 For example, see *SKS* 9, 124 / *WL*, 120–121.

65 *SKS* 9, 265 / *WL*, 266.

66 *SKS* 9, 376 / *WL*, 383.

notion of love penetrated by the commercial logic of symmetrical exchange: what the partners of the relationships do is conditioned by their expectation of receiving something in return—payment and repayment.[67] However, this specific kind of reciprocity is difficult to achieve because both sides of the relationship demand *first of all* to be recognized by the other *before* recognizing their counterpart. Thus, in Kierkegaard's words, both selves *enter* and *remain* in the relationship *seeking their own, seeking to be loved.*[68] Hence, they hinder the other from being aware of *their distinctiveness* (*Eiendommelighed*).[69]

In the course of *Works of Love*, Kierkegaard outlines several definitions of the neighbor. Scholars distinguish and dwell on five of them: (1) the *redoubling of the self*, (2) the *other I*, (3) *the man we see*, (4) *spiritual being*, and (5) the *first You*. A sixth definition is, however, very often overlooked in Kierkegaard studies: the neighbor is *the other "You"* (*det andet "Du"*). If Kierkegaard qualifies the neighbor as the other "You" or rather, the *second* "You," then there is a first "You." Therefore, it is necessary to ask in what sense there is a first "You" when this first "You" is not the neighbor. The answer: the self is not to be defined essentially as an "I" but as a "You": both the self and the neighbor are qualified as "You." That means that the same demand addresses the self (first "You") and the neighbor (second "You"): *You shall love*. Nevertheless, it is not the neighbor who exhorts the self to love, nor is it the self that requires the neighbor to love. If I become a "You" relative to you, and you become a "You" relative to me, then each of us still begins our relationship as an "I." The A - B relationship is the relation "I" (A) - "You" (B) from A's point of view, and also the relation "I" (B) - "You" (A) from B's point of view. Even if A understands that it is B's "You" and B understands that it is A's "You," they remain in an "I" - "I" relationship. Only insofar as there is someone who distinguishes himself from both A and B is it possible for them to relate to each other in a "You" - "You" relationship. Therefore, A and B have to see themselves not only as each of them sees himself or as the other sees him but from a new perspective. On the other hand, both A and B have to see the other not merely as "*their You*" (relative to each of them) but also, and, more essentially, as a "You" from the perspective of the one who

67 See SKS 9, 238 and 343 / WL, 237 and 349. In his analysis of erotic love and friendship, Kierkegaard observes and denounces the fact that in modern bourgeois society, under the guise of the romantic rhetoric of passion and feeling as pure waste and gift, lies the reciprocally fruitful exchange of contractual intercourses: everything is really about potential losses or benefits.

68 See SKS 9, 263 / WL, 264.

69 See SKS 9, 268 / WL, 269.

makes it possible for A and B to see themselves as a "You."[70] *Common duty is prescribed by God.*[71]

Thus, Christianity teaches that human relationships are not dichotomous but a trichotomy: *person-God-person*. It is tempting to understand God, in a Feuerbachian way, as a third party who interrupts the bond between the lover and the beloved. That is what usually happens in worldly relationships. The circumstances may confront the individual with a complicated decision: *Either she/he (the third party) or me! Choose!*[72] This understanding of the term "third party" turns the relationship into a triangle and wrongly places God at the same level as the two partners of the relationship. In a worldly threesome, two of its members are rivals who vie for the lover's care and attention. So Kierkegaard allows himself to say that *all the members of a worldly triadic relationship seek their own*. But when God is the third party, everything is different because He does not need the affirmation of his own selfhood from the other members of the relationship. God does not demand anything for himself. On the contrary, He requests that the partners of the relation show their love for him by looking after each other.[73] What Kierkegaard means is that God as a "third party" is not a third element of the relation but rather its *intermediate-determinant*.[74] For this reason, the relationship which Kierkegaard has in mind is not a triangle but rather a *circle* in which God keeps the partners of the relation *in* the relation and continually maintains their activity of relating. Understanding God as *intermediate-determinant* turns him into a means to the goal and "places the neighbor as the direct object of our love."[75] *To relate to God in relating to*

70 See Ingolf Dalferth, "Selfless Passion: Kierkegaard on True Love," *Kierkegaard Studies Yearbook*, 2013, p. 174.

71 See *SKS* 9, 95 / *WL*, 90.

72 This is the very structure of what happens in every erotic or friendship relationship. There is *always* a third party. This third party may take part in the relationship and stand between the self and the other, or it may be outside of the relationship. However, in both cases the third party claims its own: in one case against the *mine* of the self and the *yours* of the other, in the other case against the *ours* of the community of the self and the other, against the *mine* of the joined I who cuts itself off from everyone else.

73 See *SKS* 9, 161 / *WL*, 160–161.

74 The Danish word is "*mellembestemmelse*" and appears on many occasions in Kierkegaard's work. The English translation of *Works of Love* by Howard and Edna Hong uses the expression "middle term."

75 M. Jamie Ferreira, *Love's Grateful Striving*, p. 75. Some scholars argue that the notion of "middle-term" is to be understood as a *logical metaphor*. In a syllogistic argument, each of the premises has respectively one term in common with the conclusion: the major term and the minor term. At the same time, both premises share one term, which is known as middle-term. The middle-term does not appear at the conclusion. But without the middle-term the conclusion would be impossible because there would be no con-

the other (*or loving the neighbor "before God"*) *does not mean relating to another person, a theological behavior, but essentially a detailed criterion* (*Maalestok*) *of how every human being should love his neighbor. Kierkegaard summarizes his position in a Feuerbachian mood:* "The love-relationship requires threeness: the lover, the beloved, the love—but the *love is God*."[76]

Why does Kierkegaard regard the love relationship as requiring three elements? If we had only two components in the love relationship (the lover and the beloved), then it would depend on the arbitrariness of its partners or on the worldly judgment of what love should be (payment and reward). Therefore, the lover and the beloved would relate to each other without relating to their relationship, that is, without relating to love as *criterion* of human relationships.[77] The individual who, in relating to the other, relates to this criterion keeps in mind the true goal and task of every authentic love relationship: to promote the real good of the other, i.e., to help the other to become itself, free, independent, its own master. The individual who forgets the *criterion*, however, runs the risk of imposing his own criterion or accepting the other's. In the first case, one wants to create the other in his image and likeness. In the second case, one consents to all the other's whims and desires (including egoistic ones). Consequently, one should reverse the initial suspicion: *relating to God* (to assume the necessity of a "third party" in human relationships) *is*, in fact, *the only way to properly relate to the other*. Kierkegaard defends an extreme unity between man's love of God and of his neighbor to such a degree that the love of God itself can be nothing else than really loving the other person for their own sake. And this is, finally, very close to Feuerbach's question: "is not my love of God, though indirectly, love of man?"[78]

At the end of *The Essence of Christianity*, Feuerbach says that all human bonds (the relationship between parents and children, between siblings, marriage, friendship) are (and should be) *sacred* in themselves. Their holy nature does not depend on God's will and blessing but on the very nature of the union that they achieve. Love, friendship, and brotherly relationships

nection between the major and the minor term (see Ingolf Dalferth, "The Middle Term: Kierkegaard and the Contemporary Debate about Explanatory Theism," *Kierkegaard Studies Yearbook*, 2015, p. 86. This interpretation is very suggestive, but it has a downside. Kierkegaard does not use the expression "*mellembegrebet*" (middle-term) but the expression "*mellembestemmelse*" (intermediate-determinant). However, in *The Concept of Anxiety*, the expression "intermediate determination" characterizes anxiety and serves to clarify the *transition* between two realms separated by a breach: innocence and guilt.

76 *SKS* 9, 124 / *WL*, 121 (the emphasis is mine). See also *SKS* 9, 299 / *WL*, 301.

77 See Sergio Muñoz Fonnegra, *Das Gelingende Gutsein. Über Liebe und Anerkennung bei Kierkegaard*, Berlin and New York: Walter de Gruyter 2010, p. 122.

78 *SW* VI, 71 / *EC*, p. 57.

are sacred because they aim for the mutual well-being and self-realization of their members.[79] Feuerbach thinks that bourgeois Christian society sacrifices these human relationships to the isolated relationship with God, i.e., they are offered for the salvation of the soul. Ultimately, this means that human bonds become subservient to the private interest of the selfish individual. Stirner's criticism of these statements is well known: *The Essence of Christianity* turns marriage, friendship, and love into new divine instances that also alienate men. Transcendence remains transcendent within immanence. Christian theology placed God above the individual man; Feuerbach, on the other hand, places human relationships over the *Einzige* (Ego).[80] Feuerbach replies in a brief article from 1845 that he does not make human relationships the measure (*Maasstab*) of man, but rather man the measure of human relationships. He states that human relationships are holy "for [their] own sake" because he is rejecting Christianity, where God consecrates relationships. However, saying that human relationships are sacred "for [their] own sake" means that they are sacred for the self-affirmation of the human being.[81] But then are these relationships *above* man? Do they *alienate* human beings? Is Stirner's accusation justified? Indeed, for the individual man who conceives himself as an isolated entity focused exclusively on his private interests (Stirner's *Einzige*), these relationships have an oppressive character. The *Einzige* does not agree to adapt its life and actions to any external legality. However, for the individual man who understands himself as a social being, these relationships constitute the condition of possibility for the development of his selfhood and the realization of his personal freedom. These relationships are not placed over the individual man but *beneath* him: they are his *ground*; they *sustain* and *contain* him.[82] Therefore, the intrinsic legality of these relationships is an *external* one but not an estranged and alien one. At this point, it is Feuerbach who approaches

79 See *SW* VI, 326 / *EC*, p. 271.

80 See Max Stirner, *The Ego and his Own*, trans. by David Leopold, Cambridge: Cambridge University Press 2000, pp. 34–35.

81 See *SW* VII, 309.

82 As Heiko Schulz points out, Anti-Climacus' notion of faith and Feuerbach's "true consciousness" are quite similar: individual self-composition must rest transparently on the power that established the self. In Anti-Climacus' view, this power is no other than God. According to Feuerbach, this power is, in Schulz's words (*The Essence of Christianity*), the species (*Gattung*), and in our words (in the later works of Feuerbach), human relationships (see Heiko Schulz, "True Consciousness Dreaming: Feuerbach's Critique of Religion Reconsidered," in *Kierkegaard and the Nineteenth-Century Religious Crisis in Europe*, ed. by Roman Králik, Abrahim Kahn, Peter Šajda, Jamie Turnbull and Andrew Burgess, Toronto, Kierkegaard Circle, Trinity College and Sala: Kierkegaard Society in Slovakia 2009 (*Acta Kierkegaardiana*, vol. 4), pp. 92–94).

Kierkegaard. Something universal encompasses and structures the "I-You relationship" beyond their partners: the *law* of love.[83]

Both Feuerbach and Kierkegaard develop their doctrines of love by critically reformulating Hegel's theory of recognition. This theory, especially the version in the *Phenomenology of Spirit*, influenced both Feuerbach and Kierkegaard.[84] The specific reference is the well-known section on dependence and independence of self-consciousness (chapter IV A). Hegel distinguishes between the (pure) *concept* of recognition and its *process*. According to his concept, recognition is a bilateral movement that demands reciprocity (recognizing and being recognized): a unilateral movement (the project of being recognized without recognizing) is useless. On the contrary, the process of recognition (the *master-slave dialectic*) begins with the project of unilateral recognition but this process fails for intrinsic reasons: to be recognized by someone that I do not myself recognize has only a partial and incomplete value.[85] In the *Phenomenology of Spirit*, the search for recognition is not a peaceful activity. Indeed, in the schema proposed by Hegel in 1807, the paradigmatic experience of recognition is the *struggle* between two contenders who are in an initial situation of symmetry. To be recognized by the other, the self has to defeat the other and impose itself on him: the initial symmetry and equality evolve *toward* an asymmetrical and unequal situation. The corrections of Feuerbach and Kierkegaard consist in offering a completely different model.

Feuerbach retains the initial Hegelian symmetry but sets out a new scenario. The "I" and the "You" are no longer opponents but erotic lovers who remain equals during and after their encounter. In his 1866 book, *On Spiritualism and Materialism, Particularly in Relation to the Freedom of the Will*, Feuerbach proposes that the sexual relationship provides the foundational model (the normative standard) for human intercourse. The centrality of sexual

83 When A loves B, A refers, first, to the beloved object (B) and, second, to an implicit notion of what love means. By loving B, A objectifies B and – if unconsciously and unwittingly – the powers and perfections of the species. Hence, the human being can not refer to an object without, at the same time, being aware of an ideal relationship with this object. The human being is not able to love without simultaneously glimpsing an ideal of love that, as Feuerbach thinks, cannot be realized by a finite and bounded human being and can only be conceived as being instantiated in the human species as a whole (see Heiko Schulz, "True Consciousness Dreaming. Feuerbach's Critique of Religion Reconsidered," p. 87). I *really* love someone only when I doubt whether I am up to the demands inherent in love. To love someone means to challenge one's finitude.

84 This is a part of the thesis in Jon Stewart's *Hegel's Century: Alienation and Recognition in a Time of Revolution*, Cambridge: Cambridge University Press 2021.

85 See Arne Grøn, "Dialectics of Recognition: Selfhood and Alterity," in *Dialectics, Self-Consciousness, and Recognition*, ed. by Asger Sørensen, Morten Raffnsøe-Møller and Arne Grøn, Malmö: Nordisk Sommeruniversitet Press 2009, pp. 117–118.

relationships derives from the fact that lovers relate to each other by *giving and receiving pleasure simultaneously*. In sexual relationships, "the self cannot make itself happy without at the same time, even involuntarily, making the other person happy; indeed, the more the self makes the other happy, the more it makes itself happy."[86] The *immanent logic* of sexual relationships implies that neither of the partners is allowed to pursue their private satisfaction: each one finds their personal satisfaction *only with* and *in* the other's satisfaction. To put it briefly, lovers act together, seeking their *common pleasure*.[87] Now, to say that sexual interactions are the foundation of social life is tantamount to establishing that the normative standard of intersubjective relations is to be the joint pursuit of common benefit. The ethical task is to assume the indissoluble link between one's *true* self-realization and the self-realization of the others.[88]

Kierkegaard understands that intersubjective relationships fail because each partner enters the relationship demanding recognition from the other. Consequently, he aims to overcome this problem by modifying the starting point. The self must enter the relationship not with a requirement but with a task: the self must recognize the other without conditions. However, Kierkegaard is not arguing for a rejection of reciprocity but rather for its reformulation.[89] Some Kierkegaard scholars have already clarified some elements of this reformulation and the reasons for it.[90] To conclude, we would like to point out only

86 *SW* X, 116. See also *SW* X, 270.

87 Engels accuses Feuerbach's lover of vulgar selfishness (see Friedrich Engels, *Ludwig Feuerbach and the Outcome of Classical German Philosophy*, New York: International Publishers 1941, pp. 40–41). However, Feuerbach is not thinking in a *zero-sum game* (two men go to the market and interact: one wins money and the other loses it) but of a *win-win situation* (both partners obtain a benefit through their intercourse). If the other loses, so do I. The happiness of the other does not add to my happiness *from the outside* and *afterwards*: I am never happy *without* the other's happiness.

88 See *SW* X, 116–117. Here, an obviously *formal* coincidence with Kierkegaard can be found: the achievement of one's authentic personality includes the achievement of the authentic personality of the neighbor (see *SKS* 9, 30 / *WL*, 22).

89 This proposal would seem to be the exact reverse of the Hegelian master's unilateral project. It is true that Kierkegaard emphasizes the one-sidedness of the task, but he does so because he concentrates on fighting against the commodification of intersubjective relationships (see Sergio Muñoz Fonnegra, *Das Gelingende Gutsein*, p. 103). His theme is not so much reciprocity, as the restoration of reciprocity.

90 See M. Jamie Ferreira, *Love's Grateful Striving*, pp. 163–167, pp. 209–227 and p. 247; see also Arne Grøn, "Gegenseitigkeit in *Der Liebe Tun?*," in *Kierkegaard Revisited: Proceedings from the Conference "Kierkegaard and the Meaning of Meaning It,"* ed. by Niels Jørgen Cappelørn and Jon Stewart, New York and Berlin: Walter de Gruyter 1997 (*Kierkegaard Studies Monograph Series*, vol. 1), pp. 223–237; see also Pia Søltoft, "Giveren, gaven, modtageren og gensidigheden," *Dansk Teologisk Tidsskrift*, vol. 76, no. 2, 2013, pp. 95–114.

two interrelated issues of this reformulated notion of reciprocity: its temporality and the concrete experience of recognition that stands at its basis.

While Feuerbach considers the sexual relationship as the foundational model of intersubjective relationships, we think that Kierkegaard finds such a model in the parent-child relationship. The latter replaces the horizontal and symmetrical interaction (agonistic or erotic) with an asymmetrical vertical relationship of a pedagogical (maieutic) nature, whose proper evolution goes *from* inequality *to* equality. This specific relationship does not begin with one self's request to the other. Instead, it starts with an invitation (*Indbydelse*) from the self to the other. Thus, initially, parents' recognition of their children is not the evaluation of their faculties or the accreditation of their successes but the confirmation of the immense worth of their existence (their *distinctiveness*) and attribution of capacities. As we have seen, this invitation is nothing other than the summoning or exhortation to "being-oneself," i.e., to become independent: the greatest good, which can be done for another person, the greatest love, which can be shown to another person.[91] In this regard, in a famous journal entry from 1846, Kierkegaard states that making someone free requires a relationship whose participants have different degrees of power. The greater the difference in power, the greater the consistency and reality of the freedom obtained. A minor power is essentially concerned with itself and does not give itself away without demanding something in response. Thus, a minor power cannot act without preserving its power over the other, and, in this way, it does not create a free being but a dependent being. Only a higher power would be able to "take itself back while it gives away, and this relationship is indeed the independence of the recipient."[92] Therefore, a higher power understands that it must *delay* seeking its recognition to preserve (or restore) the relationship. However, a power is able to make someone free only because it is the power of true love. Parents' love (the model of love) is convinced of the willingness and ability of their children to return love. Thus, *love must presuppose* (not demand) *love* for the relationship to become an *endless alternating relationship* (*Vexel-Forhold*).[93]

Bibliography

Arbaugh, George, "Kierkegaard and Feuerbach," *Kierkegaardiana*, vol. 11, 1980, pp. 7–10.
Brun, Jean, "Feuerbach et Kierkegaard," *Cahiers de Sud*, vol. 50, no. 371, 1963, pp. 34–43.

91 See *SKS* 9, 275 / *WL*, 277–278.
92 *SKS* 20, 58, NB:69 / *KJN* 4, 57.
93 See *SKS* 9, 219 and 181 / *WL*, 216–217 and 181.

Czakó, Istvan, "Feuerbach: A Malicious Demon in the Service of Christianity," in *Kierkegaard and his German Contemporaries*, Tome 1, *Philosophy*, ed. by Jon Stewart, Aldershot and Burlington: Ashgate 2007; Abingdon and New York: Routledge 2016 (*Kierkegaard Research: Sources, Reception and Resources*, vol. 6), pp. 25–48.

Dalferth, Ingolf, "Selfless Passion: Kierkegaard on True Love," *Kierkegaard Studies Yearbook*, 2013, pp. 159–179.

Dalferth, Ingolf, "The Middle Term: Kierkegaard and the Contemporary Debate about Explanatory Theism," *Kierkegaard Studies Yearbook*, 2015, pp. 69–90.

Dip, Patricia, *Teoría y Praxis en* Las obras del amor. *Un recorrido por la erótica kierkegaardiana,* Buenos Aires: Editorial Gorla 2010.

Engels, Friedrich, *Ludwig Feuerbach and the Outcome of Classical German Philosophy*, New York: International Publishers 1941.

Ferreira, M. Jamie, *Love's Grateful Striving: A Commentary on Kierkegaard's* Works of Love, New York: Oxford University Press 2001.

Feuerbach, Ludwig, *Sämtliche Werke*, vols. 1–12, ed. by Wilhelm Bolin and Friedrich Jodl, Stuttgart-Bad Cannstatt, Fromman Verlag – Gunther Holzboog 1959–1964.

Feuerbach, Ludwig, *Das Wesen des Christenthums*, vol. 5 in *Gesammelte Werke*, vols. 1–21, ed. by Werner Schuffenhauer, Berlin: Akademie Verlag 2000–2022.

Feuerbach, Ludwig, *The Fiery Brook: Selected Writings,* trans. and ed. by Zawar Hafi, London: Verso 2012.

Feuerbach, Ludwig, *The Essence of Christianity,* trans. by George Elliot, New York: Prometheus Books 1989.

Feuerbach, Ludwig, *The Essence of Faith according to Luther,* trans. by Melvin Cherno, New York: Harper & Row 1967.

Feuerbach, Ludwig, *Lectures on the Essence of Religion,* trans. by Ralph Manheim, New York: Harper & Row 1967.

Grøn, Arne, "Dialectics of Recognition: Selfhood and Alterity," in *Dialectics, Self-consciousness, and Recognition*, ed. by Asger Sørensen, Morten Raffnsøe-Møller and Arne Grøn, Malmö: Nordisk Sommeruniversitet Press 2009, pp. 113–139.

Grøn, Arne, "Gegenseitigkeit in *Der Liebe Tun?*," in *Kierkegaard Revisited: Proceedings from the Conference "Kierkegaard and the Meaning of Meaning It,"* ed. by Niels Jørgen Cappelørn and Jon Stewart, New York and Berlin: Walter de Gruyter 1997 (*Kierkegaard Studies Monograph Series*, vol. 1), pp. 223–237.

Kern, Udo, " 'Nur der *ist etwas*, der *etwas liebt*.' Zu Ludwig Feuerbachs dialogisch-ontologischer Philosophie der Liebe," in *Liebe in Zeiten pädagogischer Professionalisierung,* ed. by Elmar Driescher & Detlef Gaus, Heidelberg: VS Verlag für Sozialwissenschaften 2011, pp. 239–259.

[Kierkegaard, Søren], Søren *Kierkegaards Skrifter*, vols. 1–28, K1–K28, ed. by Niels Jørgen Cappelørn, Joakim Garff, Jette Knudsen, Johnny Kondrup and Alastair McKinnon, Copenhagen: Gad Publishers 1997–2012.

Kierkegaard, Søren, *Either/Or, Part 1,* trans. by Howard and Edna Hong, Princeton: Princeton University Press 1988 (*Kierkegaard's Writings*, vol. 3, Part I).

Kierkegaard, Søren, *Either/Or, Part 2,* trans. by Howard and Edna Hong, Princeton: Princeton University Press 1988 (*Kierkegaard's Writings*, vol. 3, Part II)

Kierkegaard, Søren, *The Concept of Anxiety,* trans. by Reidar Thomas, Princeton: Princeton University Press 1981 (*Kierkegaard's Writings*, vol. 8)

Kierkegaard, Søren, *Stages on Life´s Way,* trans. by Howard and Edna Hong, Princeton: Princeton University Press 1989 (*Kierkegaard's Writings*, vol. 11).

Kierkegaard, Søren, *Works of Love,* trans. by Howard and Edna Hong, Princeton: Princeton University Press 1998 (*Kierkegaard's Writings*, vol. 16).

Kierkegaard, Søren, *The Sickness unto Death,* trans. by Howard and Edna Hong, Princeton: Princeton University Press 1980 (*Kierkegaard's Writings*, vol. 19).

Kierkegaard, Søren, *Kierkegaard's Journals and Notebooks*, vols. 1–11, ed. by Niels Jørgen Cappelørn, Alastair Hannay, David Kangas, Bruce H. Kirmmse, George Pattison, Vanessa Rumble and K. Brian Söderquist, Princeton and Oxford: Princeton University Press 2007–2020.

Krishek, Sharon, *Kierkegaard on Faith and Love,* New York: Cambridge University Press 2009.

Malesic, Jonathan, "Illusion and Offense in *Philosophical Fragments*: Kierkegaard's Inversion of Feuerbach's Critique of Christianity," *International Journal for Philosophy of Religion,* vol. 62, no. 1, 2007, pp. 43–55.

Muñoz Fonnegra, Sergio, *Das Gelingende Gutsein. Über Liebe und Anerkennung bei Kierkegaard*, Berlin and New York: Walter de Gruyter 2010.

Schulz, Heiko, "True Consciousness Dreaming: Feuerbach's Critique of Religion Reconsidered," in *Kierkegaard and the Nineteenth-Century Religious Crisis in Europe*, ed. by Roman Králik, Abrahim Kahn, Peter Šajda, Jamie Turnbull and Andrew Burgess, Toronto, Kierkegaard Circle, Trinity College and Sala: Kierkegaard Society in Slovakia 2009 (*Acta Kierkegaardiana*, vol. 4), pp. 84–104.

Søltoft, Pia, "Giveren, gaven, modtageren og gensidigheden," *Dansk Teologisk Tidsskrift*, vol. 76, no. 2, 2013, pp. 95–114.

Stewart, Jon, *Hegel's Century: Alienation and Recognition in a Time of Revolution,* Cambridge: Cambridge University Press 2021.

Stirner, Max, *The Ego and his Own,* trans. by David Leopold, Cambridge: Cambridge University Press 2000.

Viallaneix, Nelly, *Kierkegaard. El único ante Dios,* trans. by Juan Llopis, Barcelona: Herder, 1977.

PART 2

Philosophy of Religion

∵

CHAPTER 4

Ich und Du ist Gott: The Impact of Ludwig Feuerbach's Philosophy of Dialogical Communication on Modern Intersubjectivity and Recognition Theory

Kristína Bosáková

Abstract

This paper examines Feuerbach's philosophy of dialogical communication based on the relationship between a concrete, corporal I and a concrete, corporal Thou, and its impact on contemporary thinking about communication and intersubjective relations. Reflections on the relationship between the I and Thou can be traced back to the times of the Old Testament, but it was only in the modern era that the issue began to be examined systematically when Hegel developed the lord-bondsman dialectic to focus philosophical thinking on the problem of mutual recognition of two different subjects. Feuerbach's efforts to discover and rehabilitate the emotional side of the human being represented a significant innovation in the philosophical reception of interpersonal relations, but it is open to question whether Feuerbach's philosophy of dialogical communication can be perceived as a specific theory of intersubjectivity. Regardless of whether we consider Feuerbach a precursor to modern intersubjectivity, the influence of his philosophy of the I and Thou is apparent in the writings of Husserl, Buber, Levinas, Honneth, and Taylor.

The problem of the relationship between the I and Thou is an ancient one. The history of the issue can be traced back to the earliest eras of human civilization and represents one of the core principles of Western culture through its explicit articulation in the Old Testament. Long before Socrates turned his attention to anthropology and questioned the nature of the good, wisdom, beauty and truth in the dialogues which Plato preserved for posterity, before Leibniz had first broached the subject, before Descartes had moved on from *cogito ergo sum* to touch upon the question, mankind had already pondered

 | DOI:10.1163/9789004689459_006

this question, which is as deep and complex as human beings themselves: the relationship between two different subjects, between an I and a Thou.

Western philosophical thinking developed from two significant traditions, Greek philosophy and Judeo-Christian thought. Vilém Flusser believed that the fundamental difference between these two perspectives that has done so much to shape our worldview and our approach towards one another lay in the distinction between the second and the third grammatical persons.[1] Flusser argued that the most important contribution of Judaism to the European religious and cultural tradition was not, as the texts of the early Christian prophets and philosophers suggested, the concept of monotheism, a belief standing in sharp contrast to the ancient Greek and Roman system of polytheism. Instead, Flusser saw as crucial the Judaic belief in the existence of a specific relationship between God and the human and therefore also between human and human.[2] This special relationship, in which neither God nor the human are objects for the other, allows a sense of trust to develop between the two autonomous subjects and can be described by the term of friendship. According to Flusser, Greek ontology typically posits that the human, a specific I, is a subject, and that the world around him is created by objects, by a specific It.[3] The human is then placed in contraposition to the world; he is opposite and sometimes even opposed to the It, represented by the world. This kind of dialectics, in which the human and the world are in contrapositions, brings metaphysics into Greek ontology and also results in, as Flusser noted, the conflict between Idealism and Realism.[4] In Judeo-Christian ontology, however, the human is made in the image of God; he is a certain Thou, because another subject, God as a certain I, is speaking to him. This act of speaking to the human and his recognition as a concrete Thou (*ansprechen, Anspruch*) is the basis for the existence of the human as a subject, as an I. For this reason, there is also no need

1 Vilém Flusser was a fascinating and versatile figure who taught philosophy and communication theory at several universities and published many significant works on philosophy, literature, and visual art, written mostly in German or Portuguese. He was born in Prague into a Jewish, German-speaking family. His father had studied mathematics and had been taught by Albert Einstein. Flusser emigrated to London in 1939 and later moved to Brazil, where he lived until 1970, spending his later years in the south of France. Flusser's cousin was the Israeli philologist and religionist David Flusser, whose research focused on the history of Judaism and early Christianity. Flusser's book *Kommunikologie* was translated into Slovak by Alma Münzová, the first wife of Teodor Münz, one of Slovakia's most influential philosophers and a leading Slovak interpreter of Feuerbach.

2 See Vilém Flusser, *Kommunikologie*, ed. by Stephan Bollmann and Edith Flusser, Mannheim: Bollmann Verlag 2007, p. 294.

3 See ibid., p. 294.

4 See ibid., p. 293.

for any logical or metaphysical proof of the Divine existence, because God can only exist to the extent that a human is willing to respond to him.[5]

While the human is not, therefore, an object, this is also true for God. Neither God nor the human are an It; they are both an I and a Thou, depending on who is speaking and who is being spoken to. On this basis, Flusser argues, the reason for human existence in Judaism and Christianity is not the world, but the call of God. Greek metaphysics asks what true reality is; it seeks out that which is hidden behind the phenomena which can be perceived by the senses. In contrast, Jewish and Christian ontology asks the questions about the purpose of human life even during one's time on earth. Flusser therefore expresses his dismay that the Judeo-Christian tradition was soon enveloped by Greek terms and concepts and consequently lost its character of anthropologically shaped ontology after it had been converted into universal metaphysics.[6]

According to Flusser, the purpose of Greek dialogue is to seek the truth, true knowledge, by overcoming the *doxa*. In contrast, the purpose of Judeo-Christian dialogue is intersubjectivity; if the human and God are two subjects, standing next to each other or facing each other, then every human being represents part of divine existence. Judeo-Christian ontology is already a form of anthropology, because the I can only see itself as an I when another person speaks to it and calls the I and Thou, if it is recognized as a Thou.[7] The only way to God, Flusser asserts, is the way to another human being. Flusser also warns against the anthropocentric and anthropomorphic understanding of Judaism and Christianity.[8] God should neither be perceived as a human without body, an approach that represents the basis of Feuerbach's critique of Christianity, nor should a human being be placed in the position of God; in Flusser's opinion, the main point of Judeo-Christian ontology is the *holiness of the Other*.[9] For

5 Ibid., p. 294.

6 Ibid. Heidegger also addresses this problem in his critique of metaphysics as onto-theology, although his approach differs from that of Flusser. While Flusser claims that it was Greek metaphysics that converted Jewish and especially Christian ontology into theology, Heidegger believes that Greek metaphysics, especially the Platonic theory of ideas, and Christian theology are responsible for borrowing the original meaning from the Greek concept of Being, thereby converting Greek ontology into metaphysics or, even worse, onto-theology. See, for example, Martin Heidegger, *Hegels Phänomenologie des Geistes*, ed. by Ingtraut Görmann, vol. 32, in *Gesamtausgabe*, Frankfurt am Main: Vittorio Klostermann 1997, p. 4. See also Martin Heidegger, "Die onto-Theo-Logische Verfassung der Metaphysik," in *Identität und Differenz*, ed. by Günter Neske, vol. 11, in *Gesamtausgabe*, Frankfurt am Main: Klostermann 2006, pp. 31–68.

7 Flusser, *Kommunikologie*, p. 295.

8 Ibid.

9 See ibid., p. 295.

this reason, there is no general, abstract, metaphysical concept of love in either Judaism or Christianity. In the Bible, notes Flusser, there is no declaration about love for humanity in general, but only the commandment to "love thy neighbor." The assertion that "love is a materialist practice"[10] means nothing more or less than the fact that love only applies to a concrete, corporal I and Thou and can only be proven and practiced in specific acts towards others.

Over the centuries, however, the European religious tradition has abandoned the principle of the I and Thou relationship as it originated in Jewish ontology in favor of Greek metaphysics and its exclusive focus on the search for the one universal truth. The idea of love and respect for one's neighbor, so deeply rooted in Judaism and rediscovered by Christ in his harsh criticism of the Jewish authorities and the religious dogma of the society of his times, was later replaced by his Christian followers with theism, dogmatism, and hierarchy. The intersubjective relationship between the human and God disappeared, and the Church hierarchy, inspired by the social structures of the Roman Empire, was no longer willing to guarantee a broadly equal treatment of all humans. The one and only truth as articulated through religious dogmas was placed beyond any doubt and was no longer considered as open for discussion. Human well-being was replaced by the correctness of ideas; God was no longer a friend to mankind but a merciless judge who would both tend to his flock and also seek out and punish any black sheep who disobeyed him and allowed themselves to make incorrect choices. Flusser also criticizes the theistic constellation of the Western religious tradition, claiming that neither Judaism nor Christianity were capable of establishing themselves as theologies in early medieval European societies, but only as religions based on the attempts to find more harmonic relationships between very concrete corporal beings, between humans.[11] Judaism and Christianity are messianic religions because they do not aim to create a utopian society based on certain ideas but instead represent the ongoing search for better intersubjective relations.

Hegel is generally considered to have been the first modern philosopher to attempt to discuss the problem of intersubjectivity and mutual recognition. In the chapter of his work *The Phenomenology of Spirit* devoted to the topic of self-consciousness, Hegel presents his famous analogy of the lord and the bondsman. The analogy begins with the struggle between an I and an Other to ensure their own survival. Those who are prepared to risk their lives in this

10 Terry Eagleton, *Materialism*, New Haven and London: Yale University Press 2016, p. 48.

11 Flusser. *Kommunikologie*, p. 296.

struggle become the winners and secure the right to decide their own existence for themselves. The Others are willing to give up their freedom in return for their lives and must therefore accept the existence of an Other. "One is self-sufficient; for it, its essence is being-for-itself. The other is non-self-sufficient; for it, life, or being for an other, is the essence. The former is the master, the latter is the servant."[12] This relationship produces mutual dependence and engenders a state of constant tension. The lord, despite having retained the right to maintain his self-sufficient existence, is unable to satisfy his needs without the bondsman; in contrast, the bondsman, despite being self-sufficient in satisfying his needs, is not able to stay alive without the consent of the lord. The lord has power over the bondsman but is at the same time entirely dependent upon him. The increasing awareness of this mutual dependence together with the bondsman's intensifying efforts to achieve a certain degree of emancipation leads to more and more conflicts which will only ever have one conclusion. This end is called *mutual recognition*:

> This twofold sense of what is distinguished lies in the essence of self-consciousness, which is to be infinitely or immediately the opposite of the determinateness in which it is posited. The elaboration of the concept of this spiritual unity in its doubling presents us with the movement of *recognizing*. For self-consciousness, there is another self-consciousness; self-consciousness is *outside of itself*. This has a twofold meaning. *First*, it has lost itself, for it is to be found as an *other* essence. *Second*, it has thereby sublated that *other*, for it also does not see the other as the essence but rather sees itself in the other. It must sublate *its otherness*. This is the sublation of that first two-sided ambiguity and is for that reason itself a second two-sided ambiguity. First, it must set out to sublate the *other* self-sufficient essence in order as a result to become certain of itself as the essence through having sublated the other. *Second*, it thereby sets out to sublate itself, for this other is *itself*.[13]

Mutual recognition is not the mere result of the conflict between the self-sufficient and the non-self-sufficient being, between the being-for-itself and being-for-an-other. It is instead an ongoing process in which both sides, the lord and the bondsman, can sublate their otherness and recognize each other as

12 G.W.F. Hegel, *The Phenomenology of Spirit*, trans. and ed. by Terry Pinkard, Cambridge: Cambridge University Press 2018, pp. 108–109, § 178–180.

13 Hegel, *The Phenomenology of Spirit*, pp. 108–109, § 178–180.

two equal, autonomous subjects. Hegel's theory of mutual recognition, established in the *Phenomenology of Spirit* and developed further in his *Philosophy of Right*, has been a significant source of inspiration for many contemporary thinkers such as Axel Honneth,[14] Charles Taylor,[15] Jürgen Habermas,[16] and Robert Pippin,[17] whose work is focused on modern recognition theory and the question of the restrictions we can justifiably place on individual freedom for the sake of recognition; or, in other words, how to "be a person and respect others as persons."[18] Hegel's theological and metaphysical approach to recognition theory established a rational basis for the mutual recognition between two subjects and represents one of the milestones in the development of his concept of the World Spirit. While this theory and its influence on modern recognition theory has been the focus of considerable academic attention,[19] the impact of Ludwig Feuerbach's anthropologically established communicative philosophy of I and Thou has still not received the attention which his novel approach deserves.

The understandings of modern intersubjectivity represented in the works of Husserl, Buber, and Levinas derive their inspiration from sources which date back much earlier than the writings of Hegel, drawing directly from the scriptures of the Old Testament. Although there are no direct connections between their work and Feuerbach's communicative philosophy, all three of these thinkers developed their understandings of intersubjectivity and intersubjective relations on the same non-theological, anthropological and not exclusively rational foundation as Feuerbach. While the theme of intersubjectivity in the philosophy of Husserl, Buber, and Levinas has been investigated either separately,[20] comparatively or within the context of other relevant

---

14 Axel Honneth, *The Pathologies of Individual Freedom: Hegel's Social Theory*, trans. by Ladislaus Löb, Princeton and Oxford: Princeton University Press 2010.

15 Charles Taylor, "The Politics of Recognition," in *Multiculturalism and the Politics of Recognition*, ed. by Amy Gutmann, Princeton: Princeton University Press 1994, pp. 25–73.

16 Jürgen Habermas, *Theorie des kommunikativen Handelns, Bd. 1. Handlungsrationalität und gesellschaftliche Rationalisierung*, Frankfurt am Main: Suhrkamp 2019.

17 Robert Pippin, *Hegel's Practical Philosophy: Rational Agency as Ethical Life*, New York: Cambridge University Press 2008.

18 G.W.F. Hegel, *Elements of the Philosophy of Right or Natural Law and Political Science in Outline*, trans. by H.B. Nisbet, ed. by Alan Wood, Cambridge: Cambridge University Press 2019, p. 69.

19 Most recently, see Jon Stewart, *Hegel's Century: Alienation and Recognition in a Time of Revolution*, Cambridge: Cambridge University Press 2021.

20 See, for example, Dan Zahavi, *Husserl and Transcendental Intersubjectivity: A Response to the Linguistic-Pragmatic Critique*, trans. and ed. by Elizabeth A. Behnke, Toledo: Ohio University Press 2001. See also the collected volume: *Husserl's Phenomenology of*

thinkers,[21] the significance of Feuerbach's impact on modern intersubjectivity remains underappreciated.[22]

1 Ludwig Feuerbach and his Communicative Philosophy of the I and Thou

Feuerbach's interest in the relationship between an individual human being, another human and humankind as a whole arose early in his studies and was inspired by the dynamic movement of self-consciousness described in Hegel's *Phenomenology of Spirit*.[23] As a former student of Hegel who was still an uncritical follower of his German teacher, the young Feuerbach presents a completely idealistic perception of communicative philosophy, where the universality of communication assumes the universal concept of humanity. Feuerbach is particularly interested in developing Fichte's concerns over the concept of an I,[24] an apprehension that, after gaining his independence from Hegel, becomes one of the two most conspicuous examples of the false understanding of the essence of the human.[25] In his contribution to the 1839 *Hallische Jahrbücher*,[26] titled "Towards a Critique of Hegel's Philosophy,"[27] Feuerbach had already taken Hegel to task for his lack of an empirical approach. In the following years

Intersubjectivity: Historical Interpretations and Contemporary Applications, ed. by Frode Kjosavik, Christian Beyer, Christel Fricke, London: Routledge 2020.

21 See, among others, the collected volume: *Intersubjectivity and Objectivity in Adam Smith and Edmund Husserl: A Collection of Essays*, ed. by Christel Fricke and Dagfinn Føllesdal, Berlin, Boston: De Gruyter 2013; or Françoise Dastur, *Questions of Phenomenology: Language, Alterity, Temporality, Finitude*, trans. by Robert Vallier, ed. by John D. Caputo, New York: Fordham University Press 2017, pp. 69–81.

22 One exception here is Susanne Rütter, *Herausforderung Angesichts des Anderen: Von Feuerbach über Buber zu Levinas*, Baden Baden: Verlag Karl Alber 2000.

23 Francesco Tomasoni, *Ludwig Feuerbach. Entstehung, Entwicklung und Bedeutungs eines Werkes*, trans. by Gunnhild Schneider, ed. by Ursula Reitemeyer, Takayuki Shibata and Francesco Tomasoni, Münster: Waxmann 2015, p. 64

24 Ibid., p. 65.

25 Ludwig Feuerbach, *Principles of Philosophy of the Future*, in *The Fiery Brook: Selected Writings of Ludwig Feuerbach*, trans. and ed. by Zawar Hanfi, Garden City, NY: Anchor Books 1972, pp. 175–245, § 13.

26 Tomasoni, *Ludwig Feuerbach*, p. 191.

27 Ludwig Feuerbach, "Towards a Critique of Hegel's Philosophy," in *The Fiery Brook: Selected Writings of Ludwig Feuerbach*, trans. and ed. by Zawar Hanfi, Garden City, NY: Anchor Books 1972, pp. 53–96. "Zur Kritik der Hegelschen Philosophie," in *Gesammelte Werke*, vols. 1–21, ed. by Werner Schuffenhauer, Berlin: Akademie Verlag 1981–2013, vol. 9, *Kleinere Schriften II (1839–1846)*, pp. 16–62.

Feuerbach became increasingly alienated from Hegel and German idealism, culminating in his 1843 work *Principles of Philosophy of the Future*,[28] which signaled Feuerbach's definitive break from Hegelian thought and his declaration of a new philosophy founded on anthropology rather than the imitation of theology.

The relationship between the I and Thou serves as the foundation and most important element of Feuerbach's thinking. In addition to his most frequently read and studied works such as *The Essence of Christianity*, *Principles of the Philosophy of the Future*, *The Essence of Religion* or *Lectures on the Essence of Religion*, evidence that Feuerbach's communicative philosophy can be found throughout almost all his writings. Nonetheless, the two works which are crucial to an understanding of Feuerbach's conception of the relationship of the I and Thou and, by extension, between the human and humanity, are *The Essence of Christianity* and *Principles of the Philosophy of the Future*. Although *The Essence of Christianity* was written before *Principles of the Philosophy of the Future*, it is the latter work which most clearly articulates Feuerbach's shift from an idealist to an anthropological perception of an I. This is particularly apparent in the critique of the self-sufficient I, represented in Hegel's and Fichte's philosophies as the highest level of the development of world spirit or self-consciousness, depicted by the relationship of I = I. Feuerbach writes,

> Wherefrom God is free, therefrom you must also free yourself if you want to reach God; and you make yourself really free when you present yourself with the idea of God. In consequence, if you think God without presupposing any other being or object, you yourself think without presupposing any external object; the quality that you attribute to God is a quality of your own thought. However, what is *activity* in man is *being* in God or that which is imagined as such. What, hence, is the Fichtean Ego which says, "I simply am because I am," and what is the pure and presuppositionless thought of Hegel if not the Divine Being of the old theology and metaphysics which has been transformed into the *actual, active,* and *thinking* being of man?[29]

The relationship of I = I can never truly work, Feuerbach claims, because not every I is an I exclusively; at the same time, it is also a Thou. For Feuerbach,

28 Ludwig Feuerbach, *Grundsätze der Philosophie der Zukunft und andere Schriften*, ed. by Michael Holzinger, Berlin: Holzinger 2016. *Principles of Philosophy of the Future*, in *The Fiery Brook: Selected Writings of Ludwig Feuerbach*, pp. 175–245.

29 Feuerbach, *Principles of Philosophy of the Future*, p. 191, § 13.

there is no such thing as a pure subject without any objects, just as there is no God without a human, no human without another human and therefore no human without God within him. It is impossible to see anything without light, surrounded only by darkness, nor can we to breath without air; similarly, there can be no I without a Thou.[30] An I is not an isolated, self-sufficient subject, but is instead "*open to the world* by no means *through itself* as such, but through itself as a corporeal being, that is, through the body,"[31] because, ultimately, our "body is nothing but the porous ego."[32] Yet, when did we lose this porosity of our ego? When did God and after God also the human become this self-sufficient I, an I without the need of a Thou? When did religion lose its anthropological character? Feuerbach outlines this process in detail in *The Essence of Christianity*, above all in the chapter titled "The Distinction between Christianity and Heathenism."[33]

According to Feuerbach, the distinction between Christianity and Heathenism does not reside in the difference between monotheism and polytheism, but in the personality of Christ alone. Christ is the representation of the almighty subject that is, nonetheless, not subject to any restriction or limit and certainly not the laws of nature. After overcoming the limits of his corporal existence, Christ's capabilities are limitless, and he therefore becomes entirely self-sufficient. Christ, the role model for Christians, transforms the human into a self-centered being, taking him out of his natural environment and freeing him from his being in the world. In the ancient religions, the human being remained a part of nature and an element of a universe which had its own rules that represented the natural limits of humans and which humans were forced to respect. In contrast, the human in Christianity is a mere subject, a supranatural being who can exist without the limits of the objective external world. Nonetheless, neither the heathens nor the Christians could escape the limits of the objective world entirely. For this reason, Feuerbach claims, Christianity

30 Ludwig Feuerbach, "On the Beginning of Philosophy," in *The Fiery Brook: Selected Writings of Ludwig Feuerbach*, pp. 135–144, p. 143.

31 Ibid.

32 Feuerbach,"On the Beginning of Philosophy," p. 143. See also Tomasoni, *Ludwig Feuerbach*, pp. 249–250; and Ursula Reitemeyer, "Das poröse Ich in der fragilen Moderne," *Vierteljahrsschrift für wissenschaftliche Pädagogik*, vol. 85, no. 1, 2009, pp. 52–65. The original term in German is *das poröse Ich*. This concept can cause some confusion in relation to the point made later in the discussion about Husserl and his perception of intersubjectivity, where an I (*Ich*) in an intersubjective relationship differs from the transcendental ego (*transcendentales Ego*).

33 Ludwig Feuerbach, *Essence of Christianity*. trans. by George Eliot, New York: Prometheus Books 1989, pp. 150–159.

decided to destroy anything that would oppose its subjectivity, which meant, in this context, nature itself.

> The heathens, on the contrary, not shutting out Nature by retreating within themselves, limited their subjectivity by the contemplation of the world. Highly as the ancients estimated the intelligence, the reason, they were yet liberal and objective enough, theoretically as well as practically, to allow that which they distinguished from mind, namely, matter, to live, and even to live eternally; the Christians evinced their theoretical as well as practical intolerance in their belief that they secured the eternity of their subjective life only by annihilating, as in the doctrine of the destruction of the world, the opposite of subjectivity—Nature.... The ancients were so enraptured by the cosmos, that they lost sight of themselves suffered themselves to be merged in the whole; the Christians despised the world;—what is the creature compared with the Creator? what are sun, moon, and earth compared with the human soul? The world passes away, but man, nay, the individual, personal man, is eternal.[34]

However, the relationship to nature was not the only difference between Christianity and Heathenism. Another, no less important distinction is that "the heathens considered man not only in connection with the universe; they considered the individual man, in connection with other men, as member of a commonwealth."[35] Christians subordinated creation to the creator and hence nature to the human soul. In doing so, they not only severed humankind from nature, but they also severed an individual human being from the community of other humans by subordinating the entire species to a single individual, to Christ. Once this has been accomplished, a single human individual became equivalent to the entirety of humankind. It was in this way that the concept of God was derived from the concept of the human, the point at which Christians "immediately identified the individual with the universal Being"[36] and attributed all the characteristics of the human to the divine subject, but none of the natural limitations. In the figure of Christ, Christianity had created a perfect, self-sufficient individual, complete in every respect, and without any need for interpersonal relations of any type.

Although Feuerbach does not agree with the total subordination of an individual to the whole of humankind, a common practice in the religions and

34 Ibid., pp. 150–151.
35 Ibid.
36 Ibid., p. 152.

cultures of the ancient world, he is clearly aware of the fact that instead of the Old Testament partnership between God and human and the cultivation of this relationship through the commandment to "love thy neighbor," Christianity offers little more than the cultivation of an individual on his lonely journey towards impossible perfection. How can we free this isolated human being from his loneliness? Feuerbach sees only one viable option: the return to "the multitude of separate, limited individuals,"[37] to "the consciousness, that the thou belongs to the perfection of the I, that men are required to constitute humanity, that only men taken together are what man should and can be."[38] However, this return might prove difficult because all interpersonal relationships, especially the most sensitive forms such as friendship or love, require a willingness to admit to our own limitations and abandon the idea of achieving individual perfection.

We must give up the idea that the purpose of human life is striving for perfection and accept the fact that no human can ever be satisfied in a state of isolation and solitude, as "he postulates the existence of another as a need of the heart."[39] Perfection is an abstract concept, an idealized state that can never be achieved; indeed, it is largely impossible to even approach the state of perfection. But feelings of completeness or satisfaction are terms that express very specific emotions, emotions that an individual is always able to experience in contact with another individual in interpersonal relationships like love and friendship, regardless of their personal limitations. "The individual is defective, imperfect, weak, needy; but love is strong, perfect, contented, free from wants, self-sufficing, infinite,"[40] and the same can be said about friendship. Nonetheless, as Feuerbach claims, friendship "cannot be based on perfect similarity; on the contrary, it requires diversity, for friendship rests on a desire for self-completion."[41] While this might appear to be somewhat idealistic at first glance and give rise to the suspicion that Feuerbach has only exchanged one unreachable ideal for another, it is clear that Feuerbach is well aware that in a truly human life, even the most satisfying interpersonal relationship brings both happiness and pain in equal measure:

> But just as being as distinguished from non-being is given to me through love or feeling in general, so is everything else that is other than me given

37 Ibid., p. 153.
38 Ibid., p. 155.
39 Ibid., p. 156.
40 Ibid.
41 Ibid.

> to me through love. Pain is a loud protest against identifying the subjective with the objective. The pain of love means that what is in the mind is not given in reality, or in other words, the subjective is here the objective, the concept itself the object.... Feelings, everyday feelings, contain the deepest and highest truths. Thus, for example, love is the true ontological demonstration of the existence of objects apart from our head: There is no other proof of being except love or feeling in general. Only that whose being brings you joy and whose not-being, pain, has existence. The difference between subject and object, being and non-being is as happy a difference as it is painful.[42]

Yet, why does the relationship between the I and Thou, whether in terms of passionate love or the love for our fellow man that can be called friendship, bring us so much pain? Quite simply, it is because by making a distinction between I and Thou, the otherness of the Other has to be maintained and respected. According to Feuerbach, love and friendship are not processes in which two individuals eventually become one body and soul; they are instead relationships in which the feeling of completeness is based upon the recognition of diversity, the painful yet satisfying difference of any I from any Thou. "I am I—for myself—and at the same time You—for others. But I am You only in so far as I am a sensuous being."[43] Hence, as Feuerbach argues in *The Essence of Christianity*, God as a pure subject can no more be called love itself than he can be said to be life itself,[44] because true love needs an interpersonal relationship and real life needs interpersonal communication, a dialogue in which both the I and Thou experience understanding and resistance, happiness and pain, presence and absence.

Christianity generally describes itself as a religion of love, but Feuerbach expresses some degree of skepticism towards this interpretation as, according to his experience, everyday religious practices in Christianity place a far greater value on faith and obedience than on love. In Feuerbach's philosophy, love is the ultimate aim of human existence: "This final aim—love—is something that the Christian seeks in faith; that is, outside love."[45] If we

42 Feuerbach, *Principles of Philosophy of the Future*, p. 226, § 33.

43 Ibid., p. 225, § 32.

44 Feuerbach, *Essence of Christianity*, p. 154.

45 Ludwig Feuerbach, "Fragments Concerning the Characteristics of My Philosophical Development," in *The Fiery Brook: Selected Writings of Ludwig Feuerbach*, pp. 265–296, p. 288.

seek love in religious faith alone, then the two most fundamental commandments of Judaism and Christianity, "You shall love the Lord your God, with all your heart, soul, mind, and strength"[46] and "You shall love your neighbor as yourself,"[47] seem to contradict each other. How can we love our neighbors as ourselves, if our hearts, souls, and minds belong to God alone? "What is left of my heart for man if I am required to love God with the whole of it?,"[48] asks Feuerbach. He goes even further when he points out the paradox that while we can truly love the brother that we can see, this is less the case with God, a being that we cannot see and in whose existence we have to believe without the evidence of our senses; in such a situation, Feuerbach argues that this relationship is one not of love but of faith, and there is only one solution to the paradox:

> Being as the object of being—and this alone is truly, and deserves the name of, being—is sensuous being; that is, the being involved in sense perception, feeling, and love. Or in other words, being is a secret underlying sense perception, feeling, and love. Only in feeling and love has the demonstrative this—this person, this thing, that is, the particular—absolute value; only then is the finite infinite: In this and this alone does the infinite depth, divinity, and truth of love consist. In love alone resides the truth and reality of the God who counts the hairs on your head.[49]

We can love God, the non-sensuous and infinite being, only through the love that we express for the sensuous and finite being of our neighbor, but not vice versa. *Ich und Du ist Gott, I and Thou is God.* Any other approach, any different explanation would require us to sacrifice the concept of real love for imaginary love, to sacrifice concrete existence in favor of an existence in fantasy and faith.[50] With an admitted degree of exaggeration, we could suggest an analogy between the idea of God and the idea of the unicorn; no-one has ever seen either of them, and there is no practical proof of their existence, yet we are all free to choose whether or not we believe in their existence. Furthermore, we should be fully entitled to question the existence of both entities, but we

---

46 Ibid.

47 Ibid.

48 Ibid.

49 Feuerbach, *Principles of Philosophy of the Future,* p. 225, § 33.

50 Feuerbach, "Fragments Concerning the Characteristics of My Philosophical Development," p. 288.

should not be made to feel ashamed for believing in them. However, if we were to treat real, living horses cruelly in the pursuit of our love for the unicorn, this would be just as unacceptable as harming, torturing, or killing humans in the name of love for our God: "Only a real being, that is, only that which is an object of the senses, can also be an object of real love."[51] Talking about love for God in the absence of love for a human will invariably convert the concrete feeling of love into an abstract and therefore empty concept devoid of any real content. It also reduces the highly abstract, elusive being of God, to the concrete objectivity of an idol. Love disappears when God becomes a golden calf or, again with a degree of exaggeration, a unicorn. In order to avoid emptiness and idolatry, love for God can only begin and end in the love for our fellow creatures.

2 Modern Intersubjectivity

2.1 *Edmund Husserl*

Edmund Husserl is widely known for his great interest in the topic of intersubjectivity. He had examined the question in his *Cartesian Meditations*,[52] but he addressed the topic in much greater detail in the three-volume work entitled *On the Phenomenology of Intersubjectivity*,[53] which was published posthumously. Husserl was fascinated with the problem of intersubjectivity due to the difficulty of integrating the issue into his phenomenology. Husserl had realized that it was impossible to apply the procedure of *epoche* in the case of intersubjective and interpersonal relations, since the roles of subject and object were unstable and subject to constant change. How could intersubjectivity be incorporated into a theory about the possibility of objective knowledge if an individual human being could be both subject and object at the same time when in contact with other humans? Husserl partially resolved this problem through the concept of the objectivity of the living body (*Leib*), although he was forced to concede that *epoche* would never be an appropriate

51 Ibid.

52 Edmund Husserl, *Cartesian Meditations: An Introduction to Phenomenology*, trans. by Dorion Cairns, The Hague, Boston, London: Martinus Nijhoff 1982.

53 Edmund Husserl, *Zur Phänomenologie der Intersubjektivität. Texte aus dem Nachlass. Erster Teil. 1905–1920*, ed. by Iso Kern, The Hague: Martinus Nijhoff 1973. Edmund Husserl, *Zur Phänomenologie der Intersubjektivität. Texte aus dem Nachlass. Zweiter Teil. 1921–1928*. ed. by Iso Kern, The Hague: Martinus Nijhoff 1973. Edmund Husserl, *Zur Phänomenologie der Intersubjektivität. Texte aus dem Nachlass. Dritter Teil. 1929–1935*, ed. by Iso Kern, The Hague: Martinus Nijhoff 1973.

approach to intersubjective relations, an admission that seems to suggest the impossibility of ever gaining objective knowledge about another person. Even if we attempt to understand another person through empathy and compassion or by trying to put ourselves in their position, any understanding we gain could not be truly considered as knowledge about the other.

Several authors have criticized Husserl for his insistence on the ego as the point of departure for seeking objective knowledge within the transcendental consciousness and examining intersubjectivity. They argue that Husserl presents a portrayal of a lonely, isolated subject and fails to take into consideration the most important aspect of interpersonal relationships and communication, the otherness of the Other.[54] Several authors see this criticism as disingenuous, suggesting that the ego always possesses an intersubjective character and thus represents an accurate way towards intersubjectivity. These authors use argumentation based on concepts such as "the mundanizing self-apperception (*verweltlichende Selbstapperzeption*) of the transcendental ego,"[55] "the transfer of sense (*Sinnesübertragung*),"[56] "the harmoniousness (*Einstimmigkeit*) of experiences,"[57] "objectivating equalization (*Gleichstellung*)"[58] or "self-mundanization (*Selbstmundanisierung*)"[59] to describe "the way the *Leib* gets into the world."[60] I firmly agree with the critique of Husserl's alienated approach to intersubjectivity which seems to incline more towards epistemology than towards phenomenological anthropology. This epistemological approach in Husserl's phenomenology does not see the main value of the Other in his otherness; instead, it strives to reach the unity of sense and experience between an ego and the other. On the other hand, Husserl also presents a clearly anthropological perception of the living body (*Leib*) and his apprehension of intersubjectivity is grounded upon the concept of corporeity (*Leiblichkeit*) in an understanding which is very similar to that of Feuerbach. In the *Cartesian Meditations* Husserl claims:

54 See, for example, James Dodd, "The Dignity of the Mind: Levinas' Reading of Husserl," *Levinas Studies*, vol. 5, 2010, pp. 19–41. See also Jan Patočka, *Body, Community, Language, World*, trans. by Erazim Kohák, ed. by James Dodd, Chicago: Open Court 1998, p. 91.

55 Alexander Schnell, "Intersubjectivity in Husserl's Work," *META: Research in Hermeneutics, Phenomenology, and Practical Philosophy*, vol. 2, no. 1, 2010, pp. 9–32, p. 15.

56 Ibid., p. 21.

57 Ibid., p. 26.

58 Ibid., p. 27.

59 Ibid., p. 28.

60 Ibid.

> After all, I do not apperceive the other ego simply as a duplicate of myself and accordingly as having my original sphere or one completely like mine. I do not apperceive him as having, more particularly, the spatial modes of appearance that are mine from here; rather, as we find on closer examination, I apperceive him as having spatial modes of appearance like those I should have if I should go over there and be where he is. Furthermore, the Other is appresentatively apperceived as the "Ego" of a primordial world, and of a monad, wherein his animate organism is originally constituted and experienced in the mode of the absolute Here, precisely as the functional center for his governing. In this appresentation, therefore, the body in the mode There, which presents itself in my monadic sphere and is apperceived as another's live body (the animate organism of the alter ego) that body indicates "the same" body in the mode Here, as the body experienced by the other ego in his monadic sphere. Moreover, it indicates the "same" body concretely, with all the constitutive intentionality pertaining to this mode of givenness in the other's experience.[61]

However, as we have already seen, there are clear differences between Husserl's and Feuerbach's definitions of the ego. Husserl sees the ego as a monad and society as a community of monads that are capable of self-development not through the help of other monads but exclusively by themselves. However, it seems somewhat inappropriate to think of the ego as a monad since, in their original Leibnizian description, monads do not interact and are thus unable to communicate with each other. A community of monads would therefore appear as a group of distant, alienated egos regardless of the constitutive role of nature,[62] which. according to Husserl. represents "the foundation for all other intersubjectively common things ... along with that of the Other's organism and his psychophysical Ego, as paired with my own psychophysical Ego"[63] or the assertion that "the sense and status of a subjectivity ... is other in its own essence."[64] Monads in the community through their living bodies are natural beings, and they share a common space without sharing truly intersubjective relations. This understanding stands in strict contradiction to Feuerbach's philosophical doctrine, in which the living body is not a monad but a porous ego (*das poröse Ich*).

61 Edmund Husserl, *Cartesian Meditations,* § 53, p. 117.
62 Ibid., § 55, pp. 120–128.
63 Ibid., p. 120.
64 Ibid., p. 121.

2.2 *Martin Buber*

The Austrian-Israeli philosopher Martin Buber was also familiar with Feuerbach's writings. In an afterword to his book, *Between Man and Man*,[65] (which was published separately in English as "The History of the Dialogical Principle by Martin Buber"),[66] Buber summarizes the history of the communicative philosophy of the I and Thou. He opens his account by mentioning Friedrich Heinrich Jacobi and the 1775 letter he wrote to an unknown person which was quoted in another letter that Jacobi sent to Lavater in 1781. In this correspondence, Jacobi lays out his understanding of the relationship between the I and Thou as the only path towards the completeness of the human being, an assertion which the thinker would develop further in his *Pamphlets* from 1785.[67] Buber moves on to a discussion of Ludwig Feuerbach, who, as Buber correctly points out, was familiar with the work of Jacobi, although he himself was not a follower of the German idealist. Feuerbach agreed with Jacobi (and Schleiermacher) on the importance of feelings and emotions,[68] but he criticized Jacobi's overestimation and divinization of the I in its relationship to the Thou.[69] Buber writes,

> Only a half century afterward, however, did Ludwig Feuerbach—a thinker of a wholly different nature from Jacobi, but one not entirely uninfluenced by him—succeed in incorporating his knowledge of the primal relationship of I and Thou in complementary philosophical theses. He finds himself at first only in the antechamber of the building that has opened itself to him: "The consciousness of the world is mediated

65 Martin Buber, *Das dialogische Prinzip*, ed. by Lambert Schneider, Gütersloh: Gütersloher Verlagshaus 2014. English translation: *Between Man and Man*, trans. by Ronald Gregor-Smith, ed. by Maurice Friedman, London and New York: Routledge 2022. The original German edition of the book contains another essay, *Ich und Du* (*I and Thou*) which was not included in the English translation and which was issued separately. See, for example, Martin Buber, *I and Thou*, trans. and ed. by Ronald Gregor-Smith, London, New York: Continuum 2004. The English version includes an *Afterword* which was translated by Maurice Friedman and two lectures given by Buber in Heidelberg in 1926 and in Tel Aviv in 1939 on the problem of education, and the text *What is Man?* (*Was ist der Mensch?*) from 1938.

66 Martin Buber, "The History of the Dialogical Principle by Martin Buber," in *Between Man and Man*, pp. 249–264. Originally, Martin Buber, "Zur Geschichte des dialogischen Prinzips," in *Das dialogische Prinzip*, ed. by Lambert Schneider, Gütersloh: Gütersloher Verlagshaus 2014, pp. 301–320.

67 See Friedrich Heinrich Jacobi, *The Main Philosophical Writings and the Novel Allwill*, trans. and ed. by Georg di Giovanni, Montreal and Kingston: McGill-Queen's University Press 1994, pp. 173–252.

68 Tomasoni, *Ludwig Feuerbach*, p. 244.

69 Ibid., pp. 144–146.

> for the I through the consciousness of the Thou." To this, one may join a later sentence, though one that does not actually go beyond Jacobi, that the real I is "only the I that stands over against a Thou and that is itself a Thou over against another I." Soon after this utterance, however, clearly inundated by one of the surging and receding waves of an inspiration of genius, Feuerbach writes, concerning the "mystery of the necessity of the Thou for the I," the statement that manifestly has for him the character of final validity, and at this point he remains without even trying to go further: "Man for himself is man (in the usual sense)—man with man—the unity of I and Thou is God."[70]

Buber, however, considers his thinking to be closer to Jacobi's theory than to Feuerbach's. He argues that Feuerbach developed a "pseudo-mystical construction that neither he himself nor anyone after him could fill with a genuine content."[71] Buber not only disagrees with Feuerbach's anthropological approach to the I-and-Thou relationship, but at the same time he accuses Feuerbach of inconsistency concerning his conflation of the human and the divine Thou, a stance which is clearly in contradiction to his own teaching. This assertion, however, betrays the fact that Buber has obviously misunderstood Feuerbach's communicative philosophy. It was never Feuerbach's intention to replace God with the human or to suggest a "coupling of the human and the divine Thou."[72] Feuerbach is instead attempting to exchange theology for anthropology by offering a strictly anthropological definition of religious faith and aims to renew the sense and meaning of religion by once again making the well-being of the human the primary focus of religious life. This understanding of the I-and-Thou-relationship does not contradict the Jewish perception of intersubjectivity; indeed, it is perhaps in perfect agreement with the spirit of Judaism. Having addressed Buber's first objection to Feuerbach's thinking, we turn now to the accusation of pseudo-mysticism, and it is clearly apparent that Buber's own communicative philosophy, established upon Hassidic teachings, contains more elements of mysticism than Feuerbach's anthropological doctrine. Even Kierkegaard's writings show a greater leaning towards Christian mysticism than Feuerbach, although Buber states that Kierkegaard

70 Buber, "The History of the Dialogical Principle by Martin Buber," p. 250.

71 Ibid., p. 251.

72 Ibid.

had eliminated "this construction from general use,"[73] despite the fact that he "preserves at the same time Feuerbach's grasp of reality."[74]

It is interesting to note that although Buber himself stated that Feuerbach's thinking had greatly influenced his own philosophy, there is not a single mention of Feuerbach in Buber's *I and Thou*, a work that is rightly considered as his key text on the problem of intersubjectivity. Buber mentions Feuerbach in the "Dialogue"[75] (*Zweisprache*), in which he emphasizes the fact that true knowledge can only be achieved through personal development in dialogue with others. In his 1936 work "The Question to the Single One" (*Die Frage an den Einzelnen*), Buber uses Feuerbach to criticize the exclusivity and isolation of the conceptions of the I in the work of Stirner and Kierkegaard.[76] Buber makes explicit reference to the influence which Feuerbach had on the development of his thinking in the work "What is Man?" (*Was ist der Mensch?*), where he not only ranks Feuerbach as one of the most significant philosophers to ever address the problem of the human, but also admits that "I myself in my youth was given a decisive impetus by Feuerbach."[77] Despite his criticisms, Buber still saw Feuerbach and Kierkegaard as the most influential nineteenth-century philosophers on the issue,[78] as can be seen in his defense of Feuerbach (and Confucius) against the objections of Karl Barth and his usurping approach to the "love thy neighbor" question.[79]

2.3 *Emmanuel Levinas*

While Husserl places the Thou in combination with the objective exterior world in opposition to the subjective consciousness of the I, and Buber draws a strict distinction between the dialogical, intersubjective relationship of I and Thou and the pragmatically grounded relationship of an I to the world of objects, represented by an It, the French philosopher Emmanuel Levinas bases his own philosophy on the difference of the Other. This otherness of the Other that persists in every kind of relationship, regardless of how close it may be, brings Levinas' approach far closer to Feuerbach than Husserl and Buber could be, despite his partially phenomenological and partially metaphysical

73 Ibid.

74 Ibid.

75 Buber, "Dialogue," in *Between Man and Man*, pp. 1–45, p. 32.

76 Buber, "The Question to the Single One," in *Between Man and Man*, pp. 46–97, p. 47.

77 Buber, "What is Man?," in *Between Man and Man*, pp. 140–244, p. 176.

78 Buber, *The History of the Dialogical Principle by Martin Buber*, p. 256. See also Peter *Šajda, Buberov spor s Kierkegaardom: o vzťahu náboženstva k etike a politike*, Bratislava: Kalligram 2013.

79 Buber, *The History of the Dialogical Principle by Martin Buber*, p. 264.

leanings. Contrary to Buber, Levinas neither endorses Feuerbach's legacy nor does he appear to see anything in his own teachings that could have arisen from Feuerbach's communicative philosophy. He only mentions Feuerbach once in *Totality and Infinity* and does so only when referring to Buber. He argues:

> Buber distinguished the relation with Objects, which would be guided by the practical, from the dialogic relation, which reaches the other as Thou, as partner and friend. This idea, central in his work, he modestly claims to have found in Feuerbach. In reality it acquires all its force only in Buber's analyses, and it is in them that it figures as an essential contribution to contemporary thought.[80]

This statement suggests that Levinas has misunderstood the stance of Buber, who perceived Feuerbach as a critical inspiration rather than a direct philosophical ancestor. However, Levinas is correct when he argues that the relationship of the subject with objects other than corporal human beings is Buber's own conception and has little in common with Feuerbach's thinking. The real reason for Levinas' underestimation of Feuerbach and his philosophy of the I and Thou lies in his inclination towards the metaphysical in heritage of Hegel. And yet when it comes to the perception of the relationship between the I and the Other, the perception of love as passion or love as compassion with one's neighbor, Levinas adopts a distinctly non-Hegelian position which more closely matches the philosophical approach of Feuerbach:

> Subjection to the order that ordains man-the ego-to answer for the other, is perhaps, the harsh name of love. Love here is no longer what this compromised word of our literature and our hypocrisies expresses, but the very fact of the approach of the unique one, and consequently of the absolutely *other*, piercing what merely *shows* itself – that is to say, what remains the individual of a genus.[81]

For both Levinas and Feuerbach, love is not merely a concept or the process whereby two become one, as is suggested in the dialectical approach of Hegel, but rather a true and honest answer to the needs of the Other as Other without any attempt to overcome or sublimate the difference between an I and a Thou,

80 Emmanuel Levinas, *Totality and Infinity: An Essay on Exteriority*, trans. by Alphonso Lingis, ed. by John Wild, Pittsburgh: Duquesne University Press 2007, p. 68.

81 Emmanuel Levinas, *Time and the Other*, trans. and ed. by Richard A. Cohen, Pittsburgh: Duquesne University Press 1987, p. 116.

the difference that can serve as the source of both happiness and frustration. The combination of happiness and frustration derives a vision of God that is only revealed to us through a glimpse in the face of the Other:

> The subject-object relation does not reflect it; in the impersonal relation that leads to it the invisible but personal God is not approached outside of all human presence. The ideal is not only a being superlatively being, a sublimation of the objective, or, in the solitude of love, a sublimation of a Thou. The work of justice—the uprightness of the face to face—is necessary in order that the breach that leads to God be produced—and "vision" here coincides with this work of justice. Hence metaphysics is enacted where the social relation is enacted—in our relations with men. There can be no "knowledge" of God separated from the relationship with men. The Other is the very locus of metaphysical truth, and is indispensable for my relation with God. He does not play the role of a mediator. The Other is not the incarnation of God, but precisely by his face, in which he is disincarnate, is the manifestation of the height in which God is revealed.[82]

Although Levinas sees metaphysics and intersubjectivity as being closely related, his understanding of the intersubjective relationship and a God that is, in its non-incarnated form, revealed in the face of the Other is much more reminiscent of Feuerbach's perspective than that of Hegel. Levinas never achieves such a high level of synthesis as Hegel did in his dialectical movement of the World Spirit. Levinas and Feuerbach perceive the otherness of the Other as a valuable contribution to the completeness of our life and not as an obstacle that needs to be overcome. Neither philosopher believes that love means a complete unity of I and Thou, but they recognize the resistance that helps to prevent the loss of the necessary otherness. They insist that there is no relationship with God beyond the relationship with humans. From this perspective, Feuerbach's communicative philosophy cannot be perceived as a philosophy of intersubjectivity in the Hegelian sense, since it does not result in the assertion that I=I, but rather in the relationship of a specific, corporal I to a specific, corporal Thou, a relationship that is simultaneously both subjective and objective, but which does not sublate the fundamental difference between the two. However, if the difference does not stand in the way of equality, if the I and Thou can

82 Levinas, *Totality and Infinity*. pp. 78–79.

be both subject and object at the same time, then it is possible to suggest that the philosophy of Feuerbach contains undeniable traces of intersubjectivity.

3 Recognition Theory: Axel Honneth and Charles Taylor

Interpretations of recognition theory have undergone a slight shift in recent years, and thinkers have begun to identify traces of Feuerbach's philosophy of I and Thou in the thinking of, for example, Axel Honneth. In his text "Recognition in Feuerbach," Jean-Philippe Deranty directly references the influence of Feuerbach's thinking, arguing that "Ludwig Feuerbach can be considered one of the most important intellectual ancestors of the contemporary theory of recognition."[83] In his 1992 work *The Struggle for Recognition*, Honneth draws inspiration from two authors in particular: Hegel through his resolution of the lord and bondsman metaphor and the psychologist George Herbert Mead. Honneth mentions Feuerbach only twice in this key text,[84] discussing his thinking in the context of Marx and his overestimation of labor and economic interests in intersubjective relations and the personal development of an individual. Although Honneth criticized Marx and agreed with Feuerbach's understanding of the community of human beings, it is possible to suggest that he does not dedicate sufficient attention to Feuerbach's communicative philosophy of I and Thou, with Feuerbach unjustly left in the shadow of Hegel in this significant work.[85] Deranty argues correctly that Honneth's theory of mutual recognition contains so many statements that had been previously formulated by Feuerbach that it would be more accurate to describe the theory as being derived from Feuerbach rather than Hegel. This is most obvious in Honneth's definition of love which closely mirrors Feuerbach's interpretation:

> First, Feuerbach made observations that were confirmed by developmental psychology in the next century, by interpreting the I/Thou/Species relationship in dynamic terms. This is the idea that recognition of the other and by the other is a structural condition for the constitution of selfhood, both for full self-consciousness and regarding the particular structure of

83 Jean-Philippe Deranty, "Recognition in Feuerbach," in *Handbuch Anerkennung*, ed. by Ludwig Siep, Heikki Ikäheimo, Michael Quante, Wiesbaden: Springer 2000, pp. 1–5, p. 1.

84 Axel Honneth, *Struggle for Recognition: The Moral Grammar of Social Conflicts*, trans. and ed. by Joel Anderson, Cambridge, MA: MIT University Press 1996, p. 68, p. 147.

85 Perhaps one small exception here is a work from Honneth's early period: Hans Joas and Axel Honneth, *Social Action and Human Nature*, trans. by Raymond Meyer, Cambridge: Cambridge University Press 1988.

> the self's psychological make-up. More specifically, Feuerbach emphasized the ontogenetic centrality of primary attachments between mother and child, as for example in this early passage: "only when the mother becomes the object of attention and therefore the object of love, only then does the distinction between subject and object arise." Some of the passages in that book directly anticipate the social psychology of George Herbert Mead, which was at the core of Honneth's first model of recognition. Feuerbach also argued, as Honneth would in his 2005 Tanner lectures on reification, that the I/Thou relationship was the constitutive condition for the subject establishing relationships to the world, including cognitive ones.[86]

No less significant is the paper by Joaquín Gil Martínez entitled "Affective Recognition as a Moral Content, Feuerbach in the Dialogue: Fichte, Hegel, Honneth," in which he shares Deranty's opinion that recognition and recollection play a central role in the philosophies of Honneth and Feuerbach. Both Gil Martínez and Deranty stress the fact that although Feuerbach had studied under Hegel and been influenced by his teacher's thinking, he had developed his own, original theory of intersubjectivity and recognition based on the satisfaction of emotional needs through intersubjective relations.[87] Love and friendship are the two paths that lead to the recognition of the Other as a Thou and thus to the feeling of completeness and the satisfaction of the emotional needs of an I. Gil Martínez also draws attention to the limitations of recognition in Feuerbach's work; for Feuerbach, recognition mainly occurs at the emotional level, while in Honneth's understanding, the concept has three different dimensions, "the affective, the legal and the solidary (afectiva, jurídica y solidaria)."[88] However, Gil Martínez insists that true recognition has to start on the affective level of an intersubjective relationship before passing on to the wider fields of solidarity and law.[89]

The importance of feelings and emotions in the process of recognition is also noted by Charles Taylor in his essay "The Politics of Recognition." Although Taylor discusses the issue of mutual recognition from the perspective of political philosophy and focuses on the opportunities and obstacles posed by cross-cultural problems in contemporary societies, he shares the opinion held

86 Deranty, "Recognition in Feuerbach," p. 3.

87 Joaquín Gil Martínez, "El reconocimiento afectivo como contenido moral. Feuerbach en diálogo: Fichte, Hegel, Honneth," *Tópicos, Revista de Filosofía*, vol. 49, 2015, pp. 53–79, p. 55–60.

88 Ibid., p. 77.

89 Ibid., pp. 77–78.

by Feuerbach and Honneth that recognition represents a fundamental human need, one which is almost as crucial for the survival and well-being of a human being as the need for food, warmth and safety. He argues:

> The demand for recognition in these latter cases is given urgency by the supposed links between recognition and identity, where this latter term designates something like a person's understanding of who they are, of their fundamental defining characteristics as a human being. The thesis is that our identity is partly shaped by recognition or its absence, often by the misrecognition of others, and a person or group of people can suffer real damage, real distortion, if the people or society around them mirror back to them a confining or demeaning or contemptible picture of themselves. Nonrecognition or misrecognition can inflict harm, can be a form of oppression, imprisoning someone in a false, distorted, and reduced mode of being.... Within these perspectives, misrecognition shows not just a lack of due respect. It can inflict a grievous wound, saddling its victims with a crippling self-hatred. Due recognition is not just a courtesy we owe people. It is a vital human need.[90]

Despite the social and political focus of Taylor's essay on recognition, there is little doubt that the consequences of misrecognition have a negative impact not only on the broader social and political level but also on the personal and emotional levels of every single human being. Everyone who experiences misrecognition as an individual or as a member of a misrecognized community suffers personal and emotional harm at the very core of their personhood. The process of mutual recognition therefore starts with an awareness of our own limitations and the need of the Other to achieve the feeling of our own completeness. In his book *Recognition: A Chapter in the History of European Ideas*, Honneth criticizes Hobbes on the grounds of the inconsistency between his psychological and anthropological insights into the problem of recognition and his political theory.[91] Like Feuerbach, Honneth is clearly aware of the fact that without the display of love for one's neighbor, there is no solidarity, and without solidarity, there is no sense of legal recognition if a new law cannot be applied effectively in the practices of everyday life. There can be no political theory without an awareness of the relevant psychological and anthropological insights.

90 Taylor, "The Politics of Recognition," p. 25–26.

91 Axel Honneth, *Recognition: A Chapter in the History of European Ideas*, trans. and ed. by Joseph Ganahl, Cambridge: Cambridge University Press 2021, p. 12.

4 Conclusion

The problem of I and Thou is an ancient issue which has perplexed humankind since the earliest attempts to construe the self-consciousness of an I as a subject in opposition to the objective awareness of the Other, of a Thou. The relationship between the I and Thou is one of the foundations of the Jewish and Christian tradition. However, the importance of intersubjective relationships was partially abandoned in Christian ontology in particular in favor of Greek metaphysics and its search for absolute, eternal truths. Hegel was the first modern philosopher to address the problem of intersubjectivity, and his work *The Phenomenology of Spirit* posits mutual recognition as the ultimate solution to the tensions between lord and bondsman and serves as a crucial stage in the development of the World Spirit. While Hegel's theory of intersubjectivity is still formulated in the theological and metaphysical tradition, his student, Ludwig Feuerbach, found the courage to transgress the boundaries of metaphysics and formulate his communicative philosophy of the I and Thou through an anthropological approach. With the notable exception of Buber, the most significant thinkers in the field of modern intersubjectivity and recognition theory such as Husserl, Levinas, Honneth, or Taylor consider themselves to be followers of Hegel, even though their non-metaphysical and anthropological approaches to love, compassion, emotions, solidarity, and recognition place them far closer to Feuerbach's position and distance them from Hegel. As Deranty has noted, "Feuerbach can thus be seen as a founding figure for contemporary philosophies linking recognition with solidarity."[92] Feuerbach revives the long-forgotten relationship between the concrete, corporal I and the concrete, corporal Thou, a relationship based on love, solidarity, and recognition, in Western thought and can rightly be considered as the direct precursor of modern intersubjectivity and recognition theory.

Acknowledgments

This paper was supported by funding from the Agency for the Support of Research and Innovations under VEGA Project 1/0232/21.

92 Deranty, "Recognition in Feuerbach," p. 4.

Bibliography

Buber, Martin, *I and Thou,* trans. and ed. by Ronald Gregor-Smith, London, New York: Continuum 2004.

Buber, Martin, *Das Dialogische Prinzip,* ed. by Lambert Schneider, Gütersloh: Gütersloher Verlagshaus 2014.

Buber, Martin, "Dialogue," in *Between Man and Man,* trans. by Ronald Gregor-Smith, ed. by Maurice Friedman, London and New York: Routledge 2022, pp. 1–45.

Buber, Martin, "The Question to the Single One," in *Between Man and Man,* trans. by Ronald Gregor-Smith, ed. by Maurice Friedman, London and New York: Routledge 2022, pp. 46–97.

Buber, Martin, "What is Man?," in *Between Man and Man,* trans. by Ronald Gregor-Smith, ed. by Maurice Friedman, London and New York: Routledge 2022, pp. 140–244.

Buber, Martin, "The History of the Dialogical Principle by Martin Buber," in *Between Man and Man,* trans. by Ronald Gregor-Smith, ed. by Maurice Friedman, London and New York: Routledge 2022, pp. 249–264.

Dastur, Françoise, *Questions of Phenomenology: Language, Alterity, Temporality, Finitude,* trans. by Robert Vallier, ed. by John D. Caputo, New York: Fordham University Press.

Deranty, Jean-Philippe, "Recognition in Feuerbach," in *Handbuch Anerkennung*, ed. by Ludwig Siep, Heikki Ikäheimo, Michael Quante, Wiesbaden: Springer 2000, pp. 1–5.

Dodd, James, "The Dignity of the Mind: Levinas' Reading of Husserl," *Levinas Studies*, vol. 5, 2010, pp. 19–41.

Eagleton, Terry, *Materialism*, New Haven and London: Yale University Press 2016.

Feuerbach, Ludwig, *Essence of Christianity*, trans. by George Eliot, New York: Prometheus Books 1989.

Feuerbach, Ludwig, "Towards a Critique of Hegel's Philosophy," in *The Fiery Brook: Selected Writings of Ludwig Feuerbach*, trans. and ed. by Zawar Hanfi, Garden City, NY: Anchor Books 1972, pp. 53–96.

Feuerbach, Ludwig, "On the Beginning of Philosophy," in *The Fiery Brook: Selected Writings of Ludwig Feuerbach*, trans. and ed. by Zawar Hanfi, Garden City, NY: Anchor Books 1972, pp. 135–144.

Feuerbach, Ludwig, *Principles of Philosophy of the Future*, in *The Fiery Brook: Selected Writings of Ludwig Feuerbach*, trans. and ed. by Zawar Hanfi, Garden City, NY: Anchor Books 1972, pp. 175–245.

Feuerbach, Ludwig, "Fragments Concerning the Characteristics of My Philosophical Development," in *The Fiery Brook: Selected Writings of Ludwig Feuerbach*, trans. and ed. by Zawar Hanfi, Garden City, NY: Anchor Books 1972, pp. 265–296.

Feuerbach, Ludwig, "Zur Kritik der Hegelschen Philosophie," in *Gesammelte Werke*, vols. 1–21, ed. by Werner Schuffenhauer, Berlin: Akademie Verlag 1981–2013, vol. 9, *Kleinere Schriften II (1839–1846)*, pp. 16–62.

Feuerbach, Ludwig, *Grundsätze der Philosophie der Zukunft und andere Schriften*, ed. by Michael Holzinger, Berlin: Holzinger 2016.

Flusser, Vilém, *Kommunikologie*. ed. by Stephan Bollmann and Edith Flusser, Mannheim: Bollmann Verlag 2007.

Fricke, Christel and Dagfinn Føllesdal (eds.), *Intersubjectivity and Objectivity in Adam Smith and Edmund Husserl: A Collection of Essays*, Berlin, Boston: De Gruyter 2013.

Gil Martínez, Joaquín, "El reconocimiento afectivo como contenido moral. Feuerbach en diálogo: Fichte, Hegel, Honneth," *Tópicos, Revista de Filosofía*, vol. 49, 2015, pp. 53–79.

Habermas, Jürgen, *Theorie des kommunkativen Handelns, Bd. 1. Handlungsrationalität und gesellschafliche Rationalisierung*, Frankfurt am Main: Suhrkamp 2019.

Hans, Joas and Honneth, Axel, *Social Action and Human Nature*, trans. by Raymond Meyer. Cambridge: Cambridge University Press 1988.

Hegel, Georg Wilhelm Friedrich, *The Phenomenology of Spirit*, trans. and ed. by Terry Pinkard, Cambridge: Cambridge University Press 2018.

Hegel, Georg Wilhelm Friedrich, *Elements of the Philosophy of Right or Natural Law and Political Science in Outline*, trans. by H. B. Nisbet, ed. by Alan Wood, Cambridge: Cambridge University Press 2019.

Heidegger, Martin, *Hegels Phänomenologie des Geistes*, ed. by Ingtraut Görmann, vol. 32, in *Gesamtausgabe*, Frankfurt am Main: Vittorio Klostermann 1997.

Heidegger, Martin, "Die onto-Theo-Logische Verfassung der Metaphysik," in *Identität und Differenz*, ed. by Günter Neske, vol. 11, in *Gesamtausgabe*, Frankfurt am Main: Klostermann 2006, pp. 31–68.

Honneth, Axel, *Recognition: A Chapter in the History of European Ideas*, trans. and ed. by Joseph Ganahl, Cambridge: Cambridge University Press 2021.

Honneth, Axel, *Struggle for Recognition. The Moral Grammar of Social Conflicts*, trans. and ed. by Joel Anderson, Cambridge MA: MIT University Press 1996.

Honneth, Axel, *The Pathologies of Individual Freedom: Hegel's Social Theory*, trans. by Ladislaus Löb, Princeton, Oxford: Princeton University Press 2010.

Husserl, Edmund, *Zur Phänomenologie der Intersubjektivität. Texte aus dem Nachlass*, vol. 1, *1905–1920*, ed. by Iso Kern, The Hague: Martinus Nijhoff 1973.

Husserl, Edmund, *Zur Phänomenologie der Intersubjektivität. Texte aus dem Nachlass*, vol. 2, *–1928*, ed. by Iso Kern, The Hague: Martinus Nijhoff 1973.

Husserl, Edmund, *Zur Phänomenologie der Intersubjektivität. Texte aus dem Nachlass*, vol. 3, *1929–1935*, ed. by Iso Kern, The Hague: Martinus Nijhoff 1973.

Husserl, Edmund, *Cartesian Meditations. An Introduction to Phenomenology*, trans. by Dorion Cairns, The Hague, Boston, London: Martinus Nijhoff 1982.

Jacobi, Friedrich Heinrich, *The Main Philosophical Writings and the Novel Allwill*, trans. and ed. by Georg di Giovanni, Montreal and Kingston: McGill-Queen's University Press 1994.

Kjosavik, Frode, Christian Beyer, Christel Fricke (eds.), *Husserl's Phenomenology of Intersubjectivity. Historical Interpretations and Contemporary Applications*, London: Routledge 2020.

Levinas, Emmanuel, *Time and the Other*, trans. and ed. by Richard A. Cohen, Pittsburgh: Duquesne University Press 1987.

Levinas, Emmanuel, *Totality and Infinity: An Essay on Exteriority*, trans. by Alphonso Lingis, ed. by John Wild, Pittsburgh: Duquesne University Press 2007.

Patočka, Jan, *Body, Community, Language, World*, trans. by Erazim Kohák, ed. by James Dodd, Chicago: Open Court 1998.

Pippin, Robert, *Hegel's Practical Philosophy: Rational Agency as Ethical Life*, New York: Cambridge University Press 2008.

Reitemeyer, Ursula, "Das poröse Ich in der fragilen Moderne," *Vierteljahrsschrift für wissenschaftliche Pädagogik*, vol. 85, no. 1. 2009, pp. 52–65.

Rütter, Susanne, *Herausforderung Angesichts des Anderen: Von Feuerbach über Buber zu Levinas*, Baden Baden: Verlag Karl Alber 2000.

Šajda, Peter, *Buberov spor s Kierkegaardom: o vzťahu náboženstva k etike a politike*, Bratislava: Kalligram 2013.

Schnell, Alexander, "Intersubjectivity in Husserl's Work," in *META: Research in Hermeneutics, Phenomenology, and Practical Philosophy*, vol. 2, no. 1, 2010, pp. 9–32.

Stewart, Jon, *Hegel's Century: Alienation and Recognition in a Time of Revolution*, Cambridge: Cambridge University Press 2021.

Taylor, Charles, "The Politics of Recognition," in *Multiculturalism and the Politics of Recognition*, ed. by Amy Gutmann, Princeton: Princeton University Press 1994, pp. 25–73.

Tomasoni, Francesco, *Ludwig Feuerbach. Entstehung, Entwicklung und Bedeutungs eines Werkes*, trans. by Gunnhild Schneider, ed. by Ursula Reitemeyer, Takayuki Shibata and Francesco Tomasoni, Münster: Waxmann 2015.

Zahavi, Dan, *Husserl and Transcendental Intersubjectivity: A Response to the Linguistic-Pragmatic Critique*, trans. and ed. by Elizabeth A. Behnke, Toledo: Ohio University Press 2001.

CHAPTER 5

The Humorist in the Face of Religious Existence

Jorge Schulz

Abstract

Irony and humor play an important role in Kierkegaard's thought. In the *Concluding Unscientific Postscript* Johannes Climacus situates them as border regions between existential spheres, with irony being the boundary between the aesthetic and the ethical and humor between the ethical and the religious. This paper seeks to explore the role of humor in the existential transitions to the religious sphere. Humor as *confinium* marks a qualitative discontinuity between the spheres and at the same time opens a space of existential transition. Thus, it is argued that the humorist dwells in proximity to the religious, and that it is precisely this proximity that constitutes him as such, providing him through the imagination with a vision of life in which the poles of jesting and earnestness can be subverted through an eventual humorous transvaluation.

Irony and humor in Kierkegaard are much more than rhetorical devices. They are categories of human existence.[1] In the pseudonymous works, especially in Johannes Climacus' *Concluding Unscientific Postscript to the Philosophical Fragments*, irony and humor appear as forms of the comic and represent existential positions marked by contradiction: "where there is life there is contradiction, and wherever there is contradiction, the comic is present."[2] Like the comic, the tragic is also characterized by contradiction. The difference is that the tragic is a "suffering contradiction," while the comic is a "painless contradiction."[3] And this is so because the comic always provides a way of escape and relief from *pathos*. Now, if the comic is characterized by contradiction, there must

1 *SKS* 7, 457 / *CUP1*, 503–504: "Irony is an existence-qualification, and thus nothing is more ludicrous than regarding it as a style of speaking or an author's counting himself lucky to express himself ironically once in a while. The person who has essential irony has it all day long and is not bound to any style, because it is the infinite within him." As we shall see below, what Climacus says here about irony could also apply to humor, since humor is not essentially different from irony, although it has different levels and scopes.

2 *SKS* 7, 465 / *CUP1*, 513–514.

3 *SKS* 7, 466 / *CUP1*, 514.

 | DOI:10.1163/9789004689459_007

be something previously established to contradict. Something is comic when it subverts some presupposed norm.[4] To be truly comic, a jest needs to be based on something that is taken seriously. Thus, in comic contradiction there is always a tension between jesting and earnestness. And this contradiction takes on different dimensions according to each existential stage. Climacus points out that each sphere of existence can be identified through its relation to the comic and its level of participation in contradiction: "the more competently a person exists, the more he will discover the comic."[5] This correlation between existential competence and the discovery of the comic suggests that both irony and humor play an important role in the development of subjectivity, being the thresholds of different existential stages: "There are three existential spheres: the aesthetic, the ethical and the religious. Between one and the other there is a *confinium*: irony is the *confinium* between the aesthetic and the ethical; humor is the *confinium* between the ethical and the religious."[6]

Humor is the perspective of the *Postscript*. Climacus identifies himself repeatedly as a humorist, approaching the problems dealt with in the work from this particular vision of life that gravitates between the ethical and the religious. Although Climacus is not himself a Christian, he places Christianity in the highest of the spheres since it expresses the ultimate paradox: that God has entered into time to save humanity. For Kierkegaard, the Christian doctrine of the incarnation expresses this contradiction in a paradigmatic way, which is why he goes as far as to say that Christianity is "the most humorous world-historical view of life."[7] Glancing at the first entries in his journals, we see that from as early as 1834 until completing his thesis in 1841, Kierkegaard was actively engaged in the study of the concepts of irony and humor.[8] However, these concepts were not forgotten when he began his pseudonymous production, quite the contrary. Jon Stewart observes that the writing on irony is essential to an understanding of Kierkegaard's thought and authorial strategy: "its importance is enhanced rather than diminished as it provides an invaluable interpretative key to the rest of his writings."[9] Even though Kierkegaard does not address the concept of humor in his thesis on irony, he concludes it

4 See Will Williams, *Kierkegaard and the Legitimacy of the Comic: Understanding the Relevance of Irony, Humor, and the Comic for Ethics and Religion*, Lanham: Lexington Books 2018, pp. 6–8.

5 *SKS* 7, 420 / *CUP1*, 462.

6 *SKS* 7, 455 / *CUP1*, 501–502.

7 *SKS* 17, 214, DD:3 / *KJN* 1, 206.

8 See K. Brian Söderquist, "Irony and Humor in Kierkegaard's Early Journals," *Kierkegaard Studies Yearbook*, 2003, p. 144.

9 Jon Stewart, *Søren Kierkegaard: Subjectivity, Irony, and the Crisis of Modernity*, Oxford: Oxford University Press 2015, p. 114.

with a reference in which he links the nature of irony to that of humor, highlighting the importance of humor in the face of religious existence.[10] As he also expresses it in an entry in his journals: "Humor is irony taken to its maximum vibration … the Christian aspect is the real primus motor."[11]

We propose here to explore the concept of humor specifically as an instance that situates the individual at the threshold of religious existence. We are interested in dealing with the way in which the humorous, as *confinium*, aims to be a means of indirect communication of the religious.[12] Being what precedes the religious sphere, humor cannot be confused with it, but it can prepare and dispose the individual for faith by promoting a greater degree of inwardness. We want to highlight the important role of the humorous as a border territory, with a special focus on the *Postscript*. We argue here that the humorist dwells in proximity to the religious, and that it is precisely this proximity that constitutes him as such, providing him through the imagination with a vision of life in which the poles of jesting and earnestness can be subverted through a possible humorous transvaluation. We will begin, then, by approaching the two types of religiousness that Climacus distinguishes. Having done that, we will seek to address the dialectical structure of humor, and, finally, we will explore how the humorous is constituted as a *confinium* that situates existence in the face of the religious sphere.

1 Religiousness A and B

The *Postscript* presents the religious sphere on two levels that Climacus calls Religiousness A and Religiousness B. Religiousness A is a religiousness of hidden inwardness, which is not specifically Christian but expresses the pathetic dimension of the sphere, while religiousness B is the specifically Christian religiousness that incorporates the dialectical and paradoxical elements of Christianity.[13] Both levels are permeated by *pathos*. Suffering in the aesthetic sphere is of an "accidental" character, a contingent matter of "good luck or bad

10 *SKS* 1, 357 / *CI*, 329: "Humor has a far more profound skepticism than irony, because here the focus is on sinfulness, not on finitude."

11 *SKS* 17, 234, DD:36 / *KJN* 1, p. 206.

12 The function of humor as incognito will not be addressed here. For this I refer to Patricia C. Dip's commentary in "El rol de Climacus en la estrategia comunicativa de Kierkegaard," *Horizontes filosóficos: Revista de Filosofía, Humanidades y Ciencias Sociales*, vol. 8, no. 8, 2018, pp. 23–36.

13 See *SKS* 7, 504–505 / *CUPI*, 555–556. Here Climacus clarifies that to speak of religiousness B as dialectical does not mean that religiousness A lacks dialectical elements; however, religiousness A "is not paradoxically dialectical."

luck," but within the religious sphere, it is "crucial."[14] Climacus states: "Whereas aesthetic existence is essentially enjoyment and ethical existence is essentially struggle and victory, religious existence is essentially suffering, and not as a transitory element but as a continual accompaniment."[15]

In Kierkegaard's thought in general, and the perspective of Climacus in particular, the concept of *pathos* is related to the "transformation of existence"[16] of the individual through his relationship with the absolute or eternal. This contrasts with "aesthetic suffering," where there is no true inner transformation, only a speculative game of possibilities that remain abstractions and are never concretized through a decision that manifests itself in existence. This is why Climacus emphasizes that "existential *pathos* is action."[17] To act religiously is to suffer. However, not all suffering is religious. Suffering is also relevant as an ethical category. In general, "suffering serves in shaping and sharpening the individual in order that he or she may learn from it to inform temporal existence with an eternal perspective."[18] In this sense, we will see how religiousness A, through suffering, can fulfill a propaedeutic function in relation to religiousness B.

Climacus defines religiousness A as the "the dialectic of inward deepening."[19] It is the relationship with an eternal happiness that is not conditioned by anything in particular or anything external to the internalization itself. One can speak of it as a merely human, immanent religiousness. It is a generic form of the religious, a kind of natural religion, since it is a universally accessible experience that dispenses with the specific content of the Christian faith. Climacus affirms that religiousness A "can be present in paganism" (he often associates the figure of Socrates with religiousness A as a paradigm), but it can also be "the religiousness of everyone who is not decisively Christian."[20]

Religiousness A goes beyond ethical self-sufficiency. Whoever has made the leap to this first level of the religious sphere is pierced by resignation, suffering and guilt. Here we see the emergence of what Climacus calls existential *pathos*, which consists in the fact that the person who is infinitely interested in his

14 *SKS* 7, 262 / *CUP1*, 288.
15 *SKS* 7, 262 / *CUP1*, 288.
16 *SKS* 7, 392 / *CUP1*, 431.
17 *SKS* 7, 392 / *CUP1*, 431.
18 Sean Anthony Turchin, "Suffering," in *Kierkegaard's Concepts*, Tome VI, *Salvation to Writing*, ed. by Steven M. Emmanuel, William McDonald and Jon Stewart, Farnham and Burlington: Ashgate 2015 (*Kierkegaard Research: Sources, Reception and Resources*, vol. 15), p. 119.
19 *SKS* 7, 505 / *CUP1*, 556.
20 *SKS* 7, 506 / *CUP1*, 557.

eternal happiness "changes everything in his existence in relation to that highest good,"[21] that is, in relation to God. "The effect that a person's conception of God or of his eternal happiness should have is that it transforms his entire existence in relation to it, a transformation that is a dying to immediacy."[22]

The initial expression of the existential *pathos* of religiousness A consists of a complete reorientation of life that leads the person to relate absolutely to the absolute *telos* and relatively to relative ends.[23] This requires a resignation that is capable of relinquishing the absolutization of the relative and the relativization of the absolute. Because if the highest good is seen as one more end among others, one is not relating oneself in an absolute way to the absolute *telos*. Religious passion is not a matter of words. It is not something that has to be expressed through discourse but rather through life itself: "the *pathos* lies not in testifying to an eternal happiness but in transforming one's own existence into a testimony to it."[24]

For Climacus, religiousness A represents a moment in a process of development towards religiousness B. He affirms that "religiousness A must first be present in the individual before there can be any consideration of becoming aware of the dialectical B."[25] Religiousness A accentuates the importance of passionate interiority focusing on the cultivation of this existential *pathos*. Nor is religious passion a matter of doctrine. Religiousness A abstracts from the *what* (of the content) of any belief to focus on the *how*, so that this *how* can then accompany the specific *what* of religiousness B. However, Climacus observes that the task of relating absolutely to the absolute *telos* and relatively to the relative ends is a very difficult and exhausting task for a human being. He considers that religiousness A "is so strenuous for a human being that there is always a sufficient task in it."[26] A person may think that he loves God above all things, but then he discovers that in reality he is merely pursuing some finite or relative good. Thus, one repeatedly finds that one is related in an absolute way to the relative, which is nothing more than the expression of an aesthetic *pathos*. Moreover, here is the reason why religious existence is essentially

21 *SKS* 7, 354 / *CUP1*, 389.

22 *SKS* 7, 438 / *CUP1*, 483.

23 *SKS* 7, 352f. / *CUP1*, 387f.

24 *SKS* 7, 359 / *CUP1*, 394.

25 *SKS* 7, 506 / *CUP1*, 556. Here Climacus goes on to say: "When the individual in the most decisive expression of existential *pathos* relates himself to an eternal happiness, then there can be consideration of becoming aware of how the dialectical in second place (*secundo loco*) thrusts him down into the *pathos* of the absurd" (*SKS* 7, 506 / *CUP1*, 556–557).

26 *SKS* 7, 506 / *CUP1*, 557.

suffering: "the individual is unable to transform himself."[27] That is why religiousness A is also permeated by guilt, accentuating the existential *pathos* in such a way that internal suffering is a constant and always present mark.

With this said, what is now the place of religiousness B? In religiousness B, we find a specifically Christian religiousness. It is a question of a transcendent religiousness, which places the person in relation to the absolute paradox. It should not, however, be considered as something opposed to religiousness A, but rather as a specification of it. Passionate subjectivity and inner deepening are a necessary condition for grasping the content of Christian teachings. Only when one has experienced in one's own existence the *pathos* of religiousness A can one properly appropriate the dialectical and paradoxical content of religiousness B. At this level, the specific content of the Christian faith is incorporated. In Climacus' view, the Christian faith integrates the *how* of subjectivity (accentuated by religiousness A) with the specific *what* of the gospel paradox: the God-man, that is, the incarnation of God in time for the salvation of humanity.

Now, there are certain aspects in which Christianity shocks and hurts religiousness A, and this is the fact that in religiousness B salvation is presented as a grace from God, as a divine gift that does not depend on human effort, even though the effort has been sincerely pursued. Referring to Anti-Climacus' *Practice in Christianity*, no. 2, David J. Gouwens highlights two types of offenses that we are interested in mentioning here. On the one hand, there is a scandal that has to do with the paradoxical character of the God-man, since "the person who is 'lowly, poor, suffering and finally powerless' offends human ideas of divine glory and grandeur."[28] On the other hand, Christianity also scandalizes by leading to one's reevaluation of oneself with "the 'absurd' suggestion that one must see oneself not only as guilty (as in Religiousness A), but also as a sinner, living in 'untruth,' in need of a savior."[29]

In religiousness B, consciousness of guilt becomes consciousness of sin,[30] for which the demand for repentance appears. Here the religious existence

27 *SKS* 7, 394 / *CUP1*, 433.

28 David J. Gouwens, *Kierkegaard as Religious Thinker*, Cambridge: Cambridge University Press, 1996, p. 131.

29 Ibid.

30 *SKS* 7, 243 / *CUP1*, 267–268: "Sin is a crucial expression for the religious existence. As long as sin is not posited, the suspension becomes a transient factor that in turn vanishes or remains outside life as the totally irregular. Sin, however, is the crucial point of departure for the religious existence, is not a factor within something else, within another order of things, but is itself the beginning of the religious order of things."

cannot be actualized through self-realization (as in religiousness A) but only through faith. However, faith should not be understood as mere intellectual assent, but instead as trust in or dependence on God. Climacus insists that "the paradox cannot and should not be understood" and even speaks of a "crucifixion of the understanding."[31] Nevertheless, this does not involve disparaging reason,[32] but rather points to the offense we mentioned earlier, to the "objective uncertainty"[33] that represents the truth of faith. This has the function of marking a discontinuity with all human self-sufficiency and signaling the necessary renunciation of all efforts to achieve the religious existence by any means other than faith in God.[34] Faith is ultimately openness to divine assistance in the acknowledgment that the human being "is nothing before God,"[35] and that by his own efforts alone he is not capable of relating in an absolute way to the absolute *telos* and in a relative way to relative ends. In *Fear and Trembling* Johannes de silentio says: "he who loves God without faith reflects upon himself; he who loves God in faith reflects upon God."[36]

2 The Earnestness of Humor

Humor, as a subspecies of the comic, expresses an existential position characterized by contradiction. For humor to be really comical, however, it needs to work on an ethical basis that is taken seriously. Otherwise, it would lack the grounding and necessary contrast to manifest the contradictory nature of the comic. Therefore, when we talk about humor, we should not think of something that excludes earnestness. For Climacus there is a "dialectical reciprocity

31 *SKS* 7, 513 / *CUP1*, 564.

32 *SKS* 7, 513 / *CUP1*, 565: "Because an individual in faith relinquishes the understanding and believes against the understanding, he should not for that reason think poorly of the understanding."

33 *SKS* 7, 186 / *CUP1*, 203–204.

34 In the context of the *Postscript*, this applies especially to the polemic against Hegelianism or the thinkers of abstraction, who believed that they could achieve—and even surpass—religious existence through pure thought.

35 *SKS* 7, 418–419 / *CUP1*, 461. Here Climacus states that the key point of faith is to die "to immediacy or existentially expressing that the individual is capable of doing nothing himself but is nothing before God, because here again the relationship with God is distinguishable by the negative, and self-annihilation is the essential form for the relationship with God."

36 *SKS* 4, 132 / *FT*, 37.

between jest and earnestness."[37] In *Stages on Life's Way*, Quidam, a character created by Frater Taciturnus (who is also a humorist), argues that "Earnestness is basically not something simple, a simplex, but is a *compositum* [compound], for true earnestness is the unity of jest and earnestness."[38] There is a kind of earnestness that is a "bigoted earnestness" that "always fears the comic," but "true earnestness itself invents the comic."[39] This earnestness is fundamental to ethical life, because it concentrates the persistent efforts the will makes so as to actualize ethical ideals in existence itself.[40] However, the poor concrete results of such efforts very soon show their comic side. An intolerant earnestness is unable to see this comic side, but true earnestness assumes it.

Humor is thus situated between the ethical and the religious. It has the peculiarity of incorporating the religious categories of Christianity, bringing into play new levels of the comic and the earnest. To clear up possible misunderstandings, however, Climacus distinguishes between two types of humor. There are both an immature humor and a mature humor. The former is characterized as "a kind of flippancy that has skipped too soon out of reflection."[41] It is a type of humorous response that only seeks relief and does so by affirming the absurd and paradoxical in a banal way, simply as a game that makes a parody of the religious. Immature humor "is so far from being religiousness that it is an esthetic subtlety that skips past the ethical."[42] This type of humor "lags behind" what Climacus calls "humor in the balance between the comic and the tragic."[43] This is mature humor. It is the concept that is developed in the *Postscript* as an existential position and a stage previous to the religious since it represents an important subjective development that "is the condition for properly embracing Christianity."[44] Humor is, for Climacus, a school that, although it cannot be identified with faith, cultivates existence by preparing the individual for faith.

Kierkegaard's notion of humor could, in principle, be elucidated through the theory of incongruity. John Lippitt has worked on this issue based on

37 *SKS* 7, 72 / *CUP1*, 71.

38 *SKS* 6, 339 / *SLW*, 365

39 *SKS* 6, 340 / *SLW*, 366

40 See John J. Davenport, "Earnestness," in *Kierkegaard's Concepts*, Tome II, *Classicism to Enthusiasm*, ed. by Steven M. Emmanuel, William McDonald and Jon Stewart, Farnham and Burlington: Ashgate 2014 (*Kierkegaard Research: Sources, Reception and Resources*, vol. 15), p. 225.

41 *SKS* 7, 266 / *CUP1*, 292.

42 *SKS* 7, 266 / *CUP1*, 292.

43 *SKS* 7, 266 / *CUP1*, 292.

44 *SKS* 7, 266 / *CUP1*, 292.

contributions of humor theorists such as D.H. Monro and M.C. Swabey.[45] In this way, it is understood that in the different types of humor there always appears some "inappropriateness" that consists of "the linking of disparates ... the collision of different mental spheres ... the obtrusion into one context of what belongs in another."[46] The incongruity would thus be marked by "strikingly contrasting qualities at the farthest extremes of the scale from one another."[47] Lippitt notes that, at least as a starting point, these notions seem to be quite adequate for understanding contradiction in the *Postscript* since they open up a broad spectrum going far beyond mere logical or formal contradiction. However, it should be noted here that humor in Kierkegaard is not an end in itself but is rather at the service of the indirect communication of the religious. In *Practice in Christianity*, Anti-Climacus argues that indirect communication arises by placing "jest and earnestness together in such a way that the composite is a dialectical knot" so that the interlocutor has to "untie the knot himself,"[48] that is to say, "the receiver is self-active."[49]

In the *Postscript*, Climacus' interest is to present a humorous vision of Christianity in which a collision of spheres is generated that are qualitatively different and incommensurable with each other. Thus, humor incorporates into the immanent plane categories that belong to the transcendent plane:

> The humorous appears when one answers the question of *Fragments* (Can a historical point of departure be given for an eternal happiness?) not with a yes or no of decision but with a sad smile (this is the lyrical in humor), which signifies that both the old man's seventy years and the almost stillborn infant's half hour of life are too little to become a decision for an eternity.[50]

The dialectic of humor is illustrated with this metaphor of the "sad smile." Faced with this dialectical knot, the humorist's response is marked by revocation.

---

45 See John Lippitt, *Humour and Irony in Kierkegaard's Thought*, London: Palgrave Macmillan 2000, pp. 8–11.

46 David H. Monro, *Argument of Laughter*, Notre Dame: University of Notre Dame Press 1963, p. 235. This quotation is taken from John Lippitt, *Humour and Irony in Kierkegaard's Thought*, p. 9.

47 Marie C. Swabey, *Comic Laughter: A Philosophical Essay*, New Haven: Yale University Press 1961, p. 111. This quotation is taken from John Lippitt, *Humour and Irony in Kierkegaard's Thought*, p. 9.

48 *SKS* 12, 137 / *PC*, 133

49 *SKS* 12, 130 / *PC*, 125.

50 *SKS* 7, 245n / *CUP1*, 270n.

Climacus states: "Humor is always a revocation"; it is "the backward perspective," in contrast to Christianity, which "is the direction forward to becoming a Christian." But "without standing still there is no humor."[51] When elements of the immanent are brought together with elements of the transcendent, a tension is produced that guides existence towards the religious sphere, that is, forward. Humor seeks to resolve this tension by stopping the march, suspending the decision. With this, the humorist revokes suffering. Humor becomes a kind of refuge from pain, a way to escape "faith's martyrdom."[52] Humor maintains the contradiction, even becoming aware of suffering, but projects it onto the immanent speculative plane without existentially appropriating it. The reason why the humorist retreats in the face of religious *pathos* is that he "comprehends the meaning of suffering as inherent in existing"; he does not advance to find its ultimate meaning in the religious sphere since for him "the explanation lies behind."[53] Although the humorist is infinitely interested in appropriating the eternal happiness that Christianity offers, he has no sense of urgency: "the humorist always has ample time, because he has eternity's amplitude of time behind him."[54]

Jest is the humorist's expression of revocation. As we have seen, however, the real jest has nothing to do with the frivolity of immature humor because it is always rooted in a component of earnestness that is not ephemeral. The humorist is rooted in immanence.[55] There he has his stable foothold that is constituted as earnestness for him. Now, is it possible to affirm that the humorist's revocation is due to the fact that he also takes the religious seriously? Here it depends on how we understand the expression "take seriously." If we understand it as the existential appropriation of a stable foothold, then the answer is no. However, this does not mean that the humorist is totally blind to the earnestness of religion. We have already said that the humorist has a certain understanding of religious *pathos* when he stops and "revokes the suffering in the form of jest."[56] The humorist "turns and withdraws" precisely because he knows what is at stake.[57] That is why Climacus maintains that in humor there is always "an incipient depth that is revoked."[58] Thus, although the humorist

51 *SKS* 7, 547 / *CUP1*, 602.
52 *SKS* 7, 266 / *CUP1*, 292.
53 *SKS* 7, 408 / *CUP1*, 449.
54 *SKS* 7, 547 / *CUP1*, 602.
55 See *SKS* 7, 410 / *CUP1*, 451.
56 *SKS* 7, 407 / *CUP1*, 447.
57 *SKS* 7, 407 / *CUP1*, 447.
58 *SKS* 7, 501 / *CUP1*, 552.

does not decisively appropriate religious earnestness by making it his base, he is able to retain such appropriation as an emerging possibility.

Although humor incorporates Christian categories,[59] Climacus constantly emphasizes that it should not be confused with Christianity: "humor is not essentially different from irony, but is essentially different from Christianity."[60] It is not faith, but "the last stage in existence-inwardness before faith."[61] The humorist is still standing on the plane of immanent speculation. When humor "uses Christian categories (sin, forgiveness of sins, atonement, God in time, etc.), it is not Christianity but a pagan speculative thought," even though it "has come to know all the essentially Christian."[62] The point here is that humor "does not take in the suffering aspect of the paradox or the ethical aspect of faith but only the amusing aspect."[63] Unlike the ironist, who "levels everything on the basis of abstract humanity," the humorist levels everything "on the basis of the abstract relationship with God, inasmuch as he does not enter into the relationship with God."[64] This is where the limits of humor, confined to an immanent activity, are revealed. The humorist does not embrace the transcendent existentially nor does he integrate the dialectic of faith into his own life, but instead revokes it with humor and, in this way, retains the reference to the religious within an aesthetic speculation that remains on the plane of a mere possibility.

Climacus writes the entire *Postscript* from the perspective of humor. Although he himself is not a Christian, he believes that one can know what Christianity is without being a Christian oneself. In fact, the entirety of this work is oriented to expounding what Christianity is since he maintains that his era has forgotten what it is about. The interesting thing is that when we get to the end of the *Postscript,* we find the following:

> Just as in Catholic books, especially from former times, one finds a note at the back of the book that notifies the reader that everything is to be

59 *SKS* 7, 458 / *CUP1*, 505: "The humorist continually ... joins the conception of God together with something else and brings out the contradiction—but he does not relate himself to God in religious passion (*stricte sic dictus* [in the strict sense of the word]). He changes himself into a jesting and yet profound transition area for all these transactions, but he does not relate himself to God."

60 *SKS* 7, 246 / *CUP1*, 271.

61 *SKS* 7, 265 / *CUP1*, 291.

62 *SKS* 7, 247 / *CUP1*, 272.

63 *SKS* 7, 265 / *CUP1*, 291.

64 *SKS* 7, 407n / *CUP1*, 448n.

> understood in accordance with the teaching of the holy universal mother Church, so also what I write contains the notice that everything is to be understood in such a way that it is revoked, that the book has not only an end but has a revocation to boot. One can ask for no more than that, either before or afterward.[65]

What is Climacus doing? As a good humorist and in a manner that is consistent with his position, he is revoking the *Postscript*. Does it mean then that all this work has been nothing other than a jest? In the secondary literature on Kierkegaard there has been much discussion of how to interpret this final revocation,[66] but when one becomes familiar with the figure of the humorist, this revocation should not be surprising. Climacus appeals to a reader who is able to understand that "to write a book and to revoke it is not the same as refraining from writing it, that to write a book that does not demand to be important for anyone is still not the same as letting it be unwritten."[67] If indeed everything written by Climacus in this work must be understood as a jest, we must not forget that it is a jest that is capable of contemplating—at least in an incipient way—the possibility of religious earnestness, but that can in no way be appropriated by mere intellectual assent. Nor can the *Postscript* condition its reader to existentially assume the earnestness of Christianity. For this reason, in the revocation of the *Postscript*, Climacus steps back to remind us of the limits of the humorous perspective and thus enhance objective uncertainty in religious matters. Humor cannot directly communicate Christianity. It can only provoke or destabilize the reader by offending his immanent categories through a confrontation with the Christian paradox. Climacus turns and withdraws, leaving his reader alone so that he does not forget himself, and to remind him that there is no objective or theoretical mediation that can untie this dialectical knot for him, not even the *Postscript* itself.

65 *SKS* 7, 562 / *CUP1*, 619.

66 See, for example, James Conant, "Kierkegaard, Wittgenstein and Nonsense," in *Pursuits of Reason: Essays in Honor of Stanley Cavell*, ed. by Ted Cohen, Paul Guyer, and Hilary Putnam, Lubbock: Texas Technical University Press 1993. Lippitt, *Humour and Irony in Kierkegaard's Thought*, pp. 49–60. Genia Schönbaumsfeld, *A Confusion of the Spheres: Kierkegaard and Wittgenstein on Philosophy and Religion*, Oxford: Oxford University Press 2010, pp. 119–139. Alastair Hannay, "Johannes Climacus' Revocation," in *Kierkegaard's Concluding Unscientific Postscript: A Critical Guide*, ed. by Rick Anthony Furtak, Cambridge: Cambridge University Press 2010, pp. 45–63.

67 *SKS* 7, 563 / *CUP1*, 621.

3 Humor as *Confinium*

The humorist, Climacus maintains, becomes "a jesting and yet profound transition area."[68] Having referred to the two types of religiousness and the concept of humor, we want to address here the function of the latter as a *confinium* between the ethical and the religious. What is a *confinium*? And how is it possible that humor can become a means of indirect communication of the religious? In an article I published on the concept of irony in Kierkegaard, I have addressed the way in which the figure of Socrates becomes a model for thinking about irony as a *confinium* between the aesthetic and the ethical.[69] We have already seen that Climacus presents irony and humor as border territories between spheres of existence. A *confinium* is an instance that has the peculiarity of being a limit and, at the same time, a transition point. This double dimension of a *confinium* is what makes a link between speculation and action possible. Robert J. Widenmann defines a *confinium* as "a twilight zone between essence and being, between thought and act, in which action is clothed in the form of possibility."[70] Widenmann emphasizes that "it is not merely a border area but a connecting link, an intermediary and communal sphere that makes an eventual qualitative transition possible while providing a point or juncture at which thought and act can hold a rendezvous."[71]

Now, the fact that something is possible does not necessarily mean that it will be done, but for something to be done, it must first be seen as possible. So, how is it possible for someone who has not yet experienced religious *pathos* in his own life to have a perspective on religious existence or to project her life as existing in such a sphere? This is where the importance of the imagination comes in. A *confinium* is an instance where existence in a higher sphere is imagined, whether to make it real or to revoke it. M. Jamie Ferreira has highlighted the role of the imagination in ethical and religious transitions. A qualitative leap is not an unprecedented event of pure will but requires prior projection or the imagination. Ferreira suggests that in the boundaries of the spheres, a transformation of vision must take place that consists in describing oneself simultaneously from two different perspectives, keeping them in

68 *SKS* 7, 458 / *CUP1*, 505.

69 See Jorge Schulz, "Kierkegaard y el Concepto de Ironía: Entre lo Estético y lo Ético," *Boletín de Estética*, no. 56, 2021, pp. 49–78.

70 Robert J. Widenmann, "Kierkegaard's Concept of a Confine," in *Irony and Humor in Søren Kierkegaard*, ed. by Niels Thulstrup and Marie Mikulová Thulstrup, Copenhagen: C.A. Reitzel 1988 (*Liber Academiae Kierkegaardiensis*, vol. 7), p. 30.

71 Ibid.

a paradoxical tension.[72] The imagination thus fulfills the function of keeping together elements in tension that are theoretically irreconcilable. Lippitt follows this same idea by arguing that "the chief instrument of existential change may not be argument, but redescription and active seeing,"[73] and that in this sense "the primary role of irony and humor as *confinia* pertains to relating oneself to a higher position that one has not—yet—embraced, but which one is attempting to identify oneself with in imagination."[74]

Commenting on the passage in John 12:32 ("And I, when I am lifted up from the earth, will draw all to myself") in *Practice in Christianity*, Anti-Climacus stresses the importance of the imagination in the context of religious transformation by affirming that "every human being possesses to a higher or lower degree a capability called the power of the imagination, a power that is the first condition for what becomes of a person."[75] The imagination exerts a force of attraction or seduction.[76] Whoever imagines brings with him a certain ideality, such as, for example, the projection of a life model which he can feel sympathy with, get excited about, and even fall in love with. Moreover, although this instance of ideality is fundamental for a religious transition, it still remains on the speculative plane of "nonactuality": "with regard to adversities and sufferings, it lacks the actuality of time and of temporality and of earthly life."[77] The imagination of humor marks a point of closest proximity to the religious sphere, but between the imagination and reality there is a qualitative discontinuity that can only be overcome through a decisive appropriation of religious *pathos*. Anti-Climacus insists that the reality of religious existence overwhelms the power of the imagination. The reality permeated by *pathos* cannot be represented, but can only be lived.[78] Commenting on the words of Jesus in John 12:32, Anti-Climacus points out: "because he wants to draw all to himself, it does not follow that all will let themselves be drawn."[79] The imagination opens

72 M. Jamie Ferreira, *Transforming Vision: Imagination and Will in Kierkegaardian Faith*, Oxford: Clarendon Press, 1991, p. 5.

73 Lippitt, *Humour and Irony in Kierkegaard's Thought*, p. 104.

74 John Lippitt, "Humor and Irony in the *Postscript*," in *Kierkegaard's Concluding Unscientific Postscript: A Critical Guide*, ed. by Rick Anthony Furtak, Cambridge: Cambridge University Press 2010, p. 162.

75 *SKS* 12, 186 / *PC*, 186.

76 Ryan S. Kemp has emphasized this aspect in "The Role of Imagination in Kierkegaard's Account of Ethical Transformation," *Archiv für Geschichte der Philosophie*, vol. 100, no. 2, 2018, pp. 202–31.

77 *SKS* 12, 187 / *PC*, 187.

78 *SKS* 12, 187 / *PC*, 187.

79 *SKS* 12, 181 / *PC*, 181.

up possibilities, but it also has its limits. It never becomes such that it completely annuls the responsibility of the qualitative leap, and, however, without the imagination there would be no place for said leap since it is what makes it possible for the individual to allow himself to be seduced or not.

Humor as *confinium* is an instance where the religious perspective on life is taken into consideration, even when it is not experienced in one's own existence. The *confinium* of humor is a threshold where the individual stops to look beyond the territory he has traversed. He observes what he has *not* lived so as to imagine it together with what he *has* lived. This tension between ideality and reality can represent for the humorist both a limit point and a transition point, both a point of return and a point of advance. The instance of revocation is fundamental to weighing the earnestness of both alternatives and avoiding taking lightly both what has been lived and what has not been lived.

Now, when we approach the concept of humor to examine how it constitutes a frontier, the following question arises: is humor to be found between the ethical and religiousness A, or between religiousness A and religiousness B? Certain elements are held in common between ethics and religiousness A. For both positions, existence has an immanent foundation, that is, becoming oneself is a task to be achieved by the individual's own efforts. That said, as we have seen, by incorporating existential *pathos* in religiousness A, the self-affirmation of ethical effort is replaced by resignation, suffering and guilt. However, neither in the ethical nor in religiousness A does the distinctiveness of religiousness B appear yet, which is characterized by an awareness of sin that has discovered its own nothingness before God and has embraced the paradox of Christianity through faith. Thus, between the ethical and religiousness A we can observe both continuous and discontinuous aspects. Between both spheres, there is a continuity in the place that immanence occupies as the foundation of existence, but there is a discontinuity in the way that the individual relates to himself. Here the self-affirmation of ethical effort contrasts with the self-denial of resignation. Between religiousness A and B, we can also observe continuity and discontinuity. What is continuous between these spheres is the existential *pathos* because, although religiousness B incorporates, for its part, a discontinuous novelty (the specifically Christian), it is absolutely essential to retaining the *pathos* of religiousness A.

So, what is the place of humor as *confinium*? Climacus is not precise about this, but he does suggest that the scope of humor is quite comprehensive when he states: "Nowadays, people have often been inclined to confuse the humorous with the religious, even with the Christian-religious, and that is why I try to return to it everywhere. In reality, this confusion is not at all unreasonable since the humorous, precisely as a *confinium* of the religious, is something quite comprehensive."[80] In this respect, C. Stephen Evans points out that the notion of humor that Climacus presents should not be understood as a slot or a gap that blocks the passage between existential positions, but "a 'slot' in a lock step of existential positions, but an existential possibility within a 'range.'"[81] That is to say, when we are told that humor incorporates religious categories, these can be either those of a generic religiousness or the specific categories of the Christian religion. As for the role played by humor, it is not essential to define whether it is a religiousness A or B because it can move within the range of both possibilities. The important thing here is not to lose sight of the fact that humor is essentially contradiction. If the humorous finds itself fulfilling a *confinium* role between the ethical and religiousness A, it will cause the discontinuous elements of both spheres to collide. In this context, humor will seek primarily to bring together, at the level of the imagination, the two exclusionary forms of self-relationship that we have mentioned: self-affirmation and self-denial. Now, if the humorous appears between religiousness A and B, it will seek to put elements of the immanent and the transcendent together on the plane of ideality to make the incongruity stand out. Even if we were to examine a broader range by placing humor as a *confinium* between the ethical and religiousness B, religiousness A could not be ignored. In this case, there could be simultaneously a double dialectic: the immanence-transcendence opposition would mark the contrast between the ethical-religious A and religiousness B at the same time that the opposition between self-affirmation and self-denial would mark the contradiction between the ethical and religiousness A. The way in which humor as *confinium* can fulfill its function in a wide spectrum has thus been illustrated.

These tensions propitiated by humor open the possibility of subverting its components of jesting and earnestness. The humorist is able to imagine a transvaluation in which the absurd can also be seen in a new light of earnestness. And this new light of earnestness projected towards the absolute *telos* is at the same time a playful light that leads to the re-evaluation of oneself and that tends to relativize relative ends. In his imagination the humorist maintains at one and the same time a misrepresented and a non-misrepresented perspective, in such a way that earnestness in one is jesting in the other and jesting in one is earnestness in the other. Humor degenerates the moment it

80 *SKS* 7, 410 / *CUP1*, 451.

81 C. Stephen Evans, *Kierkegaard's "Fragments" and "Postscript": The Religious Philosophy of Johannes Climacus*, Atlantic Highlands: Humanities Press 1983, p. 201. The quotation is taken from Lippitt, "Humor and Irony in the *Postscript*," p. 154.

loses one of these perspectives, but true humor holds them together, so that it can only laugh at what it simultaneously perceives as deeply serious.

Climacus considers that the ethicist's despair is the "moment of decision" in which "the individual needs divine assistance."[82] The ethicist still does not see it, however, for he is still "enduring the despair"[83] and has no clear consciousness of sin.[84] Instead, the humorist expresses himself in a deeper sense that our need for divine assistance is much more radical than the ethicist admits. And it is just that the ethicist has not yet transformed the vision that he has of himself, while the humorist person has done so. This change in self-perception is what had begun to be cultivated by humor, and this is the reason for its important propaedeutic function. Humor offers the individual an imaginative space from which he perceives himself from two opposing perspectives. Thus, the humorist can get an idea of what an appropriation of the religious implies, even if he does not take the decisive step towards it. Any possible leap into the religious sphere presupposes the previous perspective of said sphere. This is where the fundamental importance of the function of humor as *confinium* makes itself felt. Humor is an instance that can be highly significant for ethical-religious development. Paraphrasing Robert C. Roberts, Lippitt says: "repeated exposure to a sense of humor that speaks from a position 'higher' than that which we currently occupy may be just what we need to provide the kind of 'attractive redescription' that makes a 'leap' to the higher perspective possible for us."[85]

However, it should be remembered that everything that the humorous perspective can offer in reference to the religious always remains on the speculative plane of the imagination. Although here we note the limits of humor, its contribution is no small thing. Just as, for Climacus, writing a book and then revoking it is not the same as not writing it, we could say here that having a dialectical vision of one's own existence cultivated by humor is not the same as not having one. When the contradiction of the comic reaches a new level in humor, it yields a further deepening of inwardness. Even when the humorist always remains a humorist without going a step further, we can say that his

82 *SKS* 7, 234 / *CUP1*, 258.

83 *SKS* 7, 234 / *CUP1*, 258.

84 Climacus comments: "Sin was not brought up in any of the pseudonymous books. The ethicist in *Either/Or* did indeed give a religious touch to the ethical category of choosing oneself ... but this was a vitiation that no doubt had its basis in the aim of keeping the work ethical ..." (*SKS* 7, 243 / *CUP1*, 268).

85 Lippitt, "Humor and Irony in the *Postscript*," p 162. The article by Roberts to which reference is made here is Robert C. Roberts, "Humor and the Virtues," *Inquiry*, vol. 31, no. 2, 1988, pp. 127–149.

subjective development has reached a higher level since he is capable of opening a space in which visions of life that are theoretically or objectively irreconcilable collide. The *confinium* of humor thus achieves an imaginative richness that is impossible on the basis of the kind of argumentation that adheres to the laws of logic. The rules of the game of humor provide an environment in which even the most absurd paradox can have a place and be considered with the utmost earnestness.

4 Conclusion

The humorist is an ethicist who has come up against his own limitations in wanting to live in accordance with the infinite ethical requirement. Desperation has worked in him in such a way that he has found himself insufficient, empty, incapable of taking up the ethical demand on his own. This situation allows him to consider the possibility of divine assistance, given that humor incorporates religious categories. The humorist does not advance towards the relationship with God, however, but rather regresses, retreating into immanence. He defers the decision about faith by revoking jesting. In this way, humor is constituted in an existential position between the ethical and the religious. Although there is still no appropriation of religious *pathos*, the humorist's perspective provides some elements of the religious perspective. In the life of the humorist, there is not yet a religious transformation, but what we can find is a vision enriched by the imagination that allows him to understand what a religious transformation implies. Moreover, the fact that the humorist begins to perceive himself in his own existential aporias already represents an approximation that reveals a greater development of subjectivity. This enables one to look beyond oneself to where the religious horizon stands as a possibility. It is essential that something be first seen as possible before that possibility is finally realized. In this way, the *confinium* of humor cultivates a transformation of the gaze that not only precedes the religious transformation but also is its condition of possibility.

By bringing together what is absolutely different, humor causes the ethical and religious spheres to collide with such a degree of tension that the humorist is led to cling to jesting so as to escape from and get relief from religious suffering. The revocation is proof that the humorist perceives the implications of religious *pathos*. However, as we have seen, jesting should not be understood as a mere triviality. The real jest has a dialectical structure that incorporates a deep earnestness. Only someone who has taken his own finitude seriously can jest. Whoever has learned to laugh at himself shows that he has passed through the school of humor and that he has been enriched with a greater inner deepening. In this sense, the ethicist lacks true humor because he fails to perceive seriously his own inadequacy. He may have some sense of humor, but he does not become dialectical enough as long as he does not take his own human condition seriously. In this way, the humorist goes one step further in subjective internalization. His sense of humor is rooted in a deep sense of earnestness whereby he makes it clear that he has grasped his human limits, but he is in no hurry to make the leap to the religious sphere.

In repentance and faith there is a transvaluation that inverts the poles of jesting and earnestness in the dialectical structure of humor. For the humorist, who has seriously assumed the precariousness of his immanent resources to face an infinite ethical demand, the proposal of transcendent divine assistance may seem like a jest. However, this divine humor sets before his eyes the possibility of a subversion in which the transcendent becomes the plane of maximum earnestness, while the precariousness of the immanent becomes a jest in light of the riches of divine grace. For this reason, humor is still present in the religious sphere, even more present than ever. However, as Anti-Climacus points out,[86] a direct communication that has decided in advance what jesting is and what earnestness is, is not possible. It is the receiver who must untie this dialectical knot by himself. Thus, in humor the earnestness of repentance and faith is not present as anything other than a possibility taken into consideration. Here is the limit where the humorist stops by maintaining the posture of revocation. This does not, however, mean that the religious is for him a mere jest since his imagination has been enriched with the ability to project himself from both perspectives. Moreover, this has enabled him to perceive not only the earnestness of his own finitude, but also the infinite earnestness that religion could take on for him in a possible humorous transvaluation propitiated by religious transformation. The fact that the humorist wavers in the face of faith shows that he is not totally blind to the earnestness of religion. Perhaps we could say that the humorist is at this point closer to God than many others who, while—as Kierkegaard perceived in his own time—calling themselves Christians, have probably not even come close to the earnestness that this implies. The humorist dwells in proximity to faith; he does not dwell in the religious, but he has it in view.

86 See *SKS* 12, 130 / *PC*, 125.

Bibliography

Conant, James, "Kierkegaard, Wittgenstein and Nonsense," in *Pursuits of Reason: Essays in Honor of Stanley Cavell*, ed. by Ted Cohen, Paul Guyer, and Hilary Putnam, Lubbock: Texas Technical University Press 1993, pp. 195–224.

Davenport, John J., "Earnestness," in *Kierkegaard's Concepts*, Tome II, *Classicism to Enthusiasm*, ed. by Steven M. Emmanuel, William McDonald and Jon Stewart, Farnham and Burlington: Ashgate 2014 (*Kierkegaard Research: Sources, Reception and Resources*, vol. 15), pp. 219–227.

Dip, Patricia C., "El rol de Climacus en la estrategia comunicativa de Kierkegaard," *Horizontes Filosóficos: Revista de Filosofía, Humanidades y Ciencias Sociales*, vol. 8, no. 8, 2018, pp. 23–36.

Evans, C. Stephen, *Kierkegaard's "Fragments" and "Postscript": The Religious Philosophy of Johannes Climacus*, Atlantic Highlands: Humanities Press 1983.

Ferreira, M. Jamie, *Transforming Vision: Imagination and Will in Kierkegaardian Faith*, Oxford: Clarendon Press 1991.

Gouwens, David Jay, *Kierkegaard as Religious Thinker*, Cambridge: Cambridge University Press 1996.

Hannay, Alastair, "Johannes Climacus' Revocation," in *Kierkegaard's Concluding Unscientific Postscript': A Critical Guide*, ed. by Rick Anthony Furtak, Cambridge: Cambridge University Press 2010, pp. 45–63.

Kemp, Ryan S., "The Role of Imagination in Kierkegaard's Account of Ethical Transformation," *Archiv für Geschichte der Philosophie*, vol. 100, no. 2, 2018, pp. 202–231.

Kierkegaard, Søren, *Kierkegaard's Journals and Notebooks*, vols. 1–11, ed. by Niels Jørgen Cappelørn, Alastair Hannay, David Kangas, Bruce H. Kirmmse, George Pattison, Vanessa Rumble and K. Brian Söderquist, Princeton and Oxford: Princeton University Press 2007–2020.

Kierkegaard, Søren, *Fear and Trembling and Repetition*, trans. by Howard and Edna Hong, Princeton: Princeton University Press 1983 (*Kierkegaard's Writings*, vol. 6).

Kierkegaard, Søren, *The Concept of Irony, with Continual Reference to Socrates/Notes of Schelling's Berlin Lectures*, trans. by Howard V. Hong and Edna H. Hong, Princeton: Princeton University Press 1990 (*Kierkegaard's Writings*, vol. 2).

Kierkegaard, Søren, *Concluding Unscientific Postscript to Philosophical Fragments*, vol. 1, trans. by Howard and Edna Hong, Princeton: Princeton University Press 1992 (*Kierkegaard's Writings*, vol. 12.1).

Kierkegaard, Søren, *Practice in Christianity*, trans. by Edna H. Hong and Howard V. Hong, Princeton: Princeton University Press 2013 (*Kierkegaard's Writings*, vol. 10).

[Kierkegaard, Søren], *Søren Kierkegaards Skrifter*, vols. 1–28, K1–K28, ed. by Niels Jørgen Cappelørn, Joakim Garff, Jette Knudsen, Johnny Kondrup and Alastair McKinnon, Copenhagen: Gad Publishers 1997–2012.

Lippitt, John, "Humor and Irony in the *Postscript*," in *Kierkegaard's Concluding Unscientific Postscript: A Critical Guide*, ed. by Rick Anthony Furtak, Cambridge: Cambridge University Press 2010, pp. 149–169.

Lippitt, John, *Humour and Irony in Kierkegaard's Thought*, London: Palgrave Macmillan 2000.

Monro, David H., *Argument of Laughter*, Notre Dame: University of Notre Dame Press 1963.

Roberts, Robert C., "Humor and the Virtues," *Inquiry*, vol. 31, no. 2, 1988, pp. 127–149.

Schönbaumsfeld, Genia, *A Confusion of the Spheres: Kierkegaard and Wittgenstein on Philosophy and Religion*, Oxford: Oxford University Press 2010.

Schulz, Jorge, "Kierkegaard y el Concepto de Ironía: Entre lo Estético y lo Ético," *Boletín de Estética*, no. 56, 2021, pp. 49–78.

Söderquist, K. Brian, "Irony and Humor in Kierkegaard's Early Journals," *Kierkegaard Studies Yearbook*, 2003, pp. 143–167.

Stewart, Jon, *Søren Kierkegaard: Subjectivity, Irony, and the Crisis of Modernity*, Oxford: Oxford University Press 2015.

Swabey, Marie C., *Comic Laughter: A Philosophical Essay*, New Haven: Yale University Press 1961.

Turchin, Sean Anthony, "Suffering," in *Kierkegaard's Concepts*, Tome VI, *Salvation to Writing*, ed. by Steven M. Emmanuel, William McDonald and Jon Stewart, Farnham and Burlington: Ashgate 2015 (*Kierkegaard Research: Sources, Reception and Resources*, vol. 15), pp. 115–119.

Widenmann, Robert J., "Kierkegaard's Concept of a Confine," in *Irony and Humor in Søren Kierkegaard*, ed. by Niels Thulstrup and Marie Mikulová Thulstrup, Copenhagen: C.A. Reitzel 1988 (*Liber Academiae Kierkegaardiensis*, vol. 7), pp. 27–41.

Williams, Will, *Kierkegaard and the Legitimacy of the Comic: Understanding the Relevance of Irony, Humor, and the Comic for Ethics and Religion*, Lanham: Lexington Books 2018.

CHAPTER 6

Hegel's Philosophy of Religion and Durkheim's Sociology of Religion: A Comparative Study

Jon Stewart

Abstract

It is usually thought that Hegel's philosophy of religion did not have much of an impact on the twentieth and twenty-first centuries. While this is generally true with regard to the field of philosophy, the influence of Hegel can be detected in the social sciences. This paper offers a comparison of Hegel's *Lectures on the Philosophy of Religion* and Durkheim's *The Elementary Forms of Religious Life*. Points of commonality are explored in the two thinkers' respective accounts of (1) the scientific methodology for the study of religion, (2) the need to establish the origin of religion and its history, (3) the understanding of the truth of religion, (4) the role of symbolism, (5) and the social basis of religion.

There is no doubt that Hegel was a major figure in the history of philosophy in the nineteenth century.[1] His influence on the twentieth century has been often discussed. He is most frequently associated with the traditions of Marxism and Critical Theory.[2] However, attempts have also been made to establish a connection between his thought and the school of existentialism.[3] Given this, the

1 See, for example, my *Hegel's Century: Alienation and Recognition in a Time of Revolution*, Cambridge: Cambridge University Press 2021.

2 See, for example, William Maker, "The Science of Freedom: Hegel's Critical Theory," *Hegel Bulletin*, vol. 21, nos. 1–2, 2000, pp. 1–17. Steven B. Smith, "Hegel's Idea of a Critical Theory," *Political Theory*, vol. 15, no. 1, 1987, pp. 99–126. Robyn Marasco, *The Highway of Despair: Critical Theory after Hegel*, New York: Columbia University Press 2015.

3 Perhaps most notably Merleau-Ponty's "Hegel's Existentialism," in his *Sense and Non-Sense*, trans. by Hubert L. Dreyfus and Patricia Allen Dreyfus, Evanston: Northwestern University Press 1964, pp. 63–70. See also Christopher M. Fry, *Sartre and Hegel: The Variations of an Enigma in "L'Etre et le Néant,"* Bonn: Bouvier 1988. Bruce Baugh, "Hegel and Sartre: The Search for Totality," in *The Palgrave Handbook of German Idealism and Existentialism*, ed. by Jon Stewart, Cham: Palgrave Macmillan 2020, pp. 499–521.

 | DOI:10.1163/9789004689459_008

twentieth-century reception of Hegel seems to run primarily along the lines of social-political philosophy or social criticism.

This stands in contrast to the immediate influence of Hegel's thought after his death in 1831, which was primarily in the field of the philosophy of religion—something that neither Marxism nor Critical Theory is particularly known for. His *Lectures on the Philosophy of Religion* were published in 1832 by the theologian Philipp Marheineke.[4] This was by far Hegel's most extensive statement on religion, and its publication evoked a controversy about exactly how orthodox he really was regarding Christian dogma. Out of the fermentation of these discussions there arose a split among Hegel's followers between what David Friedrich Strauss dubbed the "right Hegelians" and the "left Hegelians" in his *Streitschriften zur Vertheidigung meiner Schrift über das Leben Jesu und zur Charakteristik der gegenwärtigen Theologie* from 1837.[5] These labels were quickly accepted by historians of ideas and became fixed points of orientation in the complex story of the Hegel reception.[6] According to the way the narrative usually runs, these discussions about Hegel's philosophy of religion took place in the 1830s and 1840s, and after this Hegel's influence gradually died out.

The thematic contrast between the reception of Hegel in the nineteenth century, with its focus on religion, and in the twentieth century, with its focus on social-political thinking, seems striking. It is not usually thought that Hegel's philosophy of religion found much of a resonance among the thinkers who lived after the heyday of his influence in the 1830s and 1840s. Apart from a few specialists dedicated specifically to this topic, there seem to have been no

4 Hegel, *Vorlesungen über die Philosophie der Religion. Nebst einer Schrift über die Beweise vom Daseyn Gottes*, I–II, ed. by Philipp Marheineke, vols. 11–12 [1832], in *Georg Wilhelm Friedrich Hegel's Werke. Vollständige Ausgabe*, vols. 1–18, ed. by Ludwig Boumann, Friedrich Förster, Eduard Gans, Karl Hegel, Leopold von Henning, Heinrich Gustav Hotho, Philipp Marheineke, Karl Ludwig Michelet, Karl Rosenkranz, Johannes Schulze, Berlin: Duncker und Humblot 1832–45.

5 David Friedrich Strauss, *Streitschriften zur Vertheidigung meiner Schrift über das Leben Jesu und zur Charakteristik der gegenwärtigen Theologie*, Tübingen: Osiander 1837, pp. 95–126. (Partial English translation as *In Defense of My Life of Jesus Against the Hegelians*, trans. by Marilyn Chapin Massey, Hamden, CT: Archon Books 1983, see pp. 38–66.)

6 For critical discussions, see Jon Stewart, *An Introduction to Hegel's Lectures on the Philosophy of Religion: The Issue of Religious Content in the Enlightenment and Romanticism*, Oxford: Oxford University Press 2022, pp. 199–231. John Edward Toews, "Right, Centre, and Left: The Division of the Hegelian Schools in the 1830s," in his *Hegelianism: The Path Toward Dialectical Humanism, 1805–1841*, Cambridge: Cambridge University Press 1980, pp. 203–254.

high-profile philosophers who adopted his views on religion as tools in their own constructive projects.[7]

I wish to suggest that this odd contrast is perhaps in part an illusion. It is true that Hegel's philosophy of religion has not enjoyed a large following among philosophers of the twentieth and twenty-first centuries. One obvious reason for this is simply that the field of the philosophy of religion today is not particularly large compared to mainstream areas such as philosophy of mind or philosophy of science. However, it would be a mistake to conclude from this that Hegel's philosophy of religion had no significant impact after the first half of the nineteenth century. In fact, Hegel's study of religion did influence the approach to the subject in different fields outside philosophy. Specifically, it played a role in the development of the field of the sociology of religion during the *fin de siècle*. I will try to demonstrate this by highlighting a couple of important points of commonality in the accounts of religion presented by Hegel and Émile Durkheim. The goal is to show that there is clear evidence of Hegel's thought in Durkheim's approach.

Some scholars are dismissive of a possible connection between Hegel and Durkheim because Durkheim rarely mentions Hegel and gives no indication that the German philosopher was a source of inspiration for him.[8] However, a more positive approach has been taken which has determined a number of links between the philosophy of Hegel and different aspects of the sociology of Durkheim.[9] Some of these studies try to see Hegel as a forerunner of social scientific methodology.[10] Others try to find common ground between the two thinkers in their understanding of the importance of society for ethics and

7 See Stewart, *An Introduction to Hegel's Lectures on the Philosophy of Religion*, pp. 232–244.

8 For example, Gillian Rose, *Hegel contra Sociology*, London and New York: Verso 2009, pp. 14–19. Ernest Wallwork, *Durkheim: Morality and Milieu*, Cambridge, MA: Harvard University Press 1972. Susan Stedman Jones, *Durkheim Reconsidered*, Cambridge: Polity 2001.

9 For example, Axel Honneth, "Hegel and Durkheim: Contours of an Elective Affinity," in *Durkheim and Critique*, ed. by Nicola Marcucci, Cham: Palgrave Macmillan 2021, pp. 19–41. Mark S. Cladis, *A Communitarian Defense of Liberalism: Émile Durkheim and Contemporary Social Theory*, Stanford: Stanford University Press 1992. Dominick LaCapra, *Émile Durkheim: Sociologist and Philosopher*, Ithaca, NY: Cornell University Press 1972.

10 See Peter Knapp, "The Question of Hegelian Influence upon Durkheim's Sociology," *Sociological Inquiry*, vol. 55, 1985, pp. 1–15. Peter Knapp, "Hegel's Universal in Marx, Durkheim and Weber: The Role of Hegelian Ideas in the Origin of Sociology," *Sociological Forum*, vol. 1, no. 4, 1986, pp. 586–609. Heike Delitz, "Durkheims Hegel. Von Korporationen zu kollektiven Affekten, vom Soziozentrismus zum Postfundationalismus," in *Korporation und Sittlichkeit. Zur Aktualität von Hegels Theorie der bürgerlichen Gesellschaft*, ed. by Sven Ellmers and Steffen Herrmann, Paderborn: Wilhelm Fink 2017, pp. 45–72.

forms of comportment.[11] However, Hegel's philosophy of religion seems to have escaped the attention of scholars, which is somewhat surprising in that Durkheim wrote one of the founding books on the sociology of religion, *Les Formes élémentaires de la vie religieuse: le système totémique en Australie*, which was originally published in 1912.[12] I believe that there is evidence that Hegel's approach to the study of religion influenced Durkheim in this important work.

In what follows, I will explore a few key themes in Hegel's philosophy of religion, and then compare these to Durkheim's sociology of religion. I will examine points of commonality in the two respective accounts of (1) the scientific methodology for the study of religion, (2) the need to establish the origin of religion and its history, (3) the understanding of the truth of religion, (4) the role of symbolism, (5) and the social basis of religion.

1 The Methodology for the Study of Religion: Conceptual and Empirical

Hegel is known for his long-winded statements about the importance of understanding philosophy as a science. But what he means by this is clearly not how we understand science today. He argues that philosophy is about concepts, which of course is nothing new since questions about the nature of concepts such as truth, beauty, and justice have been the core of philosophical thinking since the Greeks. Hegel's special twist on this theme is the idea that concepts are related to one another in necessary ways. Pure being cannot exist on its own. For the concept of being to exist, there must also exist the concept of nothing, which is its necessary mirror image. In Hegel's language, the one concept implicitly *posits* its opposite. From one concept, another or its other arises. But then the thus produced opposite pairs also imply a higher concept in their unity. This produces the third concept that makes a triad. In the case of the opposites of being and nothing, the concept of becoming appears as that which the two share.

---

11 See Spiros Gangas, "Social Ethics and Logic: Rethinking Durkheim through Hegel," *Journal of Classical Sociology*, vol. 7, no. 3, 2007, pp. 315–338. Spiros Gangas, "Hegel and Durkheim: *Sittlichkeit* and Organic Solidarity as Political Configurations," *Hegel-Jahrbuch*, 2009, pp. 222–226. Louis Carré, "Die Sozialpathologie der Moderne. Durkheim und Hegel im Vergleich," *Hegel-Jahrbuch*, 2013, pp. 318–323.

12 In this article, I refer to the following edition: Émile Durkheim, *Les Formes élémentaires de la vie religieuse. Le système totémique en Australie*, 4th ed., Paris: Presses Universitaires de France 1960. The English translations are taken from *The Elementary Forms of Religious Life*, trans. by Karen E. Fields, New York: The Free Press 1995.

This is Hegel's famous dialectical logic. His *Science of Logic* maps out these relations among the concepts in great detail. In this book, Hegel is clearly working with concepts alone without any empirical aspect. Admittedly, he occasionally makes use of concrete examples in his explanations, but his methodology is that of a rationalist, trying to deduce the truth of concepts on their own without the use of experience. According to his account, what makes this approach *scientific* is the fact that it reveals necessary relations. Being must have the concept of nothing as its opposite, and this holds for every pair of opposites. For Hegel, there is no contingent element in this. The goal of science is to discover these necessary relations.

However, there is another side of Hegel. In his thought on the philosophy of history, aesthetics, the philosophy of religion, and the history of philosophy, he is obliged to make use of the empirical experience. For a study of these fields, he gives accounts of concrete historical periods, religions, works of art, etc. He has studied the main works in these different fields and has gathered as much empirical information about the subject matter as possible based on the original sources that were available to him.

The question then is how his rationalist side fits with his empiricist side. Hegel's answer is that it is a false dichotomy. In fact, dialectical thinking means that the one side must necessarily imply the other. He calls "dogmatism" the kind of thinking which insists on the one side or the other and fails to see the necessary connection between the two.[13] Hegel's point is perhaps most clearly illustrated by his theory of the concept (*Begriff*).[14] As was just seen, concepts are not fixed, static ideas for Hegel. Instead, they are always in movement and development. The concept moves through three distinct phases: the universal, the particular and the singular. The universal is the abstract idea, which then becomes concrete in the real world in the form of a particular. For example, one might have an idea of a house, but this is just an abstraction. Only when one builds the house does it become real and enter the realm of actuality. However, very often the reality of our projects does not match our original idea and thus the particular is separate from the universal. However, in those cases

13 Hegel, *The Encyclopaedia Logic: Part One of the Encyclopaedia of the Philosophical Sciences*, trans. by T.F. Gerats, W.A. Suchting, and H.S. Harris, Indianapolis: Hackett 1991, § 32, Remark. *Sämtliche Werke. Jubiläumsausgabe*, vols. 1–20, ed. by Hermann Glockner, Stuttgart: Friedrich Frommann Verlag 1928–41, vol. 8, p. 106. See Jon Stewart, *Kierkegaard's Relations to Hegel Reconsidered*, New York: Cambridge University Press 2003, p. 186.

14 Hegel, *The Encyclopaedia Logic*, § 163, pp. 239–241; *Jub.*, vol. 8, § 163, pp. 358–361. *Hegel's Science of Logic*, trans. by A.V. Miller, London: George Allen and Unwin 1989, pp. 600–622; *Jub.*, vol. 5, pp. 35–65.

where it is successful to realize the idea in actuality, then the universal and the particular coincide, and this is what Hegel means by the third step in the triad.

In his approach to religion, Hegel tries to apply this approach. True to his dialectical methodology, Hegel divides his *Lectures on the Philosophy of Religion* into three parts: first, the abstract or universal part, then the particular part, and finally their unity, where the particular matches the universal.[15] With regard to the subject matter of religion, this means that the first part is dedicated to the concept of God or the divine in the abstract. The second part, called "The Determinate Religion," concerns the particular conceptions of the gods in the different religions. The third and final part is concerned with Christianity, which, according to Hegel, is the one particular religion that matches the universal, that is, the concept of the divine as such, and thus represents the culmination of the development of this concept.

Most important for our purposes is "The Determinate Religion" since it is here that Hegel comes closest to an actual empirical investigation of religion in the way that Durkheim pursues in his study. For this part of his lectures, Hegel made a detailed study of what was written on the different religions, some of which were new and foreign to the Europe of his time. In fact, he got so carried away with his study of ancient China, Eduard Gans, the editor of the *Lectures on the Philosophy of History*, felt himself obliged to cut a large number of pages:

> In the first delivery of his lectures on the philosophy of history, Hegel devoted a full third of his time to the Introduction and to China—a part of the work which was elaborated with wearisome prolixity. Although in subsequent deliveries he was less circumstantial in regard to this Empire, the editor was obliged to reduce the description to such proportions as would prevent the Chinese section from encroaching upon, and consequently prejudicing the treatment of, the other parts of the work.[16]

This can be seen as evidence that Hegel was concerned with empirical information and not just with the abstract movement of conceptual thought.

How then does Hegel's conception of scientific methodology compare to that of Durkheim? At the time when Durkheim was making his study of religion,

---

15 See Jon Stewart, *Hegel's Interpretation of the Religions of the World: The Logic of the Gods*, Oxford: Oxford University Press 2018, pp. 19–22.

16 Hegel, *Vorlesungen über die Philosophie der Geschichte*, ed. by Eduard Gans, vol. 9 [1837], in *Hegel's Werke*, p. XVII. See the useful reprint of the translation of this Preface in Michael Hoffheimer, *Eduard Gans and the Hegelian Philosophy of Law*, Dordrecht: Kluwer Academic Publishers 1995, pp. 97–106; p. 104.

social-scientific methodology was only just starting to be established, and he himself played an important role in this. Durkheim had extensive knowledge of the history of philosophy, which was one of the fields of instruction that he offered.[17] He was thus well versed in philosophy and had no problem borrowing ideas from philosophy. However, he was keen to establish sociology, and specifically the sociology of religion as a truly empirical scientific study. A part of his goal was to carve out an independent sphere for this new discipline. For this reason, Durkheim explicitly contrasts what he intends to do in *Les Formes élémentaires de la vie religieuse* with a traditional philosophical approach:

> If it is useful to know what a given religion consists of; it is far more important to examine what religion is in general. This is a problem that has always intrigued philosophers, and not without reason: It is of interest to all humanity. Unfortunately, the method philosophers ordinarily use to solve it is purely one of dialectic: All they do is analyze the idea they have of religion, even if they have to illustrate the results of that mental analysis with examples borrowed from those religions that best suit their model.[18]

It might be tempting to take the word "dialectic" as an allusion to Hegel, but, unfortunately, it remains unexplained here. In any case, it is clear that Durkheim's objection to philosophy is that it confines itself to the world of abstract ideas and concepts. It thereby does not take into account the actual empirically existing practices of religions that can be studied scientifically. Clearly, Durkheim is not interested in tracing a necessary conceptual development of opposites in the way that Hegel does. Sociology is not just about concepts and their interrelations in this sense.

But in what he goes on to say, Durkheim makes it clear that his approach is far from antiphilosophical. He explains that religions can be studied comparatively in order to determine what they have in common, that is, their essence or concept. Thus, even in sociology one tries to answer the question about the nature or essence of religion. In this sense, he is not so far away from Hegel after all. The main difference is clearly that Durkheim thinks that the subject matter should be approached in an empirical manner.

17 See, for example, Émile Durkheim, *Durkheim's Philosophy Lectures: Notes from the Lycée de Sens Course, 1883–1884*, ed. and trans. by Neil Gross and Robert Alun Jones, Cambridge: Cambridge University Press 2004.

18 Durkheim, *Les Formes élémentaires de la vie religieuse*, p. 6; *The Elementary Forms of Religious Life*, p. 4.

While it might be said that Hegel is concerned primarily with conceptual thinking and Durkheim with empirical data, these two elements are not mutually exclusive. In fact, the difference can be regarded as one of degree or focus and not of absolute opposition. It is clear that Hegel acknowledges the importance of the empirical and makes use of it; indeed, it is a constitutive part of the concept. Likewise, Durkheim believes that ultimately sociology is also concerned with the determination of concepts, although it goes to work empirically. Despite their methodological differences, there are also some important commonalities.

2 The Origin of Religion and the Role of History

It is well known that in his *Lectures on the Philosophy of History* Hegel traces the idea of spirit or freedom through the historical peoples of the world. In "The Determinate Religion" from his *Lectures on the Philosophy of Religion*, he, much in the same way, makes an attempt to trace the history of the conception or idea of the divine in the different world religions. He identifies specific religions that he associates with different world historical peoples.[19] This corresponds to the way in which he treats the development of spirit in the *Lectures on the Philosophy of History*, where, for example, the Greeks have a conception of freedom different from and more developed than that of the Chinese and the Persians. Likewise, in his *Lectures on the Philosophy of Religion* Hegel claims that each people has its own specific deities that are unique to them.

To begin his account, Hegel wants to go back to the very start of religion, to a time before there was even any real organized cult as such. In "The Determinate Religion," he provides an analysis of what he calls "magic" as a kind of forerunner for religion proper.[20] There are discussions in the secondary

19 In this regard, Hegel has the most trouble placing Buddhism, which is not a national religion but instead is practiced in many countries. See Stewart, *Hegel's Interpretation of the Religions of the World*, pp. 92–108.

20 Hegel, *Lectures on the Philosophy of Religion*, vols. 1–3, ed. by Peter C. Hodgson, trans. by Robert F. Brown, P.C. Hodgson and J.M. Stewart with the assistance of H.S. Harris, Berkeley et al.: University of California Press 1984–87, vol. 2, pp. 272–299 (hereafter abbreviated as *LPR*); *Vorlesungen über die Philosophie der Religion*, Parts 1–3, ed. by Walter Jaeschke, Hamburg: Felix Meiner (1983–85) 1993–95, Part 2, pp. 176–203 (hereafter as *VPR*). *LPR*, vol. 2, pp. 535–547; *VPR*, Part 2, pp. 433–445. *LPR*, vol. 2, pp. 724–725; *VPR*, Part 2, pp. 613–613. See also Hegel's account in his *Lectures on the Philosophy of World History*, vols. 1–3, ed. and trans. by Robert F. Brown and Peter C. Hodgson, with the assistance of William G. Geuss, Oxford: Clarendon Press 2011ff., vol. 1, pp. 196–197; *Vorlesungen über die Philosophie der Weltgeschichte: Berlin 1822–1823*, ed. by Karl Heinz Ilting, Karl Brehmer and Hoo Nam

literature about to what degree Hegel regards "Magic" as a religion or whether the ancient Chinese worship of T'ien, which he treats next, should be regarded as a real religion,[21] but these discussions are a bit beside the point. The key is that Hegel believes that in order to understand the concept of God or the divine, one must go back and determine how such a concept first arose and then see how it developed over time. It is only possible to understand the concept in its developmental context.

With his study of the different world religions Hegel turns to the past to examine the specific belief systems, practices, and representations of the divine of, for example, the Chinese, the Persians, the Egyptians, etc. All these ancient cultures left behind written records and works of art that can be studied. By contrast, for his analysis of magic Hegel is obliged to make a study of several peoples that were still living in his own time. He mentions the Eskimos, along with the native tribes of North America, Mongolia, and Africa.[22] His implicit claim is that these groups have not progressed beyond the most basic form of religion, and for this reason a study of them can be insightful. Here again we can see the important empirical element in Hegel's approach that can be seen as foreshadowing the sociology of religion. It will be noted that there is debate among Hegel scholars about the degree to which there is an empirical element in Hegel's philosophy of religion and what role it plays in his conceptual thinking.[23]

When we turn to Durkheim's *Les Formes élémentaires de la vie religieuse*, we can immediately see some commonality in the basic points of departure. As

Seelmann, Hamburg: Felix Meiner 1996, vol. 1, pp. 98–101. *The Philosophy of History*, trans. by J. Sibree, New York: Willey Book Co. 1944, pp. 91–99; *Jub.*, vol. 11, pp. 135–145. See Stewart, *Hegel's Interpretation of the Religions of the World*, pp. 42–62.

21 See Andrew Komasinski, "Response to History and Philosophical Method: Hegel, Stewart, and Chinese Religion." *The Owl of Minerva*, vol. 53, nos. 1–2, 2022, pp. 1–29. Jon Stewart, "Hegel's Account of the Chinese Religion: Interpretative Challenges" *The Owl of Minerva*, vol. 53, nos. 1–2, 2022, pp. 31–46.

22 For an account of Hegel's sources of information on these peoples, see Stewart, *Hegel's Interpretation of the Religions of the World*, pp. 43–47. See the "Editorial Introduction," in *LPR*, vol. 2, pp. 4–5.

23 I cannot pursue this discussion here but instead simply refer the interested readers to the following articles: Allen Speight, "The Sphinx and the Veil of Isis: Enigmas of Interpretation in Hegel's Determinate Religion and Its Relation to Hegel's History of Art," *The Owl of Minerva*, vol. 52, nos. 1–2, 2021, pp. 11–26. Dale M. Schlitt, "Hegel on Determinate Religion: Claims, Challenges, Conclusions," *The Owl of Minerva*, vol. 52, nos. 1–2, 2021, pp. 27–50. Kevin Thompson, "Hegel's History of Religions: The Speculative Method in the Philosophy of Religion," *The Owl of Minerva*, vol. 52, nos. 1–2, 2021, pp. 117–135. Jon Stewart, "The Significance of the Determinate Religions," *The Owl of Minerva*, vol. 52, no. 1–2, 2021, pp. 159–192.

his title indicates, Durkheim too is interested in finding the true beginning of religion. In his Introduction, he explains the goal of his work:

> I propose in this book to study the simplest and most primitive religion that is known at present, to discover its principles and attempt an explanation of it. A religious system is said to be the most primitive that is available for observation when it meets the two following conditions: First, it must be found in societies the simplicity of whose organization is nowhere exceeded; second, it must be explainable without the introduction of any element from a predecessor religion.[24]

Durkheim wants to study the most basic form of religious thinking, which he believes can be found among the indigenous peoples of Australia. He takes their system of totems to be the precursor of all later religious thinking. Like Hegel, Durkheim thus makes a study of people living in his own day and not in the ancient past. His study, like that of Hegel, is confined to reading scholarly studies about these peoples and drawing conclusions from these. In this sense, both thinkers work empirically, although neither does any actual field work.

It might sound like the objectives of Hegel and Durkheim are different in the sense that the former is interested in tracing the broad development of the idea of the divine conceptually in history, whereas the latter is only interested in the first part of this story, that is, the origin of religion. But, on the contrary, Durkheim claims that while in a sense looking into the past, his study ultimately aims to provide insight into the human being today:

> Sociology sets itself different problems from those of history or ethnography. It does not seek to become acquainted with bygone forms of civilization for the sole purpose of being acquainted with and reconstructing them. Instead, like any positive science, its purpose above all is to explain a present reality [*une réalité actuelle*] that is near to us and thus capable of affecting our ideas and actions. That reality is man. More especially, it is present-day man, for there is none other that we have a greater interest in knowing well.[25]

24 Durkheim, *Les Formes élémentaires de la vie religieuse*, p. 1; *The Elementary Forms of Religious Life*, p. 1.

25 Durkheim, *Les Formes élémentaires de la vie religieuse*, pp. 1–2; *The Elementary Forms of Religious Life*, p. 1.

Here we could easily replace Durkheim's "man" (*l'homme*) with Hegel's "*Geist*." The object of both thinkers is the human mind and its products, and the goal is to find some kind of system, regularity, or λόγος, in it. Both agree that our present condition is the result of a long development, and therefore to understand the present, we must understand this development.

For Hegel, it was necessary to trace the entire history of the world religions in order to understand the truth of Christianity, that is, the point that has been reached in religious development in his own day. While Durkheim does not embark on this same ambitious task, he is in complete agreement with the basic idea that this is the way to understand religious phenomena. He explains,

> we cannot arrive at an understanding of the most modern religions without tracing historically the manner in which they have gradually taken shape. Indeed, history is the only method of explanatory analysis that can be applied to them. History alone enables us to break down an institution into its component parts, because it shows those parts to us as they are born in time, one after the other. Second, by situating each part of the institution within the totality of circumstances in which it was born, history puts into our hands the only tools we have for identifying the causes that have brought it into being.[26]

Here it is clear that, for Durkheim (as well as for Hegel), the importance of discovering the origin of religion lies in the fact that it will allow us to trace its further development up until our own day. Likewise, Durkheim shares Hegel's systematic intuition according to which individual things are only rightly understood in their proper context and in relation to other things and not as abstractions. It is imperative that one seek the origins of the thing under examination.

3 The Truth of Religion

In the time of both Hegel and Durkheim, there was a trend to try to debunk religion. Since the Enlightenment there were attempts to demonstrate that religion was nothing but simple-minded superstition that should be immediately discarded by reason. According to this view, traditional religion was simply antithetical to scientific thinking. Philosophers such as Reimarus, Lessing,

26 Durkheim, *Les Formes élémentaires de la vie religieuse*, p. 4; *The Elementary Forms of Religious Life*, p. 3.

Voltaire, and Hume used different methods to undermine traditional religious belief. In their view, only Deism was compatible with the modern scientific view. Against this background, Hegel gave his *Lectures on the Philosophy of Religion*.[27]

Hegel's explicit goal here is to restore the truth of Christianity by putting it back on a solid footing after the attacks on religion in the Enlightenment.[28] Given this, it is no surprise that he believes that religion, namely, Christianity contains truth. But what about the other religions that are serially *aufgehoben* as spirit marches along its historical path? It might seem that they are devoid of truth and are hardly worth the trouble to study. Hegel is attentive to this issue and is concerned that it might discourage his students from taking seriously the nonEuropean religions that he presents in his class.

Hegel explains in his lectures that religion, like any other form of human culture, is a product of the mind, but this does not mean that it is just a fiction or is untrue. On the contrary, every religious practice is an external expression of the given culture to which it belongs. Each culture has its own divinities and its own practices. Each of them produces a conception of the divine that is in harmony with its own level of the realization of spirit or human freedom. Each religion possesses the truth about a particular people.

At the beginning of his lectures, Hegel explains to his students that they should give up their prejudices about religions that seem foreign or strange to them. Instead, he claims, a philosophical approach has to see beyond what might appear as outward absurdities and penetrate to the deeper truth:

> A survey of these religions reveals what supremely marvelous and bizarre flights of fancy the nations have hit upon in their representations of the divine essence and of their [own] duties and modes of conduct. To cast aside these religious representations and usages as superstition, error, and fraud is to take a superficial view of the matter....[29]

Hegel thus acknowledges the ethnocentric intuition in his students and is quick to criticize it as unreflective and unphilosophical. Such a dismissal of

27 See Stewart, *An Introduction to Hegel's Lectures on the Philosophy of Religion*, pp. 22–78.

28 There are of course detracting views to this. Richard J. Bernstein discusses how Hegel's concept of religion can be understood as either pantheistic or atheistic. See Richard J. Bernstein, "Hegel: The Healing of the Spirit," in his *Radical Evil: A Philosophical Interrogation*, Cambridge, UK and Maldon, MA: Polity Press 2002, pp. 46–75.

29 Hegel, *LPR*, vol. 1, p. 198; *VPR*, Part 1, p. 107.

what might appear as strange or unusual stands in the way of learning. The true philosophical approach demands more from us.

In his lectures from 1827 in his treatment of Buddhism and Lamaism, he addresses himself to this issue again: "It is easy to say that such a religion is just senseless and irrational. What is not easy is to recognize the necessity and truth of such religious forms, their connection with reason, and seeing that is a more difficult task than declaring something to be senseless."[30] Here he strikes the same tone as before. It would be wrong to cast aside a study of the world religions as a waste of time since in fact all religions contain key insights into what it is to be human: "The higher need is to apprehend what it [sc. the history of religions] means, its positive and true [significance], its connection with what is true—in short, its *rationality*. After all it is human beings who have lighted upon such religions, so there must be reason in them—in everything contingent there must be a higher necessity."[31] Hegel insists that there is an underlying λόγος that is accessible to the human mind if the correct philosophical method for discovering it is applied.

Even if a given religion is not the end point of the development of the concept of the divine, it still marks an important step along the way that is worthy of careful study. Hegel thus emphasizes to his students, "However erroneous a religion may be, it possesses truth, although in a mutilated phase. In every religion there is a divine presence, a divine relation; and a philosophy of history has to seek out the spiritual element even in the most imperfect forms."[32] Here again it is clear that Hegel values the empirical and regards a study of it as important for philosophical understanding, even though philosophy goes beyond the purely empirical.

In his disposition towards the truth of religion, Durkheim is in complete agreement with Hegel. He too wants to defend the idea that there is more to religion than simply superstition and ignorance. Durkheim anticipates the objection of a critic who claims that his approach has a hidden antireligious agenda; specifically, by putting Christianity on the level of what at the time were regarded as "more primitive" religions, Durkheim, it is claimed, aims to undermine the truth of Christianity. Durkheim strongly rejects this view:

> ...such could not possibly be a sociologist's point of view. Indeed, it is a fundamental postulate of sociology that a human institution cannot rest upon error and falsehood. If it did, it could not endure. If it had not been

30 Hegel, *LPR*, vol. 2, p. 570; *VPR*, Part 2, p. 467.
31 Hegel, *LPR*, vol. 1, p. 198; *VPR*, Part 1, p. 107.
32 Hegel, *The Philosophy of History*, pp. 195f.; *Jub.*, vol. 11, p. 261.

> grounded in the nature of things, in those very things it would have met resistance that it could not have overcome. Therefore, when I approach the study of primitive religions, it is with the certainty that they are grounded in and express the real.[33]

Like Hegel, Durkheim believes that there must be good reasons for the religious beliefs and practices in any given culture. Even though they might appear odd or even offensive to our sensibilities today, this does not mean that they are in themselves irrational. It only means that human sensibilities are different or have changed over the course of time, which is perfectly normal and understandable.

Durkheim's plea here sounds strikingly similar to that of Hegel to his students. Durkheim concludes, "Fundamentally, then, there are no religions that are false. All are true after their own fashion: All fulfill given conditions of human existence, though in different ways."[34] Likewise for Hegel, every religion represents a truth at its particular stage in the development of spirit. Hegel and Durkheim are thus in agreement that religion contains something true and should not be dismissed simply because it might strike us as odd sometimes. The question remains about where exactly we can find the deep underlying truth of religion.

4 The Role of Symbolism: Conceptual Thinking and Picture Thinking

For Hegel, the truth of *history* is the development of spirit to freedom. This means that the truth of *religion* is found in the development of the concept of the divine, which is the pendant of spirit. The different versions of the divine that are seen in the different cultures reflect the different historical stages of a given people. This would suggest that, for Hegel, the deep underlying truth of religion lies not in its mutable, empirical aspect but rather in its concept. However, as we have noted, it is impossible to understand this concept without having some knowledge of the empirical which must be studied in a different way. Since the empirical is a reflection of the concept, it too contains something of the truth. The abstract aspect, the universal, is only a part of the concept. For

33 Durkheim, *Les Formes élémentaires de la vie religieuse*, p. 3; *The Elementary Forms of Religious Life*, p. 2.

34 Durkheim, *Les Formes élémentaires de la vie religieuse*, p. 3; *The Elementary Forms of Religious Life*, p. 2.

its development, the concept also needs its incarnation or realization in the actuality of space and time.

This means that the truth of religion is in a sense like the truth of history. It appears in the empirical sphere but expresses a deeper truth. Hegel explains, "We must, therefore, comprehend religion, just like philosophy, which means to know and apprehend it in reason; for it is the work of self-revealing reason and is the highest form of reason."[35] Religion thus presents the truth to us in the empirical sphere of representation.

Hegel insists that it is necessary not to take things at face value when we are concerned with religious phenomena. Instead, they should be understood as symbolic, and the job of the philosopher is to understand what the symbol represents. In this context, Hegel, in his *Lectures on Aesthetics*, defends the controversial work of his friend, Georg Friedrich Creuzer,[36] entitled *Symbolik und Mythologie der alten Völker, besonders der Griechen*.[37] Hegel's discussion of Creuzer is insightful for an understanding of his own approach to religion. He explains Creuzer's methodology as follows:

> On this view mythology must therefore be interpreted *symbolically*. For "symbolically" means here only that the myths, as a product of spirit (no matter how bizarre, jocular, grotesque they may look, no matter how much too of the casual external caprices of fancy is intermingled with them) still comprise meanings, i.e., general thoughts about the nature of God, i.e., philosophical theories. On these lines in recent times Creuzer especially has begun again in his *Symbolik* to study the mythological ideas of the ancients not, in the usual manner, externally and prosaically, nor according to their artistic value; on the contrary, he has sought in them inner rational meanings.[38]

35 Hegel, *Lectures on the History of Philosophy*, vols. 1–3, trans. by E.S. Haldane, Lincoln and London: University of Nebraska Press 1995, vol. 1, p. 62; *Jub.*, vol. 17, pp. 93f.

36 For Creuzer and his account of mythology, see René Gérard, *L'Orient et la pensée romantique allemande*, Nancy: Georges Thomas 1963, pp. 173–181.

37 Friedrich Creuzer, *Symbolik und Mythologie der alten Völker, besonders der Griechen*, vols. 1–4, Leipzig and Darmstadt: Karl Wilhelm Leske 1810–12. See also *Symbolik und Mythologie der alten Völker, besonders der Griechen*, vols. 1–4, 2nd fully revised edition, Leipzig and Darmstadt: Heyer und Leske 1819–21. *Abbildungen zu Friedrich Creuzers Symbolik und Mythologie der alten Völker. Auf sechzig Tafeln*, Leipzig and Darmstadt: Heyer und Leske 1819.

38 Hegel, *Hegel's Aesthetics. Lectures on Fine Art*, vols. 1–2, trans. by T.M. Knox, Oxford: Clarendon Press 1998, vol. 1, p. 310; *Jub.*, vol. 12, p. 417.

Hegel takes this again as an occasion to explain to his students the need to search for the rational in what appears to have no rationality. As the product of the human mind, the conceptions of religion must contain some inner logic:

> In this enterprise he [sc. Creuzer] is guided by the presupposition that the myths and legendary tales took their origin in the human spirit. This spirit may indeed make play with its ideas of the gods, but, when the interest of religion enters, it treads on a higher sphere in which reason is the inventor of shapes, even if it too remains saddled with the defect of being unable yet at this first stage to unfold their inner core adequately. This hypothesis is absolutely true: religion has its source in the spirit, which seeks its own truth, has an inkling of it, and brings the same before our minds in some shape or other more closely or distantly related to this truthful content. But when reason invents the shapes, there arises also the need to know their rationality.[39]

This is of course not to say that the religious worshipers at the time understood this deeper rationality. This is Hegel's doctrine of the difference between religious representation or *Vorstellung* and conceptual thinking. The religious myths are stories, that is, representations, which the believers take to be true at face value. This is sometimes referred to as "picture thinking," a free translation of *Vorstellung*. The religious worshipers do not seek further. But there is a rationality in these stories that is a necessary reflection of spirit. Hegel explains,

> In conscious thought the ancients did not have such theories before them, nor did anyone maintain them, yet to say that such content was not implicitly present, is an absurd contention. As the products of reason, though not of thinking reason, the religions of the people, as also the mythologies, however simple and even foolish they may appear, indubitably contain as genuine works of art, thoughts, universal determinations and truth, for the instinct of reason is at their basis.[40]

It would be a mistake to regard everything about religion simply as contingent or arbitrary and thus bearing no truth at all. While the believers use picture thinking, the philosophers think in terms of concepts, and in this way they can discern the deeper, necessary truth of religion.

39 Hegel, *Aesthetics*, vol. 1, pp. 310f.; *Jub.*, vol. 12, p. 417.
40 Hegel, *Lectures on the History of Philosophy*, vol. 1, p. 82; *Jub.*, vol. 17, p. 115.

Durkheim's approach is strikingly similar on this point. Again in his account of his methodology, he explains, "Therefore, when I approach the study of primitive religions, it is with the certainty that they are grounded in and express the real."[41] Precisely along the same lines as Hegel, he continues,

> No doubt, when all we do is consider the formulas literally, these religious beliefs and practices appear disconcerting, and our inclination might be to write them off to some sort of inborn aberration. But we must know how to reach beneath the symbol to grasp the reality it represents and that gives the symbol its true meaning.[42]

Durkheim's claim is that the religious believer's view is usually wrong, but this is not to say that there is no rationality behind it.

Durkheim explains that it is necessary, by means of sociological methodology to get beyond the surface of religious phenomena, which often strike us as simply incoherent. But once we do this, we can see that there is in fact a deeper underlying rationality that the religious followers are usually entirely unaware of. He explains,

> The most bizarre or barbarous rites and the strangest myths translate some human need and some aspect of life, whether social or individual. The reasons the faithful settle for in justifying those rites and myths may be mistaken, and most often are; but the true reasons exist nonetheless, and it is the business of science to uncover them.[43]

The new field of the sociology of religion thus holds great promise in revealing the deeper underlying truth of religion. Like Hegel, Durkheim claims that there is a difference between the beliefs of the faithful, taken at face value, and the understanding of these beliefs by the scientist. While the faithful takes the religious myths to be contingent stories, the scientist can see in them an expression of some deeper human need or desire. It would therefore be wrong to take the beliefs of the faithful uncritically as true on their own terms, but this does not mean that they should be dismissed as false or meaningless superstitions.

41 Durkheim, *Les Formes élémentaires de la vie religieuse*, p. 3; *The Elementary Forms of Religious Life*, p. 2.

42 Durkheim, *Les Formes élémentaires de la vie religieuse*, p. 3; *The Elementary Forms of Religious Life*, p. 2.

43 Durkheim, *Les Formes élémentaires de la vie religieuse*, p. 3; *The Elementary Forms of Religious Life*, p. 2.

5 The Social Basis for Religion

Although more is needed to develop the issue, I will suggest one final point of comparison. Both Hegel and Durkheim are in agreement that religion is a social phenomenon and that the society itself is the source of the different conceptions of the divine. The key term for Hegel is "spirit." Each people has its own spirit which represents its collective culture. Religion is one part of this. Religion is not something that isolated individuals create. On the contrary, it is the work of a group of people sharing a common way or life and experience. This is the reason that the different peoples of the world have different religions and different conceptions of the divine. According to Hegel, there is a national element to this. The Egyptians have specifically Egyptian gods, just as the Greeks have specifically Greek gods. They look different since the cultures that created them represent different levels of the development of spirit.

Durkheim, of course, does not employ the concept of spirit, but he does believe that the conceptions of the gods have their origin in the demands of social life in a community. In his analysis of totemism, Durkheim claims that the conception of the divine is a reflection of the society in general. He argues,

> ...the totem expresses and symbolizes two different kinds of things. From one point of view, it is the outward and visible form of what I have called the totemic principle or god; and from another, it is also the symbol of a particular society that is called the clan. It is the flag of the clan, the sign by which each clan is distinguished from the others, the visible mark of its distinctiveness, and a mark that is borne by everything that in any way belongs to the clan: men, animals, and things. Thus, if the totem is the symbol of both the god and the society, is this not because the god and the society are one and the same? How could the emblem of the group have taken the form of that quasi-divinity if the group and the divinity were two distinct realities? Thus the god of the clan, the totemic principle, can be none other than the clan itself, but the clan transfigured and imagined in the physical form of the plant or animal that serves as totem.[44]

Here it is clear that Durkheim too sees the connection between a specific conception of a totem and a specific group, clan, or nation. The different conceptions of the divine are a part of what makes it possible to distinguish one group from another, just as it does not take long training to recognize the difference between the Egyptian and the Greek gods. For the believers themselves, this

44 Durkheim, *Les Formes élémentaires de la vie religieuse*, pp. 294f.; *The Elementary Forms of Religious Life*, p. 208.

is completely intuitive and constitutes an important part of their self-identity. Durkheim, like Hegel, claims that the divine principle is itself a reflection of the society. On this point Durkheim can be seen as following in the tradition of Hegel's student Feuerbach, who also argues for the human origin of the divine and for the ultimate and necessary unity of the two.[45]

For Hegel, religion represents one of the three highest forms of human culture and thought. The highest triad, which he calls "absolute spirit," consists of art, religion, and philosophy. All of these are collective human products that are produced by societies as a whole. Conceptions of the divine are among the highest forms of human thought. Likewise, Durkheim concludes that religion is a fundamental part of social life:

> In short, then, we can say that nearly all the great social institutions were born in religion. For the principal features of collective life to have begun as none other than various features of religious life, it is evident that religious life must necessarily have been the eminent form and, as it were, the epitome of collective life. If religion gave birth to all that is essential in society, that is so because the idea of society is the soul of religion.[46]

For Durkheim, religion plays an important part in the creation of society. Indeed, society could not function as it does without religion.

Hegel and Durkheim thus hold positions that are very close with respect to the important and necessary role of society in religious beliefs and practices. For Hegel, there is a conceptual unity of society and religion since both are a part of the same spirit. The *Volksgeist* of a given people is a natural, organic whole. Therefore, its individual parts cannot be separated. It is the same concept or spirit that produced both the society and its religion. For Durkheim, the idea seems to be very much the same. The institutions that arose from social life came from common religious practices and beliefs. So at the very beginning of society, religion was there as an integral part of it. Like Hegel, Durkheim seems to believe that this is not something contingent or accidental that just so happened to take place among the indigenous people of Australia, whom he is studying. On the contrary, he takes this to be a universal claim, a fact of the matter about every society. Durkheim seems to want to use this idea to establish the scientific credentials of the sociology of religion by showing that this new field can produce real, enduring results that have a universal validity.

---

45 See Stewart, *Hegel's Century: Alienation and Recognition in a Time of Revolution*, pp. 89–117.

46 Durkheim, *Les Formes élémentaires de la vie religieuse*, pp. 598f.; *The Elementary Forms of Religious Life*, p. 421.

What can be concluded from these points of commonality between Hegel and Durkheim in the sphere of religion? Philosophy in the nineteenth century has had a great influence on the twentieth century. When this is explored, we should not forget that this influence is not confined to the field of philosophy itself. In fact, it would seem that Hegel played an important role in the development of the methodology of the social sciences. This is especially interesting since, among philosophers today, Hegel's pretension to be doing *science* with his philosophy is usually rejected and even derided. If Hegel's idea of science is ever mentioned in modern treatments of the philosophy of science, it is only as an example of an utterly mistaken and confused view. However, Durkheim's use of specific Hegelian ideas seems to suggest that in fact Hegel's idea of science was not so far-fetched after all and might be worth a fresh look.

Acknowledgments

This paper was written at the Institute of Philosophy of the Slovak Academy of Sciences, V.V.I. It was supported by the Agency for Research and Development under the project APVV-20-0137 Philosophical Anthropology in the Context of Current Crises of Symbolic Structures. This article is dedicated to the memory of Judy Vichniac, who first drew to my attention the connection between Hegel and Durkheim at a lecture that I gave at Harvard University on October 19, 2016.

Bibliography

Baugh, Bruce, "Hegel and Sartre: The Search for Totality," in *The Palgrave Handbook of German Idealism and Existentialism*, ed. by Jon Stewart, Cham: Palgrave Macmillan 2020, pp. 499–521.

Bernstein, Richard J., *Radical Evil: A Philosophical Interrogation*, Cambridge, UK and Maldon, MA: Polity Press 2002.

Carré, Louis, "Die Sozialpathologie der Moderne. Durkheim und Hegel im Vergleich," *Hegel-Jahrbuch*, 2013, pp. 318–323.

Cladis, Mark S., *A Communitarian Defense of Liberalism: Émile Durkheim and Contemporary Social Theory*, Stanford: Stanford University Press 1992

Delitz, Heike, "Durkheims Hegel. Von Korporationen zu kollektiven Affekten, vom Soziozentrismus zum Postfundationalismus," in *Korporation und Sittlichkeit. Zur Aktualität von Hegels Theorie der bürgerlichen Gesellschaft*, ed. by Sven Ellmers and Steffen Herrmann, Paderborn: Wilhelm Fink 2017, pp. 45–72.

Durkheim, Émile, *Les Formes élémentaires de la vie religieuse. Le système totémique en Australie*, 4th ed., Paris: Presses Universitaires de France 1960

Durkheim, Émile, *The Elementary Forms of Religious Life*, trans. by Karen E. Fields, New York: The Free Press 1995.

[Durkheim, Émile], *Durkheim's Philosophy Lectures: Notes from the Lycée de Sens Course, 1883–1884*, ed. and trans. by Neil Gross and Robert Alun Jones, Cambridge: Cambridge University Press 2004.

Fry, Christopher M., *Sartre and Hegel: The Variations of an Enigma in "L'Etre et le Néant,"* Bonn: Bouvier 1988.

Gangas, Spiros, "Hegel and Durkheim: Sittlichkeit and Organic Solidarity as Political Configurations," *Hegel-Jahrbuch*, 2009, pp. 222–226.

Gangas, Spiros, "Social Ethics and Logic: Rethinking Durkheim through Hegel," *Journal of Classical Sociology*, vol. 7, no. 3, 2007, pp. 315–338.

Hegel, G.W.F., *Vorlesungen über die Philosophie der Religion. Nebst einer Schrift über die Beweise vom Daseyn Gottes*, I-II, ed. by Philipp Marheineke, vols. 11–12 [1832], in *Georg Wilhelm Friedrich Hegel's Werke. Vollständige Ausgabe*, vols. 1–18, ed. by Ludwig Boumann, Friedrich Förster, Eduard Gans, Karl Hegel, Leopold von Henning, Heinrich Gustav Hotho, Philipp Marheineke, Karl Ludwig Michelet, Karl Rosenkranz, and Johannes Schulze, Berlin: Duncker und Humblot 1832–45.

Hegel, G.W.F., *Vorlesungen über die Philosophie der Geschichte*, ed. by Eduard Gans, vol. 9 [1837], in *Georg Wilhelm Friedrich Hegel's Werke. Vollständige Ausgabe*, vols. 1–18, ed. by Ludwig Boumann, Friedrich Förster, Eduard Gans, Karl Hegel, Leopold von Henning, Heinrich Gustav Hotho, Philipp Marheineke, Karl Ludwig Michelet, Karl Rosenkranz, and Johannes Schulze, Berlin: Duncker und Humblot 1832–45.

Hegel, G.W.F., *Georg Wilhelm Friedrich Hegel's Werke. Vollständige Ausgabe*, vols. 1–18, ed. by Ludwig Boumann, Friedrich Förster, Eduard Gans, Karl Hegel, Leopold von Henning, Heinrich Gustav Hotho, Philipp Marheineke, Karl Ludwig Michelet, Karl Rosenkranz, and Johannes Schulze, Berlin: Duncker und Humblot 1832–45.

Hegel, G.W.F., *Sämtliche Werke. Jubiläumsausgabe*, vols. 1–20, ed. by Hermann Glockner, Stuttgart: Friedrich Frommann Verlag 1928–41.

Hegel, G.W.F., *The Philosophy of History*, trans. by J. Sibree, New York: Willey Book Co. 1944.

[Hegel, G.W.F.], *Hegel's Science of Logic*, trans. by A.V. Miller, London: George Allen and Unwin 1989.

Hegel, G.W.F., *Vorlesungen über die Philosophie der Religion*, Parts 1–3, ed. by Walter Jaeschke, Hamburg: Felix Meiner (1983–85), 1993–95. (This corresponds to vols. 3–5 in the edition, Hegel, *Vorlesungen. Ausgewählte Nachschriften und Manuskripte*, vols. 1–17, Hamburg: Meiner 1983–2008. Part 1, *Einleitung. Der Begriff der Religion* = vol. 3. Part 2, *Die Bestimmte Religion. a: Text* = vol. 4a. Part 2, *Die Bestimmte Religion. b: Anhang* = vol. 4b. Part 3, *Die vollendete Religion* = vol. 5.)

Hegel, G.W.F., *Lectures on the Philosophy of Religion*, vols. 1–3, ed. by Peter C. Hodgson, trans. by Robert F. Brown, P.C. Hodgson and J.M. Stewart with the assistance of H.S. Harris, Berkeley et al.: University of California Press 1984–87.

Hegel, G.W.F., *The Encyclopaedia Logic: Part One of the Encyclopaedia of the Philosophical Sciences*, trans. by T.F. Gerats, W.A. Suchting, and H.S. Harris, Indianapolis: Hackett 1991.

Hegel, G.W.F., *Lectures on the History of Philosophy*, vols. 1–3, trans. by E.S. Haldane, Lincoln and London: University of Nebraska Press 1995.

Hegel, G.W.F., *Vorlesungen über die Philosophie der Weltgeschichte: Berlin 1822–1823*, ed. by Karl Heinz Ilting, Karl Brehmer and Hoo Nam Seelmann, Hamburg: Felix Meiner 1996. (This corresponds to vol. 12 in the edition, Hegel, *Vorlesungen. Ausgewählte Nachschriften und Manuskripte*, vols. 1–17, Hamburg: Meiner 1983–2008.)

[Hegel, G.W.F.], *Hegel's Aesthetics. Lectures on Fine Art*, vols. 1–2, trans. by T.M. Knox, Oxford: Clarendon Press 1998.

Hegel, G.W.F., *Lectures on the Philosophy of World History*, vols. 1–3, ed. and trans. by Robert F. Brown and Peter C. Hodgson, with the assistance of William G. Geuss, Oxford: Clarendon Press 2011ff.

Hoffheimer, Michael, *Eduard Gans and the Hegelian Philosophy of Law*, Dordrecht: Kluwer Academic Publishers 1995.

Honneth, Axel, "Hegel and Durkheim: Contours of an Elective Affinity," in *Durkheim and Critique*, ed. by Nicola Marcucci, Cham: Palgrave Macmillan 2021, pp. 19–41.

Knapp, Peter, "Hegel's Universal in Marx, Durkheim and Weber: The Role of Hegelian Ideas in the Origin of Sociology," *Sociological Forum*, vol. 1, no. 4, 1986, pp. 586–609.

Knapp, Peter, "The Question of Hegelian Influence upon Durkheim's Sociology," *Sociological Inquiry*, vol. 55, 1985, pp. 1–15.

Komasinski, Andrew, "Response to History and Philosophical Method: Hegel, Stewart, and Chinese Religion." *The Owl of Minerva*, vol. 53, nos. 1–2, 2022, pp. 1–29.

LaCapra, Dominick, *Émile Durkheim: Sociologist and Philosopher*, Ithaca, NY: Cornell University Press 1972.

Maker, William, "The Science of Freedom: Hegel's Critical Theory," *Hegel Bulletin*, vol. 21, nos. 1–2, 2000, pp. 1–17.

Marasco, Robyn, *The Highway of Despair: Critical Theory after Hegel*, New York: Columbia University Press 2015.

Merleau-Ponty, Maurice, "Hegel's Existentialism," in his *Sense and Non-Sense*, trans. by Hubert L. Dreyfus and Patricia Allen Dreyfus, Evanston: Northwestern University Press 1964, pp. 63–70.

Rose, Gillian, *Hegel contra Sociology*, London and New York: Verso 2009.

Schlitt, Dale M., "Hegel on Determinate Religion: Claims, Challenges, Conclusions," *The Owl of Minerva*, vol. 52, nos. 1–2, 2021, pp. 27–50.

Speight, Allen, "The Sphinx and the Veil of Isis: Enigmas of Interpretation in Hegel's Determinate Religion and Its Relation to Hegel's History of Art," *The Owl of Minerva*, vol. 52, nos. 1–2, 2021, pp. 11–26.

Smith, Steven B., "Hegel's Idea of a Critical Theory," *Political Theory*, vol. 15, no. 1, 1987, pp. 99–126.

Stedman Jones, Susan, *Durkheim Reconsidered*, Cambridge: Polity 2001

Stewart, Jon, *Kierkegaard's Relations to Hegel Reconsidered*, New York: Cambridge University Press 2003.

Stewart, Jon, *Hegel's Interpretation of the Religions of the World: The Logic of the Gods*, Oxford: Oxford University Press 2018.

Stewart, Jon (ed.), *The Palgrave Handbook of German Idealism and Existentialism*, Cham: Palgrave Macmillan 2020.

Stewart, Jon, *Hegel's Century: Alienation and Recognition in a Time of Revolution*, Cambridge: Cambridge University Press 2021.

Stewart, Jon, "The Significance of the Determinate Religions," *The Owl of Minerva*, vol. 52, no. 1–2, 2021, pp. 159–192.

Stewart, Jon, "Hegel's Account of the Chinese Religion: Interpretative Challenges" *The Owl of Minerva*, vol. 53, nos. 1–2, 2022, pp. 31–46.

Stewart, Jon, *An Introduction to Hegel's Lectures on the Philosophy of Religion: The Issue of Religious Content in the Enlightenment and Romanticism*, Oxford: Oxford University Press 2022.

Strauss, David Friedrich, *Streitschriften zur Vertheidigung meiner Schrift über das Leben Jesu und zur Charakteristik der gegenwärtigen Theologie*, Tübingen: Osiander 1837.

Strauss, David Friedrich, *In Defense of My Life of Jesus Against the Hegelians*, trans. by Marilyn Chapin Massey, Hamden, CT: Archon Books 1983.

Thompson, Kevin, "Hegel's History of Religions: The Speculative Method in the Philosophy of Religion," *The Owl of Minerva*, vol. 52, nos. 1–2, 2021, pp. 117–135.

Toews, John Edward, *Hegelianism: The Path Toward Dialectical Humanism, 1805–1841*, Cambridge: Cambridge University Press 1980.

Wallwork, Ernest, *Durkheim: Morality and Milieu*, Cambridge, MA: Harvard University Press 1972.

PART 3

Philosophical Anthropology and Social Sciences

CHAPTER 7

The Concept of Anxiety and *The Sickness unto Death*: A Theory of Frustrated Subjectivity

Yésica Rodríguez

Abstract

Kierkegaard's pseudonymous works mean a rupture with the philosophical modern ideas about subjectivity. This rupture can be appreciated in *The Concept of Anxiety* and *The Sickness unto Death*. These psychological works presuppose a theory of the subjectivity of sin. Both show that the freedom in which the self was once constituted cannot respond to possibility, since it opens the door to sinfulness. Thus, man must plunge into the desperate realization that before God he will lose, rendering useless his attempts at self-foundation.

In the *Concluding Unscientific Postscript to Philosophical Fragments* (1846), the pseudonymous Climacus defines truth as subjectivity.[1] With this definition, he does not intend to reject the value of objective truth *per se* but rather aims to point out that the objective thinker is mistaken when he assumes that he holds the truth by virtue of the fact that his beliefs are objectively true. That is why, if there is a truth, it must be given in the process of the actualization of possibilities that constitutes the very existence of the existent itself. The relationship with the new reality that faith discovers demands of the subject a type of communication that goes beyond immediate communication, placing the religious subjective thinker in a new relationship, which Kierkegaard calls "the double nature of existence."[2] The double reflection of the subjective thinker implies the appropriation of his becoming a subject, downplaying the importance of obtaining objective results. The difference between the objective and the subjective thinker is expressed in the form of communication since the subjective thinker must be attentive to the implication of truth in his own existence, i.e., to communicate a truth he must exist in it. With this

1 See *SKS* 7, 158 / *CUP1*, 189.
2 See *SKS* 7, 58 / *CUP1*, 75.

 | DOI:10.1163/9789004689459_009

in mind, we interpret Kierkegaard's pseudonymous works as a novel proposal in relation to the structures that modernity has made use of to think about subjectivity. This novelty is evident, fundamentally, in the books *The Concept of Anxiety* and *The Sickness unto Death*. This fundamental shift can be thought of in terms of the replacement of the first ethics by the second ethics. The ethics that Haufniensis calls "the first ethics" not only presents the individual with a universal task that would not address his or her uniqueness, but also assumes that the individual possesses the capacity to perform it and that his or her existential performance should therefore be evaluated without concessions. The *first* ethics conceives reality as the "place" in which ideality has to be realized but fails to understand that reality is not determined by the fulfillment of this requirement. Haufniensis explains that the first ethics is ultimately based on a metaphysical conception of the human being, i.e., it operates on the assumption that man is a rational agent, fully capable of self-determination. The *second* ethics, by contrast, abandons the metaphysical conception and builds itself on a dogmatic conception of man. This understanding of humanity is based on a central idea: the individual to whom the first ethics addresses its demand is not in a position to fulfill what is expected of him because he is a subject who is constrained to a power that exceeds his capacity for rational self-determination. For this reason, the movement that the second ethics implies must be of an ascending character, for it is a question of raising reality to ideality. Therefore, it has to begin with a description of the phenomena that reveal the inherent limits of the human condition. We can say, then, that the fundamental purpose of the pseudonymous books devoted to anxiety and despair is to provide a self-understanding for the individual, which will be a necessary, but not sufficient, condition for the realization of his ethical task.

The Concept of Anxiety and *The Sickness unto Death*, as their respective subtitles make clear, are psychological works. The "psychology" that Kierkegaard deploys through his pseudonyms has two clearly defined strands. We have works and fragments that are characterized by Kierkegaard with the expression "experimental psychology," which appears as the subtitle of the book, *Repetition* (1843) and of "Guilty/Not Guilty?," the third part of *Stages on Life's Way* (1845). In these passages the pseudonyms proceed to a detailed description of the origin and unfolding of different states of mind. These moods are presented either by recreating figures from history and world literature or by poetically producing clearly defined personalities. The psychological experiment is a tool for philosophical argumentation that makes possible the representation of existential movements. However, the "psychology" that Kierkegaard proposes is not limited to the study of the particular but rather is capable of contributing to the formulation of general psychological statements about the human being. Haufniensis himself states that both the construction of the psychological experiment and its observation are defined by conceptual categories. Thus, Kierkegaard also develops a "theoretical psychology," the main goal of which is the clarification of the particular conditions of the human being.

If we concentrate on *The Concept of Anxiety* and *The Sickness unto Death*, it is precisely because in these works we find the clearest conceptual articulation of this "theoretical psychology," that is, of the most complete philosophical treatment of what we consider the Kierkegaardian rupture with the modern model of the subject. One of the main grounds of modernity is confidence in the capacity of the individual to define his or her behavior freely and without being forced. Every individual can, by virtue of being human, attain a degree of personal development that enables him to organize his existence in which interests, needs and personal and social commitments are integrated. In other words, the subject postulated by modernity is fully cognizant of that over which he exercises his capacity of determination. The psychology handled by the Kierkegaardian pseudonyms makes the opposite assumption.

1 The Psychology of Sin

The central category of "theoretical psychology" is sin. This is the concept that determines the dogmatic conception of the human being assumed by the second ethics. However, both Haufniensis and Anti-Climacus desist from a direct treatment of sin on the grounds that this notion cannot be dealt with by science but only from a non-scientific perspective. Instead of an open and direct investigation of sin, the pseudonyms opt for the approach that Dip calls "parallel phenomena,"[3] i.e., anxiety and despair. It is the theoretical relationship of psychology to sin that makes it possible to distinguish between the approach of *The Concept of Anxiety* and that of *The Sickness unto Death*. Haufniensis' book on anxiety is thought of as "A Simple Psychologically Orienting Deliberation on the Dogmatic Issue of Hereditary Sin."[4] The pseudonym conceives his proposal as an investigation directed towards the revealed fact; it remains, nevertheless, within the limits of strictly human considerations. The subject of *The Concept of Anxiety* is not sin; for, as the pseudonym states, this is a book on psychology, and sin belongs to the realm of theological preaching. The pseudonymous author points out that, understood merely as a synthesis between the corporeal and the psychic, the human being is no different from the animal. What, as a matter of fact, makes a man human is the irruption of

3 Patricia Dip, "La paradoja del análisis conceptual del cristianismo en *El concepto de la angustia*," *Enfoques*, vol. 17, 2005, p. 126.

4 *SKS* 4, 309 / *CA*, 1.

the spirit, the third party that transforms the immediate natural synthesis into a mediated free synthesis. Anxiety is precisely that strictly human experience which confronts the individual with his essential condition: only a free being, and one who experiences himself as such, can suffer anxiety, because only a free being can differ from himself.

On the other hand, Anti-Climacus' work devoted to despair is subtitled "A Christian Psychological Exposition for Upbuilding and Awakening."[5] The study developed in *The Sickness unto Death* takes a dogmatic assumption as its starting point and invites us to reflect on man from that perspective. This dogmatic assumption is, obviously, sin. For the pseudonymous author, the real dimension of the human becomes manifest when the individual is aware of his sinful character "before God." The analysis of subjectivity in the pages of the treatise on despair no longer conceives the structure of the human self as *The Concept of Anxiety* still did, that is, in terms of the possibility of sin, but rather from the actual reality of sin. Once again, we are faced with an investigation of freedom. It is, however, an indirect analysis since freedom is shown to us from the perspective of those phenomena in which the ego experiences its loss.

2 A Sinful Subjectivity

With the introduction of sin in *The Concept of Anxiety* there is a shift in the understanding of the subjective that presents to us a new horizon. As Dupré says, no study has adequately demonstrated that "the originality of Kierkegaard's philosophy of the self lies not so much in the identification of the self with freedom, but in the fact that it relates this freedom to a transcendent principle beyond freedom."[6] On the one hand, freedom is linked to the intermediate concept of anxiety within possibility; on the other hand, the epistemological approach to subjectivity becomes defined by sin. The incorporation of sin produces a reconfiguration of the discourse on subjectivity since no science is capable of dealing with it because it is not a conceptualized phenomenon. Hence Haufniensis proposes an auxiliary method to ethics and dogmatics, which allows access to this phenomenon by means of the intermediate category of anxiety, since intermediate determinations possess the characteristic of dialectical ambiguity, and precisely for this reason, in contrast to

5 *SKS* 11, 115 / *SUD*, 1.
6 Louis Dupré, "The Constitution of the Self in Kierkegaard's Philosophy," *International Philosophical Quarterly*, vol. 3, no. 4, 1963, p. 506.

German Idealism, the categories of the analysis of the pseudonym are psychological and not logical.

In explaining neumatic psychology, Haufniensis rejects the method of empirical psychology, which would entail an indifferent stance that leads to failure. This is because the observation of inner phenomena from an empirical phenomenological approach is insufficient to access the understanding of parallel phenomena. There are three main flaws in the attempt to understand distress and sin through the observation of the behavior of others. First, distress and sin are only known in their fullness when one experiences them directly, which is why Haufniensis writes: "How sin came into the world, each man understands solely by himself. If he would learn it from another, he would *eo ipso* misunderstand it. The only science that can help a little is psychology, yet it admits that it explains nothing, and also that it *cannot* and *will not* explain more."[7] Secondly, one's own affections and psychological states are presented at first hand; describing sin by this means will be richer and less diluted than by means of descriptions of another's affections. A traditional means of acquiring examples for psychological analysis was through characters in literature, something that the pseudonymous author criticizes. He rejects this method, along with the methods of empirical psychology, for as he understands it, the psychologist must duplicate the affect himself, so that he has no need to take his examples from literary repertoires and offer half-dead reminiscences.[8] Finally, empirical psychology's attempt to understand human beings by observing the behavior of others leads to another undesirable consequence: it forces the psychologist to engage in a mindless search for people so as to be able to observe what they are experiencing. As Beabout puts it, using the method of double reflection or what he calls "Kierkegaard's phenomenology of self-reflection, 'one' will have to run to death to become conscious of something."[9] However, experts such as Nordentoft argue that there is no absolute rejection of "third party observation."[10] This reading indicates that this third party is not an empirical individuality, but a personality elaborated by the psychologist himself, something like a "pure type" that allows for the observation of an uncontaminated affect. In this sense, the "third party observation"

7 *SKS* 4, 356 / *CA*, 51.

8 See *SKS* 4, 329 / *CA*, 21.

9 Gregory Beabout, *Freedom and its Misuses: Kierkegaard on Anxiety and Despair*, Milwaukee: Marquette University Press 1996, p. 32.

10 Kresten Nordentoft, *Kierkegaard's Psychology*, trans. by Bruce H. Kirmmse, Pittsburgh: Duquesne University Press 1972, pp. 7–10.

that is discredited is in fact indifferent. Haufniensis argues that the intention of the psychology he proposes requires flexibility in observation.

Haufniensis' type of neumatic psychological discourse assumes that the subject is spirit, and it is in its territory that the problem of freedom is found, because, ultimately, anguish appears before freedom. There is anxiety because there is freedom, and it is possible to access freedom through anguish, because freedom cannot be conceptualized, as it is the overdetermination of subjectivity. There are very few straight lines in *The Concept of Anxiety*, but two points are fixed: anxiety is practically synonymous with possibility and, more specifically, with the possibility of freedom. And again, anxiety is defined as the possibility of freedom revealing itself. Yet, very early on, Haufniensis makes it clear that freedom is never merely possible; as soon as it exists, it is real. And so, while anxiety is the possibility of freedom revealing itself, freedom, like God, is never a mere possibility, but it is simply a process of becoming. Faced with this situation, Haufniensis' concern will be to seek an epistemological tool in psychology, since, although sin cannot be explained, the anxiety which it manifests provides the possibility of access to the self by means of psychology. Haufniensis is committed to the task of trying to disarm some rather attractive forms of confusion about sinfulness and, more particularly, about hereditary sin (*arvesynd*). On this point Haufniensis himself states that some accounts of original sin suggest that, unlike the first man, humans, Adam's descendants, are corrupt by nature and therefore cannot resist it. Thus, Kierkegaard's theory of subjectivity was born. In this sense, *The Concept of Anxiety* can be seen as a foundational work for the themes that he would later address, mainly in *The Sickness unto Death*. These themes are no longer focused on fundamentally aesthetic categories but rather on generic concepts of the human linked to the ethical and religious spheres.

We can be sure that from 1844, Kierkegaard's pseudonyms will abandon two typically modern assumptions. The pseudonyms will attempt to develop an understanding of the subject that leaves behind both the notion of a self-transparent subjectivity and ethical intellectualism. One of the fundamental pillars of modernity is confidence in the capacity of the concrete individual to define his or her conduct freely and without being coerced: every individual can, by virtue of being human, attain a degree of personal development that enables him to organize his existence in which interests, needs, and personal and social commitments are integrated. However, this possibility rests on the assumption that the subject has an undistorted knowledge of his own being and of the motivations for his actions. In other words, the subject is fully aware of that over which he exercises his capacity of determination. The psychology that the Kierkegaardian pseudonyms handle assumes the opposite. For Haufniensis and Anti-Climacus, the phenomena of anxiety and despair are indications that actually existing subjectivity is not exhausted in its conscious and rational aspect but instead contains hidden elements that resist manifestation. In this way, the modern project of radical self-determination is seriously challenged by Kierkegaard's work. At the same time, however, the approach of the Kierkegaardian pseudonyms also exceeds the modern horizon in the sense that the subject's lack of clarity about himself, which would weaken the capacity for human self-determination, can no longer be attributed to a failure or confusion of thought, presumably caused by the sensible and empirical dimension of the subject, but has its origin in a negative activity of freedom. For this reason, Anti-Climacus will argue that modern philosophers, from Descartes to Hegel, are wrong when they ultimately reduce evil to ignorance or intellectual confusion. Kierkegaardian psychology, therefore, goes beyond modernity when it asserts that evil is not a matter of ignoring the good or knowing it incorrectly, but of not wanting to know the good.[11]

Anti-Climacus differs from both Climacus and Haufniensis in that he assumes a point of view which, according to Kierkegaard, is higher than that of those pseudonyms. The theme that Climacus claims as his own is not that of the Christian existent, but that of the existent that orients its existence in the direction of Christianity. The author of the *Concluding Unscientific Postscript to Philosophical Fragments* does not set out to tell us about being a Christian; he is only interested in showing how one can become one. For this reason, Climacus is only in a position to offer us an image of man, an anthropology, compatible with Christianity; however, strictly speaking, this image of man is not yet Christian. The same is true of Haufniensis. His book does not provide an understanding of the human subject from a Christian perspective since such a perspective would have to assume the reality of sin and not its possibility. Haufniensis' book, as Haufniensis himself points out in its subtitle, is only oriented towards a Christian understanding of existence. Anti-Climacus, on the other hand, portrays the ideality of a Christian existence as such, as he is a high-ranking Christian. Anti-Climacus is against what is non-Christian, opposing the non-Christian existence. However, Anti-Climacus should not be understood as a simple negation of the pseudonym Johannes Climacus. On the contrary, in many important respects, Anti-Climacus continues the works of Climacus and Haufniensis as he takes up much of what both pseudonyms try to convey in their works, but does so from a decidedly Christian point of view.[12]

11 See *SKS* 11, 207 / *SUD*, 32.

12 See Jakub Marek, "Anti-Climacus: Kierkegaard's 'servant of the word,'" in *Kierkegaard's Pseudonyms*, ed. by Jon Stewart and Katalin Nun, Farnham: Ashgate Publishing 2015 (*Kierkegaard Research: Sources, Reception and Resources*, vol. 17), pp. 40–41.

Anti-Climacus draws the reader's attention to the problem of Christian existence, helping him to become aware of the seriousness of the main Christian categories, demanding self-reflection, focusing on the individual and examining a person critically and forcing him to return within his limits.

3 A Frustrated Subjectivity

Only after the idea that man occupies his place in a universe ordered hierarchically by God had faded away, and only after modern interpretations of man as a self-conscious being had developed, could man's contradiction with himself appear at the center of the anthropological structure of the concept of sin. In his analysis of the phenomena of anxiety and despair, this point of view was adopted by Kierkegaard. Man is a synthesis of soul and body, and also of spirit in so far as he relates to himself as such. On the other hand, however, this synthesis is given; it is not a question of "realizing" it. What has to be realized is "spirit," and for such an undertaking of freedom, anxiety is linked. The clinging to one's own finitude corresponds to the loss of infinity, to which man is destined, and which occurs when the spirit wants to realize the synthesis of its finite body with the soul, attached to the infinite, and can only realize it on the basis of its own finitude. However, this step would not be possible if man were only a finite being; nor would it be possible if man, as a finite being, were in any relation to the infinite only factually. With this intuition, Kierkegaard goes beyond *The Concept of Anxiety*, where the spirit was still added to the body and soul as the *tertium* which is the synthesis of them, but which at the same time must produce it. Kierkegaard still thought then that the synthesis of time and eternity lacked a *tertium*. By contrast, in *The Sickness unto Death* it is argued that in the relation itself, the synthesis of infinity and finitude (equivalent to the synthesis of the temporal and the eternal) is the *tertium*, and not only as a negative unity by which the extremes are distinguished, but as a positive unity, which in turn enters into relation with the relation of the two opposite members.[13] But this way the "spirit" is also understood as self-consciousness, for the relation of the self to itself, as a synthesis of finitude and infinity, takes place as the self-consciousness of being itself. On the other hand, the concept of self-consciousness refers to that of the relation between the finite and the infinite; hence, man, as a relation to the infinite, has not established himself, but has been established by another, and relates to that other as the power

---

13 See Wolfhart Pannenberg, *Antropología en perspectiva teológica. Implicaciones religiosas de la teoría antropológica*, trans. by García Baro, Salamanca: Ediciones Sígueme 1993, p. 172.

that has established him. The existence of despair is a "negative unity," which is why, in describing the state of innocence, Haufniensis refers to man as *psychically determined in immediate unity with his naturalness*. Here the relation to the heterogeneous elements of man's primitive constitution is realized in an immediate unity with his naturalness. There is unity, but it is negative; that is to say, it lacks the relation of the elements being related to the relation itself, in which the spirit is present, unconscious, dreaming. The intermediate determinations lead us from the bodily dimension to the psychic dimension. The truth, however, is not to be found in any of these polarities. There is a discontinuity that reveals that the spirit has been forgotten as the unthinkable element of the relationship. However, "spirit" and "I" are two identical concepts; what makes the spirit possible is the self-awareness that man is a synthesis and that he is a synthesis thanks, ultimately, to God. Understanding this paradoxical relationship between the heterogeneous elements that constitute the self can be seen only through the spiritualist psychology which Haufniensis makes use of.

When the spirit is dreaming, i.e., present but absent, absent but present, then the spirit relates to itself by acting in an ambiguous way. The Kierkegaardian dialectic of freedom, within dogmatics, implies that the condition of the possibility of freedom is the anxiety that psychology thematizes. The reader is thus immediately alerted to the fact that this is not a theological treatise but a psychological treatment of the concept of anxiety that deals with the dogma of hereditary sin. According to Haufniensis, sin is not a subject that falls under the domain of any "science," but rather, sin is an actuality that must be dealt with in a personal or existential manner, not in an academic context. The latter alters the true concept of sin by subjecting it to the non-essential refraction of reflection, thus transforming it into a state that is nullified (*ophævet*) by thought rather than overcome (*overvundet*) in the actuality of the individual. In this way, psychology works in concert with dogmatics, explaining the real or actual possibility of sin so that dogmatics can begin its work of explaining the ideal or conceptual possibility of sin through the concept of inherited sin. With this explanatory framework, Kierkegaard stresses that the ultimate foundation of the indecipherable character of action, intention, is heteronomy, for it rests on obedience to God. Even when preceded by deliberation, action finds its limits in reason and transcends the explanatory problem by putting an end to it in the action itself or the "leap," whereby the didactic continuity of the chain of reasoning that justifies the action is interrupted.[14]

14 See Patricia Dip, *Ética y "límites del lenguaje" en Kierkegaard y Wittgenstein*, PhD thesis, Buenos Aires, Facultad de Filosofía y Letras de la Universidad de Buenos Aires: Buenos Aires 2003, p. 44.

Here the ambiguous relation of anxiety and despair is revealed. In anxiety, what stands out most is the character of movement, of the leap in its relation to nothingness and possibility. When sin, evil, is introduced, then it can happen that anxiety ceases because the possibility provoked by the spirit of self-determination taking form, a form of being, would no longer exist. When sin is introduced, the situation moves from possibility to reality, i.e., to a state. The individual, psychologically trapped in a state, does not move any more, but only persists in insisting on what he has imposed on himself. But then, suddenly, anxiety reappears, raising the possibility of relating to the given reality as if it were an improper reality. Thus, the leap "with the suddenness of the enigmatic" bursts forth, and now possibility has the power to bring man out of a state of fact, into a mold, to give a new form to the spirit.

At this point, it is worth pausing to consider a discussion implied by the categories of anxiety and despair themselves and their ambiguity that this presents. Broadly speaking, we can distinguish two points of view: on the one hand, that of those who understand anxiety and despair as fundamental categories of the ontological constitution of the existent, as the possibility of opening up being in its infinite possibilities of being; and on the other, that of those who understand that, as symptomatic manifestations, the categories represent a negative phenomenon that accounts for what must be remedied, realized, or assumed in order to become an authentic existence. Beabout, for example, argues that the term "anxiety" is sometimes used by Haufniensis to refer to an affective state, as for example when a person looking over the edge of a cliff feels an attack of anxiety. In that case, we find both the giddy sensation at the possibility of falling, with the accompanying sense of repulsion, and the silent impulse to lean out further, to jump. However, according to Beabout, Haufniensis' analysis of anxiety goes beyond a description of these affective states, by understanding the human being as a synthesis of the psychic and the physical united by the spirit, thus providing an analysis of the structure of the human being.[15]

Given this structural analysis of the human being, i.e., thanks to the synthesis of the self, which Kierkegaard proposes, it is the psychic aspect which can imagine future possibilities based on the present and the past of the individual. That is to say, the structural relationship between one's own present and imagined future possibilities is part of the human mode of being that always relates to the future through the ambiguity of attraction and repulsion simultaneously, thus producing anxiety. In this sense, anxiety is not a description

15 See Beabout, *Freedom and its Misuses*, p. 48.

of how the individual feels, but of the individual's very relation to the future; and this relation remains, even when the affect is not felt. On the other hand, Malantschuk considers both distress and despair to be incorrect relations in the individual. He sees distress as the wrong relationship at the lower levels of human existence and claims that when the eternal, and therefore the spiritual in the individual, is excluded, the wrong relationship is distress. In support of this, he claims that in *The Concept of Anxiety*, the eternal in man has been bracketed in the discussion.[16] Therefore, his position is that Kierkegaard conceives of distress as a wrong relationship in the self on the physical-mental level. However, with the inclusion of the spiritual element, the wrong relationship in the individual is transformed into despair. Malantschuk's view, then, is that distress and despair are both wrong relations in the self. He sees distress as the wrong relationship on the physical-mental level, before the spiritual element is actualized, and despair as the wrong relationship in the self after the spiritual element is actualized.[17] In the same vein, Rodríguez argues that, insofar as Kierkegaard, on the basis of his theory of the "choice of the self," understands the human being as a constant effort towards the self-knowledge and self-formation of a singular self, his philosophical production is included, with its own peculiar stamp, in the post-Hegelian program of detranscendentalisation of the subject.[18] However, Kierkegaard considers that the process by which the individual comes to be himself is not guaranteed and can indeed become shipwrecked. In order to elucidate this failure, he describes a series of negative psychological phenomena (melancholy, anxiety, and despair) in an attempt to account for the spiritual pathology of the human self. The determination to detect and deal with these phenomena will lead him to use, to an increasing extent, a clinical vocabulary (symptom, illness, cure, etc.), culminating, "as can be read in the Prologue to *The Sickness unto Death*, with the express identification between his philosophical project and medicine."[19]

In response to both questions, our hypothesis is, on the one hand, as we have already stated, that *The Concept of Anxiety* is linked to *The Sickness unto Death* in the sense that both develop, in the period 1844–1849, a theory of subjectivity. Haufniensis' approach makes it possible to show the intermediate determinations present in the self, conceived as freedom, by means of the concept of

16 See Gregor Malantschuk, *Kierkegaard's Thought*, trans. by Howard H. Hong, Princeton: Princeton University Press 1971, p. 339.

17 See Beabout, *Freedom and its Misuses*, pp. 7–8.

18 See Pablo Rodríguez, "Kierkegaard y Freud: enfermedad, terapéutica y cura," *Revista de Filosofia Moderna e Contemporânea Brasília*, vol. 1, no. 2, 2013, pp. 50–75.

19 Ibid., pp. 55–56.

anxiety, that allows it, as a symptom, to approach sin. This will be important in the development of Kierkegaard's theory of the subject since Anti-Climacus presupposes sin and concentrates on showing what sin produces. Each pseudonymous author represents a different sphere of existence, and this must not be forgotten; anxiety and despair, understood as negative manifestations of the becoming self, are approached from different spheres. Despair will be left to be studied by a Christian. This brings us to the second question, which concerns the discussion of whether these are ontological affective tonalities. Although they show their positivity in the sense of bringing the symptom of discomfort to the plane of the psychophysical, insofar as they are sufferings of the subject that manifest themselves in the highest degree of discomfort and disorientation of interiority, preventing the development of the uniqueness of the self, we agree with Anti-Climacus that they are symptomatic of a disease. It is therefore appropriate to present them, like any other symptom, in order to heal them. By relating to himself in his self-consciousness, man also establishes himself, since self-consciousness is at the same time freedom, and therefore the synthesis of finitude and infinitude in the self presents itself as the task, that of becoming itself. This is something that can only be accomplished by the relation to God: "The self is a relation that relates itself to itself or is the relation's relating itself to itself in the relation; the self is not the relation but is the relation's relating itself to itself."[20] In this understanding of the self as synthesis, the self that the pseudonym has in mind is a self that is not yet.[21] Since the self is "[i]n the relation between two," the relation being "the third as a negative unity,"[22] there can be the form of despair that is about wanting to be oneself and not only the kind of despair that is about wanting to stop being oneself, eliminating one's self. This, in turn, shows that man is created by a greater power, since the existence of this despair, which consists in wanting to be oneself, leads man to rely on that power which has created him. With the introduction of Christianity, the concept of spirit is introduced into the classical duality of man, thought of in terms of body and soul. The relationship between body and soul, temporality, and eternity, exists only in fact, in reality, by virtue of, by force of, the spirit. It is therefore the spirit that makes the relationship possible. The spirit relates to itself and to its condition of unconsciousness and ignorance as anxiety.

Since paganism did not know the concept of spirit, it also lacked the possibility of dealing with the concept of despair. Therefore, Christianity discovered

20 *SKS* 11, 129 / *SUD*, 13.

21 See *SKS* 11, 129 / *SUD*, 13.

22 *SKS* 11, 130 / *SUD*, 13.

a miserable condition unknown to the natural man: the sickness unto death.[23] The possibility of this illness is therefore an advantage that Christianity has over paganism, for only through it is it possible to find happiness, i.e., redemption through faith. This is why the Socratic definition of sin exposes the emptiness of Greek thought by not specifying that ignorance does not refer to the state of innocence, but has to do not only with the consciousness of the person who does what is just or unjust but also with his intentions. On the other hand, paganism within Christianity is not unaware of the spirit,[24] does not ignore it, and therefore chooses to distance itself from it, making its denial all the more rigorous. Therefore, in the Christian understanding, sin lies in the will, not in knowledge; and this corruption of the will is something that goes beyond the conscience of the individual. There is sin when, after a divine revelation it has made clear what sin is, one does not want desperately and before God to be oneself, or when, also desperately and before God, one wants to be oneself.[25]

In having to achieve through his freedom what he ultimately cannot do, because his foundation, his self, cannot be achieved without the presence of the third party in the relationship, God, man perverts himself. This is what Anti-Climacus calls *the despair of wanting to be oneself.*[26] It is the attempt to found oneself apart from God. Despair, being a discordance in the relation of the synthesis, leads man to spoil his true self. Thus, the self that he desperately wants to be, is a self that is not himself. It wants, in effect, to tear itself away from the power that has established it. In order not to despair, the individual must at every moment annul the possibility of succumbing to this perversion, which is what happens when the self is clearly grounded in the power that has established it.

The almost inevitable consequence that follows from this is the illusion that the synthesis of being must itself be an act of an already existing subject, a creation of its freedom. Kierkegaard's own expressions often suggest this flawed interpretation. This is so, for example, when he speaks of the synthesis of the self as a task to be accomplished, or when he describes sin as produced by an action of freedom. But a closer examination shows that it is not freedom itself, but only its possibility, that precedes the event in which the subject both gains himself and, at the same time, loses himself. Sin, being a spiritual category, shows itself under psychological determinations, which are manifested through anxiety in the face of this possibility and the consequent

23 See *SKS* 11, 125 / *SUD*, 8.
24 See *SKS* 11, 159 / *SUD*, 44.
25 See *SKS* 11, 209 / *SUD*, 64–65.
26 See *SKS* 11, 130 / *SUD*, 34.

despair produced by the realization that the ultimate foundation cannot be extracted from the subject himself if he does not become aware of the presence of a foundation that transcends the self, and to which he ultimately owes his existence.

If sin manifests itself in the possibility of choosing, every man as a member of the species participates with his freedom in the history of the genus, through the psychological manifestation of anxiety. If in *The Concept of Anxiety* the manifestation of the possibility of sin was shown through neumatic psychology, in *The Sickness unto Death* sin is also defined by the symptomatic manifestation of the sick spirit of despair, which consists, on the one hand, of wanting to affirm oneself without God and, on the other hand, of wanting to put an end to the existence of the self. This latter form of despair implies that the subject first of all wants to put an end to something that he has not founded in the first place. The paradox lies in the fact that this mode of despair is doubly problematic since, if one does not acknowledge that the foundation of the self is God, there is no self to want to do away with.

Anxiety presupposes a constituted personality. However, Haufniensis shows the error of starting with this presupposition, which says that hereditary sin is the historical beginning of humanity, by attending to the explanation of sin, but not to the personality that realized it, that is, without taking Adam into account. Explaining sin as hereditary is not the same as talking about the first sin since this would imply taking Adam into account, something that, as the pseudonym explains,[27] has not been done. Referring to sin as hereditary excludes Adam, and, as such, "If innocence is ignorance, it might seem that, insofar as the quantitative determinability of the race's guilt is present in the ignorance of the unique individual and by his act manifests itself as his guilt, there will be a difference between Adam's innocence and that of every subsequent person."[28] Therefore, to speak of original sin implies the need to explain Adam, which is impossible, since, as with any man, his interiority cannot be explained. Adam is himself the species, that is why one cannot speak of the species or the beginning of the history of the species without referring to him at the same time. The first man commits the first sin, i.e., Adam also acquires his personality through a choice, and then, after a personality is constituted, he receives the baptism of the will, becomes conscious of freedom, of possibility, and chooses to sin. Therefore, the inherited hereditary or inherited "human condition" is the possibility of choice, i.e., freedom, and not sin. The story of Adam shows us the dynamics of freedom and subjectivity in which

27 See *SKS* 4, 297 / *CA*, 25.
28 *SKS* 4, 334 / *CA*, 30.

every human being takes part as a member of the species.[29] Sin introduces sinfulness into the species through the figure of Adam; the first sin is included in the history of the species and is not located outside it. In that sense, the first man is an individual of the species, and so he operates like any other individual within the human conditions that are present in him as a member of his species. The importance of Adam consists in the introduction of the concept of the first sin, of origins.

However, the first man's participation in the species means that subsequent men, as human descendants of him, inherit the possibility of sin, the sinfulness, but not sin itself. Sin is the possibility, and men are aware of it by means of the leap, not by mere hereditary or genetic transmission. Adam cannot be separated from the species, something that happens when he is explained as a paradigmatic myth, in which he is shown as "someone" who is outside the species as its origin but without being part of it. This dogmatic explanation of the myth of Adam does not take into account the fact that he is the first man and falls under the determinations proper to any other man; he must become his personality, he must be given, for the first time, the baptism of his will. Adam is made with his self, and, with this act, possibility is introduced into the world, and thus sinfulness too.

Modern science has tried to explain sin as selfishness. However, egoism cannot be conceived from a universal point of view since it affects only the singular individual and the singular individual knows only what egoism means for his self. The ego refers to the individual; therefore, it consists in the universal standing for the individual, which is why one can only speak of the egoistic if the concept of the individual is given in the first place. Since no science can explain individuality, egoism cannot explain sin any more than sexuality can explain it; moreover, no science can explain interiority. This is why a new science is needed, psychology, which, through the approach to the limits of spiritual manifestations, can account for individuality, but which no science has yet been able to show.

If sin appears with the introduction of the conception of man as synthesis, then sin will have to do with disobedience with respect to the foundations of subjectivity. Anti-Climacus introduces the category before God in order to close the debate on sin initiated in *The Concept of Anxiety* seen from the dogmatic point of view. Sin, seen as a transgression against God, cannot account for what God is. God, being part of the human synthesis, is not something exogenous to the subject himself, and so man, being conscious of existing

29 See *SKS* 4, 335 / *CA*, 31.

before God, sins when he transgresses with his actions that which is the basis of his existence. To disengage from despair implies wanting to disengage from oneself. However, to be aware of despair requires an awareness on the part of the subject that he or she is suffering from despair. In despair there is darkness and ignorance, knowledge and will.

As we have already argued, the despair of not wanting to be oneself is defined as weakness since it includes in turn the despair of wanting to be oneself, the despair of obstinacy.[30] The despair of wanting to be oneself implies being aware of the self, and so, rather than a form of suffering, this kind of despair is an act of the subject that will bring forth the obstinacy to be a self and transcend despair. Despair drives the desperate person to the most abstract of possibilities, so that this self, which the desperate person wants to be, without the power that founds it, attempts to found itself as its own creator.[31]

There is a joy in despair, which manifests itself in the false belief in being master of oneself. The conclusion of a self that defines itself as synthesis cannot be exhausted by the work and grace of the subject. Even though, driven by the precarious understanding of his self, this desperate subject attempts to master himself, and by rejecting God he falls into the deepest arrogance, and finally through his despair he will fall into the demonic.

The subject who is conscious of being spirit, conscious of his interiority, falls into the demonic, not out of mere obstinacy, as a challenge to himself, but because he rejects with malice the power that founds him:

> He is offended by it, or, more correctly, he takes it as an occasion to be offended at all existence; he defiantly wills to be himself, to be himself not in spite of it or without it (that would indeed be to abstract himself from it, and that he cannot do, or that would be movement in the direction of resignation)—no, in spite of or in defiance of all existence, he wills to be himself with it, takes it along, almost flouting his agony.[32]

That is why the individual wants to run aground the torment of his existence and reject it completely. On the other hand, in the despair of not wanting to be oneself, there is no awareness of the infinity of the self, so there is no awareness that what manifests itself is despair.[33] In this description of despair in terms of one's awareness of it, Kierkegaard shows how important the elective dimension is for the theory of subjectivity, i.e., the subject's awareness of the

30 See *SKS* 11, 163 / *SUD*, 49.
31 See *SKS* 11, 181 / *SUD*, 23.
32 *SKS* 11, 187 / *SUD*, 71.
33 See *SKS* 11, 178 / *SUD*, 63.

self. Although it is God who is the foundation and the realization of the self in the world, the individual must constitute himself in his freedom in order to be able to be directed by his own spirit to recognize that, in his constitution, something transcends him and makes him a special being.

In contrast to the animals, man possesses a spirit that bursts forth when he assumes his freedom. This spiritual character of man is the generic human characteristic that brings with it the possibility of sin. This approach by means of spiritualistic psychology offers the possibility of showing the consequences of sin in human existence. These consequences are not presented as a transgression of the divine law, thought of as an external law, but rather, the definition of man that Kierkegaard gives us incorporates God as the third party, which is the foundation of the relation of the self to itself. This way of understanding man leads Kierkegaard to formulate a theological anthropology, since he incorporates God into the very definition of man through the use of dialectical concepts. Man, defined as a synthesis that relates to himself, and of which he is aware, pushes to the limits the approach to what subjectivity is by means of the paradox of being an existent.

Within the framework of this proposed approach, Kierkegaard shows the limits and impossibilities of constructing a theory of subjectivity that claims to bring to an end the discussion of what subjectivity is. On the one hand, the pretension of knowing what the self is from an external point of view is precluded from the outset by the incorporation into anthropology of the concept of spirit with a theological foundation; on the other hand, interiority can only be shown under negative symptomatic manifestations of the subject who suffers from them. In these negative manifestations there is, for Kierkegaard, as idealism claims, no possibility of rational mediations that would permit complete knowledge of what lies behind that which is manifested, since the ultimate foundation is given by something that transcends the manifested and is located in the realm of paradox. In this way, there is something that is never concluded, neither for the subject itself nor for anyone who wants to access subjectivity outside of it.[34]

Man does not immediately have a self (personality) but rather obtains one by his own action of choosing, but he is called to live a relational life, integrating himself, conquering a self (*Selv den Enkelte*), that is to say, referring his action to its foundation. This transition from a fragmented and disparate self to a relational and integrated self that the ethical way of life proposes does not, however, seem to overstep its own limits in the concept of becoming, since man is not a self, but must become one. To understand the situation in which

34 See Jon Stewart, *Kierkegaard's Relations to Hegel Reconsidered*, New York: Cambridge University Press 2003, pp. 378–418.

the individual (*Individet*) struggles to achieve his singularity (*Enkeltheden*), Kierkegaard assumes the determination of man as spirit, and, therefore, for the appropriation of the subjectivity of the self, anxiety, and despair, those intermediate determinations forgotten by tradition will be essential, anxiety for the success of this determination or despair for its failure. In this transition, intermediate determinations appear, the affective tones that possess man, mobilize him, placing him in the movement of becoming the self.

This is why subjectivity will be limited, and the theory of subjectivity will be a theory of limits, which will show the failure of modernity, while at the same time proposing new ways of thinking about the subject from small points of light that will be constructed for the existing subject itself in the course of its existence. The constitution of self-consciousness is limited by wanting, defined doubly as despair and as a preliminary step to faith. In *The Concept of Anxiety*, not only does an epistemological redistribution take place, but it is emphasized that this becomes possible when the object of knowledge is not defined on the basis of the use of a particular method, but on the basis of the appropriate mood (*Stemming*). The new science, based on mood, does not aim at objective truth, but at subjective certainty, by means of the ambiguity of psychological concepts.[35]

4 The Frustrations of the Self

Faced with the situation in which the existent finds itself, what kind of subjectivity is developed in this theory? It is a subjectivity that is glimpsed but cannot be accounted for, because it is always in the process of becoming, in the face of God, fearful. For before God, whatever one does, one loses. *The Big Other*, God, imposes an absolute and infinite criterion on the subject, and the subject, unable to fulfill the great expectation, begins to manifest psychological symptoms of frustration, such as wanting or not wanting to be himself. With this in mind, Kierkegaard proposes a cure that demands a surrender. Ultimately, the great sin of speculative philosophy was to elevate the ego above God.[36]

What is a real me? If I am honest and authentic enough with myself and acknowledge my character traits and my limitations and flaws, can I gain absolute transparency about who I am? The answer is no. No approximation will ever accurately reflect the true self, firstly because authenticity and honesty cannot escape fiction and self-deception. One instinctively believes oneself

35 See Dip, *Ética y "límites del lenguaje" en Kierkegaard y Wittgenstein*, p. 46.

36 See Jon Stewart, "Kierkegaard's Phenomenology of Despair in *The Sickness unto Death*," *Kierkegaard Studies Yearbook*, 1997, pp. 117–143.

to be unique and special. One wants to believe that one is free to create oneself according to one's interests and abilities. One longs to say that there is something irreducible about one's personality and character, but as soon as one tries to define it, a barrier appears. In this sense, the subjectivity shown in this theory always exists within the limits and at the same time develops, so that admitting a theory of subjectivity in Kierkegaard means showing those limits, which make the individual remain a secret. Appearing, almost forcibly, in the form of symptoms that individuality manifests, these limits can be visualized through the use of psychology. Anxiety approached through psychology is connected with the anthropological-theological-spiritual conception since anxiety as a symptom makes possible the awareness that there is a spirit present in the classical body-soul duality of philosophical anthropology. With the assumption and awareness of the self, sin breaks through, and in time, with the birth of the self, awareness of the possibility of death falls like a bolt of lightning. In between, the *inter-essence*, existence, is a continuous doing, a being that is but has not come to be in all its potentialities, not because it does not want to, but because it is not possible, given that the very constitution of the individual is to be halfway between being and nothingness, a synthesis of finitude and infinity.

Although the constitution of the self is given by a choice, which the subject makes in freedom, subjectivity must be won, not definitively, but as a task. With his theory of selfhood and freedom, Kierkegaard came very close to the dissolution of the transcendental notion of the subject of idealist philosophy since, if the subject is in the process of becoming of selfhood, its freedom cannot then be the precondition and foundation of all experience. However, Kierkegaard did not follow this path to the end, but limited himself to his famous paradoxical statements about subjectivity. The fact that the existent always faces possibilities makes him an aspirant. The entry of the sphere of faith into existence determines the approach to subjectivity since the religious dimension projects new horizons of possibility. Faith is the ultimate passion of subjectivity, and, therefore, the limit of appropriation coincides with the limit of passion, and the latter is infinite. The fact that he keeps this indeterminacy in abeyance is what safeguards the individuality of the leap, that is, the fact that the leap is not in the name of anything other than the individual himself, for if the leap is objectified, with a name or an image, it will free the individual from the anxiety of realizing himself in terms of a pure possibility, in order to realize himself instead in virtue of this or that particular thing. By virtue of its indeterminacy, anxiety is safeguarded as the reality of freedom, as possibility in the face of possibility, becoming the affection *par excellence* of individuation.

The task of existence is to establish and maintain distinctions, and reject, as incorrect, incursions into the sphere of actuality, developing, through the continuous assimilation of what lies beyond, the specific characteristics of individuality. The discontinuous leaps of the personality, the actual growth of individuality, expands the sphere of actuality by successively incorporating more and more non-existence into itself. The "aesthetic" individual is thus an insubstantial creature in which doubt and dread touch and intermingle as melancholy. The ethical individual, on the other hand, manages to distinguish and set aside these dangerously entangled elements, opening up a larger and more expansive area of inner freedom. However, the ultimate goal of individuality, i.e., the conquest of despair that is identified with the task of becoming a Christian, implies a fuller expansion of the sphere of existence, pushing doubt and despair further and further away by transforming and incorporating into experience the pure alien forms that lie beyond its boundary zone.[37]

Thus, although the presence of freedom as a modern topic is central, at least at the beginnings of his thought, the theory of subjectivity presented both in *The Concept of Anxiety* and in *The Sickness unto Death*, strongly suggests Kierkegaard's abandonment and rejection of modern pretensions to find solutions based on man himself. The Kierkegaardian subject takes responsibility for itself, is born with vigor, only to soon crash into the wall of possibility. The starry sky is not a good sign, the many possibilities imply a horizon of anxiety. Possibility brings sin, a sin that occurs before God, that God before whom we must surrender ourselves as guilty: before God I am always in error. According to Anti-Climacus, just as everything is possible for God, there is too much impossibility for finite beings since each individual is subject to personal and social limitations and is essentially defined as a self by God. However, if possibility is lacking in a person's life, if from a merely human perspective there seems to be no hope and a personal collapse or a fall is certain, then out of necessity the disparity takes the form of despair.

The psychological delineation of the above-mentioned forms of despair is preliminary to the ultimate aim of Anti-Climacus, which is to provide a theological analysis of despair as sin, for the edification of the particular individual. Although despair is identified from the outset as a disparity in one's relationship, not only with oneself, but also with God, this latter disparity does not come to light until the second part of *The Sickness unto Death*, where sin is associated with the intensification of the two forms of conscious despair (despair in weakness and despair in defiance), by virtue of being conscious of existing before God or with the conception of God.[38] With this qualification,

37 See Harvie Ferguson, *Melancholy and the Critique of Modernity: Søren Kierkegaard's Religious Psychology*, New York: Routledge 1995, pp. 98–99.

38 See *SKS* 11, 169 / *SUD*, 53.

the deliberation dialectically takes a new direction. The above-mentioned gradations in the consciousness of the self, presuppose a purely human conception of the self, whose criterion for what it means to be a self is the human being himself. By becoming conscious of existing before God, the self acquires "a new quality and qualification"[39] as a theological self or infinite self in the sense that it acquires an infinite reality by having God as its qualitative measure and ethical goal. The greater the conception of God one has, the more self there is, and the more self there is, the greater the conception of God. But the greater the conception of self and God, the more despair intensifies as a result of not becoming one's infinite self before God. Before God, therefore, despair is defined as sin or willful disobedience to God, a definition that applies to all forms of sin.

Both *The Concept of Anxiety* and *The Sickness unto Death*, works that are closely related in terms of content, are didactic rather than narrative in form. This is not because Kierkegaard believes that he can address the issues he raises here in a clearer or more "logical" way than in the case of the major "aesthetic" works, but rather because he begins here with sensuality rather than actuality. Later, when he approaches the relation between existence and ideality from the side, so to speak, of ideality, he again adopts a more conventional philosophical form of discourse. The realm of actuality is the realm of individuation and must always be represented by means of a personality. Kierkegaard is well aware of the difficulty, and his mode of presentation, which is always sensitive to the internal character of the world he hopes to represent, becomes compressed, dense, and obscure.[40]

The relationship with the new reality that faith discovers demands of the subject a type of communication that goes beyond immediate communication. It places the religious subjective thinker in a new relationship that Kierkegaard calls the "double nature of existence."[41] The difference between the objective and the subjective thinker is expressed in the form of communication, as the subjective thinker must be attentive to the implication of truth in his own existence, for in order to communicate a truth, one must exist in it. Sin poses an epistemological problem. Modern science has tried to explain sin as egoism, but egoism cannot be thought of from the point of view of the universal since it affects only the singular individual and only the singular individual knows what egoism means for his or her self. The ego refers to the individual and therefore consists in the universal being situating itself as the individual.

---

39 *SKS* 11, 191 / *SUD*, 97.

40 See Ferguson, *Melancholy and the Critique of Modernity*, p. 95.

41 See *SKS* 7, 58 / *CUP1*, 75.

Hence one can only speak of egoism if the concept of the individual is given in the first place. Since no existing science can explain individuality, neither egoism nor sexuality can explain sin since no science can explain interiority. Therefore, only the man who is conscious of being a self knows what no science knows. This is why a new science, psychology, is needed, which through the approach to the limits of spiritual manifestations can account for that which is individuality, but which no science has been able to demonstrate.

If "self-knowledge" can only be approached by means of the limits it expresses, and if the task of the existent itself is to come to terms with a self that is always in the process of becoming, another problem presents itself, and that is the problem of communication. Self-knowledge, as equivalent to knowledge of God insofar as one is supposed to have an innate knowledge and an essential unity with the divine, has something communicable about it. However, for genuine communication to take place and true understanding to be achieved, the receiver of the communication must be able to do more than grasp in an abstract way what the communicator says. The receiver must somehow think about the meaning of what is said concretely in relation to his or her own life. In this case, the effort that the communicator has made to reach this understanding cannot be conveyed directly or immediately as a "result," but the "path" that the communicator has taken to reach the understanding must be duplicated by the receiver, and this requires the "double reflection" of the communicator.[42] Genuine subjective understanding requires that a person first grasp the relevant concepts (the first reflection), but then go on and think about what it means to apply those concepts to their own life (the second reflection). Climacus claims that objective communication, communication that does not require this second reflection, can lead to only a rote understanding. Kierkegaard's critique of "Christianity" stems partly from this point, since many Danes of his time had only a verbal knowledge of the faith. They knew what they were supposed to know about how to live their lives as Christians, but they did not understand what it is to be a Christian. It is the same for the existing person, who cannot understand who he or she is, without being involved in understanding what his or her interiority is. For this reason, the communication that affects human existence essentially must be indirect because the "second reflection" that must be made requires a kind of active participation and appropriation on the part of the person who receives the communication, and this means that direct communication has no value, at least for communicating in words what the interiority of the existent is.[43]

42 See *SKS* 7, 233 / *CUP1*, 274.

43 See C. Stephen Evans, *Kierkegaard on Faith and the Self: Collected Essays*, Waco, Texas: Baylor University Press 2006, pp. 30–31.

The question of silence appears here as the impossibility of expressing in words the secret that interiority represents. A paradigmatic example is the figure of the father of faith. This silence is not merely *keeping silent* but not *being able to speak*. This distinction makes it possible to consider the difference between the *silence* of the aesthetic sphere and that of the "paradox of faith."[44] When individuals are not satisfied with turning inwards but, in a relationship of reflection, seek the external and others, chatter appears, but when this passes, silence emerges. Chatter fears silence, as it makes emptiness evident. Silence is interiority, which is why he who knows how to be silent knows how to speak. In developing the third problem, Kierkegaard redefines "ethics." This time, it will be thought of as the overt, while the individual will turn out to be an expression of the *hidden*. It is proper to the ethical sphere to possess *pure* categories that do not leave space for games of chance, thus condemning those who try to replace providence with their own initiatives and acts. For this reason, ethics demands "manifestation" and punishes concealment, whereas aesthetics not only demands concealment but also rewards it. So here, too, it is necessary to recognize the presence of the dialectic of the silence of concealment, which is justified only in the sense of paradox.

As we have shown, speech presupposes a relation in which the individual can *translate* his state of interiority to other individuals, who understand him insofar as they *reflexively* possess the same capacity, that of carrying out, among themselves, a double reflection. The problem of language in terms of *communication*, when conceived in the realm of the religious, causes the communicative function to be transcended by the *paradoxical*. Since the individual cannot translate his *second kind of interiority*, language cannot account for it. This is why none of the common "uses" of language is capable of expressing the paradox of faith, which is why it constitutes the "limit" of all language, the "inexpressible."[45]

5 Conclusion

The Concept of Anxiety is linked to *The Sickness unto Death* to the extent that both works develop a theory of subjectivity from a psychological point of view. In this theory, Haufniensis' approach makes it possible to show the intermediate determinations in the self, conceived as freedom; thus, the analysis of the phenomenon of anxiety makes possible an approach to sin. This point will be of vital importance in the development of Kierkegaard's theory of the

44 See *SKS* 4, 103 / *FT*, 127.

45 See Patricia Dip, "La paradoja del juicio de responsabilidad moral en *Temor y Temblor*," *Revista de Filosofía*, vol. 28 no. 1, 2003, pp. 188–189.

subject, since Anti-Climacus will presuppose sin and concentrate on showing what it produces and generates in the existence of the concrete human being. However, it is important to stress that the psychological approaches of the two pseudonyms are not identical, although both define man as spirit. It is the fact that man is "spirit" that makes it possible to account for the irruption of sin, since, if man were to remain within the limits of the immediate relationship between body and soul, subjectivity in the strict sense would not arise. Man can become what he truly is, a "singular individual," because he is "spirit" and not nature. In this framework, anxiety is an account of man's spiritual character, for in the face of the freedom to constitute himself, man falls into sin. The anxiety of which Haufniensis speaks comes into existence in the face of the possibility of sin, so that the psychology of 1844 is simply oriented towards the central dogmatic categories of Christianity. In contrast, the despair to which Anti-Climacus alludes is identical with the reality of sin; so the psychology of 1849 is Christian, i.e., it takes for granted the fundamental dogmas of Christianity.

Man defined as spirit is aware of being in relation to himself. In *The Sickness unto Death*, it is precisely the awareness of this relation that gives rise to the emergence of the "I." Since self-consciousness is also freedom, the synthesis of finitude and infinitude in the self presents itself as a task, the task of becoming itself, something that can be fulfilled only through the relation to God. The self that the pseudonym Anti-Climacus has in mind is a relation that relates to itself as a synthesis: "a human being is still not a self."[46] If the self were exclusively a relation to itself, then it could only despair by not wanting to be itself, that is, by wanting to eliminate its being. However, the self is a relation that relates to itself and, at the same time, relates to Another (i.e., God) and, therefore, the form of despair that consists in wanting to be oneself can occur.[47] This, in turn, shows that man has been posited by a power that transcends him and that the existence of this despair, which consists in wanting to be oneself, leads man to lean on that power. If anxiety is the psychological precursor and consequence of the freedom of a human being, understood as spirit, despair is the psychological expression of the disparity or misunderstanding in the relationship of the human being to himself as spirit. Anti-Climacus speaks as a Christian psychologist, diagnosing, at the bedside of a patient, despair as a disease of the human spirit that can be cured only by faith, i.e., by a proper relationship with God. In this way, we were able to present Kierkegaardian subjectivity as a subjectivity of frustration, of the suffering of always being unfinished before God, since one cannot speak of a subjectivity achieved once and for all. Despair, then, is the failure of the self to become itself; it is the product of the inability of the

46 *SKS* 11, 129 / *SUD*, 13.

47 See *SKS* 11, 130 / *SUD*, 13.

self to constitute, solely from its own forces, a harmonious synthesis of the disparate factors of which it is composed (body and soul). This means that one can become oneself only through a relationship with God, who defines what it means to be a human self and makes it possible for one to become that self.

In Kierkegaard's "psychological" turn in thinking about the problem of subjectivity and its relation to the world, there is a departure from the modern way of understanding the question in terms of "autonomy." Anxiety is the object of psychology since the history of an individual life progresses through states that are exposed by the leap. In each state, possibility is present and, therefore, anxiety as well. When anxiety establishes itself as reality, it does so in the form of repentance. However, repentance does not liberate the individual because it cannot eliminate sin, but merely reveals it and suffers it. Therefore, in the theological anthropology of Anti-Climacus, man is always constituted before God. Anxiety sets man in motion in the realization of his freedom; that is to say, it impels man to exist, to appropriate a way of being, making him become what he is existentially. Anxiety, from the proposed methodological framework, as a unifying concept of the human race, which shows the manifestation of interiority in the face of possibility, will be the starting point of the rupture with the theoretical approach from which modern philosophy starts. As a human manifestation, anxiety has the role of revealing signs that guide the articulation of individual interiority with the history of humanity. This self, born with the force of its own choice, with the appearance of God, bows down and becomes anxious. The freedom in which the self was constituted cannot respond to possibility, since this opens the door to sinfulness. While anxiety is the suffering in the face of what is not yet, despair, concentrated in the self, makes the individual aware of his own limitations. Man's frustration becomes apparent when, after his glorious birth, he must plunge into the desperate realization that before God he will lose, and his efforts will be rendered futile.

Bibliography

Beabout, Gregory, *Freedom and its Misuses: Kierkegaard on Anxiety and Despair*, Milwaukee: Marquette University Press 1996.

Dip, Patricia, "La paradoja del análisis conceptual del cristianismo en *El concepto de la angustia*," *Enfoques*, vol. 17, 2005, pp. 123–148.

Dip, Patricia, *Ética y "límites del lenguaje" en Kierkegaard y Wittgenstein*, PhD thesis, Buenos Aires, Facultad de Filosofía y Letras de la Universidad de Buenos Aires: Buenos Aires, 2003.

Dip, Patricia, "La paradoja del juicio de responsabilidad moral en *Temor y Temblor*," *Revista de Filosofía*, vol. 28 no. 1, 2003, pp. 171–195.

Dupré, Louis, "The Constitution of the Self in Kierkegaard's Philosophy," *International Philosophical Quarterly*, vol. 3, no. 4, 1963, pp. 506–526.

Evans, C. Stephen, *Kierkegaard on Faith and the Self: Collected Essays*, Waco, Texas: Baylor University Press 2006.

Ferguson, Harvie, *Melancholy and the Critique of Modernity: Søren Kierkegaard's Religious Psychology*, New York: Routledge 1995.

[Kierkegaard, Søren], *Søren Kierkegaards Skrifter*, vols. 1–28, K1-K28, ed. by Niels Jørgen Cappelørn, Joakim Garff, Jette Knudsen, Johnny Kondrup and Alastair McKinnon, Copenhagen: Gad Publishers 1997–2012.

Kierkegaard, Søren, *The Sickness unto Death*, trans. by Howard V. Hong and Edna H. Hong, Princeton: Princeton University Press 1980 (*Kierkegaard's Writings*, vol. 19).

Kierkegaard, Søren, *Fear and Trembling*, trans. by Howard and Edna Hong, Princeton: Princeton University Press 1983 (*Kierkegaard's Writings*, vol. 6).

Kierkegaard, Søren, *The Concept of Anxiety*, trans. by Reidar Thomte in collaboration with Albert B. Anderson, Princeton: Princeton University Press 1980 (*Kierkegaard's Writings*, vol. 8).

Kierkegaard, Søren, *Concluding Unscientific Postscript to Philosophical Fragments*, vol. 1, trans. by Howard and Edna Hong, Princeton: Princeton University Press 1992 (*Kierkegaard's Writings*, vol. 12.1).

Marek, Jakub, "Anti-Climacus: Kierkegaard's 'servant of the word,'' in *Kierkegaard's Pseudonyms*, ed. by Jon Stewart and Katalin Nun, Farnham: Ashgate Publishing 2015 (*Kierkegaard Research: Sources, Reception and Resources*, vol. 17), pp. 39–51.

Malantschuk, Gregor, *Kierkegaard's Thought*, trans. by Howard H. Hong, Princeton: Princeton University Press: Princeton 1971.

Nordentoft, Kristen, *Kierkegaard 's Psychology*, trans. by Bruce H. Kirmmse, Pittsburgh: Duquesne University Press 1972.

Stewart, Jon, "Kierkegaard's Phenomenology of Despair in *The Sickness unto Death*," *Kierkegaard Studies Yearbook*, 1997, pp. 117–143.

Stewart, Jon, *Kierkegaard's Relations to Hegel Reconsidered*, New York: Cambridge University Press 2003.

Pannenberg Wolfhart, *Antropología en perspectiva teológica. Implicaciones religiosas de la teoría antropológica*, trans. by García Baro, Salamanca: Ediciones Sígueme 1993.

Rodríguez, Pablo Uriel, "Kierkegaard y Freud: enfermedad, terapéutica y cura," *Revista de Filosofia Moderna e Contemporânea Brasília*, vol. 1, no. 2, 2013, pp. 50–75.

CHAPTER 8

Encore Cassirer: Meta-Worlds of Symbolic Forms

František Novosád

Abstract

Philosophical conceptions elaborated by the representatives of the Marburg School of Neo-Kantianism, Herman Cohen, Paul Natorp, and Ernst Cassirer, admit of characterization as an endeavor to give a contemporary answer to Kant's principal problem—the quandary of the possibility of the mutual coexistence of science (causality), ethics (norms), and aesthetics (purposefulness). Neo-Kantians were conscious of the fact that fundamental forms of our being-in-the-world—which Cassirer dubs "symbolic forms"—obey distinct and irreducible principles. The response to Kant's question of the "harmony in contrariety" existing among science, ethics, and art is just a theory of culture as a concurrence of diverse forms—equally valid and legitimate—of humans' bestowing of sense and world-building. Through the power of symbolic thought, as a coping mechanism for survival in the indifferent materiality of the cosmos, humanity builds up, Cassirer proposes, a spiritual cosmos, an "ideal" world of their own.

The philosophical landscape of the latter part of the nineteenth and the beginning of the twentieth century served as a stage for the drama of ideas, where varying intellectual motifs of different provenance and unequal vigor were mingling together—either coherently or not. The last third of the nineteenth century saw, as if in a nutshell, the recapitulation of all the disputes which, from the seventeenth century onwards, had animated modern philosophy. It was a time of the sharpening of all the antinomies that philosophers had discovered, thematized, and sought to resolve. Hegel attempted to erect a coherent philosophical system that, underpinned by dialectical logic, would synthesize within itself the antithetical trends, the rivalry of which had been pushing forward the development of Western philosophical thought, but his attempt proved unsuccessful. This then led to the resumption of the dispute between empiricism and rationalism (the controversy was renewed as a dispute between psychologism and logicism),[1]

1 As the masterpiece of the noted disputes on psychologism, one is safe to mention Edmund Husserl's *Logische Untersuchungen I*, Leipzig: Von Veit & Comp. 1900.

 | DOI:10.1163/9789004689459_010

subjectivism and objectivism, speculative and scientific thinking as well as religion and philosophy. These traditional controversies were augmented with one more—perhaps, the most distinctive of the day—a dispute between irrationalism, represented, above all, by the philosophy of life,[2] and scientism, most ardently embraced by positivism and naturalism.[3] Yet all the wrangling—whether traditional, revised, or freshly instigated—came to be seen in a new light. The point is that the shared ground where it happened to occur was no longer an effort to remove the residua of medieval scholastic metaphysics, but, instead, such a common platform was, step-by-step, being recognized in the endeavor to understand the distinctiveness of the modern culture.[4]

1 Objectives of Neo-Kantians

As a fairly heterogeneous intellectual movement, Neo-Kantianism belongs to the most dominant philosophical conceptions of the last third of the nineteenth century and the first third of the twentieth. Its mainstream arose and spread in Germany, while its influences spilled over the borders of the country and the German-speaking area as a whole. Consequently, then, Neo-Kantianism and other conceptions akin to it exerted their influence and gained authority throughout nearly all European countries, with Russia and France topping the list.

Understanding the causes of the rise, structure, and impact of Neo-Kantian philosophical conceptions is only possible against the backdrop of the economic, social-political, and spiritual development of the then-Western societies. The point is that philosophical reflection as such is always boosted by the compelling needs of the present. Philosophical thinking, however, despite the fact that its processes occur within the realm of generalities and abstractions, is ever particular in the sense that it is keen to articulate itself by means of concepts and resolve issues posed by social concerns. Put otherwise, a philosopher who only speaks on her own behalf advocates merely for herself. Resonance and influence are prerogatives of just such a philosophy that effectively engages in a social struggle; a philosophy that has succeeded in having

2 Its main proponents are considered to be thinkers such as Arthur Schopenhauer, Friedrich Nietzsche, Wilhelm Dilthey, and Georg Simmel.

3 It was exactly stimuli and insights stemming from Charles Darwin's writings that proved to become a major impulse for the development of naturalism.

4 For the outline of the problematic of the period's philosophical thinking, see J.W. Burrow, *The Crisis of Reason: European Thought 1848–1915*, New Haven: Yale University Press 2002.

expressed via the medium of ideas interests whose clashes and rivalry are, in the end, responsible for a specific character of social life.

At first blush, Neo-Kantianism, so to speak, was anxious to stand aloof from the ferment of its era, and so it is not surprising that many a commentator of the *Critique of Pure Reason* would perceive the announced return to Kant as nothing more than just turning its back on the compelling contemporary issues, an escape from the current social-political reality. Yet the visitation of the past does not necessarily imply a flight from the present, it may betoken—which is the case of Hermann Cohen and Paul Natorp—a critical coming to terms with the degrading and increasingly ominous reality of Western societies, above all, that of Germany as it used to be at the turn of the nineteenth and the twentieth century.

Also, when it comes to theoretical thinking, the Neo-Kantians themselves would account for their return to Kant citing the need to ensure the immanent lineage of philosophical thought that culminated in Kant's *oeuvre* but ended up as misappropriated by the systems of post-Kantian speculative philosophy. Already Otto Liebmann's programmatic announcement—"it is necessary to have the genuine content of Kant's teaching separated from impure additives"[5]—makes explicit the Neo-Kantian effort to give attention to an expressly immanent, purely conceptual analysis. Later on, the Neo-Kantians would work out a theoretical grounding for such a standpoint on the history of thinking—actually, their conception of the immanent development of philosophy and spiritual culture as a whole. Overall, the Neo-Kantians take the history of philosophy as a history of problems, which, at that, are for them no more than "particularizations of the in-itself integral reason in its partial areas."[6]

In philosophy, tradition acts not necessarily as a burden that encumbers the present, but it does mute into a hindrance in case of an uncritical—be it uncritically dismissive or uncritically sympathetic—attitude to it. A critical approach to tradition will facilitate the understanding of the past as embroiled in its conflicts and disputes, plagued by its immanent inconsistences (also, as a complex of possibilities, only some of which are tested, others but partially so, while still others left intact). That being so, it is not implausible that the headway made in the evolution of cognition should *ex post* empower humans

5 Otto Liebmann, *Kant und Epigonen*, Stuttgart: C. Schrober 1910, p. 20.

6 Nicolai Hartmann, *Kleinere Schriften*, vols. 1–3, Berlin: De Gruyter 1955–58, vol. 3, *Vom Neukantianismus zur Ontologie*, p. 9. The most insightful achievement in the area of treating history of philosophy as a history of problems was probably Wilhelm Windelband's *Die Geschichte der neueren Philosophie in ihrem Zusammenhange mit der allgemeinen Cultur und den besonderen Wissenschaften dargestellt*, vols. 1–2, Leipzig: Breitkopf und Hartel 1878–80. Bd.1: *Von der Renaissance bis Kant* (1878), Bd. 2: *Die Blüthezeit der deutschen Philosophie. Von Kant bis Hegel und Herbart* (1880).

to grasp the gravity of issues brought up by the thinkers of the past, to enable people to set apart questions and answers, and, perhaps, recognize and take over some of the former, while dismissing the latter.

Specifically, Neo-Kantianism takes itself as an immediate response to the maelstrom of ideas, the "philosophical unmindedness" of its epoch, and as an attempt at finding a way out of the quandary. This is how Otto Liebmann, one of the originators of the movement, portrayed the condition of German philosophy at the time:

> In any case, one must be taken aback by the fact that, while speculation within a number of celebrated systems seems to have achieved nearly everything that is thought conceivable in this domain, still the majority of intellectuals remain little moved, behaving towards the spirit of these systems in part indifferently, in part gravitating towards superficial and ungrounded opinions of materialism.[7]

Otto Liebmann was convinced that the crisis in philosophy had been precipitated by exclusively ideational factors, seeing thereby the remedy to get things right in rectifying the common "thought error," the hypertrophy of which had been culpable, he maintained, for the rise of the grand post-Kantian systems. He assumed that the latter were just attempts at the explication of the main principles of Kant's system; therefore, it was Kant alone who might serve as a foolproof touchstone for the validity and worth of the post-Kantian systems. The return to Kant could by no means imply just prescinding from the entire post-Kantian philosophical development. The comeback, for Liebmann, also should involve a sort of purification of the Kantian system from all foreign elements which were in discord with the kernel of Kant's thought. This core of Kant's teaching Liebmann sees in the "transcendental aesthetics," where "the subject and the object of knowledge depend on each other—via shared transcendental forms of their existence—so immanently and necessarily that they can, thus, only exist together as necessary correlates."[8] Kant's system can only be consistently taken to its completion when we come to the understanding that "whatever would be taken to exist beyond time and space, is once and forever—nonsense."[9]

Neo-Kantian thinkers were alive to the fact that it was imperative for philosophy to look for the justification of its own existence solely within the horizon

7 Liebmann, *Kant und Epigonen*, p. 3. All translations from German are mine, unless otherwise noted.

8 Ibid., p. 24.

9 Ibid., p. 22.

of the most authoritative spiritual power of the day, that is, within the ambit of science. The snag was that the picture of the world furnished by physics, chemistry, and biology bore an obviously naturalistic character, on principle denying any specificity to the "spiritual." Such an attitude to things ideational was conveyed, in a grossly caricatured fashion, by Du Bois-Reymond:

> Prosaic as that may sound, it is true, nevertheless, that Faust, instead of going to the royal court, issuing unbacked paper money, or descending to the fourth dimension, the realm of the "Mothers," would have done better if he had married little Gretchen, got the child adopted, and invented the electric machine or the air compressor.[10]

The Neo-Kantians were fully cognizant of the fact that a direct attack on such unconstrained naturalism was in advance condemned to failure, and that an antidote capable of uprooting it could only be found in science itself. The matter was that giving scientific thinking a new direction (in such a fashion that it could "not only satisfy the computing reason but also even respond to the most difficult and deep-seated doubts and questions of the soul")[11] required placing the emphasis on disciplines that explicitly pointed to "the display and manifestation of principal cognitive functions within the material of the senses itself."[12] And the sciences that used to be the most defiant against both materialistic and naturalistic interpretations were for the Neo-Kantians, in the first instance, logic and mathematics.

In this context, Neo-Kantianism constitutes an endeavor to wed traditional German idealism with the "spirit" of natural science. Admittedly, the attempt at synthesis was just one of the facets of a more broadly envisioned undertaking: Neo-Kantianism was one of the last attempts to restore the classical modern spiritual culture by its own means alone. Its philosophical systems were touting the vitality of rationalistic ideational motifs—ultimately, those of the Enlightenment—at a time that was far more favorably disposed towards irrational and clearly anti-Enlightenment conceptions.[13]

10 Cited according to Paul Hühnerfeld, *In Sachen Heidegger*, Munich: P. List Verlag 1961, p. 34.

11 Paul Natorp, *Philosophie, ihr Problem und ihre Probleme*, Göttingen: Vanderhoeck und Ruprecht 1911, p. 1.

12 Ernst Cassirer, *Philosophie der symbolischen Formen*, vol. 1, *Die Sprache*, Berlin: Bruno Cassirer 1923, p. 47.

13 On the political and ideological dimensions of the contemporary irrationalism, Georg Lukács writes, in a quite exaggerated manner, in his *Die Zerstörung der Vernunft*, Berlin: Aufbau-Verlag 1955.

2 Old Questions, New Answers

In the beginning, the Neo-Kantians used to see the kernel and the only vital element of Kant's system in his theoretical philosophy, above all, the transcendental aesthetics. In interpreting the *Critique of Pure Reason,* Liebmann insists: "It is the content of the transcendental aesthetics that makes the proper groundwork and the epoch-shaping element of Kant's philosophy."[14] Friedrich Albert Lange committed to quite a similar view when he claimed that "All practical philosophy is, however, a protean and transient element in Kant's philosophy.... the whole sense of Kant's reform has to be sought in his critique of theoretical reason."[15] Such an outright dismissive stance on ethics would be surmounted in the course of the movement's further development: the Baden school even came to see in the *Critique of Practical Reason* the kernel of Kant's philosophizing.[16]

Yet let's revert to the beginnings of Neo-Kantianism. Why was the updating of Kant's theoretical philosophy even possible? The query can be primarily answered by considering the philosophical problems arising from the developments in natural science. The latter part of the nineteenth century saw conspicuous changes to the social status and structure of the sciences. They expanded, their technological applications multiplied, and technology became an objectified scientific theory. It is just then that science entered the stage as an immediate productive force. What was being changed, however, was not just the outward circumstances of science. Crucial shifts were happening inside it, with the revision of the understanding of the foundations of individual disciplines as well as the methodological and epistemological status of scientific theories. Modifications in the functions and structure of the latter reanimated discussions about the assumptions, the method, and the relevant implications of scientific knowledge for one's worldview. There reappears the problem of the relationship obtaining between the empirical and the rational in cognition, that is, the interface of philosophy and science.

Regarding the philosophy-science relationship, the philosophy of the period in question would generally show favor towards Kant's style of untangling the difficulty, while renouncing, more or less, solutions offered by Fichte, Schelling and Hegel. At the time, the chief complaint about them was to the effect that

14 Liebmann, *Kant und Epigonen*, p. 20.

15 Friedrich Lange, *Geschichte des Materialismus und Kritik seiner Bedeutung in der Gegenwart*, vols. 1–2, Leipzig: Alfred Kröner Verlag 1926, vol. 2, p. 2.

16 To its prominent representatives belong, in the first instance, Wilhelm Windelband (1848–1915) and Heinrich Rickert (1863–1936).

in his system, they had failed to elucidate the interrelation of competences between science and philosophy, positioned philosophy above science, and made the methods of the specific sciences subordinate to that of philosophy. Hermann Cohen, summarizing in his *Logik der reinen Erkenntnis* the positions of Fichte, Schelling and Hegel on the relation between concept und idea (science and philosophy) writes: "According to such non-respect to reason in science, even the old pantheism was healing herb." [17] Kant, conversely, was not keen on rendering science submissive to philosophy; what he was after was, instead, the coordination of the two, a clear-cut demarcation of the object of science and that of philosophy, and an unequivocal differentiation of the methods employed in science from those fitting for philosophy. Kant proceeded from the exact delimitation of their competencies. Philosophy's main concern, for Kant, is analyzing science, its foundations and methods, instead of inquiring into "reality." Philosophy, with him, plainly cannot be ontology, a theory of Being, but merely and exclusively a theory of knowledge.

The materialization of Hegel's solution to the problem of the relationship existing between science and philosophy indubitably aggravated, in terms of content, the "alienation" which segregated the two. As a consequence, the philosophy of nature, in the latter part of the nineteenth century, clearly became a hindrance to the development of the natural sciences. On the other hand, however, faults plaguing Hegel's treatment of the relationship between science and philosophy in terms of their respective subjects obscured the fact that Hegel had offered a more fruitful and profound method of analyzing science than Kant did.[18]

Yet the repudiation of Hegel cannot be taken as an exclusively immanent affair of scientific and philosophical thinking. Hegel's disciples had already recognized the self-sufficiency of science *versus* philosophy. Karl Rosenkranz, too, in his *Logic*, deleted everything which could cause collisions with the special sciences.[19] The advancement of the natural sciences of the day primarily rocked the Cartesian-Baconian understanding of the objective character of scientific knowledge. It was becoming ever more obvious that a scientific image of the world could not be made purely of its "subjective moments," that

17 Hermann Cohen, *Logik der reinen Erkenntnis*, Berlin: Bruno Cassirer Verlag 1922, p. 314.

18 Methodological prospects of the dialectical tradition are presented in the work of Pirmin Stekeler-Weihofer, *Philosophie des Selbstbewußtseins. Hegels Systems als Formanalyse von Wissen und Autonomie*, Frankfurt am Main: Suhrkamp Verlag 2005. Further possibilities drawing on Hegel are addressed in Robert Brandom, *Making It Explicit*, Cambridge: Harvard University Press 1994.

19 Karl Rosenkranz, *Wissenschaft der logischen Idee*, Königsberg: Gebrüder Bornträger 1859.

consciousness is no mirror, which, upon appropriate cleansing procedures, would be capable of reflecting things-in-themselves.

The very first note of caution—and, in fact, the strongest one—against the subjective contingency of our understanding of objective reality came from the works in the field of physiology of the sense organs by Johannes Müller. He conceived the so-called receptor theory of perception, according to which the specific quality of sensations following the stimulation is determined by the peculiarities of the respective receptor and the relevant neural pathways rather than by the mode of the stimulation. Considered from the abstract historical-philosophical point of view, Müller's conception furnishes nothing new: it is actually a mere extrapolation of the principles of classical empiricism on the level of particular physiological research. The conception owes its credit and impact, though, just to the fact that it no longer treats the problem of the objectivity of knowledge on the philosophical level but, on the face of it, on the "purely" empirical one—that of physiology as a specific empirical discipline.

Herman von Helmholtz, drawing on Müller, tries to mitigate the agnostic implications of the latter's receptor theory of perception. All the same, a sensation, for him, is not a reflection but a sign of external reality. Our focus here is not to furnish a detailed analysis of Müller's and Helmholtz's positions. What we pursue here, instead, consists in calling attention to the fact that it was exactly how the two brought up the issue of the physiological mechanism of sensory perception that proved to be one of the strongest catalysts for the revision of Kant's theoretical philosophy.[20]

Multiple alterations punctuate the understanding of the nature of physical research. Framing the principles of thermodynamics and field theory shattered the exclusive position of classical mechanics. Even the historical-philosophical analysis of Newtonian physics, which had stood until then as the exemplar of science as such, revealed that classical physics is not without "metaphysical" presumptions. Ernst Mach, in his *Die Mechanik in ihrer Entwicklung historisch-kritisch dargestellt*, stated that basic assertions of Newtonian natural philosophy had not been obtained exclusively through induction, and therefore they also had been contaminated by the "metaphysical" additive, which rendered their claims to purity but conditional: "Of absolute space and

20 Both psychologists and philosophers will claim today that Helmholtz, and above all Müller, underrated the importance of motor skills in the process of creating sensations, which stemmed from their erroneous passive understanding of a sensation as a "state" of a sense organ, as well as from their attribution of activity exclusively to consciousness, intellect. The receptor theory of perception thus led to the revival of the discrepancy existing between the receptivity of sensibility and the spontaneity of thought, which was at the epistemological level most explicitly formulated by Kant.

absolute motion, none can say anything, these being pure thought entities that cannot be shown in experience. All principles of mechanics are... experiences of the relative positions and motions of bodies."[21] The concrete evolution of the natural sciences, then, demonstrated the limitedness of the methodological ideal in whose ambiance those disciplines were unfolding. The traditional metaphysical reflection theory, which used to be just the epistemological exploitation of the Newtonian methodological program, was not equipped for the interpretation of the new situation in the sciences. The philosophy of the day found itself facing an alternative: knowledge is either reality's reflection or it is our construction. As late as the twentieth century, there appeared conceptions that seek to grasp cognition as the coordination of spontaneity and receptivity.[22] The mainstream of the philosophy of the second half of the nineteenth century decided, by and large, to conceive knowledge as the subject's construction, and did so along two epistemologically contradictory lines. Knowledge is seen either as the voluntarist construction of the subject, while science is interpreted conventionally, or as a rational and the only possible construction of the subject (the latter perspective requiring a commitment to the quest for an *a priori* law governing the development of knowledge). Thus, what provided an impetus for the return to Kant was the fact that it was none other than Kant himself who had consistently comprehended and philosophically unfurled the subject's agency in the process of cognition. It was just there and then that, while looking for the solutions to the epistemological difficulties of the contemporary sciences, the Neo-Kantians inferred that exactly Kant's philosophy contains insights that would also be fruitful and helpful in figuring out the then topical issues of scientific thinking.

3 Another Kind of Idealism

Yet it was not science alone that preoccupied the minds of the Neo-Kantians. What they were keen to do—Kant being their basic inspiration—was to demonstrate how the coexistence of science, morality, and art was possible. So the questions of how science is possible, how morality is possible, and

21 Ernst Mach, *Die Mechanik in ihrer Entwicklung*, Leipzig: F.A. Brockhaus 1883, p. 213.

22 In the first instance, at issue are conceptions of critical realism. In the field of German philosophy, these are most prominently represented by Nicolai Hartmann in his *Grundzüge einer Metaphysik der Erkenntnis* (Berlin: Walter de Gruyter 1921). Nowadays, the idea of knowledge as an interaction between the subjective and the objective is suggested in Hubert Dreyfus and Charles Taylor, *Retrieving Realisms*, Cambridge, MA: Harvard University Press 2015.

how art is possible were replaced by the question of how culture is possible. Hermann Cohen suggested that "exposing the connections, collisions, correspondences, and the genetic evolution of the three areas of consciousness has to become a proper object of philosophy."[23] In Cohen, again, the task of reconstructing culture as a unity of forms of objectification of pure reason is entrusted to a discipline concerned with the subjective—psychology: "Laws of thinking constitute the groundwork for the unity of human spirit, yet culture, in its entirety and unity, is the peak of human development. Displaying this development and this unity is a great task of systematic psychology, the highest task of systematic philosophy."[24] In this Cohenian vein, Natorp carried on his undertaking to create "reconstructive psychology" as a discipline that would systematically analyze the subjective modes of the grounding of objective formations. Against objectifying thinking in logic, ethics, and aesthetics, Natorp posits the subjectifying thinking of psychology, while letting the two procedures of thought maintain a constant mutual correlation. To summarize, Cohen develops transcendental thinking in two directions: the analysis of objective forms of consciousness is correlated with the analysis of subjective ways of grounding objective forms of consciousness—with the primacy being given to the analysis of the objective.

Cassirer's philosophical conception did not, however, make its appearance as a linear, purely immanent honing of the principles formulated by his predecessors and mentors. The contours of his system appeared in the continual confrontation of the principles of transcendental idealism with the actual intellectual events occurring throughout different realms of spiritual activity—in the natural and social disciplines, art, and philosophy. What distinguishes Cassirer's philosophical system from those of Cohen and Natorp is not just its "openness" to the issues in the spiritual culture of the era. The divergences are equally conditioned by the circumstance that Cassirer's thinking was being constituted in a different intellectual ambit—that is, no longer exclusively in the dispute with materialism and naturalism, but as a part of the anti-positivistically oriented intellectual surge, which was quite characteristic of the first third of the twentieth century.

The anti-positivistic movement involved various streams of thought, all too often quite diverging and reciprocally controverting in terms of their motives and goals. In disputes with the positivists, advocates of the philosophy of life

---

23 Hermann Cohen, *Logik der reinen Erkenntnis*, p. 17.

24 Ibid., p. 610.

would encounter a reforming Thomism and phenomenology in turn—various attempts at the "resurrection of metaphysics."[25]

Yet Cassirer did know that Neo-Kantian transcendentalism and positivism shared certain assumptions and were in accord about denying the claims regarding transcending, through the medium of either intuition or understanding, the boundaries of science. In addition, both streams of thought shared the conviction that philosophy could not be a theory of Being but just a theory of knowledge. What was more, they were hand in glove with each other in the trend to reduce the theory of knowledge to the theory of the method of scientific cognition. The awareness of these mutual assumptions in Neo-Kantianism and positivism, was for Cassirer, nevertheless, just a prelude to the scathing critique of the positivistic way of thinking.

The point is that positivism worms its way into everyday consciousness not as a conception that offers guidance on how to ameliorate society, but as a certain methodological algorithm designed to avert attention from metaphysical speculations and apply it to the inquiry into facts and their relationships. Positivism, though, was not only ill-disposed to metaphysics but skeptical about theory as such, and therefore the positivists' exhortations on being wary of generalizing ended up in a mistrust of any generalizations whatsoever.

The positivistic ideal—its core comprised of observed facts—as drawn up by Auguste Comte defaulted with regard to the actual trends of development in the positive sciences, that is, in such scientific disciplines that made for Comte and his followers a paragon to look to in designing their methodological theories. Cassirer's philosophical system in turn may be regarded, in a sense, as a consistent employment of the principle that "the image of the natural reality we create depends not just on the data of sensory perception but also on the ideational standpoints and requirements with which those data are approached."[26]

The positivistic ideal, however, failed to deliver on its promises not just in the field of natural science. In very much the same situation—in many respects even a more serious one—it would find itself in the sphere of the sciences concerning man, society, and culture. Here too, it was realized, upon

25 The term "resurrection of metaphysics" is a reference to the *oeuvre* of the Catholic existentialist Peter Wust (1884–1940). Attempts at the revival of metaphysics in Germany were made, above all, by the representatives of the "new ontology" Nicolai Hartmann (1882–1950) and Günther Jacoby (1889–1969). Hartmann summarized his investigations in the work *Neue Wege der Ontologie* (Stuttgart: Kohlhammer Verlag 1943) and Jacoby in his *Allgemeine Ontologie der Wirklichkeit*, vols. 1–2 (Halle: Niemeyer 1925–1955).

26 Ernst Cassirer, *Substanzbegriff und Funktionsbegriff*, Berlin: Bruno Cassirer Verlag 1923, p. 225.

the undermining of the authority of speculative idealism, that the difficulty resides not in the paucity of facts, but, instead, in the manner how they are interpreted. While positivism with its cult of "small facts" succeeded in attenuating speculative idealism, it proved incapable of conceptualizing the methodological and categorial apparatuses that would permit the transformation of the constantly burgeoning variety of disparate empirical findings into the unity of systematic knowledge.

A turn to idealism primarily implies a reevaluation of the role of theory in the process of the spiritual appropriation of reality. Most articulately, perhaps, this trend was imparted by Karl Vossler (1872–1949) in his text *Positivism and Idealism in Linguistics*.[27] For him, positivism means "the death of human thinking.... what remains is just the chaos of raw material, bereft of form, bereft of order, bereft of relationships. Remove the notion of causality from linguistics, and it is dead."[28]

True, as far as linguistics is concerned, Vossler's requirement to switch from positivism to idealism was an extreme response to the exclusively historically oriented positivistic linguistics. Far more promising turned out to be the structurally oriented (and less freighted with philosophical idealism) conception of Ferdinand de Saussure. It insisted on the synchronic analysis of language as a system that "is a self-contained whole and a principle of classification."[29]

Cassirer's philosophy of symbolic forms tries to extend its goodwill just to such anti-positivistic and anti-empiricist conceptions in the natural and social disciplines; it endeavors to justify philosophically the turn from facts to theoretical interpretations, from genesis to significance, and from history to structure. In this effort, the philosophy of symbolic forms mingles with the manifold thought streams flowing from other intellectual sources. That holds mostly for Husserl's phenomenological conception presented in his *Logical Investigations* and even for certain trends within the framework of positivistic thinking and for those that over time would morph into logical empiricism. (Although, to tell the truth, Cassirer valued Schlick's and Carnap's treatments of logic rather than their interpretations of the scientific *empiria*).

Underscoring the significance of the rational ingredients of scientific theory also implies, for Cassirer, the distinct understanding of the relationships

27 Karl Vossler, *Positivismus und Idealismus in der Sprachwissenschaft*, Heidelberg: C. Winter 1904.

28 Cited according to Gerhard Helbig, *Geschichte der neuern Sprachwissenschaft*, Leipzig: Bibliographisches Institut 1973, p. 22.

29 Ferdinand de Saussure, *Course in General Linguistics*, trans. by Wade Baskin, ed. by Perry Meisel and Haun Saussy, New York: Columbia University Press 1959, p. 9.

obtaining between philosophy and the special sciences. Positivism is generally known for its aversion to philosophy. It renounces any attempts to go beyond the boundaries of the perceptually given as a mere playing with words. Had its representatives recognized the validity of philosophy, then that would have happened exclusively under the psychological aspect. Cassirer's approach to metaphysics is much more nuanced. Although also straightforwardly denying the claims of metaphysics, he goes as far as to attract attention to the inspiring nature of metaphysical notions. Of course, having learned the lesson from Kant, he does not treat it on the historical-psychological plane, but on that of methodology. Notions of metaphysics, if adequately conceived, do not inform us about how "things-in-themselves" are, but govern our cognition, performing a regulative function.

The emphasis placed on the regulative function of metaphysical notions in the overall process of cognition coheres with the account of the genesis of metaphysical conceptions. In Cassirer's view, metaphysics does not make an appearance where we venture beyond the realm of the empirically knowable. Metaphysics begins where something that in the overall process of cognition functions as an inseparable unity of conditions and reciprocally supplementing viewpoints is hypostasized, owing to the metaphysical style of thinking, into the dispute of things, therefore "the logically correlative is transformed into the substantially contradictory."[30] The concern of the critique of knowledge, then, cannot involve just a rejection of metaphysics; it is instead imperative to translate substantially antithetical entities into the network of correlative relationships, hence transforming anew hypostases into hypotheses.

Cassirer identifies, without qualifications, with the paradigm of transcendental reflection developed by Cohen and Natorp: "We find ourselves standing in the framework of the general transcendental question," writes Cassirer, "that takes the '*quid facti*' of the particular forms merely as a departing point for asking about their meaning, their '*quid iuris*.'"[31] In a piecemeal fashion, Cassirer widens the scope of transcendentalism and stresses that understanding the world as it is presented in science represents just one of the possibilities; myth, religion, art, and history provide the parallel pictures of the world. That is to say that man's attitude to the world is not mediated by science alone; reality is also revealed to man through language, art, myth, or history. Cassirer sees as his goal to show that each of these symbolic forms is in possession of a certain logic of its own that is irreducible to any other within the scope of scientific

30 Cassirer, *Substanzbegriff und Funktionsbegriff*, Berlin: Bruno Cassirer Verlag 1923, p. 359.

31 Ernst Cassirer, *Philosophie der symbolischen Formen*, vol. 3, *Phänomenologie der Erkenntnis*, Berlin: Bruno Cassirer Verlag 1929, p. 58.

knowledge. Along the way, he indicates that the entirety of those forms of representing reality makes up a historically and logically self-differentiating complex of culture. The unity of culture is given as the specific configuration of symbolic forms, and philosophy's task consists in the explication of the logic of those constellations, to wit, the laws governing the formation of culture. Cassirer is in search of a notion that would allow the command of the "view" of all areas of culture; a view that would open up access to the variety of ways of the apperception of the world and would enable the understanding of the immanent law of constructing individual symbolic forms, and would not, at the same time, erase the singularity of their particular nature. Such a notion appears to be just that of the symbol.

4 Symbols as Key to Culture

Cassirer names the human being an *animal symbolicum*.[32] This very definition illustrates his effort to position man within the two worlds: as an *animal*, the human being is the child of nature and the product of the evolutionary process; as an animal *symbolicum*, the human being is the creator of her own world. "No longer in a merely physical universe, man lives in a symbolic universe. Language, myth, art, and religion are parts of this universe.... All human progress in thought and experience refines upon and strengthens this net."[33] This combination of naturalism and transcendentalism points to man's fundamental duality, to her belonging to the animal kingdom, and to her ability to overcome her own animality.

In identifying man's specifics and her distinctions from other animals, Cassirer focuses on the structural rather than the genetic problem.[34] The question of genesis is subordinated to that of structure. To put it more precisely,

32 The definition of man as *animal symbolicum* was forged by Ernst Cassirer in his *An Essay on Man: An Introduction to the Philosophy of Human Culture*, the first edition of which was released in 1944 by Yale University Press.

33 Ernst Cassirer, *An Essay on Man: An Introduction to the Philosophy of Human Culture*, New Haven and London: Yale University Press 2021, p. 25.

34 Identifying the specifics, the particularities of any entity are possible only by way of comparison. When making comparisons, one can lay stress either on likenesses or on divergences. Naturalistic schools are engaged with commonalities shared by humans and animals, while cultural ones, in turn, with dissimilarities dividing them. In his analyses of human beings, Cassirer explicitly concerns himself with the incongruities, even, lastly, extreme ones. The methodological thrust on the extremes may well prove productive since it facilitates a crisper identification of that which constitutes the "substance" of the entity examined.

only upon elucidating—on the phenomenological, systematic plane—the peculiarities of the human approach to the world, a relevant response to the question of the genesis can be hoped for. So it is necessary, in the first place, to thematize the difference between a human and an animal, and only afterward can one pose the question of how a particular symbolic form has evolved.[35]

According to Cassirer—who herein considers Jacob von Uexküll's view—the relationship of an animal to its environment is conditioned by its anatomy, that is, the structure of its receptors and effectors. The examination of their structures shows which is "real" for the particular animal and which is not. Of course, the evolutionary "ladder" involves the widening of the "degrees of freedom" enjoyed by individual animals regarding their relations to external reality. It is just in humans that we can see a radical change in the degree of distance from the reality. The symbolic system, sandwiched between receptors and effectors, steeply heightens the degree of human freedom from the binding immediacy of the surroundings. For human beings, their reality is created in the domain of the symbolic, which accounts for the fact that the human "world image" cannot be derived from the anatomical structure of humans. Our picture of the world is just in part conditioned by the faculties of our sense organs; its defining portion is formed at the level that has set itself free from our biologically given possibilities. The "reality" consists not just in what humans can perceive through their senses but equally in what they reflect and imagine. Thinking and imagination, though, turn out to be ambivalent gifts: they not only help humans obtain a better orientation in the world, but they are also to blame for our falling into errors, and letting illusions—or delusions—get the better of us. It is, then, exactly the symbolic function that always problematizes our relations with reality.

To summarize, the symbolic function enables the following: (1) It opens up access to the differentiation between possibility and facticity, thereby getting us to take decisions and make choices. All our choices are the outcomes of selection that is commonly spontaneous and "subconscious," but under certain circumstances, it may become conscious. (2) It makes it possible to expand our notion of reality, namely, in its relatedness towards "things" as well as regarding humans. Human communication implies an ability to put oneself in another's place, to retrieve for oneself what things look like for her. I, as it

35 When it comes to determining the direction to be taken in the process of examining the genesis of the symbolic function, Cassirer rested content with a suggestive, indicative answer to the effect that the symbolic function is there due to the emergence, the specific recombination of conditional reflexes. It is they, to all appearances, that are the "material" out of which, under certain circumstances, the symbolic function emerged.

were, can see something she also can, but there is also something I can see yet she cannot. (3) It empowers humans to constitute new dimensions of the surrounding reality that are unchained from the sphere of facticity, the yoke of immediacy. One such example is the aesthetic function that makes it possible for us to discriminate between the beautiful and the ugly. (4) It enables us to attain a distance from external pressures, to say "no" to those coming from both the outside and the inside, securing a break in the immediate relationship with the external—to be filled with thought, which in turn promotes an unmediated animal reaction to a symbolically mediated human response. (5) Not only does the symbolic function modify our reactions, it equally impacts the ways how we receive sensory signals. It "opens up" our senses, widening thereby the palette of the stimuli we gain the capacities to discern. Where animal sensibility reacts merely to the stimuli crucial for the survival under specific circumstances, the human receptive organs react to "more" than it is necessary for bare survival. (6) The symbolic function allows us to build up different types of society, viz. ones founded on the common language, and shared values and norms.

For Cassirer, just as for Cohen and Natorp, the notions of spiritual functions are identical with the notion of the synthesis of the manifold. Thus he writes: "In all the human activities and across all the guises of human culture, we encounter the 'unity of the manifold.' Art affords us the unity of contemplation, science gives us the unity of thinking, while religion and myth provide the unity of emotion."[36] The fulcrum of Marburg Neo-Kantianism is shifted to the analysis of multifarious forms and degrees of unifying the manifold. That process, never complete, is, for Cohen and Natorp, coextensive with one of positing relationships.

Gradually, Cassirer works through to the view that Cohen and Natorp's immanent justification of the foundations of science is too narrow. Although it enables interpreting the progression of advanced disciplines, it incapacitates the adequate treatment of connections from which scientific thinking stems. Cassirer holds that the conceptualization of scientific notions always proceeds from certain assumptions and draws on a certain pre-arrangement of phenomena, which are mediated for us by the various forms of the pre-scientific understanding of the world, such as language, myth, and art. Although science, indeed, builds on the pre-scientific forms of understanding the world rather *per negationem*, nonetheless should these pre-scientific forms of

36 Ernst Cassirer, *The Myth of the State*, New Haven and London: Yale University Press 1946, p. 37.

understanding the world lack their firm and stable structure and be just pure chaos and contingency, that would entail a denial of the unity and spontaneity of consciousness, re-animating, consequently, the ancient dualism of the given and the constituted, which Cohen and Natorp strove to collapse.

What Cassirer is anxious to perform is to surmount the dualism of the rational and the sensory via the notions of symbol and symbolic forms. A symbol as such is the synthesis of the sensory and the intelligible, and a symbolic form is "that very energy of the spirit by virtue of which a certain spiritual content gets synthesized with a specific sensory sign."[37] The notion of a symbolic form thus makes it possible to capture the totality of the forms of the synthesis of the manifold, namely, to capture the forms, degrees, and types of processes through which "any impression [is] related to and permeated by the activity of expression."[38] Cassirer's chief aim, then, comes to be the working out of a general theory of expressive forms—one which would make it possible to formulate explicitly the connections and particularities of the individual forms of the synthesis of the manifold.

The individual symbolic forms—those that objectify spirit—make up a certain whole of human culture that is never a pure unity. Instead, it is the integration of the manifold and the harmonization of even reciprocally discordant trends. On that account, the notion of the synthetic unity of the manifold will not merely aid Cassirer as a key to understanding the individual forms of the spiritual appropriation of reality, but equally as an instrument for comprehending relations—both accordant and discordant—in the framework of the total process of forming human culture as one whole.

Cassirer's notion of culture is evidently established in the vein of Neo-Kantian idealism. The particular forms of "getting the world" are not ones of appropriating it, or the ways of reflecting the objectively existing material reality manifest in the multiple types of human activity. They are exclusively the forms of the objectivation and externalization of consciousness: "Spirit understands itself, and it is in antagonism with the 'objective' world in the sense that it attributes to the phenomena only certain differences in reflection that are lodged in itself."[39] Hence the source and subject of the syntheses of the manifold is the spiritual activity materialized in the process of the creation of culture as a complex of symbolic forms.

---

37 Ernst Cassirer, *Wesen und Wirkung des Symbolbegriffs*, Darmstadt: Wissenschaftliche Buchgesellschaft 1969, p. 175.

38 Ibid., p. 175.

39 Cassirer, *Philosophie der symbolischen Formen*, vol. 1, p. 123.

Cassirer's characterization of the symbolic function and symbolic forms retains its relevance nowadays. What has changed, however, is the context within which the symbolic function and its performance are treated. First and foremost, current approaches—encouraged by the development of systems theory and the theory of complexity—overcome the stark differentiation between genetic and structural analyses. At the same time, the characteristics definitive of a human being and the divergences between humans (sapience) and animals (sentience) are no longer looked for just in the area of cognitive performance but also in bodily gestures and corporeality at large. Cassirer takes symbolic forms primarily as externalizations, as modes of sense-bestowal.

Current anthropological thought perceives symbolic forms above all as modes of communication. Expression, locution, and speech acts are primarily communication acts. Evolutionary psychology concluded that the most powerful urges towards the formation of intelligence issue not from our relations to objects but from the intersubjective sphere. A human being is a social creature, and she achieves more via cooperation than through an individual effort. She takes care that her share of the product of the cooperation is optimal. It is necessary to strike the best possible balance between cooperation and egoism. We need to know what others think, what intentions they have, and what they make of us. Fondness for stories, then, is at once the product of and the booster for the evolution of social intelligence.

The differentiation of the bodily and the spiritual in contemporary thinking is overlaid by one between the implicit and the explicit, while the former is taken as the sedimentation of communicative acts. Where we primarily consider a human being as relying on her "higher" spiritual achievements, the necessary outcome, then, will be the dualism of the bodily and the mental. The unified image of human beings can only be attained if the analysis proceeds in a bottom-up direction, that is to say, from human corporeality.

It is the body that delimits a framework for our orientation in the world. To the right, to the left, up, down, near, far—all of these are content structures bound to our corporeality, our specific localization in the world. Similarly, the primary identifications of things and relationships among them are given by our needs and the capacity of our sense organs. Giving us our bearings in the world, cognition in the broadest sense is determined by practice, which implies assessment. We take "things," first and foremost, as useful or useless, as those aiding us in meeting our objectives or preventing us from so doing. "Pure" knowledge—cognition that is no longer immediately tethered to the mundane exigencies and interests, that is, knowledge as a "symbolic form"—is already a product of a highly differentiated culture.

Acknowledgments

This paper was written at the Institute of Philosophy of the Slovak Academy of Sciences, v.v.i. It was supported by the Agency for Research and Development under the project APVV-20-0137 Philosophical Anthropology in the Context of Current Crises of Symbolic Structures.

Bibliography

Brandom, Robert, *Making It Explicit*, Cambridge: Harvard University Press 1994.

Burrow, J.W., *The Crisis of Reason: European Thought 1848–1915*, New Haven: Yale University Press 2002.

Cassirer, Ernst, *An Essay on Man: An Introduction to the Philosophy of Human Culture*, New Haven and London: Yale University Press 1944.

Cassirer, Ernst, *Philosophie der symbolischen Formen*, vol. 1, *Die Sprache*, Berlin: Bruno Cassirer 1923.

Cassirer, Ernst, *Philosophie der symbolischen Formen*, vol. 3, *Phänomenologie der Erkenntnis*, Berlin: Bruno Cassirer Verlag 1929.

Cassirer, Ernst, *Substanzbegriff und Funktionsbegriff*, Berlin: Bruno Cassirer Verlag 1923.

Cassirer, Ernst, *The Myth of the State*, New Haven and London: Yale University Press 1946.

Cassirer, Ernst, *Wesen und Wirkung des Symbolbegriffs*, Darmstadt: Wissenschaftliche Buchgesellschaft 1969.

Cohen, Hermann, *Logik der reinen Erkenntnis*, Berlin: Bruno Cassirer Verlag 1922.

Dreyfus, Hubert and Charles Taylor, *Retrieving Realisms*, Cambridge, MA: Harvard University Press 2015.

Hartmann, Nicolai, *Grundzüge einer Metaphysik der Erkenntnis*, Berlin: Walter de Gruyter 1921.

Hartmann, Nicolai, *Kleinere Schriften*, vols. 1–3, Berlin: De Gruyter 1955–58.

Hartmann, Nicolai, *Neue Wege der Ontologie*, Stuttgart: Kohlhammer Verlag 1943.

Helbig, Gerhard, *Geschichte der neuern Sprachwissenschaft*, Leipzig: Bibliographisches Institut, Leipzig 1973.

Hühnerfeld, Paul, *In Sachen Heidegger*, Munich: P. List Verlag 1961.

Husserl, Edmund *Logische Untersuchungen*, Leipzig: Von Veit & Comp. 1900

Jacoby, Günther, *Allgemeine Ontologie der Wirklichkeit*, vols. 1–2, Halle: Niemeyer 1925–1955.

Lange, Friedrich, *Geschichte des Materialismus und Kritik seiner Bedeutung in der Gegenwart*, vols. 1–2, Leipzig: Alfred Kröner Verlag 1926.

Liebmann, Otto, *Kant und Epigonen*, Stuttgart: C. Schrober 1910.

Lukács, Georg, *Die Zerstörung der Vernunft*, Berlin: Aufbau-Verlag 1955.

Mach, Ernst, *Die Mechanik in ihrer Entwicklung*, Leipzig: F.A. Brockhaus 1883.

Natorp, Paul, *Philosophie, ihr Problem und ihre Probleme*, Göttingen: Vanderhoeck und Ruprecht 1911.

Rosenkranz, Karl, *Wissenschaft der logischen Idee*, Königsberg: Gebrüder Bornträger 1859.

Saussure, Ferdinand de, *Course in General Linguistics*, trans. by Wade Baskin, ed. by Perry Meisel and Haun Saussy, New York: Columbia University Press 1959.

Stekeler-Weihofer, Pirmin, *Philosophie des Selbstbewußtseins. Hegels Systems als Formanalyse von Wissen und Autonomie*, Frankfurt am Main: Suhrkamp Verlag 2005.

Vossler, Karl, *Positivismus und Idealismus in der Sprachwissenschaft*, Heidelberg: C. Winter 1904.

Windelband, Wilhelm, *Die Geschichte der neueren Philosophie in ihrem Zusammenhange mit der allgemeinen Cultur und den besonderen Wissenschaften dargestellt*, vols. 1–2, Leipzig: Breitkopf und Hartel 1878–80. Bd.1: *Von der Renaissance bis Kant* (1878), Bd. 2: *Die Blüthezeit der deutschen Philosophie. Von Kant bis Hegel und Herbart* (1880).

CHAPTER 9

Anxiety and Sexuality in Kierkegaard and Freud: From the Psychology of Spirit to *Neurosenpsychologie*

Patricia C. Dip

Abstract

Although some commentators have drawn attention to the relationship between Freud and philosophy, particularly the influence of Schopenhauer and Nietzsche on the Viennese psychoanalyst, the same emphasis has not been placed on highlighting the importance of Kierkegaard's thought as a theoretical antecedent of the future field of psychoanalysis. The aim of this article is to reveal the central formulations of *The Concept of Anxiety* as a thematic and conceptual anticipation of Freud's early writings. Freud's first writings from the end of the 19th century, in which an intimate link between anxiety and sexuality is proposed, can be considered as a deepening of the issues raised in *The Concept of Anxiety*, a consideration that assumes a certain thematic continuity between the psychology of spirit and *Neurosenpsychologie*.

In *Fear and Trembling*, the concept of "anxiety"—a key notion both for existential philosophy and for the subsequent development of psychoanalysis—is announced.[1] The announcement is made by Johannes de Silentio upon highlighting the fact that in the biblical story of Abraham no one took into consideration the problem of anxiety. However, this problem is conceptualized only a little later by Vigilius Haufniensis, who places it at the center of his psychology. Two related consequences can be drawn from Haufniensis' decision. The first has to do with something new in relation to the understanding of psychological phenomena in the strict sense, since, although since ancient times philosophy had taken the soul as its theme, it had not done so from the

1 For an analysis of the announcement and appearance of the concept of anxiety in Kierkegaard's work and its relationship with Lacanian psychoanalysis, see Patricia Dip, "De Kierkegaard a Lacan: el surgimiento de la angustia en *Temor y temblor*," *Estudios kierkegaardianos. Revista de Filosofía*, vol. 7, 2021, pp. 91–120.

 | DOI:10.1163/9789004689459_011

point of view of anxiety. Looking at it from this analytical perspective has an effect on contemporary thought about the understanding of the meaning of human subjectivity since from the moment the concept of anxiety is introduced, subjectivity can no longer be conceived from the point of view of its full constitution. It will begin to be thought of as a task to be realized, but it cannot be determined *a priori*, nor can it be fully constituted in the sense of the modern subject-substance. The introduction of the concept of anxiety implies a discussion of the modern point of view of the subject. Within the framework of this discussion, the second consequence appears, namely, the possibility of proposing a connection between existential philosophy and psychoanalysis on the basis of the effect produced when the concept of anxiety is taken into account in the analysis of the meaning of human subjectivity as an open "task" that is fundamentally of a future order.

In this context, Vigilius Haufniensis, the pseudonymous author of *The Concept of Anxiety* (1844), introduces four issues relevant to future psychoanalytic research: (1) sexuality as a discursive field; (2) the difference between instinct and impulse; (3) the "concept" of anxiety; and (4) the psychological understanding of the relationship between the psychic and the physical. As is well known, towards the end of the 19th century, Freud began to think about a theme that would reappear throughout his life at different stages of his work: "anxiety." Simultaneously, he concentrated on the meaning of sexuality in the etiology of the neuroses. In 1894, when the unconscious had not yet been discovered and the rudiments of a sexual theory had not yet been advanced, the relationship between anxiety and sexuality—emphasized by Haufniensis in *The Concept of Anxiety*—would be the key to Freud's definition of the origin of this "affect." This was taken up as a theme for the first time in a work published in the author's lifetime, namely, "On the Grounds for Detaching a Particular Syndrome from Neurasthenia under the Description 'Anxiety Neurosis.'"

Although Kierkegaard is responsible for having drawn attention to the importance of the treatment of sexuality in the field of psychology, his theoretical framework, through which sexuality is explained, is conditioned by the logic of religious discourse, which is focused on the theological problem of evil and based on the assumption of hereditary sin. Kierkegaard's psychology arises in the context of an epistemological discussion of the impossibility of conceiving of or defining the concept of sin.[2] This implies a displacement from the metaphysical understanding of the problem of evil to the dogmatic

2 To get an understanding of the epistemological discussion in *The Concept of Anxiety*, see Darío González, "The Triptych of Sciences in the Introduction to *The Concept of Anxiety*," *Kierkegaard Studies Yearbook*, 2001, pp. 15–42.

assumption as the basis of guilt and the consequent introduction of anxiety as an intermediate psychological category typical of a new science and which is capable of approaching the limits of sin, which in a sense strict is inexplicable. Since the concept of sin lacks determination, dogmatics can only presuppose it, but not explain it. What Haufniensis calls "the second ethics"—because its starting point is the dogmatic presupposition of hereditary sin—will face the reality of the evil really produced. In this context, only anxiety, as an intermediate category of psychology, will be able to account for how sin "comes into existence"—not the fact that it "exists." The new psychological science focuses on anxiety to account for freedom defined in terms of possibility. Precisely, "Freedom's possibility announces itself in anxiety."[3]

Unlike Kierkegaard, who introduces the question of sexuality within the framework of the discussion of hereditary sin, the Freudian notion of sexuality implies a "cultural revolution," since it frees the former from its immediate relationship with sinfulness and allows it to be displaced to a profane sphere. In this way, he distances it from merely reproductive purposes and incorporates it into the analysis of human personality, emphasizing the psychophysical development of the individual, the starting point of which is the new terrain of infantile sexuality.

With regard to the analysis of the issue of the relationship between sexuality and anxiety, there is a displacement of the discursive logic used by Kierkegaard to present it—which is based on sin and its relationship with "second ethics," on the basis of a spiritualist psychology concentrated on anxiety—to the Freudian approach—which starts from the discursive logic of the psychology of neurosis, the first articulating concept of which is anxiety. This displacement has important consequences for the understanding of the question of sexuality. It implies liberation from the ethical-religious field of analysis, which supposes (1) the Freudian understanding of human sexuality as a psychophysical process, in such terms that in childhood sexuality is already manifested, (2) the distinction between genitality and sexuality, (3) the approach to the theme of homosexuality, freed from the "anomaly of perversion," since the child is described as polymorphously perverse, because for Freud, neurosis is the conceptual scheme through which what can be very cautiously called "normality" is understood, and not the other way around. The change in discursive logic produces effects in the meaning that sexuality will assume throughout the 20th century, not only in individual but also in social terms.[4] The Freudian drive

3 *SKS* 4, 378 / *CA*, 74.

4 Paul L. Assoun, *El freudismo*, trans. by Tatiana Sule Fernández, Buenos Aires and Mexico City: Siglo XXI editores 2003, p. 28: "The knowledge of the unconscious is not psychoanal-

comes to respond to the Kierkegaardian search for a relationship between body and soul on the basis of a third term. While, for Kierkegaard, the mediator is the spirit, in the case of Freud, this will become the drive as the limit between the psychic and the organic. This subtle difference in emphasis or approach allows the field of sexuality to gradually free itself from religious guilt and the anomaly to which it was condemned by the opinion of bourgeois double standards. In theoretical terms, it manifests itself as a shift from the psychology of spirit, which starts from sin, to the psychology of neurosis, which arises from the limitations that Freud found in the explanatory model of physiology.

1 Anxiety as an Intermediate Category: From Innocence to Guilt

According to Haufniensis, anxiety arises from the individual's possibility of sinning, framed in a generational context in which evil is perceived as destiny, since the history of the generations has thus determined it. The qualitative leap that the individual makes when starting from innocence and arriving at guilt is a free act since only the individual can be held responsible for the evil that he himself has done, but at the same time, he is conditioned by the history of the species, which shows that every individual since Adam has lost his innocence and will continue to lose it in the same way that the first man did. This state of vulnerability of the individual in the face of freedom provokes anxiety and, simultaneously, shows the relationship between the latter and the history of sexuality. From this perspective, according to Haufniensis, when born into a determined historical nexus, the individual is both "himself and the species."[5] It is not possible to understand individuality except within the more general framework of the history of the generations, and therefore, of sexuality.

Haufniensis derives two consequences from sin: sexuality and history. Once the individual is understood as being both himself and the species, that is, conditioned by a historical nexus, sexuality and history are interrelated. This is because what it is a question of developing, ultimately, is not the nature of the species but the history of the human race, which would not be possible without presupposing the sexual difference understood in terms of the impulse from the man to the woman and vice versa. We cannot lose sight of the fact that the starting point for Haufniensis' analysis is the apparent inconsistencies

ysis applied to culture, but *ipso facto* social theory, either as a diagnosis of 'modern nerves' recovered by repression, as a study of the destiny of the ideal, in short and above all, as pointing out the effects of the death drive on the destinies of *Kultur*."

5 *SKS* 4, 335 / *CA*, 29.

of the biblical account of the Fall. In this framework, Haufniensis seeks to make the story consistent; psychology as a science of ambiguity, with all the correct intuitions that it reveals for the future psychoanalytic treatment of the concept of anxiety, is conditioned by the dogma of hereditary sin. This implies that the way to approach the discussion of anxiety and sexuality will be from a "religious," more specifically, Christian, perspective, even when consequences that transcend this viewpoint are derived from the discussion itself.

Haufniensis' psychology can be conceived in terms of "pneumatic psychology," since it tries to understand the human being defined as body and soul sustained by spirit. Man is distressed because his ultimate foundation has a spiritual character.[6] "That anxiety makes its appearance is the pivot upon which everything turns. Man is a synthesis of the psychical and the physical; however, a synthesis is unthinkable if the two are not united in a third. This third is spirit."[7] If man were reduced to being an immediate unity of body and soul, his destiny would be determined by the world of nature. Anxiety presupposes a rupture with the natural world and an anticipated "consciousness" of the possible "disruption" of the synthesis of body and soul when this unity is not experienced by the individual in a harmonious way.

The immediate unity of body and soul founded on the spirit seeks to respond to the dualism of the modern tradition, which fails to resolve the relationship satisfactorily, or in any case, does so by giving the soul priority over the body in line with the Platonic tradition. Faced with this explanatory model, Haufniensis conceives man as a "synthesis" of body and soul, advancing towards understanding the psychophysical unity of man, while he vindicates the body in its materiality by conceiving it as "sexed," as we will see below. Human sexuality presupposes awareness of "sexual difference" in terms of drive.[8] Unlike the animal, whose sexuality is determined by instinct, human sexuality is determined by the drive. From sin, which makes sense because man is not an immediate natural relationship between body and soul, but spirit, Haufniensis deduces both sexuality and history. And, in turn, the fact that man is defined as spirit explains the emergence of anxiety. Already in innocence man is spirit and not merely an animal. However, in this state the spirit is present as something immediate; it is "like dreaming."[9] This spirit, already present in innocence, is ambiguous. On the one hand, it behaves as a "hostile power" that disturbs the

6 SKS 4, 347 / CA, 41: "Anxiety is a qualification of dreaming spirit, and as such it has its place in psychology."

7 SKS 4, 349 / CA, 43.

8 SKS 4, 373 / CA, 69.

9 SKS 4, 349 / CA, 43.

relationship between body and soul. On the other, it behaves as a "friendly power" whose purpose is to establish the relationship: "What, then, is man's relation to this ambiguous power? How does spirit relate itself to itself and to its conditionality? It relates itself as anxiety."[10]

Human history presupposes a generic link to the first man and at the same time the understanding of the individual as an always new self with which the species renews itself and not a mere specimen of nature as in the case of the animals. In the animal world there exist examples of the species, not individuals. Animal nature has no history. Unlike animal nature, man, understood as a synthesis sustained by the spirit, has a history. It is, then, within the framework of "the history of the spirit" that Haufniensis conceives the theme of sexuality:

> So sinfulness is by no means sensuousness, but without sin there is no sexuality, and without sexuality, no history. A perfect spirit has neither the one nor the other, and therefore the sexual difference is canceled in the resurrection, and therefore an angel has no history.[11]

The object of psychology is man as an "imperfect spirit," who, being neither mere nature—like the animal—nor pure perfection—like the angels—develops his existence as a task of freedom whose achievement produces "anxiety."[12] Pneumatic psychology or the science of ambiguity treats the concept of anxiety in a scenario whose backdrop is represented by the dogma of hereditary sin, which is not explained, but assumed. In this sense, psychology, as a doctrine of the "subjective spirit"—in the line of Hegel and Rosenkranz—refers to the absolute spirit, understood in terms of dogmatic assumption.

The psychology of the subjective spirit is based on an anthropological presupposition that Anti-Climacus will soon explain in greater detail by identifying the spirit with the self and deepening the debate with the modern philosophical tradition, especially with Cartesianism. According to Haufniensis, the human being (*Mennesket*) is an individual and, as such, is both himself and the entire species. What psychology describes is how the human being develops his existence in the transition from innocence to guilt, that is, the significance of the loss of the state of innocence to the constitution of subjectivity, when it is not yet thought of as a "self." For Haufniensis, the spirit is the third term that sustains the immediate synthesis between body and soul, but

10 *SKS* 4, 349 / *CA*, 43.
11 *SKS* 4, 354 / *CA*, 49.
12 *SKS* 4, 354 / *CA*, 49.

it is not a "relationship that relates to itself,"[13] as it is for Anti-Climacus in *The Sickness unto Death.*

This subtle change of perspective on the understanding of the spirit explains the difference between the psychological category of anxiety and the anthropological category of "despair," which supposes the emergence of the self in terms of "self-awareness." The function of the former is to demonstrate human freedom as a condition for the appropriation of "oneself," while that of the latter is to determine the condition of the human existential structure of the self before God. While anxiety represents the way in which man relates to freedom, despair refers to man's relationship with God. Together they define the history of man in terms of the history of the subjective spirit, and the method with which to approach this history is precisely "psychological."

This method begins to be applied in *The Concept of Anxiety*, where the notion of "spirit" occupies a central role with regard to the definition of man: "Innocence is ignorance. In innocence, man is not qualified as spirit but is psychically qualified in immediate unity with his natural condition. The spirit in man is dreaming."[14] Human history supposes a progressive spiritual determination, the point of departure of which is innocence, and its point of arrival is guilt. In innocence there is no knowledge of good and evil, nor is there awareness of sexual difference because man lives in an immediate relationship with his naturalness. However, that does not mean that the spirit is not present, only that it does not yet determine the relationship. It is precisely anxiety that accounts for the presence of spirit in the state of innocence in which there is peace and rest. And this happens because in that state, besides peace and rest, there is nothing to fight with. And it is nothingness that causes anxiety:

> The concept of anxiety is almost never treated in psychology. Therefore, I must point out that it is altogether different from fear and similar concepts that refer to something definite, whereas anxiety is freedom's actuality as the possibility of possibility.[15]

Anxiety has no object. Unlike fear, that is produced by something definite, anxiety is caused by the reality of freedom, the latter not being understood as a pure abstraction—as in the case of free will—nor as a necessity, in the terms in which philosophical idealism explains it, but as "possibility." With anxiety, what Haufniensis seems to take as his theme is the effect of concrete

13 *SKS* 11, 129 / *SUD*, 13.

14 *SKS* 4, 347 / *CA*, 41.

15 *SKS* 4, 348 / *CA*, 42.

freedom on the particular individual, that is, the feeling of being able to lean both towards good and towards evil, without this depending on either destiny or necessity. From innocence to guilt there is a transition that causes anxiety. Ignorance generates anxiety because it is an ignorance of "nothing" since there is no knowledge of good and evil. However, if there is anxiety in innocence, it is because, even if it is identified with ignorance, what appears is the "premonition" of the Fall and not the "consciousness" of it.[16] This premonition would not occur if man were not defined as spirit within the framework of a historical link. Since the individual is not only himself but also the species, we can say that, in ignorance, what the individual senses and what makes him anxious, is the anticipation of the guilt that appears insofar as he forms part of the species, although this bond with the species is not constituted by sin, and in that sense it is not inherited by nature, but becomes present through the fault committed by the individual himself. The inheritance of sin is in this sense spiritual in character. A person is not born guilty, but he always becomes guilty.

In the description of anxiety that Haufniensis presents, certain features that will be taken up by the psychoanalytic tradition become evident. In the first place, emphasis is placed on the lack of an object for anxiety and on its difference from fear and other affects. Secondly, he shows its ambiguous nature that is manifest in the language itself, when he speaks of worrying about nothing.[17] Finally, anxiety, the meaning of which is dialectical, since it lacks an object but not effects, is presented as a hostile power that the individual does not control and for which he is not responsible, but which at the same time forces him to take responsibility since it is not a power alien to him. The hostility of the power of anxiety is typical of "selfhood."[18] It is a question of the effect that freedom, understood as a possibility of realization, provokes in the individual. The anxiety that freedom causes is the fact of knowing that if the individual becomes guilty, it is by his own hand. Anxiety is a hostile power that confronts the individual with himself, causing in him fear and desire simultaneously:

> The qualitative leap stands outside of all ambiguity. But he who becomes guilty through anxiety is indeed innocent, for it was not he himself but anxiety, a foreign power, that laid hold of him, a power that he did not love but about which he was anxious. And yet he is guilty, for he sank in anxiety, which he nevertheless loved even as he feared it.[19]

16 *SKS* 4, 348 / *CA*, 42.
17 See *SKS* 4, 348–349 / *CA*, 43.
18 *SKS* 4, 349 / *CA*, 43.
19 *SKS* 4, 349 / *CA*, 43.

In addition to these general features of the notion of anxiety, which the psychoanalytic tradition will take up again, the Kierkegaardian idea of the relationship between anxiety and the "disruption" of the elements of the synthesis—physical and psychic—seems to be applicable to describing both hysteria and the anxiety neurosis in the early writings of Freud. This is because in both neuroses the proper organization of the phenomena of a physical and psychic nature is lacking, although in a different way in each of them.

2 The Introduction of the Field of Sexuality in *The Concept of Anxiety*

In the second chapter of *The Concept of Anxiety*, Haufniensis draws attention to the importance of the theme of sexuality, to speak of which requires an "art" that Socrates would understand. We believe that Haufniensis introduces here the "field of sexuality" that psychoanalysis will later deal with. The Danish psychologist understands that "the whole question of the significance of the sexual, as well as its significance in the particular spheres, has undeniably been answered poorly until now; moreover, it has seldom been answered in the correct mood."[20] Otherwise, "to speak humanly about it is an art."[21] Moreover, the only thing the pseudonymous author knows is that "had Socrates lived now, he would have reflected on such things."[22]

Haufniensis understands that he has no interlocutors to whom he can address himself to give them an account of his discovery; for this reason he goes back to Socrates, whom he considers a true teacher with respect to the understanding of "merely human" issues, such as sexuality as the first moment of the realization of the subjective spirit, and anxiety as an intermediate category of psychology that allows us to account for the transition from innocence to guilt. Although the starting point was the biblical story, it is clear that Haufniensis' discourse moves from the dogmatic presupposition to the discovery of a "new science," psychology, which highlights, perhaps for the first time, the close links between anxiety and sexuality.

Although the biological nature of man is not rejected, neither humanity nor sexuality is reduced to nature. The transition from innocence to guilt accounts

20 *SKS* 4, 371 / *CA*, 67.

21 *SKS* 4, 371 / *CA*, 67.

22 *SKS* 4, 372 / *CA*, 68.

for a foundational moment in human history, understood in spiritual terms.[23] Haufniensis explains,

> In animals the sexual difference can be developed instinctively, but this cannot be the case with a human being precisely because he is a synthesis. In the moment the spirit posits itself, it posits the synthesis, but in order to posit the synthesis it must first pervade it differentiatingly, and the ultimate point of the sensuous is precisely the sexual.[24]

The deepening of the spirit in the body-soul synthesis, which assumes its "realization," implies at first "dissociation." The dissociation of the psychic and the somatic elements supposes the understanding of sexuality as being at the bodily or sensitive extreme.[25] In this sense, the first moment of the realization of the subjective spirit consists in the "sexuation" of the body, whose consequence is the determination of human sexuality in terms of "drive." Man can reach that extreme only "in the moment the spirit becomes actual."[26] "Before that time he is not animal, but neither is he really man. The moment he becomes man, he becomes so by being animal as well."[27] The important thing to note at this point is that before the Fall "there is no sexual distinction" properly speaking.

Sin, then, introduces the possibility of realizing what is properly human in terms of the "history of sexuality," which, since it is not exhausted in natural immediacy, has love as its *telos*. Hence, the natural place of overcoming the "anxiety" of sexuality is love, and from the beginning of the description of the determinations or history of the spirit, the intimate link between anxiety and eroticism is raised, since "the proportion of sensuousness corresponds to that of anxiety."[28]

With Adam's sin, sinfulness came into the world, and sexuality remained. Ignorance, properly speaking, is reserved for the animal alone. Therefore, it walks blindly, subjected to the blindness of instinct. Innocence, however, is a

23 *SKS* 4, 354 / *CA*, 48–49: "In innocence, Adam as spirit was a dreaming spirit. Thus the synthesis is not actual, for the combining factor is precisely the spirit, and as yet this is not posited as spirit."

24 *SKS* 4, 354 / *CA*, 49.

25 At this point it is striking that Haufniensis only highlights the "sensual" or bodily extreme of the synthesis, by defining sexuality as the "extreme" of sensuality, without leaving any indication of its psychic "extreme."

26 *SKS* 4, 354 / *CA*, 49.

27 *SKS* 4, 354 / *CA*, 49.

28 *SKS* 4, 368 / *CA*, 64.

knowledge that means ignorance. What is the content of that ignorant knowledge? Its content is precisely sexual, since "spirit is not merely qualified as body but as body with a generic difference."[29] The body is not only the organ of the soul but is also established as a gender, and it is the sexual determination of the spirit that causes anxiety: "the sexual is the expression for the prodigious *Widerspruch* [contradiction] that the immortal spirit is determined as genus."[30]

The fact that sexuality is presented in terms of "contradiction" is explained on the basis of the relationship between Paganism and Christianity. The latter, by introducing "reconciliation," approaches sexuality from a perspective unknown to the happy Pagan mentality. However, this does not mean that Christianity rejects sexuality out of hand.[31] Rather, it understands it as a "moral task" consisting in granting it a *telos* that transcends the contradiction of the "embodied spirit." The "neighbor" as a "purely spiritual" concept,[32] as defined in *Works of Love*, can be thought of as the other, which transcends the sphere of otherness in terms of impulse, which appears in *The Concept of Anxiety* with the introduction of the field of sexuality.

In analyzing the concept of modesty,[33] Haufniensis describes it precisely as a knowledge "of gender distinction" in which the impulse is not present as such and anxiety appears, so there is no trace of sensual desire, but there is a shame of "nothing." "In modesty, the generic difference is posited, but not in relation to its other. That takes place in the sexual drive."[34] Modesty, as the first determination of sexuality, does not refer to another, but to oneself. Only in the impulse does the other appear as an object.

Evidently, anxiety and sexuality are directly proportional. The greater the sensitivity—and sexuality is its peak—the greater the anxiety. The spirit cannot express itself in the erotic; it feels foreign in its presence and that causes anxiety. In this sense, anxiety can be understood as "the concealment of the spirit," which, although it is present, cannot be expressed. Sexuality, as an

---

29 *SKS* 4, 372 / *CA*, 68.

30 *SKS* 4, 373 / *CA*, 69.

31 *SKS* 4, 383 / *CA*, 80: "Here, as everywhere, I must decline every misunderstood conclusion, as if, for instance, the true task should now be to abstract from the sexual, i.e., in an outward sense to annihilate it."

32 *SKS* 9, 63 / *WL*, 69.

33 For an analysis of the importance of this concept in Haufniensis' theory of sexuality, see Pablo Uriel Rodríguez, "El concepto de pudor en Kierkegaard: análisis de la determinación sexual en *El concepto de angustia*," *Universitas Philosophica*, vol. 72, no. 36, 2019, pp. 251–277.

34 *SKS* 4, 373 / *CA*, 69.

extreme of the synthesis, then implies an imbalance or disorganization of the latter, which causes anxiety:

> When the sexual is once posited as the extreme point of the synthesis, all abstraction is of no avail. The task, of course, is to bring it under the qualification of the spirit (here lie all the moral problems of the erotic). The realization of this is the victory of love in a person in whom the spirit is so victorious that the sexual is forgotten, and recollected only in forgetfulness. When this has come about, sensuousness is transfigured in spirit and anxiety is driven out.[35]

The happy Greek mentality, being ignorant of sin, does not assume the task of transfiguring sexuality into love and finds its maximum expression in the concept of "beauty," which, from the Christian point of view, is nothing other than an "aesthetic expression" of the erotic. This explains why the anxiety of eroticism can only be eradicated through education in love. However, the love that brings anxiety under control is not of an aesthetic nature, and this allows us to establish a relationship between *The Concept of Anxiety* and *Works of Love*. Love out of duty is the only love that would allow the anxiety of eroticism to be neutralized by forgetting the sexual, which the presence of spiritual love would make possible. The neighbor, as an "other" that supposes a spiritual determination and not only as another determined emotionally and sensitively, would leave the sexual impulse between the genders in the background.

3 The Freudian Conception of Sexuality

The outlines of what we could call a "Freudian theory of sexuality" were established only at the beginning of the 20th century in "Three Essays on the Theory of Sexuality" (1905) and "Instincts and their Vicissitudes" (1916). At the end of the 19th century, Freud was going through a stage of transition from medical knowledge, especially physiological knowledge, to the discovery of psychoanalysis. At this stage, sexuality already played a decisive role in his understanding of neurotic phenomena since Freud not only posited causal links between sexuality and neurosis, but also sought to give them scientific support. However, sexuality was still conceived in "material terms," as it generally refers to disorders arising from sexual practice itself. Later there would be a transition to what we can call a kind of "symbolism of sexuality." This transition from

35 *SKS* 4, 383 / *CA*, 80.

materialism to the symbolism of sexuality implies a gradual distancing from medicine, which is evident in the introduction of the Oedipus and castration complexes into the explanatory framework of the sexual phenomenon,[36] and at the same time the development of the link between sexuality and eroticism, the latter being understood through the logic of "desire."

In "The Sexual Life of Human Beings," Freud seeks to define "the sexual" by expanding the concept beyond the limits of "reproduction," showing the relationship between perversion and normal sexual life, while also extending the terrain of human sexual life to childhood, showing the link between perversion and childhood sexuality. If one falls into the error of reducing sexuality to reproduction, then one fails to understand the relationship between sexuality, perversions, and neuroses. In other words, it would not be possible to elucidate the meaning of the human sexual phenomenon, and the nature of human sexuality would remain unknown. According to Freud himself, the two novelties that he posits in his "sexual theory" are the following: (1) the perverse inclinations of normal sexual life, and (2) the existence of an "infantile sexuality," in which "perversion"—which survives in adult sexual life—originates.[37]

There is an implicit debate between historians and psychoanalysts over the reception of Freud's work. While the former (Delgado and Foucault) tend to point out the continuity between Freud's ideas and issues that were already being raised in psychiatry and sexology at the time, the latter (Assoun, Rudinesco, and Davidson) emphasize the rupture that the Viennese thinker introduces in sexual science. The distinction between instinct and drive plays a significant role in this dispute. For the defenders of continuity, the understanding of human sexuality on the basis of the vicissitudes of the instincts became possible due to changes in conceptualization within psychiatry, particularly when the mental patient was no longer conceived in terms of alienation but rather from the perspective of abnormality. The shift from the paradigm of alienation to that of anomaly implied the liberation of patients from confinement and isolation in order to turn the anomaly into a social problem based, so to speak, on the "deviation" of drives, which all human beings experience in some way, and not only those who suffer from a mental illness.

---

36 Freud worked on both the Oedipus complex and the castration complex in the first decade of the 20th century. Although the Oedipal theme appears in the context of Freud's self-analysis, after the death of his father, the term "Oedipus complex" was introduced in 1910 in "A Special Type of Object Choice Made by Men." See Sigmund Freud, "Contributions to the Psychology of Love," in *The Standard Edition of the Complete Works of Sigmund Freud*, vols. 1–24, trans. from the German under the General Editorship of James Strachey, in Collaboration with Anna Freud, assisted by Alix Starchey and Alan Tyson, London: The Hogarth Press 1953–74, vol. 11 (1957). (This edition is hereafter abbreviated as *SE*.)

37 See *SE*, vol. 16, pp. 303–319.

In turn, this paradigm shift from alienation to abnormality later produced effects in terms of the extension of the abnormal to the realm of "normality." Freud plays a central role in this second movement. In this context, Delgado points out the "paradoxical" situation of the theory of the drives, which, although it allows us to distinguish the fixed and inherited character of the animal instinct from the non-univocal and dynamic direction of the drive, proposes at the same time a certain "normativity." For Delgado, when it considered human psychosexual development from the perspective of the journey through different phases (oral, anal, phallic, latency, genital), Freudianism would fall, in spite of itself, into a normative model.[38]

In "A Reply to Criticisms of my Paper on Anxiety Neurosis" (1895) we find Freud's own point of view on the dispute between psychoanalysts and historians over the revolutionary character of his thesis regarding sexuality:

> I know very well that in putting forward my "sexual aetiology" of the neuroses, I have brought up nothing new, and that undercurrents in medical literature taking these facts into account have never been absent. I know, too, that official academic medicine has also been aware of them. But it has acted as if it knew nothing of the matter. It has made no use of its knowledge and it has drawn no inferences from it.[39]

Although Freud acknowledges not having discovered "the etiology of neuroses," which the medicine of his time was aware of, by highlighting its importance he reveals the gesture of concealment made by official medicine, which made no effort to draw any consequences from this fact. Freud's denunciation makes clear his revolutionary position, even when the subject dealt with had been previously considered, since it had been set forth in a way that actually conceals the phenomenon.

Confronted with French neurology—particularly with Charcot, as can be deduced from "Heredity and Aetiology of the Neuroses" (1896)—and with German psychiatry—as evidenced in the answers to Löwenfeld's objections that appeared in "A Reply to Criticisms of my Paper on Anxiety Neurosis" (1895)—Freud discusses the inherited nature of nervous diseases. Although he accepts the idea that heredity is the "condition" of the neuroses, Freud emphasizes

38 For a discussion of the disruptive character of the Freudian conception in relation to sexological discourse, see Rigoberto Hernández Delgado, "El instinto y la pulsión sexual. El lugar del psicoanálisis freudiano en la historia de la sexualidad," *Teoría y Crítica de la Psicología*, vol. 8, 2016, pp. 33–71.

39 *SE*, vol. 3, p.124.

sexual life as the specific etiological cause of the latter. This emphasis provoked Löwenfeld's reaction and Freud's consequent response, which is based on the distinction between the conditions, concurrent causes and "specific cases" of neuroses: "There has been too little research into these specific and determining causes of nervous disorders, since the attention of physicians has remained dazzled by the grandiose prospect of the etiological precondition of heredity."[40]

4 Anxiety as a Key to Neurosis in Freud's Early Writings (1892–1897)

Freud's early texts introduce psychological discussions conditioned by a neurological approach.[41] As the branch of medicine that deals with the anatomy, physiology, and diseases of the nervous system, neurology was the point of departure for the psychology of neurosis, originally focusing on the multiple functions of the nervous system. The hypothesis that places sexual life at the center of the etiology of neuroses will be of great significance for the progressive, properly "psychoanalytic," approach to "neuroses," previously conceived exclusively as "nervous diseases," that is, as pathologies of the nervous system, since it makes possible the passage from the analysis of the "nervous system" to the analysis of the "psychism." Although Freud takes neurological problems as a starting point, the need to introduce a new field of analysis—the psychological—appears, however, so as to account for phenomena of a "border-like" nature between the physical and the psychic. While in the "borderline" period,[42]

40 *SE*, vol. 3, p. 145.

41 In "An Autobiographical Study," distinguishing current neuroses as a direct toxic expression and psychoneuroses as a psychic expression of disturbances of sexual function, Freud maintains: "My medical conscience felt pleased at having arrived at this conclusion. I hoped that I had filled up a gap in medical science, which, in dealing with a function of such biological importance, had failed to take into account any other injuries beyond those caused by infection or by gross anatomical injury. The medical aspect of the matter was, moreover, supported by the fact that sexuality was not something purely mental. It had its somatic side as well, and it was possible to ascribe specific chemical processes to it and to attribute sexual excitement to the presence of some particular, though at present unknown, substances." *SE*, vol. 20, p. 25.

42 We call the "borderline period" the one that encompasses the writings produced between 1892 and 1897. At this time, Freud discussed sexual issues on the border between the psychic and the organic, without having yet introduced "the unconscious." Furthermore, he seems to think that the libido is a phenomenon of a psychic nature, without clearly defining whether it reduces the psyche to consciousness, as he would later criticize philosophical thought of doing. According to Strachey, "'libido' is regarded in these early writings

Freud emphasizes the link between anxiety and sexuality,[43] years later he will emphasize the relationship between anxiety and castration, as can be seen in "Inhibition, Symptom and Anxiety."[44]

Freud deals with anxiety very early on. The first appearance of the theme is framed in the context of an analysis of the link between physical and mental factors in the triggering of this "affect." The perspective is physiological, and what it tries to do is differentiate neurasthenia from "anxiety neurosis." With respect to this first appearance of the subject, it is important to bear in mind certain issues: (1) from the beginning he suggests a relationship between anxiety and sexuality in the etiology of neuroses (anxiety appears as a result of poor psychic "treatment" of somatic sexual tension); (2) sexuality is not conceived in "representative or symbolic" terms (explanations based on the Oedipus complex or the castration complex are not yet in play), but rather "material" terms since the analysis of sexuality focuses on intercourse and what causes anxiety has to do with the impossibility of practicing it fully.

By considering sexuality as the "etiology of the neuroses," Freud presents an intimate relationship between anxiety neuroses and sexuality, based on the link between the psychic and the somatic, since anxiety results from the lack of psychic processing of sexual tension or excitement, in a context in which the notion of "drive" itself had not yet appeared in Freudian terminology. The relationship between anxiety and sexuality occupies a prominent place in Freud's early writings. Even before formulating an outline of a sexual theory, he has already set out the close link between the two: "This sexual aetiology of the anxiety neurosis can be demonstrated with such overwhelming frequency that I venture, *for the purpose of this short paper*, to disregard those cases where the aetiology is doubtful or different."[45]

Within the framework of the aetiology of the neuroses, a distinction appears between the current neuroses (neurasthenia and anxiety neurosis) and the psychoneuroses (hysteria and obsessional neurosis). Although all the neuroses ultimately seem to have, as a determinant, a cause of sexual origin, neurasthenia and anxiety neurosis are differentiated by the fact of having a "temporary" nature. While current neuroses are due to disturbances in current sexual life,

as essentially 'psychical,' though it is not yet clear whether that still means the same as 'conscious.'" *SE*, vol. 1, p. 193.

43 For an analysis of the separation of anxiety and sexuality in post-Freudian psychoanalysis, see Héctor Garbarino et al., "Las diferentes concepciones psicoanalíticas sobre la angustia," *Revista uruguaya de Psicoanálisis* (online), vol. 114, 2012, pp. 15–26.

44 *SE*, vol. 20, pp. 71–175.

45 *SE*, vol. 3, p. 99.

psychoneuroses are caused by issues related to past sexual life, originating in childhood:

> By laying stress on the supposed aetiological factors, it was possible at that time, to draw a contrast between the common neuroses as disorders with a *contemporary* aetiology and the psychoneuroses whose aetiology was chiefly to be looked for in the sexual experiences of the remote past.[46]

In this period, Freud distinguishes physical sexuality from psychic sexuality and links the issue of sexuality to the customs of the time—as evidenced by the cases he describes—and to the difficulties bourgeois society encounters in achieving a pleasurable sexual practice, due fundamentally to the cumbersome methods required to prevent conception. "Anxiety" is thus manifested when the free expression of sexuality is hindered. Within this framework, Freud highlights the importance that the full development of sexuality has for psychic life, even though he has not yet unfolded the fundamental principles of psychoanalysis.

The years 1894 and 1895 are particularly relevant for the analysis of the relationship between anxiety and sexuality, since during those years Freud proposes, on the one hand, to consider the symptomatology of anxiety in an autonomous way with respect to neurasthenia; that is, he identifies anxiety as a specific symptom of a type of neurosis caused by the impossibility of processing coitus normally. And, on the other hand, in this period he places sexuality at the base of what for the moment he calls "the aetiological equation,"[47] when referring to the different classes of causes that contribute to the genesis of the neurosis.

For our purposes, the analysis of "Draft E" and of "On the Grounds for Detaching a Particular Syndrome from Neurasthenia under the Description 'Anxiety Neurosis'" (1895 [1894]) is fundamental. In "Draft E," of uncertain date, but probably written in June 1894, not only is the problem of the "genesis" of anxiety formulated for the first time, but in addition the immediate link between anxiety and sexuality is introduced so as to account for neurosis. At the same time, the importance of anxiety is underlined in the work of 1895: "I call this syndrome 'anxiety neurosis,' because all its components can be grouped around the chief symptom of anxiety; because each one of them has a definite relationship to anxiety."[48] In turn, in "Draft E," he insists on the

46 SE, vol. 3, pp. 273–274.
47 SE, vol. 3, p. 136.
48 SE, vol. 3, p. 91.

relationship between anxiety and sexuality.[49] He explains, "It quickly became clear to me that the anxiety of my neurotic patients had a great deal to do with sexuality; and in particular it struck me with what certainty *coitus interruptus* practiced on a woman leads to anxiety neurosis."[50] As we can see, the link between anxiety and sexuality is expressed from the beginning in relation to neurosis. *Coitus interruptus* is identified as a cause of anxiety,[51] and its origin is distinguished in women from its origin in men; in women it is based on the fear of pregnancy, and in men, on the fear that their contraceptive "artifice" will fail. Although at first Freud conceived of anxiety as "the heir of what is felt in the sexual act,"[52] and understood it as a "hysterical symptom,"[53] on confirming that in many cases the "anxiety neurosis" appeared without the mediation of any concern about pregnancy, he concluded that this neurosis could not be identified with hysterical anxiety or be remembered and continued.

In this period, the origin of anxiety is found in the lack of psychic processing of physical tension:

> Where there is an abundant development of physical sexual tension but this cannot be turned into affect by psychical working-over because of insufficient development of psychical sexuality or because of the attempted suppression of the latter (defense), or of its falling into decay, or because of habitual alienation between physical and psychical sexuality—the sexual tension is transformed into *anxiety*. Thus a part is played in this by the accumulation of physical tension and the prevention of discharge in the psychical direction.[54]

49 *SE*, vol. 1, p. 91.

50 *SE*, vol. 1, pp. 189–190.

51 The specific causes of anxiety neurosis are voluntary withdrawal, frustrated excitement, and *coitus interruptus*. Although at first Freud believed that anxiety in the practice of *coitus interruptus* was caused by the fear of pregnancy, he later found that it was not due to this, but rather to sexual dissatisfaction. That is why he clarifies that if in this practice the man waits for the woman's satisfaction, it becomes normal intercourse for her, but the man is the one who becomes sick with anxiety, because looking after the woman's satisfaction, he voluntarily directs intercourse, postponing ejaculation. The problem then does not lie in the practice of *coitus interruptus* itself, but in the frustration that it generates, depending on the case, in the woman or the man. It is the frustration caused by sexual dissatisfaction that generates anxiety.

52 *SE*, vol. 1, p. 190.

53 *SE*, vol. 1, p. 190.

54 *SE*, vol. 1, p. 194.

For his part, observing that anxiety afflicted both anesthetic women and sensitive women in normal intercourse, he deduces that the source of anxiety is to be looked for not in a psychic but in a physical factor of sexual life. This factor that allowed unity to be given to all the observed cases turned out to be abstinence. Anxiety is defined as the accumulation of sexual tension as a result of a blocked discharge, and then turns out to be a "neurosis of damming-up,"[55] just like hysteria. Since anxiety is not contained in what is stagnant, it arises from a "modification" of somatic sexual tension. Why does the accumulation of sexual tension change into anxiety? To answer this question, Freud needs to consider the normal mechanism of the processing of accumulated tension, that of "endogenous excitation."[56] In exogenous excitation, the increase is simpler, since the excitatory source is external, and it sends to the psyche an increase of excitation that is processed in accordance with its quantity. For that purpose, any reaction that reduces psychic excitation by the same quantum is sufficient. With endogenous tension, the source of which is located in the body itself (hunger, thirst, sexual drive), the same does not happen. Here only the "specific reactions" prevent further excitement, which becomes evident once a certain "threshold" is reached.[57] Freud explains,

> Thus physical sexual tension above a certain value arouses psychical libido, which then leads to *coitus*, etc. If the specific reaction fails to ensue, the physic-psychical tension (the sexual affect)[58] increases immeasurably. It becomes a disturbance, but there is still no ground for its transformation.[59]

However, in anxiety neurosis this change occurs, which would be explained by the following derailment. When sexual tension grows and reaches the threshold value with which it could awaken a psychic affection, which is not awakened due to the lack of psychic conditions, "the physical tension, not being psychically bound, is transformed into anxiety."[60] In anxiety neurosis, dyspnea

55 SE, vol. 1, p. 191.

56 SE, vol. 1, p. 192.

57 "It is only above this threshold that it is turned to account (*verwerten*) *psychically*, that it enters into relation with certain groups of ideas which thereupon set about producing the specific remedies." SE, vol. 1, p. 192.

58 Sexual affection is presented in Letter 18, dated Vienna, May 21, 1894, as "an excitation of definite quantity." SE, vol. 1, p. 189.

59 SE, vol. 1, pp. 192–193.

60 SE, vol. 1, p. 193.

and palpitations of *coitus* are observed, but in this case they are the only outlets of excitement, while in intercourse they are used as collateral discharges:

> Anxiety is the sensation of the accumulation of another endogenous stimulus, the stimulus to breathing, a stimulus which is incapable of being worked over psychically apart from this; anxiety might therefore be employed for accumulated physical tension in general.... There is a kind of *conversion* in anxiety neurosis just as there is in hysteria (another instance of their similarity); but in hysteria it is *psychical* excitation that takes a wrong path exclusively into the somatic field, whereas here it is a *physical* tension, which cannot enter the psychical field and therefore remains on the physical path.[61]

In the vocabulary used by Freud in these years (1894–1895) to account for the fact that anxiety arises from the poor psychic processing of a somatic sexual tension, the notion of drive—as a limit between the organic and the psychic—does not yet appear, nor does the distinction, which will be so important later, between ego libido and object libido.[62] The definitions of the anxiety neurosis that Freud elaborates are the following: in "A Reply to Criticisms of my Paper on Anxiety Neurosis," he maintains that, "anxiety neurosis is created by everything which keeps somatic sexual tension away from the psychical sphere, which interferes with its being worked over psychically."[63] In "On the Grounds for Detaching a Particular Syndrome from Neurasthenia under the Description 'Anxiety Neurosis'" (1895 [1894]) he states that "*the mechanism of anxiety neurosis is to be looked for in a deflection of somatic sexual excitation from the psychical sphere, and in a consequent abnormal employment of that excitation.*"[64] In the summary of this work, it is defined as "the deflection of somatic sexual excitation from the psychical field and a consequent abnormal employment

61 SE, vol. 1, pp. 194–195.

62 "On Narcissism: An Introduction" (1914) is the key work on the distinction between ego libido and object libido. According to Strachey (SE, vol. 14, p. 70), "this is one of Freud's most important works," since in it he not only summarizes his previous elucidations on the subject of narcissism, but also examines its place in sexual development. We believe that the separation of the sexual drives from the ego reflects the dual function of the individual, that is, the fact of being, as Kierkegaard pointed out in *The Concept of Anxiety*, under the identity of Haufniensis, "himself and the species." In a similar way, Freud maintains "the individual does actually carry on a twofold existence: one to serve his own purposes and another as a link in a chain, which he serves against his will, or at least involuntarily." SE, vol. 4, p. 78.

63 SE, vol. 3, p. 125.

64 SE, vol. 3, p. 108.

of that excitation. *Neurotic anxiety is transformed in sexual libido*."[65] Lastly, in "Draft G" (1895),[66] he maintains that the condition of anxiety is found in the diverse use of somatic sexual arousal on the border between the somatic and the psychic.

In these years, Freud uses the notions of "discharge," "somatic sexual tension," "sexual arousal," and "endogenous stimulus." That is, he makes use of a materialist vocabulary typical of the natural sciences. This should not surprise us if we remember that during 1895 Freud was busy formulating a *Psychology Project* "for neurologists."[67] Neurology, physiology, biology, and medicine were all part of the concerns that organized the Freudian "psychological" discourse at the end of the 19th century. They focused on the relationship between the somatic and the psychic rather than on the intervention of consciousness or, later, of the unconscious in the understanding of human sexuality. It is precisely the treatment of anxiety as the emergence of a conflictive relationship between the somatic and the psychic that will lead him to abandon psychology to the neurologists and to analyze the influence of unconscious processes in the explanation of phenomena of a sexual nature.[68]

In "A Reply to Criticisms of my Paper on Anxiety Neurosis," Freud makes a detailed analysis of what he calls the "aetiological equation," that is, the relationships between the different classes of causes involved in the genesis of anxiety neuroses:

> The factors which may be described as *preconditions* are those in whose absence the effect would never come about, but which are incapable of producing the effect by themselves alone, no matter in what amount they may be present. For the specific cause is still lacking. The *specific cause* is the one which is never missing in any case in which the effect takes place, and which moreover suffices, if present in the required quantity or intensity, to achieve the effect, provided only that the preconditions are also

65 SE, vol. 3, p. 251.

66 SE, vol. 1, p. 203.

67 SE, vol. 1, pp. 281–397.

68 Unlike Stewart, who considers that the first concept of anxiety introduced by Freud was a "mistake" corrected thirty years later, and regardless of the discussions of the existence of one or more theories of anxiety in Freud, we believe that the first appearance of the concept is not the product of an error, but of a border theorization between the neurological and psychological fields. The "psychology of neurosis" is the previous step to the discovery of the psychoanalytic field itself. Hence the importance of the texts of this time for a full understanding of Freud's contributions. See Walter A. Stewart, *Psychoanalysis: The First Ten Years 1888–1898*, London and New York: Routledge 1969, p. 43.

> fulfilled. As *concurrent causes* we may regard such factors as are not necessarily present every time, nor able, whatever their amount, to produce the effect by themselves alone, but which operate alongside of the preconditions and the specific cause in satisfying the aetiologial equation.[69]

In the case of neuroses, heredity tends to be the condition; the specific cause is given by sexual factors; everything else, overwork, emotions, physical illness, is only an auxiliary cause. The aetiological problem supposes "a *number* of aetiological factors" that support each other.[70] It is not necessary to look for the etiology of the neuroses exclusively in heredity or constitution since this would imply a relapse into unilaterality.[71] In turn, the fulfillment of the aetiological equation, that is, the contraction of a neurotic affection, depends on a quantitative factor, the total ballast of the nervous system in proportion to its capacity of resistance. Anything that helps keep this factor below a certain threshold has therapeutic efficacy. The full extent of the neurosis depends, first of all, on the hereditary ballast since heredity acts as an interpolated "multiplier" in the current circuit, which in the multiple increases the deviation of the needle: "but what *form* the neurosis assumes—what direction the deviation takes—is solely determined by the specific aetiological factor arising from sexual life."[72]

Both the "current neuroses" (neurasthenia and anxiety neuroses) and the "psychoneuroses" (hysteria and obsessive neurosis) have their origin in sexual life. Now, while Freud finds the specific causes of neurasthenia in masturbation and spontaneous ejaculation, he finds the causes of anxiety neurosis in forced abstinence, frustrated genital irritation, which is not fulfilled by the sexual act, and in *coitus interruptus*, which does not culminate in satisfaction. Those sexual efforts that exceed the psychic capacity of the subject "disturb the equilibrium of the psychical and somatic functions in sexual acts, and … they prevent the psychical participation necessary in order to free the nervous economy from sexual tension."[73]

In anxiety neurosis we find a lack of harmony, a kind of inadequacy or disorganization between the somatic and psychic libido. When somatic arousal fails to achieve a normal development that converts it into affect, as a consequence of this mismatch, anxiety occurs. If sexual tension had become affect or sexual desire (psychic libido), anxiety would not occur since it appears as

---

69 *SE*, vol. 3, p. 136.
70 *SE*, vol. 3, p. 138.
71 *SE*, vol. 7, p. 279.
72 *SE*, vol. 3, p. 139.
73 *SE*, vol. 3, p. 151.

a manifestation of the lack of normal development of somatic sexual tension. If there is anxiety, it is because the sexual tension failed to turn into pleasure:

> The psyche finds itself in the *affect* of anxiety if it feels unable to deal by the appropriate reaction with a task (a danger) *approaching from the outside*; it finds itself in the *neurosis* of anxiety if it notices that it is unable to even out the (sexual) excitation originating *from within*....[74]

What we are interested in emphasizing in anxiety neurosis is precisely the relationship between the somatic and the psychic. It is the lack of harmony or disorganization between these two areas or spheres, between these terms of synthesis, according to Haufniensis, which causes anxiety. Unlike neurasthenia, the specific cause of the anxiety neurosis is, then, the accumulation of somatic excitation that does not become affect, that is, the imbalance that causes the frustration of the adequate relationship between the psychic and the somatic since only specific or adequate action produces psychic relief from sexual tension. And at this point there is a coincidence in the treatment of anxiety as a "symptom," because both for Kierkegaard and for Freud, anxiety is a symptom of the imbalance in the synthesis of the somatic and the psychic, which is what defines what is properly human.

This question becomes the subject both of Haufniensis' psychology of spirit and of Freud's psychology of neurosis. That is why it can be said that at the origin of *Neurosenpsychologie* lies the discovery of Haufniensis, namely, the concept of anxiety. This concept has made it possible to grant autonomy to the subjective spirit, placing psychology in a prominent place among the sciences that deal with man. In any case, both for Kierkegaard and for Freud, anxiety is the concept that enables the epistemological development of the "new science."

5 Final Considerations

Despite the apparent confrontation that may at first glance appear between the spiritualist psychology of Haufniensis and the *Neurosenpsychologie* of Freud, particularly considering that the starting point of the former is dogmatics,

---

74 *SE*, vol. 3, p. 112. In the first Lecture dedicated to the subject of anxiety (Lecture 25, 1916), Freud will return to the question of danger to define "real anxiety." Real anxiety is presented as a reaction to a danger that comes from outside, while "neurotic anxiety" has no visible foundation in an external danger. See *SE*, vol. 16, pp. 391–411.

while that of the latter is medicine, a more detailed analysis leads us to think of each proposal in terms of what they have in common.

In this sense, many of the issues raised by the pseudonymous author of *The Concept of Anxiety*, who in the introduction to the work gives an account of the emergence of a "new science,"[75] psychology, are taken up and deepened by Freud. One of the aspects in which both proposals coincide has to do with the expansion of the concept of "sexuality," which arises from the fact that human sexuality is not reduced to its biological "reproductive" function. Both Kierkegaard and Freud deal with the theme of sexuality in the context of "the discourse of love."[76] While for Kierkegaard this discourse implies the determination of a principle of spiritual order, for Freud it refers primarily to the register of pleasure.[77] They also agree in establishing the understanding of human psychology in the context of the relationship between the individual and the species, with Freud posing it in terms of ontogenesis and phylogenesis, and Haufniensis in terms of the relationship between the self and the species, even though Kierkegaard completely dismisses evolutionism, while Freud reserves a certain esteem for it.[78]

Although both psychologies understand the human being in psychophysical terms, spiritualist psychology, assuming sin as a starting point, finds a spiritual resolution of the synthesis between the somatic and the psychic, while the evolution of the theory of neurosis concludes by offering an explanation based on the discharge of the drive. In turn, in both authors the issue of sexuality is approached by disputing the explanatory field of biological reductionism. In the case of Kierkegaard, this involves rejecting the theories that support the idea that man is born guilty since sin is inherited by nature. And in

75 *SKS* 4, 328 / *CA*, 24.

76 I suggest that both authors consider sexuality in the context of what Barthes calls "the discourse of love." See Roland Barthes, *Fragments d'un discours amoreux*, Paris: Seuil 1977, p. 10.

77 The theme of the impact of the pleasure/displeasure duo in the understanding of the drive phenomenon is developed in Freud's thought until it reaches the postulation of the "pleasure principle." In any case, under Freud's pen, sexuality enters the field of "the discourse of love," which complicates its primitive "biological" determination, and implies a successive series of reconsiderations of the physical or psychic sense of the drive.

78 In this context, it should be noted that the continuity between the issues raised by spiritualist psychology and the psychology of neurosis is interrupted by the Darwinian hypotheses, some aspects of which Freud makes his own. Assoun, *El freudismo*, p. 89: "Even more precisely, the idea of a phylogenetic dimension (at the level of the 'species'), correlative to ontogenetic development (at the level of the individual)—an idea specified by embryology, following in the footsteps of Darwin, through his German disciple Ernst Haeckel (1834–1919)—played an essential role in Freudian thinking."

the case of Freud, it means confronting psychoanalysis with the explanations of sexology.[79] Both agree in reducing the explanation of human sexuality to biological naturalism.

Nevertheless, Kierkegaard emphatically rejects any evolutionary assumption, because if man had been an animal at some point in his development, he could never become a man. In Freud's case, however, evolutionary premises are incorporated into the description of human psychosexual development.[80] At this point, it is important to note the evolution of the concept of sexuality in Freud's work. Towards the end of the 19th century, in "Draft E," a difference between hysteria and anxiety is established. While the former has a psychic origin that produces physical symptoms, the anxiety neurosis has a physical origin that causes a psychic effect. The idea of "psychic libido" appears there, and it is argued that anxiety arises from the impossibility of psychically processing the physically originating sexual affection. At this time, a sexual theory proper had not yet been formulated; such a theory only begins to be outlined in the *Three Essays on the Theory of Sexuality* (1905).[81] In its formulation, the notion of drive as a limit between the organic and the psychic will be of the greatest relevance. In the psychology of Haufniensis, a mediation between the organic and the psychic is also sought, but it is of a spiritual nature. The spiritual sense of sexuality will be displaced by its instinctual sense. But in both explanatory structures the rupture or human transcendence of the "immediate" world of nature prevails. However, while in Freud elements of an evolutionary nature are incorporated into the analysis, for Kierkegaard, the idea that at some point in his history man can be identified with the animal cannot be defended. Man is neither mere animal nature nor pure angelic spirit, but "imperfect spirit."[82]

Despite their disagreement over the evolutionary hypotheses, we observe a line of thematic continuity between the psychology of spirit introduced by Kierkegaard in *The Concept of Anxiety* and the origins of *Neurosenpsychologie*.

---

79 Assoun, *El freudismo*, p. 27: "The science of the sexual reality is, then, an objection to and obstruction of the sexological imaginary: this is the meaning of 'Freudism' in the clinical and therapeutic field to the point where it becomes the ethics of the analytic act. This opens the way to a Freudian teaching." Ibid., p. 95: "In fact, sexology adheres to a general theory of sexuation that serves as a framework and on the basis of which the 'anomalies' are established.... In addition, psychology remains deeply linked to a genital conception of sexuality and cannot approve or assimilate the 'extension' of the concept of sexuality that Freudianism makes."

80 Freud's bold hypotheses caused psychoanalysis to be accused of pansexualism. In relation to this accusation, Assoun replies: "psychosexuality" makes us lose the biological and social evidence of the sexual, rather than "putting sex everywhere." Ibid., p. 20.

81 *SE*, vol. 7, pp. 123–245.

82 *SKS* 4, 354 / *CA*, 49.

We consider the concept of "anxiety" as the link that makes it possible to propose this line of thematic continuity between both psychologies. This is based on the common epistemological understanding of the border function of the concept of anxiety. It is this concept, as a limit between ethics and dogmatics, which allows Haufniensis to introduce psychology as a "new science." In turn, it is also this concept although it has taken on a new meaning[83]—that allows Freud, in his "borderline" period, to pose the aetiology of neuroses on the border between the neurological field and the psychological field, and to then advance to the introduction of the novel psychoanalytic field. In sum, anxiety appears in both authors as a demarcation line of an embryonic knowledge linked to the importance of the psychological field for the understanding of the phenomena of human nature.

Bibliography

Assoun, Paul L., *El freudismo*, trans. by Tatiana Sule Fernández, Buenos Aires and Mexico City: Siglo XXI editores 2003.

Barthes, Roland, *Fragments d'un discours amoreux*, Paris: Seuil 1977.

Delgado, Rigoberto Hernández, "El instinto y la pulsión sexual. El lugar del psicoanálisis freudiano en la historia de la sexualidad," *Teoría y Crítica de la Psicología*, vol. 8, 2016, pp. 33–71.

Dip, Patricia, "De Kierkegaard a Lacan: el surgimiento de la angustia en *Temor y temblor*," *Estudios kierkegaardianos. Revista de Filosofía*, vol. 7, 2021, pp. 91–120.

Freud, Sigmund, "Extracts from the Fliess Papers" (1950 [1892–99]), "Project for a Scientific Psychology" (1950 [1895]), in *The Standard Edition of the Complete Works of Sigmund Freud*, vols. 1–24, trans. from the German under the General Editorship of James Strachey, in Collaboration with Anna Freud, assisted by Alix Starchey and Alan Tyson, London: The Hogarth Press 1953–1974, vol. 1 (1953), pp. 175–280, pp. 281–397.

Freud, Sigmund, "On the Grounds for Detaching a Particular Syndrome from Neurasthenia under the Description 'Anxiety Neurosis'" (1895 [1894]), "A Reply to Criticisms of my Paper on Anxiety Neurosis" (1895), "Heredity and Aetiology of the Neuroses" (1896), "The Aetiology of Hysteria" (1896), "Abstracts of the Scientific Writings of Dr. Sigm. Freud, 1877–1897" (1897), "Sexuality in the Aetiology of the Neuroses" (1898), in *The Standard Edition of the Complete Works of Sigmund*

83 In any case, what produces anxiety, even if it is defined in another way, is the same as in Haufniensis, namely, the disharmony in the body-soul synthesis, the lack of harmony between the somatic and the psychic.

Freud, vols. 1–24, trans. from the German under the General Editorship of James Strachey, in Collaboration with Anna Freud, assisted by Alix Starchey and Alan Tyson, London: The Hogarth Press 1953–1974, vol. 3 (1962), pp. 87–117, pp. 118–139, pp. 140–156, pp. 180–221, pp. 222–257.

Freud, Sigmund, "Three Essays on the Theory of Sexuality" (1905), "My Views on the Part Played by Sexuality in the Aetiology of the Neuroses" (1906 [1905)]), in *The Standard Edition of the Complete Works of Sigmund Freud*, vols. 1–24, trans. from the German under the General Editorship of James Strachey, in Collaboration with Anna Freud, assisted by Alix Starchey and Alan Tyson, London: The Hogarth Press 1953–1974, vol. 7 (1953), pp. 123–245, pp. 268–279.

Freud, Sigmund, "Civilized Sexual Morality and Modern Nervous Illness" (1908), in *The Standard Edition of the Complete Works of Sigmund Freud*, vols. 1–24, trans. from the German under the General Editorship of James Strachey, in Collaboration with Anna Freud, assisted by Alix Starchey and Alan Tyson, London: The Hogarth Press 1953–1974, vol. 9 (1957), pp. 177–204.

Freud, Sigmund, "A Special Type of Choice of Object made by Men" (Contributions to the Psychology of Love, I) (1910), in *The Standard Edition of the Complete Works of Sigmund Freud*, vols. 1–24, trans. from the German under the General Editorship of James Strachey, in Collaboration with Anna Freud, assisted by Alix Starchey and Alan Tyson, London: The Hogarth Press 1953–1974, vol. 11 (1957), pp. 163–175.

Freud, Sigmund, "On Narcissism: An Introduction" (1914), "Instincts and their Vicissitudes" (1915), in *The Standard Edition of the Complete Works of Sigmund Freud*, vols. 1–24, trans. from the German under the General Editorship of James Strachey, in Collaboration with Anna Freud, assisted by Alix Starchey and Alan Tyson, London: The Hogarth Press 1953–1974, vol. 14 (1957), pp. 67–102, pp. 108–140.

Freud, Sigmund, "Introductory Lectures on Psychoanalysis" (1916–1917), "Lecture XX: The Sexual Life of Human Beings," "Lecture XXV: Anxiety," in *The Standard Edition of the Complete Works of Sigmund Freud*, vols. 1–24, trans. from the German under the General Editorship of James Strachey, in Collaboration with Anna Freud, assisted by Alix Starchey and Alan Tyson, London: The Hogarth Press 1953–1974, vol. 16 (1963), pp. 303–319, pp. 391–411.

Freud, Sigmund, "Beyond the Pleasure Principle" (1920), "Two Encyclopaedia Articles: "Psychoanalysis," and "The Libido Theory" (1923 [1922]), in *The Standard Edition of the Complete Works of Sigmund Freud*, vols. 1–24, trans. from the German under the General Editorship of James Strachey, in Collaboration with Anna Freud, assisted by Alix Starchey and Alan Tyson, London: The Hogarth Press 1953–1974, vol. 18 (1955), pp. 1–64, pp. 233–259.

Freud, Sigmund, "An Autobiographical Study" (1925 [1924]), "Inhibitions, Symptoms and Anxiety" (1926), in *The Standard Edition of the Complete Works of Sigmund Freud*, vols. 1–24, trans. from the German under the General Editorship of James

Strachey, in Collaboration with Anna Freud, assisted by Alix Starchey and Alan Tyson, London: The Hogarth Press 1953–1974, vol. 20 (1959), pp. 1–70, pp. 71–175.

Garbarino, Héctor et al., "Las diferentes concepciones psicoanalíticas sobre la angustia," *Revista uruguaya de Psicoanálisis* (online), vol. 114, 2012, pp. 15–26.

González, Darío, "The Triptych of Sciences in the Introduction to *The Concept of Anxiety*," *Kierkegaard Studies Yearbook*, 2001, pp. 15–42.

[Kierkegaard, Søren], *Søren Kierkegaards Skrifter*, vols. 1–28, K1–K28, ed. by Niels Jørgen Cappelørn, Joakim Garff, Johnny Kondrup, et al., Copenhagen: Gad Publishers 1997–2012.

Kierkegaard, Søren, *The Concept of Anxiety*, trans. by Reidar Thomte in collaboration with Albert B. Anderson, Princeton: Princeton University Press 1980.

Kierkegaard, Søren, *Works of Love*, trans. by Howard V. Hong and Edna H. Hong, Princeton: Princeton University Press 1995.

Kierkegaard, Søren, *The Sickness unto Death*, trans. by Howard V. Hong and Edna H. Hong, Princeton: Princeton University Press 1980.

Rodríguez, Pablo Uriel, "El concepto de pudor en Kierkegaard: análisis de la determinación sexual in *El concepto de angustia*," *Universitas Philosophica*, vol. 72, no. 36, 2019, pp. 251–277.

Stewart, Walter, A., *Psychoanalysis: The First Ten Years 1888–1898*, London and New York: Routledge 1969.

PART 4

Politics and Social Criticism

∵

CHAPTER 10

Morning and Noon Political Observations: Kierkegaard on Liberalism and the Issue of Press Freedom

Nassim Bravo

Abstract

Despite living in one of the most politically turbulent times in European history, the age of revolutions, Kierkegaard, as is well known, showed little interest in politics, both national and international. An exception to this was the debate he engaged in with Johannes Ostermann in late 1835, in which Kierkegaard developed his position regarding contemporary political issues such as the role of the press and the monarchy, the transition to liberalism, the nature of revolutions, etc. In this article, I would like to argue that these political considerations were not disconnected from Kierkegaard's early philosophical reflections, especially with his interest in the existential question on the development of selfhood.

One of the legacies of 19th-century philosophical thought that had the most profound and direct impact not only on Western culture, but on the entire world, was the theories of revolution. The French Revolution of 1789, as well as the dramatic episodes that followed—the execution of Louis XVI, the Terror, the Napoleonic Wars—shook Europe and America not only in a political sense, but also intellectually.

When one thinks of theorists of revolution, it is common to refer to thinkers such as Alexis de Tocqueville, Mikhail Bakunin or Karl Marx. Søren Kierkegaard (1813–1855) is not usually placed in this group. In fact, the Danish writer was reluctant not only to speak specifically about the phenomenon of revolution, but about political issues in general. This reluctance may seem strange in such a prolific author who, moreover, was a contemporary of the revolutions of 1830 and 1848, and witnessed the transformation of Denmark into a constitutional monarchy, a fact that acquires greater historical relevance if one considers that constitutionalism was at that time the object of revolutionary efforts in multiple European nations.

 | DOI:10.1163/9789004689459_012

One of the few works in which Kierkegaard develops a political discussion with some seriousness is his paper "Our Journalistic Literature: A Study from Nature in Noonday Light,"[1] a speech delivered before the Student Union of the University of Copenhagen on November 28, 1835. It is thus an early writing that appeared well before the "official" beginning of the so-called authorship in 1843. The paper was a reply to a speech by another student, the liberal Johannes Ostermann (1809–1888), and so the whole can be regarded as a kind of debate. The subject was the recent restrictive measures that King Frederick VI (1768–1839) had imposed on the freedom of the press, and the discussion took place in a context in which Danish liberal activists, including Ostermann, were beginning to represent a major political force, partly spurred by the excitement of the still recent July Revolution in Paris.

In his paper, Kierkegaard attempts to adopt a historical perspective in order to examine the true achievements of the liberal press in Denmark. He looks at the historical evolution of the liberal journals, the role that the government played during this process, and the impact that the French Revolution of 1830 had on Danish society.

However, after this historical account, Kierkegaard offers a kind of political theory. He argues that in every epoch there must be a balance between what he calls the form and the idea. The point is that each idea possesses a form that is its own. A historical example of this balance is precisely the July Revolution of 1830. Thanks to its historical experience, France—whose social life represents the content of the idea—was ready for a structural transformation, a new form, which manifested itself through the July Revolution. The form, Kierkegaard suggests, must conform to the idea; in other words, the social transformation, the revolution, can only occur successfully when social life is ready for it. For Kierkegaard, the Danish liberals try to force that transformation and insist on imposing a form—that of French revolutionary liberalism—on an idea that does not correspond to it, namely, the social reality of Denmark.

This early work has been largely neglected.[2] It is a little-known text, which would seem to justify the little attention it has received from scholars. It is, after all, a work from 1835, when Kierkegaard was a twenty-two-year-old theological student and still far from making a name for himself as a writer. Moreover, some might argue that it is not worth investing too much effort into this kind of text. For example, Julia Watkin, who translated "Our Journalistic Literature" into English, argues that, while it is true that Kierkegaard conveys a political

1 *SKS* 27, 189–204, Papir 254 / *EPW*, 35–52.

2 A notable exception to this is Teddy Petersen's monograph, *Kierkegaards polemiske debut*, Odense: Odense Universitetsforlag 1977.

position here, the more important purpose of the paper was to demonstrate his ability to polemicize and find the weak points in the speech of his opponent.[3] Although Watkin does not directly say that Kierkegaard's speech lacks serious content, her focus on the polemical aspect of the work may lead the reader to think that he or she will not find deeper insights there.

In this article, however, I would like to argue that the study of Kierkegaard's "Our Journalistic Literature" can offer us useful and interesting information. For example, a careful observation allows us to see that Kierkegaard's political theory, if it is possible to call it that, uses categories and insights taken from Hegel's philosophy. The most notable case of this is the recurrent use of the dialectics between form and idea. This may suggest that the historical-philosophical reading Kierkegaard offers of the July Revolution and the rise of liberalism in Denmark may have similarities with the interpretation of the development of revolutions by thinkers such as Marx, Engels, and Bakunin,[4] who also employ categories from Hegel's philosophy in their own theories. The impact of these thinkers on the political sphere of the twentieth century is undeniable, and while Kierkegaard's influence is not comparable—at least not in the political sense—it is revealing to discover this common thread between such seemingly different authors.

Moreover, I wish to suggest that in this early text one can observe some ideas or intuitions that Kierkegaard had begun to work out in a fragmentary way in earlier writings, such as the famous journal of Gilleleje,[5] and that he would later develop in a deeper and more detailed manner in his mature works. From a very early stage, Kierkegaard rejected the radical subjectivism of the Romantic intellectuals, whom he called "ironists,"[6] and their notion of a world that revolved around the individual human subject. Instead, he suggested that the world is an organic totality of which the human individual is an essential part. For Kierkegaard, the most important thing was to discover and understand what the role of the individual is within that totality. This integral understanding of actuality and its relation to the individual he will call a "life-view" in a later work.[7]

3 See Julia Watkin, "Historical Introduction," in Søren Kierkegaard, *Early Polemical Writings*, ed. and trans. by Julia Watkin, Princeton: Princeton University Press 1990, pp. XVII–XVIII.

4 On the influence of Hegelian philosophy on several European intellectuals, including the ones mentioned above, within the context of the Age of Revolutions, see Jon Stewart, *Hegel's Century: Alienation and Recognition in a Time of Revolution*, Cambridge: Cambridge University Press 2021.

5 See *SKS* 17, 7–30, AA:1–12 / *KJN* 1, 3–25.

6 For Kierkegaard's criticism of Romantic irony, see *SKS* 1, 308–352 / *CI*, 272–323.

7 See, for example, *SKS* 1, 32 / *EPW*, 76–77.

The notion that the individual must choose him- or herself and that this must happen by a reconciliation with actuality is a central and recurring theme in the Kierkegaardian corpus. We can find it in the works of 1843, such as *Either/Or, Fear and Trembling* and *Repetition*, but also in his later writings like *The Sickness unto Death*. In this article, I want to argue that Kierkegaard employs this same approach in his 1835 paper, only applying it to the political and social sphere. Liberals, in this view, cannot arbitrarily impose a new social structure on Denmark; rather, Danish society must find what structure is right for it, find what place it should occupy in actuality.

The article consists of four parts. In the first, I describe the historical context in which the discussion on the freedom of the press in Denmark arose; to understand Kierkegaard's position, it is important to know what the political and social situation was in Denmark, as well as the government's stance regarding the growing influence of the liberal press and politicians. In the second part of the article, I will analyze the main ideas in Johannes Ostermann's paper, which represents in this debate the position of the liberals. In the next section I would like to examine the discussion about the development of selfhood in the so-called journal of Gilleleje, in the months prior to the debate on the freedom of the press. Finally, in the fourth part, I will analyze the political theory that Kierkegaard proposes in his 1835 speech.

1 The Question on the Freedom of Press and the Rise of Liberalism in Golden Age Denmark

The first years of the rule of Crown Prince Frederick (1768–1839),[8] regent of the crown since 1784, were characterized by its liberal orientation and reforming enthusiasm. However, this enthusiasm began to wane in the last decade of the 18th century. The Danes were satisfied with the regent's rule, but the troublesome situation in Europe, especially after the execution of the king of France, had a decisive impact on the prince's reaction. On September 27, 1799,

8 For a more detailed discussion on Crown Prince Frederick, later Frederick VI, as a ruler of Denmark, see Alex Linvald, *Kronprins Frederik og Hans Regering 1797–1807. Bidrag til Danmark-Norges inden- og udenrigske Historie omkring begyndelsen af det 19. aarhundrede*, Copenhagen: Gads forlag 1923; Marcus Rubin, *Frederik VI's Tid. Fra Kielerfreden til Kongens Død. Økonomiske og historiske Studier*, Copenhagen: P.G. Philipsens Forlag 1895; Thomas Munck, "Absolute Monarchy in Later Eighteenth-Century Denmark: Centralized Reform, Public Expectations, and the Copenhagen Press," *The Historical Journal*, vol. 41, no. 1, 1998, pp. 201–224. Jens Vibæk, *Reform og Fallit, 1784–1830*, Copenhagen: Politikens Forlag 1964 (*Danmarks Historie*, vol. 10, ed. by John Danstrup and Hal Koch); Bruce H. Kirmmse, *Kierkegaard in Golden Age Denmark*, Bloomington and Indianapolis: Indiana University Press 1990, pp. 9–63.

the Danish government issued a severe decree concerning the press laws.[9] One of the first consequences of the decree was the exile of Peter Andreas Heiberg (1758–1841), one of Denmark's most important liberal authors.[10]

On August 16, 1807, the British Royal Navy bombarded Copenhagen.[11] The British punished Denmark's insistence on maintaining its position of neutrality during the wars with France. The Danes had to give up their fleet. After Napoleon's defeat, severe measures were taken against Denmark, because of Frederick's decision to enter an alliance with the French emperor. In the Treaty of Kiel in 1814, the Danish crown had to cede Norway to its rival, Sweden. The following year, at the Congress of Vienna, the Duchy of Holstein was incorporated into the newly created German Confederation, an event that was to have serious consequences for Denmark. During the Napoleonic wars, the British blockade had triggered inflation and the vast majority of the Danish trading houses were ruined. In 1813, Denmark would have to declare bankruptcy.

In the face of these developments, the Copenhagen intellectuals adopted a rather conservative and, in many cases, even apolitical stance. Faced with financial and military disaster, it was understandable that they believed that the only real alternative for Denmark was a kind of cultural renaissance. Thus began the period known as Denmark's Golden Age, an era of flourishing arts, literature, philosophy and theology. In this context, even the Danish press put aside political issues and devoted its pages to philosophical and literary discussions.

In this context, the July Revolution of 1830 in Paris exerted an indirect influence. In Denmark, one of the first consequences concerned the border duchy of Schleswig-Holstein. With a German population, Holstein had joined the German Confederation in 1815. One of the clauses of this membership was that Holstein was to have an assembly to represent it in the Confederation. Frederick, now King Frederick VI, had postponed the fulfillment of this measure for fifteen years, but after the July Revolution, the Prince of Metternich, faced with the complaints of the German inhabitants of Holstein, began to put pressure on the Danish monarch and the latter finally had to give in.

Thus, two consultative assemblies were created in Holstein and Schleswig. Since the king did not wish to provoke the jealousy of the rest of the Danish provinces, he created two other assemblies, one for Jutland, in the city of

9 See Petersen, *Kierkegaards polemiske debut*, p. 103.

10 See Henning Fenger, *The Heibergs*, trans. by Frederick J. Marker, New York: Twayne Publishers 1971, pp. 28–29.

11 See Gareth Glover, *The Two Battles of Copenhagen 1801 and 1807: Britain and Denmark in the Napoleonic Wars*, Barnsley: Pen & Sword Military 2018; Carl J. Kursrud, "The Seizure of the Danish Fleet, 1807: The Background," *The American Journal of International Law*, vol. 32, no. 2, 1938, pp. 280–311.

Viborg, and one for Zealand and the Danish islands (the Faroe Islands and Greenland), in Roskilde.[12]

The king was careful. First, the representatives of the Assemblies would be chosen by ballot from three different sectors: one part would be appointed directly by the crown, another by the host city, and the third by the people of the province. Since the king was confident that the rural sector would always act in harmony with the government, he could thus be assured of a majority of seats in the Assemblies. Second, he had given the Assemblies a consultative power, i.e., they had the ability to suggest reforms in matters of taxation and property rights. In this way, the king, who reserved the right to listen to such advice, offered the people a representative body, but without giving them any real power. Third, Frederick kept the Zealand Assembly out of Copenhagen, which was where most of the liberal activists were located. With these measures, the Assemblies called for an election in 1834.

But against all odds, when the elections were concluded in the fall of 1834, the vote favored the Liberals. Next, the Assembly started to obtain some small victories. It succeeded, for example, in getting the government to disclose to the representatives the state budget. It was shown that expenditure exceeded revenue, and that one of the reasons for the deficit was the excessive spending of the court and the budget for the army. The Assembly suggested to the king that he should implement some fiscal restrictions. If this was not enough to irritate the king, on December 9 of the same year the liberal newspaper *Fædrelandet* published an anonymous article—written by Orla Lehmann (1810–1870)—in which it was proposed that the Assemblies should use their right of petition more vigorously, thus hinting at the transformation of the body into a kind of parliament.[13]

The king did not want to hear any more about the matter and reacted severely.[14] First, he removed Christian Nathan David (1793–1874), the editor of *Fædrelandet*, from his post at the university and initiated proceedings against him for violation of the press laws. Then, on December 14, he proposed an

---

12 See Kirmmse, *Kierkegaard in Golden Age Denmark*, pp. 45–47.

13 See Anonymous [Orla Lehmann], "Hvad kan det hjælpe?", *Fædrelandet*, no. 11, December 7, 1834. The article was the continuation of another piece published in the same journal: Anonymous [Orla Lehmann], "Om Provindsialstændernes Petitionsret," *Fædrelandet*, no. 7, November 9, 1834.

14 See Harald Jørgensen, *Trykkefrihedsspørgsmaalet i Danmark, 1799–1848*, Copenhagen: Munksgaard 1944, pp. 177–192. See also Julie K. Allen, "Orla Lehmann: Kierkegaard's Political Alter-Ego?," in *Kierkegaard and His Danish Contemporaries. Tome I: Philosophy, Politics and Social Theory*, ed. by Jon Stewart, Farnham and Burlington: Ashgate 2009 (*Kierkegaard Research: Sources, Reception and Resources*, vol. 7), p. 92.

amendment to the decree of 1799 that amounted in practice to a state of total censorship.

The liberals met to compose a petition against the legislation. The petition was delivered on February 21, 1835. The negative reply came a few days later, on February 26, in the form of the famous sentence attributed to the king: *Vi alene vide*, "we alone know,"[15] that is, only the monarch can know what is or is not in the interest of his people and the State. The liberals immediately responded. On March 6 they founded The Free Press Society (*Trykkefrihedsselskabet*), headed by Joakim Frederik Schouw (1789–1852), who was also the president of the Roskilde Assembly. The Society grew rapidly, and in the following years began to spread throughout the rest of the country through chapter houses. The nascent national liberal party now constituted a real power, and the question of the freedom of the press was the huge topic of discussion, especially among the students at the University of Copenhagen.

2 Johannes Ostermann

On November 14, 1835, a student of philology named Johannes Ostermann presented to the Student Union[16] a paper entitled "Our Latest Journalistic Literature."[17] In the first part of his paper, Ostermann attempts to present a history of the development of the journalistic tradition in Copenhagen. He acknowledges that, until recently, the press played a minor role in the life of society. However, from 1830 onwards, people began to take an interest in newspapers, as they discovered there a means of expressing themselves. Ostermann gives as an example the newspaper *Raketten* of Mathias Winther (1795–1834), a tabloid founded in 1831, which, despite its indecorous tone, had the virtue of popularizing the press among the people, offering them an outlet for their discontent. Outside Copenhagen, too, particularly in the duchies (Schleswig-Holstein), the press had been of decisive importance. Ostermann goes so far

15 Literally, Frederick VI's words were, "No one but us can judge what is best and most beneficial for both [the State and the people]." See *Collegial Tidende*, no. 9, February 28, 1835. See also Petersen, *Kierkegaards polemiske debut*, pp. 57–58; Christian Kirchoff-Larssen, *Den Danske Presses Historie*, vols. 1–3, Copenhagen: Munksgaard 1962, vol. 3, pp. 80–89.

16 For more on the Student Union, see Hans Carl August Lund, *Studenterforeningens Historie, 1820–1870*, vols. 1–2, Copenhagen: Gyldendal 1896–1898.

17 Ostermann's paper was later published by *Fædrelandet*. See Johannes Ostermann, "Vor nyeste Journalliteratur," *Fædrelandet*, no. 71, January 22, 1836. In the following discussion I will use Julia Watkin's translation of the paper. See Johannes Ostermann, "Our Latest Journalistic Literature," in EPW, pp. 189–199.

as to suggest that it was thanks to the pressure from the local press that the king had decided to establish the Consultative Assemblies.[18] Thus, the growing interest and participation of the people in the press, as well as the creation of the first representative institution in Denmark, could be seen as triumphs of the nascent liberal press.

These achievements, of course, worried the crown. Frederick VI's reaction to the aforementioned publications of *Fædrelandet* was an unmistakable sign of the king's antagonism towards the growing freedom of the press: "The edict concerning the authors punished for violation of the press-freedom ordinance shows the misgivings the government had about permitting those attacks. Thus it is quite unlikely that it can have been so absolutely pleased with the greater freedom that gradually spread among a better-class public."[19]

Ostermann was not saying anything that was not true. It was clear to everyone that Frederick VI was concerned about the increasingly bold demonstrations of liberal journalists. However, perhaps he was exaggerating when he referred to the spread of press freedom "among a better-class public." Most of the important intellectuals were still on the side of the king. With a few exceptions—such as Schouw and Henrik Nicolai Clausen (1793–1877), a reputed professor and theologian—the liberal group consisted mainly of student leaders who were at the same time engaged in journalistic work.

As far as the less educated public was concerned, it was a fact that the people were uncomfortable with the radical discourse of the liberals, and the liberals, in turn, when dealing with the subject of popular representation, had their doubts about the promotion of universal (male) suffrage, for they knew only too well the conservative tendency of the people. Ostermann was undoubtedly aware of this. Indeed, he had to acknowledge that there is "a general dissatisfaction that has expressed itself among the public, if not against the Liberal tendency on the whole, then against particular expressions of this to be found in our Liberal papers."[20] What does he mean by a "general dissatisfaction"? It was mainly two very specific accusations concerning the form of the discourse; or, rather, the tone of the discourse. First, Ostermann notes, liberals are accused of expressing themselves with "acrimony and an unseemly tone,"[21] and, second, they are attributed with "a certain lack of honesty and openness so dear to the Dane."[22]

18 See Ostermann, "Our Latest Journalistic Literature," pp. 190–191.
19 Ibid., p. 191.
20 Ibid., p. 195.
21 Ibid.
22 Ibid.

One can imagine that, to the liberals, who were so impetuous and inspired by such lofty ideals, such trivialities about the tone must have made them impatient, especially when so much was at stake. But Ostermann was a man of moderation and did not wish to appear unreasonable:

> We declare that we are so far from blindly being worshippers of every utterance bearing the sign of the Liberal party that we, on the contrary, are often compelled to admit what was true and well founded in those complaints. But it has nevertheless been unpleasant for us daily to hear these lamentations, daily to hear much Good demolished, often only because the form of utterance was weak.[23]

Nonetheless, Ostermann is confident that the great aims of the liberal struggle justify its means. The reading public will no doubt be forgiving of a certain lack of delicacy in speech, for "it is a truth that we must never forget, that where an energetic and powerful character speaks, his words acquire a special form because the thought is special."[24] The tone, then, is not harsh or unseemly, but energetic and powerful. The discourse that is to express the special thought of the liberal struggle must possess at least the same force as the idea it expresses; on the other hand, it would be undesirable that because of a calm tone the listeners should be put to sleep.[25]

With regard to the second accusation, that of a lack of honesty, Ostermann declares that when a man is firmly convinced that he has the truth on his side, "it is entirely natural, at least very forgivable, if by means of the press he uses a sort of circuitous route in order to have his opinion expressed."[26] The Danes, who normally prefer things to be said in a straightforward manner, will understand that, in the realm of politics, the shortest route to the goal is not the straight line, but a necessarily circuitous route with several stopovers. To be fair, Ostermann was far from being a radical liberal, and in his paper, brief and concise, we do not find anywhere the harshness that he has tried to justify. On the contrary, he recommends not to engage in a "one-sided deification of this or that party,"[27] and encourages his listeners to open their eyes "to recognize the good wherever we can find it."[28] With respect to conservatives, Ostermann

23 Ibid.
24 Ibid., p. 196.
25 Ibid.
26 Ibid., p. 198.
27 Ibid., p. 199.
28 Ibid.

invites the opponents into the journalistic fray: "If our Conservatives themselves believe in the tenets they profess, how, then, can they tolerate that another party influences the people in a direction that is the exact opposite of the one they themselves profess?"[29] Ostermann's invitation to debate would be heeded, although he probably did not imagine the kind of opponent he would have to face.

3 Kierkegaard's Discussion of the Development of Selfhood in His Earlier Journals

In December 1834, when the king threatened to establish a state of censorship in Denmark, Kierkegaard was busy with his notes on the dramatic project of the Master-Thief.[30] His idea here was to develop in a modern context the popular myth of the "good thief," the Robin Hood-like hero who steals from the rich to give to the poor. Although one can only speculate about the relationship between the actual situation in Copenhagen and the "political" stance of this imaginary Master-Thief, a closer look at this parallel between reality and literature may perhaps yield some interesting insights into Kierkegaard's own political perspective. The Master-Thief is indeed dissatisfied with the established order. However, in a note dated March 15, nine days after the founding of The Free Press Society, Kierkegaard writes that his bandit is not strictly speaking a social fighter, unlike the Italian thief, the revolutionary Fra Diavolo.[31] Fra Diavolo, the nickname of the real thief Michael Pezza (1771–1806), was the leader of a resistance group in Naples against the occupation of revolutionary France.

29 Ibid., p. 196.

30 See *SKS* 27, 118–121, Papir 97:1–6 / *KJN* 11, 119–122. *SKS* 27, 121, Papir 98 / *KJN* 11, 122. *SKS* 27, 123, Papir 103 / *KJN* 11, 124. For a more detailed discussion about Kierkegaard's Master-Thief project, see Henning Fenger, "Mestertyven. Kierkegaards første dramatiske forsøg," *Edda*, no. 71, 1971, pp. 331–339; Sara Katrine Jandrup, "The Master Thief, Alias S. Kierkegaard, and his Robbery of the Truth," *Søren Kierkegaard Newsletter*, no. 43, 2002, pp. 7–11; Nassim Bravo, "The Master-Thief: A One-Man Army against the Established Order," in *Kierkegaard's Literary Figures and Motifs*, Tome II, *Gulliver to Zerlina*, ed. by Katalin Nun and Jon Stewart, Farnham and Burlington: Ashgate 2015 (*Kierkegaard Research: Sources, Reception and Resources*, vol. 16) pp. 111–120; Nassim Bravo, "Reinterpreting Medieval Lore through the Modern Prism: The Myth of Robin Hood in Kierkegaard's Early Journals," in *The Bounds of Myth: The Logical Path from Action to Knowledge*, ed. by Gustavo Esparza and Nassim Bravo, Leiden and Boston: Brill Rodopi 2021, pp. 195–220.

31 See *SKS* 27, 123, Papir 103 / *KJN* 11, 124.

But Kierkegaard's hero is different. The force that drives him is of an individual character: an idea for which he is willing to do anything. And while the thief is aware of the injustices of the current established order and opposes its abuses,[32] it is by virtue of his idea that "he acknowledges the reality of the State and does not deny it, as one perhaps could say."[33] Like many other intellectuals in Denmark, Kierkegaard thought that the solution to these issues had to do more with inwardness and self-awareness than with revolutionary efforts or even political journalism.[34]

The above does not mean that Kierkegaard proposed a state of political passivity. It is rather a reordering of priorities. First, it is necessary to achieve inner harmony. Once this indispensable center of gravity has been achieved, the individual can and must concentrate on achieving a balance between him or herself and actuality. The key word here is "balance." The task of Kierkegaard's thief is not to demolish the State or the established order, i.e., actuality, but to reveal its flaws through humor and satire, like the mythical prankster Till Eulenspiegel.[35]

The struggle in which the individual finds this balance is a constant task that admits no leaps. In his journal of Gilleleje,[36] Kierkegaard discusses in some detail the question on how to find that Archimedean point,[37] as he will call it. In the summer of 1835, a few months before the debate with Ostermann at the Student Union, Kierkegaard traveled to Gilleleje in northern Zealand. Although at first glance it looks like a simple travel diary with descriptions of landscapes and provincial life,[38] a more careful observation shows that the journal deals with the existential question about the discovery and development of selfhood. The reader soon finds out that Kierkegaard assumes in this journal a worldview in which the universe is not a place devoid of sense, containing only meaningless particularities disconnected from each other, but rather suggests that it is an organic totality. In this context, the human self

32 See *SKS* 27, 118, Papir 97:1 / *KJN* 11, 119.

33 *SKS* 27, 119, Papir 97:2 / *KJN* 11, 120.

34 See Bravo, "Reinterpreting Medieval Lore Through the Modern Prism," p. 213.

35 See *SKS* 27, 119, Papir 97:3 / *KJN* 11, 120.

36 See *SKS* 17, 7–30, AA:1–12 / *KJN* 1, 3–25. For a more detailed discussion on the journal of Gilleleje, see Nassim Bravo, "In Search of 'That Archimedean Point': The Development of Selfhood in Kierkegaard's Journal of Gilleleje," *Kierkegaard Studies Yearbook*, vol. 26, no. 1, 2021, pp. 3–24.

37 See, for example, *SKS* 17, 15, AA:6 / *KJN* 1, 10.

38 Henning Fenger suggested indeed that this was no ordinary journal, but rather an attempt by Kierkegaard to write a *Bildungsroman*. See Henning Fenger, *Kierkegaard, The Myths and Their Origins: Studies in the Kierkegaardian Papers and Letters*, trans. by George C. Schoolfield, New Haven and London: Yale University Press 1980, pp. 89–115.

is likewise not an isolated and autonomous thing, separated from everything else, but an essential element within the totality of the world.[39]

In one passage, for example, Kierkegaard writes about his visit to one of his favorite sites in Gilleleje, Gilbjerget. There he describes his encounter with boundless nature:

> When the whole, seen thus in perspective, presented only the larger, bolder outlines and I didn't lose myself in detail as one so often does, but saw the whole in its totality, I gained the strength to grasp things differently, to admit how often I myself had made mistakes and to forgive the mistakes of others.[40]

The point here is that the intuition of totality prevents the individual from losing him- or herself in isolation: "As I stood there, without depression or despondency making me see myself as an enclitic of those by whom I am usually surrounded, or without pride making me the constitutive principle in a small circle."[41] As the individual grasps the organic totality of the world, he or she becomes aware that his or her character is at the same time contingent and necessary; not a mere relative thing, like an enclitic, but neither an isolated self who creates his or her own world. Kierkegaard suggests this is a marriage between "pride and humility,"[42] a vantage point from which the individual can adequately understand how he or she should relate to the world.

In another part of the journal, we see the author struggling to find his place in the world, what he calls his destiny (*Bestemmelse*).[43] To illustrate this, he offers a botanical metaphor:

> Our early youth is like a flower in the light of dawn, cupping a lovely dewdrop in which all surroundings are reflected with a melancholy harmony. But soon the sun rises above the horizon and the dewdrop evaporates, life's dreams vanish with it, and then the question (to resort again to a floral metaphor) is whether like the oleander one is able on one's own account to produce a drop that can stand as the fruit of one's life.[44]

39 This universe in which everything is interconnected is very similar to the view that Hegel develops in his *Phenomenology of Spirit*. [G.W.F. Hegel], *Hegel's Phenomenology of Spirit*, trans. by A.V. Miller, Oxford: Clarendon Press 1977. See Stewart, *Hegel's Century*, pp. 19–22.

40 *SKS* 17, 14, AA:6 / *KJN* 1, 9–10.

41 *SKS* 17, 14, AA:6 / *KJN* 1, 10.

42 *SKS* 17, 14, AA:6 / *KJN* 1, 10.

43 See *SKS* 17, 18, AA:12 / *KJN* 1, 14.

44 *SKS* 17, 18, AA:12 / *KJN* 1, 14.

First, the character of the individual is only a reflection of his or her surroundings. But then comes the awakening of consciousness, represented by the evaporation of the dewdrop, and the individual must take charge of him- or herself, of finding "the soil to which one really belongs, but that is not always so easy to find."[45] Kierkegaard suggests that one way to find this is through science. However, he does not refer here to science as it is usually understood, i.e., as an accumulation of knowledge about particularities, but rather what he argues is true science, a sort of Hegelian *Wissenschaft* that comprehends totality and its dialectical interconnections, and is practiced by investigators "who through their speculation have found, or tried to find, that Archimedean point which is nowhere in the world and from which they have surveyed the whole and seen the details in the proper light."[46] We see here the theme of the "proper light," which will reappear in Kierkegaard's debate with Ostermann.

The journal of Gilleleje ends with one of the most famous passages in Kierkegaard's *oeuvre*, in which he enthusiastically claims that what really matters is to "understand my own *destiny*, of seeing what the Deity really wants me to do; the thing is to find a truth which is truth *for me*, to find *the idea for which I am willing to live and die*."[47] While the passage undoubtedly speaks about the existence of the individual and the idea of subjective truth, it also assumes the worldview that Kierkegaard has developed throughout the journal, namely, that the world is an organic totality of which the individual is a part. In this sense, the "truth for me" that Kierkegaard mentions here is not about the individual being able to arbitrarily choose what is true for him- or herself; rather, it is about him or her finding what his or her proper place is in the totality that is the world. As we will see in the next section, Kierkegaard will also apply this principle to the political sphere.

4 A Study from Nature in Noonday Light

In 1867, Ostermann offered Hans Peter Barfod an account of what happened in 1835:

> In those days, the movements of the times tore some of us young people out of our poetic dreams and hurled us into political life, because in those days only a few individuals—at least among the trend-setting group in

45 *SKS* 17, 18, AA:12 / *KJN* 1, 14.

46 *SKS* 17, 20–21, AA:12 / *KJN* 1, 16.

47 *SKS* 17, 24, AA:12 / *KJN* 1, 19.

> the Student Union—were taken with the idea [of politics]. But the alpha and omega of politics in those days was freedom of the press, which was exposed to persecution from above and to grumbling criticism from the public. Under these conditions I read my essay to a large crowd.... In those days, or just before then, I was often (almost daily, in fact) in the company of Kjerk., who was as little interested in politics then as he would be later. But his lively intellect took hold of any issue in those days, and he exercised his brilliant dialectical skill and wit upon it, without bothering himself much about the reality of the matter. The fact that my defense [of the freedom of press] was met with sympathy pushed him into the opposite camp, where he allied himself more or less as a matter of indifference. He borrowed my essay after having informed the leadership of the Student Union that he wanted to "give a reading," and the manuscript which you have found can scarcely be—indeed, I would say it is impossible that it can be—anything other than the essay which he read aloud at the Student Union shortly thereafter, perhaps fourteen days after I did. There was a very large crowd present. People had expected a debate between us on the issue. But for one thing, I had only fleetingly heard him read his essay; and for another, as an eager politician I had no desire to take on such opponent, whom I knew had only a slight interest in the reality of the matter. As far as I can remember it, Kierkegaard's essay was rather ponderous; it bore the hallmark of his unique intellectual talents and was received with great applause.[48]

Ostermann states bluntly that Kierkegaard, who was not interested in political affairs, had entered the debate out of a desire to polemicize. He does not even think he is a genuine conservative: the alliance with the other side is due to his natural impulse to controversy. No one denied his "brilliant dialectical skill," but this hardly harmonized at this time with the earnestness of the discussion on the freedom of the press. The members of the Student Union must have been surprised when Kierkegaard informed them of his intention to deliver a speech.

On November 28, 1835, Kierkegaard appeared before the Union to read an essay entitled, "Our Journalistic Literature: A Study from Nature in Noonday Light." The title of the piece had been carefully chosen; it summed up Kierkegaard's approach in a nutshell. What does it mean to see something in the light of noon? Kierkegaard explains it by evoking the image of a painter. Artists often paint in the morning light. This is because, at that time of day,

48 Bruce H. Kirmmse (ed.), *Encounters with Kierkegaard: A Life as Seen by His Contemporaries*, trans. by Bruce H. Kirmmse and Virginia R. Laursen, Princeton: Princeton University Press 1996, pp. 20–22.

the constant movement of light and shadow produces a special impression in which each particular point, because of the quivering in the illumination, appears as if dissociated from the whole.[49] On the contrary, under the noon light things appear as they are. The visual illusion created by the morning illumination is pleasant in the plastic arts, but in other spheres, where a difference of perception can be decisive, it is more convenient to contemplate events under the sober and impartial light of noon. Thus, Kierkegaard begins his speech by calling for objectivity and calm reflection: "On the whole, I believe it is beneficial, as much for every form of individual life as for the individual man, to stop the wheel of development, to look back over the past, and to see how much progress has been made, whether dust and other such things have not caused detrimental frictional resistance to quicker progress."[50]

Kierkegaard is no stranger to the idea of a prior state of circumspection upon which the course of action is to be built and then guided. He had reflected on the subject in his journal of Gilleleje, and the most satisfactory answer he had arrived at was precisely that first one must put one's feet firmly on the ground and find out what one's place in the world is. Of course, the questions raised during that summer concerned the life of the individual (and, more specifically, Kierkegaard himself), but it was logical to transfer the approach to the broader sphere of life in society. In his paper, Kierkegaard adds to his scheme an essential point: in the struggle for progress, one must not lose sight of the historical situation, and one must look to the past. Here, Kierkegaard intends to assume the role of a reflective and impartial observer. He is not on the side of the liberals, whose excessively optimistic hopes he finds suspicious; but he is likewise not on the side of the conservatives, as most suppose, for it is not his intention to climb Mount Tabor to announce that the passage to the Promised Land is closed.[51]

It is true that Ostermann had also given a historical account in his speech. However, his approach was too local, and the examples he had used to illustrate it were dubious. It had been especially unfortunate to refer to the newspaper *Raketten* as the historical predecessor of the liberal press. Winther, the editor of the newspaper, had never shown any signs of being dissatisfied with the established order, which is demonstrated by the fact that nowhere in the pages of his tabloid is it possible to find any criticism of the government.[52] Kierkegaard's hypothesis is that the rise of the liberal press is a phenomenon posterior to the creation of the Consultative Assemblies a year earlier. To prove

49 See *SKS* 27, 189, Papir 254 / *EPW*, 36.
50 *SKS* 27, 190, Papir 254 / *EPW*, 36–37.
51 See *SKS* 27, 191, Papir 254 / *EPW*, 37.
52 See *SKS* 27, 191–192, Papir 254 / *EPW*, 38.

his point, Kierkegaard examines the order of events in Europe and Denmark since 1830. The starting point, of course, is the July Revolution in Paris.

Kierkegaard diagnoses the revolution with a clinical eye. Revolutions, he points out, behave much like diseases. When they get out of control and their contagion is rampant, the consequences can be terribly violent, as was the case with the French Revolution of 1789. The July Revolution, on the other hand, had been an endemic case. The French, like an experienced surgeon, had successfully carried out the operation and sutured the wound; indeed, "the July Revolution stands as a remarkable example of a clean, pure, revolution, free of extraneous elements."[53] In this situation, the rest of the European nations had no choice but to sit and wait. Finally, the Revolution triumphed, but only a few were aware of the difficulty of the internal process; the great majority, at least in the case of Denmark, only saw—or only wanted to see—the apparent ease with which the result had been achieved, which made it difficult to resist the temptation to imitate the French. Meanwhile, the Danish press remained silent: "the government and the Liberals faced each other as two entities that, because of the July Revolution, had a great deal to say to each other but did not rightly know how to begin until the government broke the silence."[54]

It was the crown which made the first move. Kierkegaard refers here to the creation of the Consultative Assemblies. From a strictly temporal point of view, the government played the active role, not the liberal press. In his speech, Ostermann had argued that one of the causes of the creation of the Assemblies was the pressure exerted by the press in Holstein. He was partly right, but that was not the same as saying that the Danish liberal press had been the active factor in the process. It was undeniable that the journalistic efforts of the people of Holstein—who wrote in German, not Danish—had had some influence on the king's decision, but it was also necessary to bear in mind that the Holstein press, while driven by liberal ideas, also had separatist pretensions: it demanded a constitution of its own. In short, its press was not a properly Danish press. Moreover, on a more realistic view, Frederick VI, who had no desire to give the Danes a representative body, had acted in this way out of fear of the threat that the Prince of Metternich might try to persuade Prussia and Austria to intervene.

It remained to be shown that the Danish liberal press had assumed a passive position. Kierkegaard argues that prior to the creation of the Assemblies, Danish newspapers had remained in a state of political inactivity.[55]

53 See *SKS* 27, 192, Papir 254 / *EPW*, 39.
54 See *SKS* 27, 193, Papir 254 / *EPW*, 40.
55 See *SKS* 27, 195, Papir 254 / *EPW*, 42.

The tabloid *Raketten* can by no means be considered a liberal publication. *Fædrelandet,* the newspaper edited by David, had come out in 1834, after the creation of the Assemblies. What about the other liberal newspaper, *Kjøbenhavnsposten,* founded in 1827 by Andreas Peter Liunge (1798–1879)? Kierkegaard reviews the contents of this journal between 1829 and May 1831, the date on which the resolution to establish the Assemblies was taken. He found articles about aesthetics, culture and literature, but little or nothing on politics.[56] From May 1831 onwards, *Kjøbenhavnsposten* suddenly began to publish articles of a more political tone.

Even so, between 1831 and 1834, the year of the Assembly elections, the demonstrations of the liberal press were rather moderate in character (suggesting, for example, that the crown's expenditures should be more frugal). It was not until December 1835, with the trial against David and the legislation concerning the press laws, that the liberals turned to a more radical stance. In other words, the liberal press did not take the initiative; its actions, as Kierkegaard's historical account shows, were always a response to the government's position. Moreover, it was important to remember that the representation in the Assemblies, particularly that of Roskilde—the most important bastion of the liberals—had been, so to speak, a gift from the crown. Kierkegaard does not wish to undermine the liberal triumphs; but he also finds it necessary to dispel the illusion that the freedom of the press had been a victory of the liberal press alone, as Ostermann suggested.

Up to this point, Kierkegaard remains an observer who recounts the order of events. His analysis is in no way a defense of conservatism—a group less defined than the liberals and far less active—but a wake-up call for the liberal movement. It is easy to lose one's compass when, faced with the appearance of some concrete results, one thinks that these have been one's own achievement rather than the fruit of the inertia of history.

Kierkegaard formulates a kind of political theory in the second part of his paper, in the section where he analyzes the current role of the liberal newspapers, *Fædrelandet* and *Kjøbenhavnsposten.* The present age, says Kierkegaard, is characterized as a "formal struggle."[57] A formal struggle is an effort whose foundation lies precisely in the form. It is because of this quality that the present age tends to "emphasize symmetrical beauty, to prefer conventional rather than sincere social relations."[58] When we adopt good manners as a rule of conduct, this means that we give primacy to form. But there are other cases of formal struggle

56 *SKS* 27, 195, Papir 254 / *EPW*, 42.
57 See *SKS* 27, 198, Papir 254 / *EPW*, 46.
58 *SKS* 27, 198, Papir 254 / *EPW*, 46.

that go beyond our everyday relationships. Thus, for example, "the attempts of Fichte and other philosophers to construct systems by sharpness of mind and Robespierre's attempt to do it with the help of the guillotine."[59] What do Fichte and Robespierre have in common? The predominance of form, according to Kierkegaard. Finally, the formal struggle is the hallmark of all revolutions in the political world,[60] because a revolution attempts to impose a form.

The concept of form has here a very particular meaning. First, it is accompanied by another key concept: the idea. The relationship between form and idea is decisive, as Kierkegaard explains below:

> I agree completely with this whole effort to cling to form, insofar as it continues to be the medium through which we have the idea, but it should be remembered that it is the idea that is supposed to determine the form, not the form that is supposed to determine the idea. One should keep in mind that life is not something abstract but something extremely individual. One should not forget that form, for example, from a poetic genius's position of immediacy, is nothing but the coming into existence of the idea in the world, and that the task of reflection is only to investigate whether or not the idea has acquired the properly corresponding form. It should always be remembered that life is not acquired through form, but form is acquired through life.[61]

It appears Kierkegaard is employing here terms from Hegelian philosophy. It is likely that he had become familiar with these concepts through Johan Ludvig Heiberg,[62] who had personally known Hegel and had tried to introduce his philosophy in Denmark. In the passage quoted, form is understood as the medium through which the idea is expressed, but this medium must be suitable for the idea. Kierkegaard offers an example that helps us better understand this relation between form and idea. He tells us to imagine a modern

---

59 See *SKS* 27, 199, Papir 254 / *EPW*, 46.

60 See *SKS* 27, 199, Papir 254 / *EPW*, 47.

61 *SKS* 27, 199, Papir 254 / *EPW*, 47.

62 For more on the importance of Heiberg in Golden Age Denmark, see Fenger, *The Heibergs*; Morten Borup, *Johan Ludvig Heiberg*, vols. 1–3, Copenhagen: Gyldendal 1973; Jon Stewart (ed.), *The Heibergs and the Theater: Between Vaudeville, Romantic Comedy and National Drama*, Copenhagen: Museum Tusculanum Press 2012 (*Danish Golden Age Studies*, vol. 7); Vibeke Schrøder, *Tankens våben. Johan Ludvig Heiberg*, Copenhagen: Gyldendal 2001; Jon Stewart, *A History of Hegelianism in Golden Age Denmark*, Tome I, *The Heiberg Period: 1824–1836*, Copenhagen: C.A. Reitzel 2007 (*Danish Golden Age Studies*, vol. 3). Jon Stewart (ed.), *Johan Ludvig Heiberg: Philosopher, Littérateur, Dramaturge, and Political Thinker*, Copenhagen: Museum Tusculanum Press 2008 (*Danish Golden Age Studies*, vol. 5).

man obsessed with Ancient Greek culture who happens to have the means to fix up his house in the Greek style. He would immediately reject this project as absurd, Kierkegaard argues, when he realized the imbalance between the form he wished to implement in his life, Ancient Greek architecture, and the real situation in which he lived, namely, that of a Danish man in the 19th century.[63] This example shows that form should adjust to the concrete situation, which in turn indicates that Kierkegaard is equating the notion of *idea* to that of *life*, and that life is understood here as the concrete and individual.

This seems to be consistent with the line of thought that Kierkegaard had begun to outline earlier with his sketch of the Master-Thief, and in his journal of Gilleleje. In his depiction of the Master-Thief, we saw that the foundation of the hero's struggle was inner harmony and self-awareness, not the desire to destroy the established order or, to use the terms employed in Kierkegaard's speech, the impulse to impose a form. In a similar way, in his journal of Gilleleje Kierkegaard asserted that the individual cannot be an isolated entity who constructs his or her own world arbitrarily. The human being is an element within the organic totality that is the world. For Kierkegaard, then, what is important is to find what is the place of the individual within that totality, that which at the end of the journal he called *truth for me*.

Thus, when it is said that the form is determined by the idea, what Kierkegaard means is that the form of a concrete action must have its foundation in life, whether it is a question of an individual or of a society. In this way, the example of Robespierre makes sense. Since the social situation of France at the end of the 18th century did not harmonize with Robespierre's revolutionary program, he decided to impose it by force, i.e., through the guillotine. Although the gesture became an object of admiration for his passionate conviction in favor of liberty, the period known as the Terror would eventually reveal that all was not well. Robespierre, unlike the French revolutionaries of 1830, was not an experienced surgeon.

By suggesting that the age in general and the press in particular are clinging to form, Kierkegaard is trying to make the point that Denmark is not ready for the reforms proposed by the liberals. This does not mean, of course, that he opposes liberal reforms (freedom of the press, constitutionalism, universal suffrage), but rather that he does not consider it wise to ignore the clause that reform has to be founded on the life of the people, and that it is not advisable to try to force the course of history: "But just as a backward leap is wrong (something which the age in general is inclined to recognize), so a forward leap is wrong; this is due, in both cases, to the fact that progress does not advance by

63 See *SKS* 27, 199, Papir 254 / *EPW*, 47.

leaps, and the seriousness of life will punish with its irony every experiment of this kind, even when it is momentarily successful."[64]

Kierkegaard, who does not wish to participate in Danish politics, prefers to advise liberals to take on this task of reflection themselves. He urges them to keep in mind that "it does not do to travel in Zealand with a map of France,"[65] and to abandon this formal quixotic struggle in which "one sounds the alarm every minute, gives Rosinante the spurs, and charges—at windmills; at the same time there is no lack of discernment to make one aware that some evil demon or other has changed the giants into windmills."[66]

When he diagnoses *Kjøbenhavnsposten*'s current situation, Kierkegaard uses a picturesque astrophysical metaphor:

> Scientists maintain that a heavenly body is formed from a cloud mass through the harmony of centrifugal and centripetal forces in combination with rotation on an axis—and to me *Kjøbenhavnsposten* seems to be just like such a fog mass, but one whose existence as a planet has still not been realized through the harmony of centrifugal and centripetal forces in combination with turning on an axis.... That I understand a competent editor to be the axis on which the planet is to rotate, and that I have intended the centrifugal and centripetal tendencies to designate what people up to now have called by the so-popular party names Liberal and Conservative, scarcely needs to be pointed out. It is quite natural and can hardly be denied that *Kjøbenhavnsposten* has acquired a somewhat greater unity recently and that the center of our solar political system, the Assembly in Roskilde, has exercised upon it some power of attraction and thereby helped it find its path and regulate its course, and that on the other hand the centrifugal force, which used to have the ascendancy, has done its best to keep it. However, to repeat, since the harmony of the forces has not taken place as yet, nor the rotation on the axis either, it easily runs the risk of being drawn into another solar system, since—seen from our solar system—the centrifugal direction in relation to another system must appear as centripetal.[67]

64 *SKS* 27, 199, Papir 254 / *EPW*, 47.

65 *SKS* 27, 200, Papir 254 / *EPW*, 48.

66 *SKS* 27, 200, Papir 254 / *EPW*, 48.

67 *SKS* 27, 200–201, Papir 254 / *EPW*, 49. It is interesting to see that Kierkegaard used this same metaphor in his journal of Gilleleje: "A person would no more want to decide the externals first and the fundamentals afterward than a heavenly body about to form itself would decide first of all about its surface, about which bodies it should turn its light side to, and to which its dark side, without first letting the harmony of centrifugal and

The planet in formation is, of course, *Kjøbenhavnsposten*; the centrifugal force is the liberal tendency; the centripetal force is the conservative tendency; finally, the axis that should balance both forces, thus culminating the formation of the body, is a competent editor, which is lacking so far (the editor of *Kjøbenhavnsposten* was Andreas Peter Liunge). It is surprising that Kierkegaard claims that the sun of this "political solar system" is the predominantly liberal Roskilde Assembly, and not the government, which he has not ceased to praise throughout his speech. One can imagine, then, that Kierkegaard in fact thinks that the political progress of Denmark must revolve around this semi-representative body and that, on the other hand, the crown, although it has played an active role in this process, is part of the "centripetal forces," that is, the conservative tendency. This is obvious, but it is surprising nonetheless coming from someone who is supposedly on the conservative side.

However, since there is still no axis, and the centrifugal force (the liberal tendency) has subjugated the centripetal force (the conservative tendency), it might happen that *Kjøbenhavnsposten* breaks away from the orbit of the Roskilde Assembly and is pulled into another solar system, from whose perspective the centrifugal force appears as centripetal. What other solar system? It is difficult to say. Perhaps it is the foreign influence (France or Holstein), which, if not properly assimilated, can bring with it terrible consequences. But what is important to note is that, having lost its compass, the newspaper in question, and the liberal movement in general, would wander aimlessly through the space of politics.

With respect to the other liberal newspaper, *Fædrelandet*, Kierkegaard's judgment is less severe. He congratulates them on having survived the storm of the trial against David and admits that, in recent times, the paper has "a vigorous and sound existence,"[68] which is due, in no small measure, to the firm and sensible leadership of its editor, Johannes Hage.[69] *Fædrelandet*, according to Kierkegaard, has managed to understand the myth of the struggle for press freedom, thanks to which it has learned "among other things to investigate more closely what freedom of the press is before sounding the alarm."[70]

Thus concludes Kierkegaard's first and only political speech. The text was heavy and too intellectually overloaded for the nature of the subject; indeed,

centripetal forces bring it into being and letting the rest come by itself. One must first learn to know oneself before knowing anything else." *SKS* 17, 27, AA:12 / *KJN* 1, 22.

68 *SKS* 27, 203, Papir 254 / *EPW*, 52.

69 After his trial, C.N. David resigned as editor. Johannes Hage edited *Fædrelandet* between 1835 and 1837, the year he committed suicide.

70 *SKS* 27, 203, Papir 254 / *EPW*, 52.

Kierkegaard barely touched on the question of the struggle for the freedom of the press. However, it might be unfair to say, as Ostermann told Barfod, that Kierkegaard did not take the problem seriously. It is remarkable how well informed he was about the political situation in Europe and the history of the press in Denmark.

5 Conclusion

At first glance, Kierkegaard's speech at the Student Union looks like a disjointed and isolated piece in relation to the rest of his early work. Kierkegaard's first published writings, *From the Papers of One Still Living* (1838) and *On the Concept of Irony* (1841), discuss literary and philosophical, not political, issues. In fact, Kierkegaard would not write again on political matters until the publication of *A Literary Review*, and even then, as the title indicates, it was within the context of a literary discussion. In addition to this, one could reasonably argue, as Ostermann or Watkin did, that Kierkegaard does not seem to take the issue under discussion, freedom of the press and the merits of liberals, seriously, but rather uses the occasion to hone his dialectical skills as a polemicist.

However, in this article I wanted to show that there is a thematic continuity between Kierkegaard's first literary projects in 1834 and 1835, such as the sketch on the Master-Thief and his journal of Gilleleje, and his paper "Our Journalistic Literature." In those, Kierkegaard begins to develop a worldview and an existential theory about the role the individual plays within actuality. For Kierkegaard, as discussed before, the world is not a composite of isolated and meaningless phenomena, but an organic totality in which every element is interconnected. In this context, the human individual must not isolate him- or herself, or reject reality. Thus, in the Master-Thief project, the hero does not attempt to destroy the established order, even though he is able to recognize its imperfections and injustices. This seems to suggest that Kierkegaard was opposed to a radical change of political structures. His thief was not a revolutionary.

In a way, the journal of Gilleleje shows an attempt to discover "that Archimedean point," that is, the place of the individual within that organic totality. Kierkegaard seems to be referring to this when he suggests that what is really important is to find a *truth for me*, which does not mean that the individual can construct his world and him- or herself arbitrarily, but that he or she must find his or her right place in the world. In this article I wished to show that Kierkegaard transfers this worldview, whose emphasis is on the existence of the individual, to the sphere of politics. A society must know itself in order to understand the form that corresponds to it: its government, its laws, its institutions. A state that ignores this balance and tries to forcefully impose an alien form would resemble, in this analogy, the isolated individual.

It is easy to recognize the importance of the intellectual legacy of 19th century theorists of revolution such as Marx or Bakunin. These are thinkers who knew how to take advantage of some of the ideas of Hegelian philosophy and apply them to the political and social sphere. The impact of these theories on our own time is undeniable. In a way, Kierkegaard is also part of that generation of thinkers who were heirs of Hegel. But, unlike the theorists of the revolution, Kierkegaard was interested not in the political sphere, but in individual existence. However, I wanted to show how Kierkegaard took this existential approach and applied it to the political realm, specifically in the discussion of revolution, liberalism and the freedom of the press. This is an inheritance from Kierkegaard that, perhaps understandably, goes unrecognized, but might be worth taking into consideration. His proposal constitutes, from this point of view, a moderate and optimistic alternative.

Bibliography

Anonymous, *Collegial Tidende*, no. 9, February 28, 1835.

Anonymous [Orla Lehmann], "Hvad kan det hjælpe?", *Fædrelandet*, no. 11, December 7, 1834.

Anonymous [Orla Lehmann], "Om Provindsialstændernes Petitionsret," *Fædrelandet*, no. 7, November 9, 1834.

Allen, Julie K., "Orla Lehmann: Kierkegaard's Political Alter-Ego?," in *Kierkegaard and His Danish Contemporaries*. Tome I, *Philosophy, Politics and Social Theory*, ed. by Jon Stewart, Farnham and Burlington: Ashgate 2009 (*Kierkegaard Research: Sources, Reception and Resources*, vol. 7), p. 92.

Borup, Morten, *Johan Ludvig Heiberg*, vols. 1–3, Copenhagen: Gyldendal 1973.

Bravo, Nassim, "In Search of 'That Archimedean Point': The Development of Selfhood in Kierkegaard's Journal of Gilleleje," *Kierkegaard Studies Yearbook*, 2021, pp. 3–24.

Bravo, Nassim, "Reinterpreting Medieval Lore through the Modern Prism: The Myth of Robin Hood in Kierkegaard's Early Journals," in *The Bounds of Myth: The Logical Path from Action to Knowledge*, ed. by Gustavo Esparza and Nassim Bravo, Leiden and Boston: Brill Rodopi 2021, pp. 195–220.

Bravo, Nassim, "The Master-Thief: A One-Man Army against the Established Order," in *Kierkegaard's Literary Figures and Motifs*, Tome II, *Gulliver to Zerlina*, ed. by Katalin Nun and Jon Stewart, Farnham and Burlington: Ashgate 2015 (*Kierkegaard Research: Sources, Reception and Resources*, vol. 16) pp. 111–120.

Fenger, Henning, “Mestertyven. Kierkegaards første dramatiske forsøg,” *Edda*, no. 71, 1971, pp. 331–339.

Fenger, Henning, *Kierkegaard, The Myths and Their Origins: Studies in the Kierkegaardian Papers and Letters*, trans. by George C. Schoolfield, New Haven and London: Yale University Press 1980.

Fenger, Henning, *The Heibergs*, trans. by Frederick J. Marker, New York: Twayne Publishers 1971.

Glover, Gareth, *The Two Battles of Copenhagen 1801 and 1807: Britain and Denmark in the Napoleonic Wars*, Barnsley: Pen & Sword Military 2018.

[Hegel, G.W.F.], *Hegel's Phenomenology of Spirit*, trans. by A.V. Miller, Oxford: Clarendon Press 1977.

Jandrup, Sara Katrine, “The Master Thief, Alias S. Kierkegaard, and his Robbery of the Truth,” *Søren Kierkegaard Newsletter*, no. 43, 2002, pp. 7–11.

Jørgensen, Harald, *Trykkefrihedsspørgsmaalet i Danmark, 1799–1848*, Copenhagen: Munksgaard 1944, pp. 177–192.

Kierkegaard, Søren, *The Concept of Irony; Schelling Lecture Notes*, trans. by Howard V. Hong and Edna H. Hong, Princeton: Princeton University Press 1989.

Kierkegaard, Søren, *Early Polemical Writings*, ed. and trans. by Julia Watkin, Princeton: Princeton University Press 1990.

[Kierkegaard, Søren], *Søren Kierkegaards Skrifter*, vols. 1–28, K1-K28, ed. by Niels Jørgen Cappelørn, et al., Copenhagen: Gad 1997–2012.

[Kierkegaard, Søren], *Kierkegaard's Journals and Notebooks*, vols. 1–11, ed. by Niels Jørgen Cappelørn, Alastair Hannay, David Kangas, Bruce H. Kirmmse, George Pattison, Vanessa Rumble and K. Brian Söderquist, Princeton and Oxford: Princeton University Press 2007–2020.

Kirchoff-Larssen, Christian, *Den Danske Presses Historie*, vols. 1–3, Copenhagen: Munksgaard 1962.

Kirmmse, Bruce H., *Kierkegaard in Golden Age Denmark*, Bloomington and Indianapolis: Indiana University Press 1990.

Kirmmse, Bruce H. (ed.), *Encounters with Kierkegaard: A Life as Seen by His Contemporaries*, trans. by Bruce H. Kirmmse and Virginia R. Laursen, Princeton: Princeton University Press 1996.

Kursrud, Carl J., “The Seizure of the Danish Fleet, 1807: The Background,” *The American Journal of International Law*, vol. 32, no. 2, 1938, pp. 280–311.

Linvald, Alex, *Kronprins Frederik og Hans Regering 1797–1807. Bidrag til Danmark-Norges inden- og udenrigske Historie omkring begyndelsen af det 19. aarhundrede*, Copenhagen: Gads forlag 1923.

Lund, Hans Carl August, *Studenterforeningens Historie, 1820–1870*, vols. 1–2, Copenhagen: Gyldendal 1896–1898.

Munck, Thomas, "Absolute Monarchy in Later Eighteenth-Century Denmark: Centralized Reform, Public Expectations, and the Copenhagen Press," *The Historical Journal*, vol. 41, no. 1, 1998, pp. 201–224.

Ostermann, Johannes, "Our Latest Journalistic Literature," in *Early Polemical Writings*, ed. and trans. by Julia Watkin, Princeton: Princeton University Press 1990, pp. 189–199.

Ostermann, Johannes, "Vor nyeste Journalliteratur," *Fædrelandet*, no. 71, January 22, 1836.

Petersen, Teddy, *Kierkegaards polemiske debut*, Odense: Odense Universitetsforlag 1977.

Rubin, Marcus, *Frederik VI's Tid. Fra Kielerfreden til Kongens Død. Økonomiske og historiske Studier*, Copenhagen: P.G. Philipsens Forlag 1895.

Schrøder, Vibeke, *Tankens våben. Johan Ludvig Heiberg*, Copenhagen: Gyldendal 2001.

Stewart, Jon (ed.), *Johan Ludvig Heiberg: Philosopher, Littérateur, Dramaturge, and Political Thinker*, Copenhagen: Museum Tusculanum Press 2008 (*Danish Golden Age Studies*, vol. 5).

Stewart, Jon (ed.), *The Heibergs and the Theater: Between Vaudeville, Romantic Comedy and National Drama*, Copenhagen: Museum Tusculanum Press 2012 (*Danish Golden Age Studies*, vol. 7).

Stewart, Jon, *A History of Hegelianism in Golden Age Denmark*, Tome I, *The Heiberg Period: 1824–1836*, Copenhagen: C.A. Reitzel 2007 (*Danish Golden Age Studies*, vol. 3).

Stewart, Jon, *Hegel's Century: Alienation and Recognition in a Time of Revolution*, Cambridge: Cambridge University Press 2021.

Vibæk, Jens, *Reform og Fallit, 1784–1830*, Copenhagen: Politikens Forlag 1964 (*Danmarks Historie*, vol. 10, ed. by John Danstrup and Hal Koch).

Watkin, Julia, "Historical Introduction," in Søren Kierkegaard, *Early Polemical Writings*, ed. and trans. by Julia Watkin, Princeton: Princeton University Press 1990, pp. XVII–XVIII.

CHAPTER 11

Jaspers' Diagnosis of the Spiritual Condition of the Age as a Continuation of Kierkegaard's Critique of *the Present Age*

Peter Šajda

Abstract

The article explores the thematic continuity between Kierkegaard's and Jaspers' social criticism. In *The Spiritual Condition of the Age* (1931) Jaspers draws substantial inspiration from Kierkegaard's *A Literary Review* (1846), claiming that Kierkegaard identified a social development which at his time was still not as disquieting as in the twentieth century when it intensified substantially. Kierkegaard's diagnosis is thus even more relevant in the first half of the twentieth century than it was at the time of its origin. Jaspers complements, develops, and updates Kierkegaard's diagnosis of the age. I discuss key concepts in Kierkegaard's and Jaspers' critiques of the age, primarily *the public* and *the mass*, as well as the related concepts of *excellence*, *envy*, *leveling* and *the modern press*. Both authors provide original and insightful analyses of the self-contradictions and degenerative tendencies of modern society.

Carl Schmitt claimed in his 1944 essay "A Pan-European Interpretation of Donoso Cortés" that the nineteenth century gave rise to a new philosophical genre which he called *the critique of the age*. The genre became popular especially after the revolutionary turbulences of 1848, and Schmitt included the Danish philosopher Søren Kierkegaard among its key representatives.[1] Kierkegaard's

1 Carl Schmitt, "Donoso Cortés in gesamteuropäischer Interpretation," in his *Donoso Cortés in gesamteuropäischer Interpretation. Vier Aufsätze*, Cologne: Greven Verlag 1950, pp. 89–91. (English translation: "A Pan-European Interpretation of Donoso Cortés," trans. by Mark Grzeskowiak, *Telos*, no. 125, 2002, pp. 104–105.) In this article I am developing ideas that I originally presented in my monograph *Kierkegaardovská renesancia. Filozofia, náboženstvo, politika* [*The Kierkegaard Renaissance: Philosophy, Religion, Politics*], Bratislava: Premedia 2016. The article is thematically linked also to another text of mine in which I explore the continuity between Kierkegaard's and Ernst Jünger's social criticism. Cf. Peter Šajda, "The Struggles of the Individual in a Nihilistic Age: Kierkegaard's and Jünger's Critiques of

 | DOI:10.1163/9789004689459_013

exploration of the self-contradictions of modernity was popularized in Germany by Theodor Haecker, who published a translation of a fragment of Kierkegaard's *A Literary Review* under the title *A Critique of the Present Age*.[2]

When Karl Jaspers presented his own diagnosis of the state of modern society in *The Spiritual Condition of the Age* (1931),[3] he continued along Kierkegaard's lines of thought in several respects. He drew inspiration primarily from Haecker's translation. In 1933 Jaspers published an amended edition of his book in which Kierkegaard's presence was even more pervasive.[4]

Jaspers was a prominent figure in the large wave of interest in Kierkegaard's intellectual legacy among German-speaking philosophers, theologians, psychologists, and littérateurs of the first half of the twentieth century, which became known as the Kierkegaard Renaissance.[5] At a time when Kierkegaard was still a rarity in the German academic discourse Jaspers, as a professor of the University of Heidelberg, published *Psychology of Worldviews* in which he devoted considerable attention to Kierkegaard's ideas. Jaspers explored a broad spectrum of Kierkegaard's concepts, paraphrased lengthy passages from his works, denoted him as a prophetic voice of nineteenth-century philosophy, and made use of his philosophical structures when discussing fundamental issues of human existence. Jaspers availed himself of Kierkegaardian motifs when describing how the individual deals with guilt, suffering, death, or paradox.[6] When analyzing the synergy of the particular and the universal he examined closely Kierkegaard's theory of the self and his doctrine of despair as the individual's defective relation to himself.[7] Jaspers' presentation of his well-known conception of *boundary situations* contained several references to Kierkegaard. In later works Jaspers highlighted the historical significance

---

Modernity," in *Modern and Postmodern Crises of Symbolic Structures: Essays in Philosophical Anthropology*, ed. by Peter Šajda, Leiden and Boston: Brill 2021, pp. 22–40.

2 Søren Kierkegaard, *Kritik der Gegenwart*, trans. and ed. by Theodor Haecker, Innsbruck: Brenner-Verlag 1914.

3 Karl Jaspers, *Die geistige Situation der Zeit*, Berlin and Leipzig: Walter de Gruyter 1931.

4 In this article I refer to the 1933 edition of the book. Cf. Karl Jaspers, *Die geistige Situation der Zeit*, 5th amended edition, Berlin and Leipzig: Walter de Gruyter 1933. (English translation: *Man in the Mondern Age*, trans. by Eden and Cedar Paul, Garden City, NY: Doubleday 1957.)

5 The term "Kierkegaard Renaissance" was first used by Werner Elert in *Der Kampf um das Christentum. Geschichte der Beziehungen zwischen dem evangelischen Christentum in Deutschland und dem allgemeinen Denken seit Schleiermacher und Hegel*, Munich: Beck 1921, pp. 430–434. I explore the phenomenon in depth in my monograph *The Kierkegaard Renaissance: Philosophy, Religion, Politics*, op. cit.

6 Karl Jaspers, *Psychologie der Weltanschauungen*, Berlin: Julius Springer 1919, pp. 217–218, pp. 225–226, p. 238, p. 242, pp. 245–247.

7 Ibid., pp. 370–381.

of Kierkegaard's existentially oriented philosophy and integrated a number of his concepts into his own philosophical projects.[8] Jaspers' explicit reception of Kierkegaard's ideas spans from the period immediately following the First World War to the late 1960s.

In the following I am going to focus on the thematic continuity between Kierkegaard's reflections in the work that was known in Germany as *A Critique of the Present Age* and Jaspers' social criticism in *The Spiritual Condition of the Age*. I am going to analyze the concepts of *the public* and *the mass* as well as the related concepts of *excellence, envy, leveling* and *the modern press*. Both texts provide original and insightful analyses of the self-contradictions and degenerative tendencies of modern society.

1 Kierkegaard: The Spread of Envy and Leveling as an Impetus for the Rise of the Public

When Kierkegaard comments on the state of modern society in 1846, he claims that *the present age* is characterized by an excess of reflection and a lack of passion.[9] This combination results in reflection losing its connection with

8 See for example Karl Jaspers, *Philosophie*, Berlin et al.: Springer 1932; Karl Jaspers, "Herkunft der gegenwärtigen philosophischen Situation (die geschichtliche Bedeutung Kierkegaards und Nietzsches)," in his *Vernunft und Existenz. Fünf Vorlesungen*, Groningen: J.B. Walters 1935, pp. 1–27. Jaspers' gradual appropriation of Kierkegaard's ideas is analyzed thoroughly by István Czakó. See especially the following articles: István Czakó, "Karl Jaspers: A Great Awakener's Way to Philosophy of Existence," in *Kierkegaard and Existentialism*, ed. by Jon Stewart, Aldershot: Ashgate 2011 (*Kierkegaard Research: Sources, Reception and Resources*, vol. 9), pp. 155–197; István Czakó, "Das Problem des religiösen Akosmismus in der Kierkegaard-Rezeption von Karl Jaspers," *Kierkegaard Studies Yearbook*, 2014, pp. 285–300. See also Hermann Schmid, "Kierkegaard og Jaspers. Forbindelsen mellem samtidskritik og spørgsmålet om muligheden for eksistens," in *Kierkegaard inspiration. En antologi*, ed. by Birgit Bertung, Paul Müller, Fritz Norlan and Julia Watkin, Copenhagen: C.A. Reitzel 1991 (*Søren Kierkegaard Selskabets populære skrifter*, vol. 20), pp. 82–95; Alessandra Granito, " 'A Great Awakener': The Relevance of Søren Kierkegaard in Karl Jaspers' *Aneignung und Polemik*," *Kierkegaard Studies Yearbook*, 2015, pp. 251–269.

9 Although Kierkegaard's primary object of analysis is the contemporary social context in Denmark, there is a tradition of interpeting the term *the present age* as referring to the broader context of European modernity. As I show below, Jaspers joins this tradition by suggesting that Kierkegaard's critique of the age is highly relevant for the twentieth century. For an excellent analysis of the intellectual context in which Kierkegaard formulated his diagnosis see the following works: Jon Stewart, *Søren Kierkegaard: Subjectivity, Irony and the Crisis of Modernity*, Oxford: Oxford University Press 2015; Katalin Nun, *Women of the Danish Golden Age: Literature, Theater and the Emancipation of Women*, Copenhagen: Museum Tusculanum 2013 (*Danish Golden Age Studies*, vol. 8).

existence. While reflection still affects the processes of deliberation, extensive communication, and everyday action, it has ceased to prompt individuals to existential decisions. The present generation is characterized by a stagnation in reflection, which can be both a conscious and an unconscious flight from resolute action. Kierkegaard maintains that "[t]he present age is a sensible, reflecting age, devoid of passion, flaring up in superficial, short-lived enthusiasm and prudentially relaxing in indolence."[10]

An accompanying phenomenon of the spread of passionless reflection is the replacement of intensiveness by extensiveness. The individual's development is characterized by the acquisition of knowledge and competence but not by a striving for personal *excellence* which is typical for a resolute person acting with passion. Respect for excellence, however, does not disappear from society even when people generally do not strive for excellence. The social pressure to choose extensiveness is unable to eliminate this respect entirely, and therefore it attempts to mask it as effectively as possible. A passionless reflective age expresses its respect for excellence in a negative way—in the form of *envy*—while making an effort not to admit it. With the help of reflection, it tries to convince itself that excellence is not what it actually is and neither is envy. The modern age "wants to degrade [excellence], minimize it, until it actually is no longer excellence."[11]

The fast-spreading envy of *the present age* is more latent than the envy of an age dominated by passion and enthusiasm. The age, in which individuals make intensive existential decisions, gives envy a certain character. Envy becomes a negative confirmation of concrete excellence. Kierkegaard mentions the practice of ostracism in ancient Greece, which was a negative distinction of a decisive person. He recalls the ostracism of the Greek statesman Aristides (ca. 525 – ca. 467 BC), who was condemned due to the envy of his virtues and the respect that he enjoyed because of them: "The man who told Aristides that he was voting to banish him, 'because he was tired of hearing him everywhere called the only just man,' actually did not deny Aristides' excellence but confessed something about himself; that his relation to this excellence was not the happy infatuation of admiration but the unhappy infatuation of envy, but

10 *SKS* 8, 66 / *TA*, 68. When referring to *Søren Kierkegaards Skrifter* (vols. 1–28, ed. by Niels Jørgen Cappelørn et al., Copenhagen: Gads Forlag 1997–2013), I use the standard abbreviation *SKS* followed by volume and page numbers. When referring to the English translation of *Two Ages: The Age of Revolution and the Present Age, A Literary Review*, trans. by Howard V. Hong and Edna H. Hong, Princeton: Princeton University Press 1978 (*Kierkegaard's Writings*, vol. 14) I use the standard abbreviation *TA*.

11 *SKS* 8, 80 / *TA*, 84.

he did not minimize that excellence."[12] Ostracism was thus a defense against excellence, but it was not its trivialization. The individuals who rejected excellence respected it, since they knew its power.

In a passionless and indecisive age envy loses character and individuals cease to be conscious of its nature. Characterless envy gives rise to a broad array of misinterpretations which cloud the fact that excellence exists, and envy is its negative acknowledgement. The negative attitude toward excellence persists, but its expression changes. Passionless envy does not have a deeper understanding of the nature of excellence, and therefore it interprets it according to its own standards: it trivializes it.[13] Veiled envious antagonism to the misinterpreted excellence creates new cohesion in the society, as latent envy unifies individuals. A synergic effect is produced, due to which the phenomenon of *leveling* arises. It is a social expansion of the originally individual envy: it is "the negative unity of the negative mutual reciprocity of individuals."[14]

Leveling spreads fastest in an age which lacks passion and enthusiasm, thus creating conditions corresponding to the nature of leveling. It does not spread in a vehement and eruptive way, but rather it is "a quiet, mathematical, abstract enterprise that avoids all agitation."[15] In an age full of fervor and revolutionary tension, eruptions of accumulated energy take place, whereas in a passionless age, leveling spreads without much ado. Although leveling in the proper sense of the word appeared first in *the present age*, it was preceded by conflicts between different kinds of excellence that weakened the social power of excellence. These conflicts, however, took place in concrete frameworks and had concrete protagonists, and therefore they lacked the power of modern abstraction.

Since leveling downplays excellence and promotes uniformity, it has no heroes. Even though it spreads due to individuals' attitudes and actions, in the final balance it is a refutation of the individual. It prompts him to deny his uniqueness and dissolve into something seemingly greater than himself. As a member of a negatively unified crowd, he participates sometimes in activities that simulate excellent actions, but even then he is motivated not by a noble goal but by the fear of the reflective judgement of others. In a leveled

12 *SKS* 8, 80 / *TA*, 83.

13 *SKS* 8, 79–80 / *TA*, 83–84.

14 *SKS* 8, 81 / *TA*, 84. The synergy of different types of envy described by Kierkegaard is explored in the following work: Milan Petkanič, *Filozofia vášne Sørena Kierkegaarda*, Cracow: Towarzystwo Słowaków w Polsce 2010, pp. 24–26. Petkanič also examines the role of passion as an antidote to leveling in his article "O vášni ako vôli k existencii," *Filozofia*, vol. 68, no. 1, 2013, pp. 62–73.

15 *SKS* 8, 80 / *TA*, 84.

environment the category of *generation* triumphs over the category of *individuality*, and the individual, instead of asserting his sovereignty and realizing his potential falls in line with the anonymous others: "The individual does not belong to God, to himself, to the beloved, to his art, to his scholarship; no, just as a serf belongs to an estate, so the individual realizes that in every respect he belongs to an abstraction in which reflection subordinates him."[16] A key determinant of the individual's actions is the mirage of the reflection's judgment. The individual is not afraid of being judged by the opinions of concrete individuals, but rather he is struck by an indeterminate fear of something that is not in the hands of any concrete person. The arbiter of the reflection's judgment is *the public*, "a negatively superior force,"[17] the limitlessness of which provides it with the aura of something colossal.

The public is a truly modern creation, and its fundamental characteristic is that it "exists only *in abstracto*."[18] It did not exist in antiquity, in which people had to be present *en masse in corpore* in order to decide about something.[19] Responsibility had a concrete form and individuals gathered physically. Also in later ages, when majorities and minorities clashed, and individuals sided with one of the parties, the element of concreteness was present throughout the decision-making process. The individual knew that he entrusts his life to actual people who will be affected by the same destiny. First in *the present age* the phantom of the public arises, and in contrast to a group, a platform, or a nation, it is not essentially determined by anything concrete. It is constituted as an abstraction without permanent identity and without an essential connection to ideas or values. For an individual to belong to it, he must negate his character. Renouncing his peculiarity, he adapts to the chimeric nature of the public and dissolves in it: "For a few hours of the day he perhaps is part of the public, that is, during the hours when he is a nobody, because during the hours in which he is the specific person he is, he does not belong to the public."[20] Despite the fact that the public is essentially ungraspable, it is often misinterpreted as an actual group of people, which can be approached and joined.

Given its limitlessness the public appears as an immense entity the sheer size of which makes it superior to concrete human communities. This limitlessness provides it with a unique authority which is claimed by individuals who seek to strengthen their positions. The public does not deny this authority

16 *SKS* 8, 82 / *TA*, 85.
17 *SKS* 8, 83 / *TA*, 87.
18 *SKS* 8, 87 / *TA*, 92.
19 *SKS* 8, 87 / *TA*, 91.
20 *SKS* 8, 88 / *TA*, 93.

to anyone, but rather it is available anytime to those claiming it. The power of the public's authority is clearly manifest in situations when someone speaks in its name and the entire nation listens.[21] Upon closer scrutiny, however, the majestic appearance of the public dissolves, and its weight becomes smaller than that of a concrete individual. This is because the public is "a corps, outnumbering all the people together, but this corps can never be called up for inspection; indeed, it cannot even have so much as a single representative, because it is itself an abstraction."[22] The public has a volatile attitude to the individuals who claim its authority and consider themselves its members. They can neither approach it personally, nor can they be sure of its favor. A concrete community or nation is rooted in responsibility, and if it breaks its commitments, it is condemned as treacherous. The public, however, can today be the individual's ally and tomorrow his enemy without ever breaking any promises. It remains the same ambivalent abstraction without any commitments.

The most efficient promoter of the public is *the modern press*, the nature of which differs from that of the press operating in the periods of concreteness. The latter supports passionate attitudes and becomes involved in social conflicts about concrete values. In a conflict between different value-oriented parties, it espouses concrete positions and defends them. A value-based division of society prompts it to resolute either-or choices. In a society, where decisiveness and passion have disappeared and excessive reflection has weakened interpersonal commitments, the press creates the pseudo-community of the public. In this way it reacts to a real relational emptiness, but the abstraction it creates only deepens the crisis of relationships. Kierkegaard suggests that "just as sedentary professionals are particularly prone to fabricating fantastic illusions, so a sedentary reflective age devoid of passion will produce this phantom [of the public]."[23] The modern press supports life without a connection to an idea and ridicules individuals who have not given up on striving for personal excellence. The public subscribes to various forms of ridicule depending on the situation: in cases where the press becomes too aggressive, it distances itself from the press, although it originally set the press against the nonconformist individual. It feels no obligation to a press medium, which is a "dog [that] has no owner"[24] and can be replaced when necessary.

Kierkegaard's largely negative description of the leveled modernity of the mid-nineteenth century includes a positive element, too. He suggests that the

---

21 Cf. *SKS* 8, 89 / *TA*, 93.

22 *SKS* 8, 87 / *TA*, 91.

23 *SKS* 8, 86 / *TA*, 90.

24 *SKS* 8, 90 / *TA*, 95.

individual, who manages to withstand the pressure of leveling, can be educated and ennobled by such experience. Just as collective solutions are inefficient in the struggle against leveling, so also the leveling is helpless vis-à-vis an individual who has not given up on passionate action based on existential either-or choices.[25] At the same time Kierkegaard refuses to answer the question to what extent the actions of such individuals will affect the development of modern society at large.

2 Jaspers: Envy and Leveling in the Apparatus of Mass-Order

Jaspers adopts a number of motifs from Kierkegaard's critique of the age and uses them to describe the problems of his own time. In *The Spiritual Condition of the Age*, he emphasizes repeatedly the topicality of Kierkegaard's insights. He claims that Kierkegaard identified a development which at his time was still not as disquieting as in the twentieth century when it intensified substantially. Kierkegaard's diagnosis is thus even more relevant in the first half of the twentieth century than it was at the time of its origin. Kierkegaard's observations are especially useful for an interpretation of the period following the First World War. Jaspers declares right in the introduction that "Kierkegaard was the first to undertake a comprehensive critique of his time, one distinguished from all previous attempts by its earnestness. This critique of his was the first to be applicable to the age in which we are now living, and reads as if it had been written but yesterday."[26]

Jaspers' productive reception of Kierkegaardian themes and accents is part of his larger project of assessing the condition of the contemporary Western civilization. His basic observation is that rapid technological development facilitated an unprecedented saturation of the life needs of the masses, thus causing a population explosion. Famines disappeared from the civilized world, public health care and social welfare were made accessible, and the standard of living increased dramatically. This development brought about an emphasis on the rationalization and mechanization of human action, which takes place in the framework of an immense high-performance apparatus that provides

---

25 Kierkegaard pays special attention to the religious individual, whose hope has an eschatological dimension. Cf. *SKS* 8, 85 / *TA*, 88–89. See also *SKS* 8, 103–104 / *TA*, 109–110.

26 Jaspers, *Die geistige Situation der Zeit*, pp. 10–11. (*Man in the Modern Age*, p. 10.) See also Jaspers' statement that "Kierkegaard and Nietzsche remain the leaders in this field ... both of them were revealers of the trend towards annihilation, [and] it was only to be expected that the war should draw unprecedented attention to their doctrines." Jaspers, *Die geistige Situation der Zeit*, pp. 13–14. (*Man in the Modern Age*, p. 15.)

for the needs of the masses.[27] The participation of individuals in the operation of this apparatus is voluntary and appears natural, since it is in their own interest. Their key contribution is the performance of functions assigned to them by the apparatus. In this framework the individual is "a part of the machinery," and his significance is derived from his performance of functions.[28] In order for the apparatus' machinery to function properly, it must conform to the nature of the mass, which is, however, essentially ambiguous.[29]

It is impossible to determine the characteristics of the mass as such since it is an indeterminate collective, the nature of which can be of any kind. Since the mass is "externally quantitative but actually unsubstantial," it appears as "a monstrosity, but when we try to seize it, it disappears."[30] It cannot be grasped by means of concrete qualitative determinations.

It is meaningful to speak of the mass' characteristics first in relation to its concrete manifestations which are constituted in certain contexts. First, there is a temporary assembly of individuals in *the crowd*, which is characterized by impulsiveness, suggestibility, intolerance, and capriciousness. Second, the mass manifests itself in the form of *the public*, which is connected by a certain opinion. In the public the individual joins the nameless others, whom he has never met but with whom he rules ideologically. The ruling instrument is *the public opinion* which is presented as the opinion of all. A concrete individual, however, never manages to appropriate this decisive instrument entirely since others claim it too, and the public opinion changes abruptly. It can turn into its opposite in an instant. It is "impalpable, illusory, transient; 'tis here, 'tis there, 'tis gone; a nullity which can nevertheless for a moment endow the multitude with power to uplift or to destroy."[31] An intellectual connection with the public is thus a tricky alliance with an unreliable abstraction, the anonymous grandiosity of which can quickly change or dissipate. The mass, as a public, is "a phantom, the phantom of an opinion supposed to exist in a vast number

27 Jaspers, *Die geistige Situation der Zeit*, pp. 26–28. (*Man in the Modern Age*, pp. 34–37.)

28 Jaspers, *Die geistige Situation der Zeit*, pp. 26–28. (*Man in the Modern Age*, pp. 33–37.)

29 When analyzing the dynamics of the mass, Jaspers was inspired not only by Kierkegaard's *A Literary Review* but also by Gustav Le Bon's *The Crowd: A Study of the Popular Mind* (1895) and possibly also by Sigmund Freud's *Group Psychology and the Analysis of the Ego* (1921). He mentions both authors in his book. Cf. Jaspers, *Die geistige Situation der Zeit*, p. 29, pp. 138–139. (*Man in the Modern Age*, p. 38, pp. 167–168.)

30 Jaspers, *Die geistige Situation der Zeit*, p. 28 (my translation). It should be noted that Martin Heidegger, who was interested in Kierkegaard's diagnosis of modern society, was highly critical of Jaspers' book. In a letter to Rudolf Bultmann from 29 August 1932, he wrote that he was "appalled" by it. Cf. Gerhard Thonhauser, "Von der Kulturkritik der 'Menge' zur existenzialen Analytik des 'Man,'" *Kierkegaard Studies Yearbook*, 2014, pp. 334–335.

31 Jaspers, *Die geistige Situation der Zeit*, p. 29. (*Man in the Modern Age*, p. 38.)

of persons who have no effective interrelation and though the opinion is not effectively present in the units."[32]

The third contextualized manifestation of the mass is *the mass articulated in an apparatus*. There are different collectives which fulfill certain functions in the apparatus for the provision of the elementary necessaries of the masses, and which are controlled by quantitative majorities. The individual represents in these collectives primarily a quantitative unit, and his contribution to the joint processes is characterized by replaceability. Every collective has specific features, and therefore it is more appropriate to speak of *the masses* rather than *the mass*.[33] Although under normal circumstances the masses tend towards mediocrity, and large collectives are governed by average norms, in rare instances the masses manage to strive for excellence. Due to their changeability, they are able to behave in surprising ways. Although such efforts are infrequent and short-lived, the efficiency of the mass is then much greater than the efficiency of a passionate and resolute individual.[34]

A basic consequence of the individual's absorption into the mass is self-alienation that generates envy. The individual no longer focuses on what is his own but on what belongs to others. He interprets himself through what the others want: "Man as member of a mass is no longer his isolated self. The individual is merged in the mass, to become something other than he is when he stands alone."[35] The suppression of the individual's uniqueness and unrepeatability means that in the mass he focuses on the comparable. The constant comparing generates envy, which leads to rivalry aimed at the maximalization of one's property, pleasure, and power. The massified individual strives to achieve what others achieved before him, his aims do not have an inner, but only an outer determination. If something is not an object of comparison, it is uninteresting and irrelevant. The ubiquitous compulsion to compare oneself with others results in the mass epoch becoming an age of advertisement and self-presentation. It is crucial that the individual achieves what everybody desires.

The individual's activity in the apparatus of mass-order is characterized by several tensions. He performs voluntarily a function that serves the mass' purposes but resists the pressure for complete reduction to a functional element. Although he lets himself be absorbed into the mass, he refuses to be fully deprived of existential self-determination. Thus, the process of the absorption

32 Jaspers, *Die geistige Situation der Zeit*, p. 29. (*Man in the Modern Age*, p. 38.)
33 Jaspers, *Die geistige Situation der Zeit*, pp. 29–31. (*Man in the Modern Age*, pp. 37–41.)
34 Jaspers, *Die geistige Situation der Zeit*, p. 31. (*Man in the Modern Age*, p. 39.) Jaspers does not explore this idea in greater detail.
35 Jaspers, *Die geistige Situation der Zeit*, p. 31. (*Man in the Modern Age*, p. 39.)

into the mass initiates an instinctive defense mechanism. The increasing dependence and awareness of one's replaceability is accompanied by a growing indifference and even hostility towards the apparatus. The more the individual becomes nullified in the mass, the closer he is to a revolt against the mass-order. The performance-driven apparatus, which provides for the needs of the masses, both protects and endangers the individual; it helps him survive and at the same time reifies him. The individual accepts the role of "a mere replaceable cog in a wheelwork,"[36] due to the advantages that it entails, but the dependence proves to be unbearable beyond a certain limit. The fragility of the apparatus of the mass-order consists in the fact that it does not have a mechanism of self-correction that would limit the massification of the individual.

The inner attitude promoted by the technological mass-order is that of practicality. Its implementation creates optimal conditions for the spread of leveling. The individual joins actions performed by others and follows rules made by others. The important factor is not his personal involvement but his practical collaboration with others and the achievement of planned results. In order to ensure smooth collaboration, it is necessary that the individual's decision-making be directed at compromise and not at the qualitative disjunction either-or. His ever firmer anchoring in the mass should ensure that the option of a struggle for his own convictions appears ever more distant. A collective effort aimed at full conformity is leveling at its most efficient, the ultimate result of which is the "the establishment of a typical behaviour which reconstructs upon a new plane something akin to the rule of taboos in primitive times."[37]

Leveling neutralizes the individual's roots which represent an integral part of his specificity and uniqueness. In contrast to the functional difference required by the apparatus of mass-order, the difference of the individuals' origin and personal rootedness represents an obstacle to their fluent incorporation into the apparatus. Leveling therefore weakens their connections to home, spouse, family, and tradition, which distance them from the mass-order. Their consciousness of the past is thereby weakened, and their focus on the present is strengthened. The more intensive the forgetting of the past is, the more the individuals are at the apparatus' disposal: "It is as if the man

36 Jaspers, *Die geistige Situation der Zeit*, p. 34 (*Man in the Modern Age*, p. 42.) In this connection István Czakó observes that "according to Jaspers, Kierkegaard's thought culminates in the uncovering of existential possibilities of the modern existing individual." Cf. Czakó, "Das Problem des religiösen Akosmismus in der Kierkegaard-Rezeption von Karl Jaspers," p. 286.

37 Jaspers, *Die geistige Situation der Zeit*, p. 38, see also pp. 64–66. (*Man in the Modern Age*, p. 47, see also pp. 80–82.)

thus deracinated and reduced to the level of a thing, had lost the essence of humanity ... As he lives on from day to day, the only desire that may stir him beyond that of performing this task is the desire to occupy the best obtainable place in the apparatus."[38] Leveling thus distances the individual from everything that directs him to existential self-determination.

In a society dominated by an overwhelming emphasis on what is common, a radical unification takes place. Natural diversity is reduced to preferred types which are normative for everybody. An example is the reduction of life cycles to *the youth* as a universally desirable type of life. Since the apparatus for the provision of the necessaries of the masses emphasizes performance, individuals are expected to be young or at least able to compete with the young. Therefore, the society is characterized by the spread of the *pretense of youth* both on the part of older people and children. This pretense is voluntary because old age and childhood are linked to a deficit of dignity. Leveling affects fashion, modes of communication as well as the system of education. The aim of education is not to create a new generation of scholars but to realize the average person's idea of education. The process of education is thus dominated by utility, limitedness, conciseness, and achievement of instant intellectual satisfaction.[39]

A prominent role in the leveled mass apparatus is played by *the press*. Its current ambition and scope of activity are far greater than its original mission of *service*, which has been complemented by the mission of *ruling*. The service of the dissemination of information has been turned into a large-scale formation of the masses and reflection of their lives: "Newspapers constitute the mental life of our day as the awareness of how things go with the masses."[40] Journalists enjoy respect in the society because they are able to express the power of the moment in a language accessible to many. The journalist's point of departure in communicating with the public is the life-view of the modern massified individual. An expression of current events on the basis of this life-view requires competence, but the effort to reflect the instincts of millions reduces the journalist's creativity and responsibility. The need for the sale of the press motivates the journalists not only to use an undemanding style of writing and search for sensations but also to be in conformity with the requirements of those who politically rule the masses. The spiritual power of the press, however, can be used to support individuals striving for the authenticity of

38 Jaspers, *Die geistige Situation der Zeit*, p. 41, see also pp. 46–49. (*Man in the Modern Age*, p. 51, see also pp. 58–62.)

39 Jaspers, *Die geistige Situation der Zeit*, pp. 38–40, pp. 103–105. (*Man in the Modern Age*, pp. 48–49, pp. 125–129.)

40 Jaspers, *Die geistige Situation der Zeit*, p. 109 (*Man in the Modern Age*, p. 133.)

existence. In the "multifarious rubbish of what is printed from day to day" we can encounter "the jewels of an amazingly terse and highly polished insight,"[41] and the press can become part of a social movement that would ultimately constitute a countertrend to leveling.

Despite the growing pressure of leveling, Jaspers anticipates that in the apparatus of mass-order a sufficient number of lacunae will remain in which independent thinking will be able to thrive. The operation of the apparatus itself generates resistance by not limiting the reduction of the individual to a function. The negation of the individual's independence is a dynamic that in the end turns against itself.

Participation in the life of the mass does not satisfy the individual in his entirety, and therefore he turns away from it at some point. Individuals who resist leveling can coordinate their actions and become a social force. Jaspers does not expect, however, an early success of such a force.

3 The Public, the Mass and the Fragility of Leveling

Jaspers' reflection on the overall condition of Western society in the 1930s confirms the accuracy of the thematic emphases that Kierkegaard presented almost a hundred years before him. The development in the second half of the nineteenth century and in the first decades of the twentieth century intensified the problems which Kierkegaard considered to be at the root of the crisis of modern society. Jaspers complemented, developed, and updated Kierkegaard's diagnosis of the age.

Jaspers draws on Kierkegaard's concept of the public in two ways. On the one hand, he adopts it when describing a specific type of the mass, and, on the other hand, he uses it when discussing the mass in general. Thus, he makes use of Kierkegaard's insights when analyzing the mass both in the narrower and the broader sense. The continuity between the concepts *the public* and *the mass* is more important because Jaspers devotes only limited attention to the contextual manifestation of the mass as a public.

It is characteristic for both Kierkegaard's *public* and Jaspers' *mass* that they appear immense, but their extent is indeterminable. Kierkegaard's public is completely phantom-like, which is a feature that Jaspers points out too, although he also describes an articulated type of the mass. The anonymous abstractness of both the public and the mass means that one cannot approach

41 Jaspers, *Die geistige Situation der Zeit*, p. 110. (*Man in the Modern Age*, p. 134.)

them personally. They remain ungraspable and distant, and it is impossible to meet them in an immediate way. From the intellectual point of view, they are unreliable and unpredictable. Although they are attractive for the individual in some respects, in the end he loses himself in them. Both entities thrive in an environment of mediocrity, lack of excellence, and lack of passion, but Jaspers points to a rare type of the mass, which in a lucid moment strives for excellence. Jaspers does not adopt Kierkegaard's motif of stagnation in reflection, but rather he emphasizes the moment of technologization, mechanization, and reduction of the individual to a function in the apparatus of mass-order. The two thinkers share the opinion that the modern massified individual aims for an extensive development of competence and knowledge, while avoiding intensive either-or decisions that represent an essential part of existential self-formation.

A crucial overlap of both diagnoses is the observation that the spread of leveling accelerates. The main protagonist of this process is the public or the mass which paralyzes existential resoluteness in the individual and motivates him to be like others. The hegemony of that which is common neutralizes qualitative distinctions which are part of the individual's uniqueness. Both Kierkegaard and Jaspers underline the connection between leveling and envy, but they explain it differently. In Kierkegaard envy is a negative expression of the persisting respect for personal excellence, while in Jaspers it is a consequence of a superficial comparing among leveled individuals.

The key communication organ of the public or the mass is the press, which is the most efficient instrument in spreading the leveling. The press is a manifestation of the vitality of the mass abstraction, and it actively suppresses excellence and promotes the cult of mediocrity. It is, however, ambivalent in its essence. Both philosophers acknowledge the fact that the press is able to oppose leveling. Kierkegaard identifies this kind of attitude in past forms of the press but does not consider it a possibility for his own age. Jaspers maintains that the press can help counter leveling even in contemporary conditions.

Although both Kierkegaard's and Jaspers' critiques of the age are oriented primarily diagnostically, they comprise allusions to potential future developments. Neither of them expects an early abating of the wave of leveling. They do not, however, suppose an absolute victory of leveling over the individual either. They agree on the point that the process of leveling contains inner contradictions that can be used against it, and that its limit is the individual who consciously resists it. Kierkegaard is skeptical about the joint efforts of nonconformist individuals, whereas Jaspers sees them positively and supports even coordinated anti-leveling activities in the field of mass media. Jaspers' overall view is more optimistic, but it is based on a controversial conviction that leveling can be defeated with its own weapons.

Acknowledgments

This article was produced at the Institute of Philosophy, Slovak Academy of Sciences. It was supported by the Slovak Research and Development Agency under the contract No. APVV-20-0137.

Bibliography

Czakó, István, "Karl Jaspers: A Great Awakener's Way to Philosophy of Existence," in *Kierkegaard and Existentialism*, ed. by Jon Stewart, Aldershot: Ashgate 2011 (*Kierkegaard Research: Sources, Reception and Resources*, vol. 9), pp. 155–197.

Czakó, István, "Das Problem des religiösen Akosmismus in der Kierkegaard-Rezeption von Karl Jaspers," *Kierkegaard Studies Yearbook*, 2014, pp. 285–300.

Elert, Werner, *Der Kampf um das Christentum. Geschichte der Beziehungen zwischen dem evangelischen Christentum in Deutschland und dem allgemeinen Denken seit Schleiermacher und Hegel*, Munich: Beck 1921.

Granito, Alessandra, " 'A Great Awakener': The Relevance of Søren Kierkegaard in Karl Jaspers' *Aneignung und Polemik*," *Kierkegaard Studies Yearbook*, 2015, pp. 251–269.

Jaspers, Karl, *Psychologie der Weltanschauungen*, Berlin: Julius Springer 1919.

Jaspers, Karl, *Philosophie*, Berlin et al.: Springer 1932.

Jaspers, Karl, *Die geistige Situation der Zeit*, 5th amended edition, Berlin and Leipzig: Walter de Gruyter 1933 (English translation: *Man in the Mondern Age*, trans. by Eden and Cedar Paul, Garden City, NY: Doubleday 1957).

Jaspers, Karl, "Herkunft der gegenwärtigen philosophischen Situation (die geschichtliche Bedeutung Kierkegaards und Nietzsches)," in his *Vernunft und Existenz. Fünf Vorlesungen*, Groningen: J.B. Walters 1935, pp. 1–27.

Kierkegaard, Søren, *Kritik der Gegenwart*, trans. and ed. by Theodor Haecker, Innsbruck: Brenner-Verlag 1914.

Kierkegaard, Søren, *Two Ages: The Age of Revolution and the Present Age, A Literary Review*, trans. by Howard V. Hong and Edna H. Hong, Princeton: Princeton University Press 1978 (*Kierkegaard's Writings*, vol. 14).

[Kierkegaard, Søren], *Søren Kierkegaards Skrifter*, vols. 1–28, K1–K28, ed. by Niels Jørgen Cappelørn, et al., Copenhagen: Gad 1997–2012.

Nun, Katalin, *Women of the Danish Golden Age: Literature, Theater and the Emancipation of Women*, Copenhagen: Museum Tusculanum 2013 (*Danish Golden Age Studies*, vol. 8).

Petkanič, Milan, *Filozofia vášne Sørena Kierkegaarda*, Cracow: Towarzystwo Słowaków w Polsce 2010.

Petkanič, Milan, "O vášni ako vôli k existencii," *Filozofia*, vol. 68, no. 1, 2013, pp. 62–73.

Šajda, Peter, *Kierkegaardovská renesancia. Filozofia, náboženstvo, politika*, Bratislava: Premedia 2016.

Šajda, Peter, "The Struggles of the Individual in a Nihilistic Age: Kierkegaard's and Jünger's Critiques of Modernity," in *Modern and Postmodern Crises of Symbolic Structures: Essays in Philosophical Anthropology*, ed. by Peter Šajda, Leiden and Boston: Brill 2021, pp. 22–40.

Schmid, Hermann, "Kierkegaard og Jaspers. Forbindelsen mellem samtidskritik og spørgsmålet om muligheden for eksistens," in *Kierkegaard inspiration. En antologi*, ed. by Birgit Bertung, Paul Müller, Fritz Norlan and Julia Watkin, Copenhagen: C.A. Reitzel 1991 (*Søren Kierkegaard Selskabets populære skrifter*, vol. 20), pp. 82–95.

Schmitt, Carl, "Donoso Cortés in gesamteuropäischer Interpretation," in his *Donoso Cortés in gesamteuropäischer Interpretation. Vier Aufsätze*, Cologne: Greven Verlag 1950, pp. 80–114 (English translation: "A Pan-European Interpretation of Donoso Cortés," trans. by Mark Grzeskowiak, *Telos*, no. 125, 2002, pp. 100–15).

Stewart, Jon, *Søren Kierkegaard: Subjectivity, Irony and the Crisis of Modernity*, Oxford: Oxford University Press 2015.

Thonhauser, Gerhard, "Von der Kulturkritik der 'Menge' zur existenzialen Analytik des 'Man,'" *Kierkegaard Studies Yearbook*, 2014, pp. 329–356.

CHAPTER 12

The Notion of Political Abstraction and the Concept of the Modern State in Marx

Ramiro Cardenes

Abstract

This paper attempts to refute the theories that deny that the domain of the political and the state constitute an autonomous and specific field of reflection in Marx's work. To this end, the paper starts with Marx's *Critique of Hegel's Philosophy of Right*. In this text, the young Marx works on the notion of the abstraction of the state, making it possible for him to identify specific aspects of the modern state. On this basis, the paper analyzes the concept of political abstraction and argues that it can be connected to Marx's analysis of modern sociability in later works. In addition, this concept can be linked with the most developed currents in Marxist state theory.

This contribution is organized as follows: It begins (1) by presenting the three principal positions on the possibility of a Marxist theory of the state. Then (2), it presents in general terms how the question of the state appears in Marx's work. Next (3), it makes preliminary observations on the importance of Marx's *Critique of Hegel's Philosophy of Right*. Then (4) it presents the concepts of political abstraction and the separation between civil society and the state. Following that (5), it discusses the concept of democracy and its relation to the abstract state. Subsequently (6), the most common interpretations of Marx's *Critique of Hegel's Philosophy of Right* are discussed. Then (7) the concept of political abstraction is linked to the possibility of a specific understanding of the modern state, and (8) it is connected to the notion of real abstraction. Finally (9), the conclusions argue for the relevance of the concept of "political abstraction" for a Marxist theory of the state and indicate its relationship to the main currents in that field of research.

1 Marxist Theory and the Problem of the State

The question of the theoretical status of the state and the political in Marx's thought is a point of controversy in the field of the social sciences, particularly

 | DOI:10.1163/9789004689459_014

in philosophy. The controversy revolves around the possibility, in Marxist thought, of a systematic theory of the state. That is, it centers on the question of whether it is possible to find a theoretical reflection on the specific form assumed by modern political domination, which is equivalent to the analysis of the capitalist social relation realized by Marx in *Capital*. In very general terms, we can point out three main ways of answering this question.

The first approach, which can be called "instrumental," affirms the existence of a Marxist theory of the state. Starting from the work of Marx and Engels, it continues in Lenin's *State and Revolution* and is then completed with the theoretical contributions of Louis Althusser and Ralph Miliband.[1]

In this conception, which starts from the opposition between structure and superstructure, the state is a passive by-product of economic relations. It takes on transhistorical and generic characteristics which are shared by the different historical periods, even to the point of partial indifference to the different modes of production. The state is conceived as an institution that, as a result of the social division of labor, has separated itself off from society to constitute a repressive instrument of the ruling classes. According to this conception, there is no theoretical space for a specific analysis of the state and the political. The classical authors provide the concepts of the state, and its characteristics are fundamentally invariable and reduced to this instrumental vision. In turn, reducing the state to a simple effect of the social division of labor inhibits the possibility of updating a Marxist understanding of the state, thus moving Marx closer to a Weberian conception of it.

---

1 Mainly, the following texts by Karl Marx: "A Contribution to the Critique of Hegel's *Philosophy of Right*: Introduction" (1844), *The Class Struggles in France, 1848 to 1850* (1850), *The Eighteenth Brumaire of Louis Bonaparte* (1852), *The Civil War in France* (1871), *The Critique of the Gotha Program* (1875), and the prologue to *Contribution to the Critique of Political Economy* (1859), in which the metaphor of base and superstructure appears. By Marx and Engels see *The Communist Manifesto* (1848) and *The Origin of the Family, Private Property and the State* (1884) written by Engels. *The German Ideology*, written between 1845 and 1846, was published complete in 1932, and the chapter dedicated to Feuerbach only appeared in 1924. For this reason, Lenin was not aware of the work when he was writing *State and Revolution* in 1917. Also, see Louis Althusser, *On the Reproduction of Capitalism: Ideology and Ideological State Apparatuses*, trans. by G.M. Goshgarian, London: Verso 2014, and Louis Althusser, "La hegemonía según Gramsci," in *Marx dentro de sus límites*, ed. by García del Campo, trans. by Beñat Baltza Álvarez, Sánchez Cedillo and García del Campo, Madrid: Akal 2003, pp. 163–176. For the instrumentalist conception, see Ralph Miliband, *The State in Capitalist Society*, London: Weidenfeld & Nicolson 1969. Also recommended is *Debates sobre el Estado capitalista 1*, ed. by Horacio Tarcus, Buenos Aires: Imago Mundi 1991, where the debate between Miliband, Poulantzas, and Laclau is presented.

The second position brings together diverse authors, including Norberto Bobbio, Claude Lefort, and Jorge Dotti.[2] This view shares the premises of the first position, namely that the state in Marx's thought would be a passive expression of economic relations, but arrives at opposite conclusions since it maintains that there is not and cannot be a specific Marxist conceptualization of the state. Indeed, starting from the analysis in terms of structure and superstructure, they argue that, for Marxism, the state is an epiphenomenon of a deeper substantial reality: the economic structure. The concept of the state, being reduced to a reflection—at best, partially distorted—of what happens in the field of economic relations, does not provide a "theoretical" space for a specific analysis within the framework of Marxist reflection. Curiously, authors such as Atilio Borón, a defender of the Marxist perspective, make similar arguments and reach similar conclusions. According to Borón, there cannot be a Marxist political theory, which would be impossible within the parameters of historical materialism, but rather a Marxist theory of politics (subordinating the political dimension to the determinations of other spheres).[3]

For our part, we argue that there is a third way of understanding the question of the state in Marxist thought. In general terms, it starts from two premises: on the one hand, it recognizes that there is no systematically developed theory of the state in Marx's work, and, on the other, it affirms that it is possible to identify a series of very relevant conceptualizations of the state. Taking this as a starting point, this third current attempts to reconstruct a theory of the state within the coordinates of Marxist thought. The referents of this position are Antonio Gramsci, Nicos Poulantzas, and the authors of the so-called "German state derivation debate" (Hirsch, Blanke, Alvater).[4]

---

2 See Claude Lefort, *L'invention démocratique*, Paris: Fayard 1981; see Norberto Bobbio "Esiste una scienza politica marxista?" *Mondoperario*, nos. 8–9, 1976, pp. 24–31; see Norberto Bobio, *Ni con Marx ni contra Marx*, Mexico City: Fondo de Cultura Económica 1999; and also see Jorge Dotti, "El hierro de madera," in his *Dialéctica y derecho*, Buenos Aires: Hachette 1983, pp. 233–258.

3 See Atilio Borón, "Teoría política marxista o teoría marxista de la política" in *La teoría marxista hoy. Problemas y perspectivas*, ed. by Atilio Borón, Javier Amadero and Sabrina Gonzalez, Buenos Aires: CLACSO 2006, pp. 175–190.

4 See Antonio Gramsci, "Algunos temas sobre la cuestión meridional" in his *El Risorgimiento*, Buenos Aires: Las Cuarenta 2008, pp. 259–291; see Antonio Gramsci, *Cuadernos de la cárcel*, vol. 3, Mexico City: ERA 1984 and *Cuadernos de la cárcel*, vol. 5, Mexico City and Puebla: ERA 1999. For Poulantzas and the structuralist view, see Nicos Poulantzas, "Estudio de la hegemonía en el Estado" and "Marx y el derecho moderno" in his *Hegemonía y dominación en el Estado Moderno*, Mexico City: Ediciones Pasado y Presente, 1986, pp. 36–86 and pp. 109–130 respectively; see Nicos Poulantzas, *Political Power and Social Classes*, trans. by Timothy O'Hagan, London: NLB 1975; and also see Nicos Poulantzas, *State, Power, Socialism*, London

It is possible to summarize their contributions as follows. First, Gramsci argues that in the West the state should not be considered only as the state apparatus or government, but as the set of activities by which the ruling class not only justifies and maintains its dominion but also obtains the consensus of the governed.[5] Thus, the state consists of the unity between state apparatus and civil society, resulting in a synthesis between coercion and consensus.[6] The notion of hegemony, then, is the one that allows us to understand that capitalist domination does not function exclusively through the coercion exercised by the state apparatus, as if it were an instrument in the hands of a particular class, but also through mechanisms of legitimization present in civil society. So, Gramsci moves away from an instrumentalist conception of the state, incorporating the concepts of "hegemony" (understood as the material, intellectual, and moral domination of one class over another) and the "extended state" (the unity between state apparatus and civil society) into Marxist reflection.

For his part, Poulantzas points out in *Political Power and Social Classes* that the concepts of politics and the state do not find a systematic theoretical treatment in the Marxist tradition but rather elaborations in a "practical state."[7] In that work and in *State, Power and Socialism*, he argues that the separation between the economic sphere of exploitation and the sphere of political domination is a distinctive feature of capitalism.[8]

For this reason, there are no conditions of possibility for a general theory of the state, which claims the invariability of its theoretical object (the sphere of "political domination") through the various historical periods. In this sense, he defends the legitimacy of elaborating a regional theory of the state-political dimension, limited to the capitalist social formation, arriving at his well-known conceptualization of the state as a specific material condensation of the relationships of forces among classes and class fractions. In Poulantzas'

and New York: Verso 2000. For the German state derivation debate, see John Holloway and Sol Picciotto (eds.), *State and Capital: A Marxist Debate*, London: Edward Arnold 1978; Alberto Bonnet and Adrián Piva (eds.), *Estado y capital. El debate alemán sobre la derivación del Estado*, Buenos Aires: Herramienta 2017. The Bonnet and Piva edition is more complete than that of Holloway and Picciotto. Also see Joam Hirsch, "¿Qué es el estado? Reflexiones acerca de la teoría del estado capitalista," in his *El Estado nacional de competencia. Estado, democracia y política en el capitalismo global*, Mexico City: Universidad Autónoma Metropolitana 2001, pp. 33–49.

5 Gramsci, *Cuadernos de la cárcel*, vol. 5, notebook 15, § 10, p. 186.

6 Ibid., notebook 13, § 18, pp. 40–47.

7 Poulantzas, *Political Power and Social Classes*, p. 19.

8 See Poulantzas, *State, Power, Socialism*, pp. 18–20.

view, this conceptualization allows us to arrive at the notion of the "relative autonomy" of politics.

In the German state derivation debate, the matrix shared by the various elaborations consists in conceiving of the state and capital as differentiated forms of existence of the same social relation. In this way, these authors seek to elude the dissolution of the political into the economic, showing how they are nothing more than particularized forms of the same social relations, dialectically deducing the necessary separation of the economic and the political. In this way, the political-state dimension does not arise from the economic base, but rather both spheres and their separation are the expressions of capitalist social relations. This conception, which derives the "state-form" from capitalist social relations, attempts to link intimately "the political" and "the economic," which assume a separate character in capitalism.

The contributions of these elaborations are fundamental to any attempt to develop a Marxist theory of the state. The Gramscian notion of hegemony, the Poulantzian conceptualization of the specific autonomy of the level of politics, and the understanding of the intimate link between economy and politics provided by the notion of "state derivation" constitute crucial elements for research within the coordinates of Marxism. However, despite the differences in their theoretical frameworks, we can identify a common factor: all three views agree in developing their reflections without working around what is known as Marx's "early" texts. In effect, the German debate develops its argument on the basis of concepts present in *Capital* (1867) and the *Grundrisse* (1857–8), while Poulantzas' work "inherits" from Althusser the dismissal of Marxian youthful reflection on the understanding that it is founded on the Feuerbachian idealist problematic of alienation. Gramsci, a prisoner of fascism, did not get to know most of Marx's posthumously published early texts, and in particular, the one written in Kreuznach in the summer of 1843 and published in 1927 by David Ryazanov, as the *Critique of Hegel's Philosophy of Right*.[9]

This paper will seek to contribute to this third current by highlighting some of the contributions of the young Marx present in the *Critique*. In particular, it will work around the concept of "political abstraction," seeking to insert it into the framework of a more general reflection on the state question. "Abstraction" will constitute the specific form of the sphere of the emergence of politics in modern society and will be the distinctive mark of the command-obedience relations that the state, as such, presupposes. In other words, starting from the concept of "political abstraction," we will try to recognize in this work of

9 Karl Marx, *Critique of Hegel's Philosophy of Right*, trans. by Annette Jolin and Joseph O'Malley, New York: Cambridge University Press 1982. This is abbreviated in the following as *Critique*.

the young Marx a conceptualization of the state that can be framed within a broader understanding: that of the social forms proper and specific to modernity.

2 Reflection on the State in Marx's Work

Before entering directly into the 1843 text and the concept of "abstraction," it is relevant to present an overview of how the state appears in Marx's work. For its part, the periodization of Marx's work is not without numerous difficulties.[10] However, we can organize Marx's different elaborations by recognizing different historical-biographical periods of his work and some theoretical patterns.

In general terms, we could identify three periods for the treatment of the question of the state in Marx's intellectual biography. In his youth, we can find a series of elaborations within the framework of a reflection of a philosophical character. The discussions with Hegelian political philosophy, Feuerbach's influence, and the break with the *Junghegelianer* are the defining characteristics of this stage. Interpretations of this period oscillate between two perspectives. On the one hand, some readings affirm that there is no Marxist perspective here but only a left Hegelian one and that the horizon proposed by Marx is not communist but that of a "radical democracy."[11] By contrast, we

---

10 For the periodization of the youth period, see Adolfo Sanchez Vazquez, *Filosofía de la praxis*, Mexico City: Siglo XXI 2003, pp. 132–133, who discusses the starting point of Marxism as a revolutionary theory. He points out that if it is a question of a break with Hegelian philosophy, then it is found in the *Critique* of 1843. If it refers to the discovery of human labor as an essential dimension of man, then one must turn to *The Economic and Philosophical Manuscripts* of 1844. If it is in the appearance of the link between productive forces and relations of production, then the break is in *The German Ideology* of 1845–6. Even if it is a question of conceptualizing revolutionary action, then the beginning of Marxism happens in the *Communist Manifesto* of 1848. Sanchez Vazquez discusses the notion of rupture and proposes that "they should be seen as phases of a continuous and discontinuous process of which they form a part, and which matures already in the *Manifesto of the Communist Party*." On the other hand, the thesis about the "epistemological rupture" between Marx's youth and maturity works is widely known. In this regard, see Louis Althusser, *Pour Marx*, Paris: Maspero 1965; see Louis Althusser and Étienne Balivar, *Lire le capital*, Paris: Maspero 1967; and also see Étienne Balivar, "The Notion of Class Politics in Marx," *Rethinking Marxism*, vol. 1, no. 2, 1988, pp. 18–51.

11 See Maximilien Rubel, *Karl Marx, ensayo de biografía intelectual*, trans. by Saul Karz, Buenos Aires: Paidos 1970, pp. 34–46. Rubel argues that Marx can be considered a radical democrat during the period corresponding to his work as a journalist in the *Rheinische Zeitung*. He abandoned this work due to the pressure of censorship, but he also breaks with the illusion of a "rational state" in his *Critique* of 1843. Moreover, it can be noted that

maintain that here we find the first rudiments of and fundamental elements for the further development of his theory.

A second period, which we could place around the Revolution of 1848, would modify Marx's level of analysis. It would no longer be found in the abstract field of philosophical reflection, but on a more historical and concrete plane where the different transformations of contemporary states appear as the scene of the class struggle. *The Communist Manifesto*, *The Class Struggles in France, 1848 to 1850*, and *The Eighteenth Brumaire of Louis Napoleon* represent classic texts of this period.

Finally, there is a third period, usually known as Marx's "mature" stage, where the critique of political economy dominates. In his investigations, Marx realizes several isolated conceptualizations of the state: the famous distinction between base and superstructure in the Prologue to the *Contribution to the Critique of Political Economy* (1859), and different allusions in the *Grundrisse* (1857–8) and *Capital* (1867) to modern law and the historical role of the state in the constitution of the capitalist economy. For some authors such as Poulantzas, reflection on the state is present in its absence: ideas about the state do not appear explicitly, but they do so in the theoretical effects that the critique of the political economy produces. Be that as it may, Marx does not systematize these reflections. In addition, the numerous exchanges of correspondence and concrete political interventions, such as the *Critique of the Gotha Program* (1875) and *The Civil War in France* (1871), correspond to these years and those following the publication of *Capital* and follow the characteristics of the preceding period.

Furthermore, we can make a classification of the different theoretical modulations in which Marx conceptualizes the question of the state in his different works, which does not necessarily coincide with the above-mentioned biographical stages.

In the first place, in the early works we can find that Marx's argumentation lies in the opposition between the concepts of the concrete, egoistic man who is a member of civil society, and the abstract, universal citizen and member of the political community. This view can be found, in particular, in the *Critique* (1843) and *On the Jewish Question* (written in 1843 and published in 1844). Moreover, the argument of *The German Ideology* (written between 1845

in "A Contribution to the Critique of Hegel's *Philosophy of Right*: Introduction," written at the end of 1843 and published in 1844, he already refers to the emancipation of the proletariat. For the relationship between Marx and Hegel, see Jon Stewart, *Hegel's Century: Alienation and Recognition in a Time of Revolution*, Cambridge: Cambridge University Press 2021, pp. 143–178.

and 1846) already constitutes an autonomous set of ideas concerning the previous reflection. Here, the state appears as the necessary result of the conflict between classes resulting from the social division of labor. The state is an "illusory community," which presents the interests of the dominant social class as those of society as a whole. Although we can see that the logic of "opposition" is maintained, the appearance of the concept of social class marks a new problematic field in Marx's thought.

In addition to these two ways of understanding the state, we could summarize Marx's reflections from the *Communist Manifesto* onwards, in which the "juridical-formal freedom and equality" of individual citizens are opposed to and are the necessary counterpart of the "capitalist exploitation" of labor, and the state functions as the guarantor of this relation of exploitation, taking on the functions of repression and of the political domination of one class over another. This is the most articulate way Marx presents the essential link between the modern state and the capitalist economy but without offering a systematic exposition of the problem. It is on the basis of these reflections that the contributions of Poulantzian structuralism and the German state derivation debate develop.

Having made these general observations, we can begin a new reading of the *Critique* of 1843 that allows us to identify elements for a theoretical understanding of the specificity of the modern state within the tradition of thought inaugurated by Marx.

3 Around the *Critique of Hegel's Philosophy of Right* of 1843

It is appropriate to clarify some essential aspects of our approach to Marx's work. On the one hand, it is not necessary to take a position in the debate on the "epistemological rupture" proposed by Althusser. Instead, it is appropriate to recover the recognition of the existence of different problematics in Marx's thought. This avoids a naive reading that sees a continual evolution from his texts in the *Rheinische Zeitung* to the *Critique of the Gotha Program* without ruptures or shocks. It is unnecessary to contrast a "young, philosophical, and idealistic" Marx with a "mature and scientific" one. Instead, it is enough to recognize the existence of diverse problematics, which allow the development of various concepts, which are neither moments of linear evolution nor mutually exclusive. In this sense, this paper's objective is to identify components of the concept of the state in the *Critique* that are relevant for contemporary reflection, which will allow subsequent research to articulate it with Marx's work as a whole.

The *Critique* occupies a singular place in Marx's work. First, the text, which was not published during his lifetime, consists of writings produced in the town of Kreuznach in the summer of 1843 and published posthumously in 1927. Although related to it, they should not be confused with "A Contribution to the Critique of Hegel's *Philosophy of Right*: Introduction," written between December 1843 and January 1844 and published in the *Deutsch Französische Jahrbücher* in 1844.[12] The 1843 *Critique* is a notebook with critical annotations to the third section (The State) of the third part (Ethical Life) of Hegel's *Philosophy of Right*. That is, it is not a systematic treatise of the problem of the state, but a set of critical observations on Hegelian theory.

These elements may explain why this text has received little attention in the field of Marxist research. Indeed, as Abensour points out, it is considered simply a moment in Marx's formative stage and not a positive source of proper concepts for Marxist reflection.[13] In his famous preface to his 1859 *Contribution to the Critique of Political Economy*, Marx alludes to the intellectual crisis that in 1843 led him to make a critical revision of the Hegelian philosophy of right:

> The first work I undertook to dispel the doubts assailing me was a critical review of the Hegelian philosophy of right, the introduction to which appeared in the *Deutsch-Französische Jahrbücher* issued in Paris in 1844. My inquiry led to the conclusion that neither legal relations nor forms of state could be grasped whether by themselves or on the basis of a so-called general development of the human mind, but on the contrary they have their origin in the material conditions of existence, the totality of which Hegel, following the example of the Englishmen and Frenchmen of the eighteenth century, embraces within the term "civil society"; that the anatomy of this civil society, however, has to be sought in political economy.[14]

A linear interpretation of these passages can reduce the contribution of the *Critique* to the inversion of the Hegelian approach to the state: instead of society being a moment of the state, as Hegel claimed, the state is the alienated expression of civil society. The quest to understand the anatomy of civil society leads

12 Karl Marx, "A Contribution to the Critique of Hegel's *Philosophy of Right*: Introduction," in *Critique of Hegel's Philosophy of Right*, trans. by Annette Jolin and Joseph O'Malley, New York: Cambridge University Press 1982, pp. 129–142.

13 See Miguel Abensour, *La dèmocratie contre l'Ètat. Marx et le moment machiavélien*, Paris: Presses Universitaires de France 1997, pp. 11–14.

14 Karl Marx, *A Contribution to the Critique of Political Economy*, Peking: Foreign Languages Press 1976, pp. 2–3.

to research into political economy. A unilateral reading of this path favors an understanding of the concept of the state in an economic understanding of the concept of the state, which will function as a foundation both for instrumentalist interpretations and for denying the possibility of a Marxist theory of the state.

Therefore, the posthumous character, the fact that it is a critical commentary, and this way of locating these reflections in Marx's intellectual development, can explain the lack of attention paid to the *Critique*. However, there are several features in this text that make it particularly interesting.

In the first place, in spite of the little interest it has aroused, the proposal is to rescue the fact that Marx places the problem of the state within the framework of the process of "political abstraction." This characteristic process of modernity allows us to approach the modern state as a necessary and concurrent institution of the relations characteristic of bourgeois society. As we shall see, the concept of "abstraction" makes it possible to understand the objectivity of the state and its real separation from civil society.

Secondly, at this moment of Marx's intellectual development, the absence of concepts linked to the notions of social class, mode of production, and class struggle stands out. Although this can be considered a limit because of their theoretical relevance and the weight they exert on Marxist reflection as a whole, this absence allows the young Marx to develop, at the same time, a concept of the state without the risk of an economic or instrumentalist gaze such as that which dominated a good part of the later Marxist tradition.[15]

Finally, the *Critique* is a critical and profound examination of Hegel's work, and this allows Marx to appropriate the profoundest moments of Hegel's reflections. Indeed, in Marx's eyes, it is Hegel's work, stripped of its illegitimate speculative inversion, that provides the closest description of the modern state.

4 Civil Society, State and Abstraction in *Critique of Hegel's Philosophy of Right*

Analyzing the argument developed by Marx, we notice that he recognizes positively in the Hegelian analysis the verification of the separation between civil society and state in modernity as a historical fact. Civil society, as a sphere of particular interest, is confronted with the political state, which is truly universal: "But Hegel proceeds from the separation of civil society and the political

15 See Poulantzas, "Estudio de la hegemonía en el Estado," p. 41.

state as two actually different spheres, firmly opposed to one another. And indeed this separation does actually exist in the modern state."[16] Indeed, for Marx, "Hegel is not to be blamed for depicting the nature of the modern state as it is, but rather for presenting what is as the essence of the state."[17] That is to say, despite the limitations of his speculative method, Hegel succeeds in giving an account of the state "as it is" in its empirical truth. Thus, there is a level at which the Hegelian description of the reality of the state is adequate, even though his attempt at grounding it metaphysically is illegitimate.

Concerning this opposition between society and state, Marx points out that Hegel fails in the attempt to overcome this split, arriving only at a false identity between the two elements, a "dualistic" and abstract identity. According to Marx, there are two reasons for the Hegelian failure: one is of the logical order and the other of the order of the real. The logical cause of this failure lies in the idealist character of the Hegelian dialectic. In turn, there is a real obstacle to the Hegelian attempt to overcome the split: the separation between state and civil society is an objective characteristic of the modern world.

Marx's acknowledgment of Hegel goes so far. Then, he criticizes the inverted form in which Hegel presents the relation between the terms of this contradiction: Hegel reasons as if the historically existing institutions were the result of the necessary development of the rationality of the Idea. With this argumentation, Hegel elevates the historically and empirically existing situation to the status of a philosophical truth, which was interpreted as the subordination of philosophical thought to the legitimation needs of the Prussian state.[18]

Thus, Hegel subordinates civil society and the family as moments of the state, but this operation hides the fact that, in reality, the state is the result of the practical activity of concrete human beings (organized in families and civil society). Marx will point out that, on the contrary, instead of civil society being a derived moment of the state, it is civil society that constitutes its condition: "Family and civil society are the presuppositions of the state; they are the really active things; but in speculative philosophy it is reversed."[19] What Marx criticizes as the inversion of subject and predicate is, then, generated: "Hegel at all times makes the Idea the subject and makes the proper and actual subject ... the predicate. But the development proceeds at all times on the side

16 Marx, *Critique*, p. 72.

17 Ibid., p. 64.

18 See Daniel Moreno Tonda, "La crítica del joven Marx a Hegel. El Manuscrito de Kreuznach," *Antítesis. Revista Iberoamericana De Estudios Hegelianos*, no. 1, 2021, pp. 111–138. Moreno Tonda polemicizes against the interpretations that see Hegel's work as an apology for the Prussian state.

19 Marx, *Critique*, p. 8.

of the predicate."[20] Then he reconstructs the Hegelian process of speculative inversion:

> Had Hegel started with the real subjects as the bases of the state it would not have been necessary for him to let the state become subjectified in a mystical way. "However, the truth of subjectivity," says Hegel, "is attained only in a subject, and the truth of personality only in a person." This too is a mystification. Subjectivity is a characteristic of subjects and personality a characteristic of the person. Instead of considering them to be predicates of their subjects Hegel makes the predicates independent and then lets them be subsequently and mysteriously converted into their subjects. The existence of the predicate is the subject.... Hegel makes the predicates, the object, independent, but independent as separated from their real independence, their subject. Subsequently, and because of this, the real subject appears to be the result; whereas one has to start from the real subject and examine its objectification. The mystical substance becomes the real subject and the real subject appears to be something else, namely a moment of the mystical substance. Precisely because Hegel starts from the predicates of universal determination instead of from the real *ens*, and because there must be a bearer of this determination, the mystical Idea becomes this bearer.[21]

Furthermore, the analysis of the split between civil society and the political state will allow us to arrive at the concept of "political abstraction." In the Middle Ages, we find an identity of civil society and political society, where social differences were immediately political differences. Marx points out that in the development and constitution of modern political states, under the absolute monarchies, the political estates became converted into civil classes. In this way, by taking apart the interweaving between the plane of political representation and the background of social relations, equality is achieved in a political heaven that coexists—in the manner of Christianity—with earthly inequality in society.

> It is a development of history that has transformed the political classes into social classes such that, just as the Christians are equal in heaven yet unequal on earth, so the individual members of a people are equal in the heaven of their political world yet unequal in the earthly existence of

20 Ibid., p. 11.
21 Ibid., pp. 23–24.

> society. The real transformation of the political classes into civil classes took place under the absolute monarchy.[22]

However, this distinction between the estates continued to be a political difference. The French Revolution concluded the social conversion of the difference between the estates by sanctioning the universality of liberty and political equality. In this way, it transformed the differences between estates into merely social differences, i.e., without immediate political significance. Consequently, social differences correspond to the sphere of private life, while equality is relegated to the domain of political life, hence consummating the separation between society and the state: on the one hand, the social life of the *bourgeois*, and on the other, the state participation of the citizen, on a plane structured by juridical equality and political freedom.

The state resulting from this process, separated from civil society (made up, then, of individuals who pursue their private interests, forming a conglomerate of particular interests), is an abstract state where there is no true unity of the general and the particular, but rather a specific form of divorce between these terms. From the point of view of the young Marx, this process is characteristic of modern, bourgeois, capitalist society: "The abstraction of the state as such belongs only to modern times because the abstraction of private life belongs only to modern times. The abstraction of the political state is a modern product."[23]

For this reason, even if there is no critique of political economy as a discourse that describes the rationality of modern social relations between individuals who exchange commodities, we find here the basis for a treatment of the modern (and, eventually, capitalist) specificity of the state.

5 Democracy and the Modern State

In addition to the separation between society and state, the other fundamental concept that emerges in the *Critique* is "democracy," which fulfills its function precisely as a real overcoming of the split between society and state.

Indeed, as Hegel fails to provide a legitimate synthesis of the split between the particular (civil society) and the universal (the state), Marx proposes the concept of "democracy" as a substantial unity between people and state. In

22 Ibid., p. 80.
23 Ibid., p. 32.

this way, it would imply the dissolution of the abstract separation of the state from society.

The separate character of the modern state is what, in Marx's view, negates its real foundation: the unity of the people with itself, through democracy as the unity of form and content. For Marx, democracy is not reduced to one particular institutional engineering of the state: democracy is the foundation of the different forms of state. In this regard, he points out:

> In democracy the abstract state has ceased to be the governing moment. The struggle between monarchy and republic is itself still a struggle within the abstract form of the state. The political republic [that is, the republic merely as political constitution] is democracy within the abstract form of the state.[24]

In other words, democracy refers to the form of sociability in which political power does not present itself in a separate way such as to dominate the social whole. Therefore, the struggle between republic and monarchy refers to the opposition between two different institutional forms within the separation of the state. Democracy, then, is not simply one form among others, but, if anything, it is the form that most adequately expresses the content (society): "Furthermore it is evident that all forms of the state have democracy for their truth, and for that reason are false to the extent that they are not democracy."[25] As the unity of form and content, Marx points to democracy as the social existence itself of human beings. In this way, every form of state will be a certain form of democracy, as a social foundation that allows statehood:

> democracy is the essence of every political constitution, socialized man under the form of a particular constitution of the state. It stands related to other constitutions as the genus to its species; only here the genus itself appears as an existent, and therefore opposed as a particular species to those existents which do not conform to the essence.[26]

Democracy is thus, for the young Marx, the secret of all forms of government. The advent of democracy will imply for Marx the disappearance of the state with its abstract and separate character.

24 Ibid., p. 31.
25 Ibid.
26 Ibid., p. 30.

Some literature affirms that Marx's concepts point to the suppression of the state and of any political dimension, so as to achieve the natural sociability of the human being in an immediate way and without institutions, realizing its essence in a non-alienated form.[27] By contrast, it has also been argued that this notion of democracy is not elementally different from the later idea of communism.[28] However, following Abensour, one can interpret Marx as proposing an overcoming of the separation of the state, which implies the transformation of the political.[29] That is to say, the overcoming of the abstract state does not imply the elimination of the political dimension as a specific sphere but rather its transformation. In other words, this conception of democracy does not necessarily imply the aspiration to immediate sociability that can dispense with political mediation. The Marxian objective in 1843 would be to try to overcome duality, which means that the political would not appear as something separate and dominant from the whole, but as one more sphere within the democratic social totality. In this light, we can interpret the following passage:

> In democracy the state as particular is only particular, and as universal it is the real universal, i.e., it is nothing definite in distinction from the other content. The modern French have conceived it thus: In true democracy the political state disappears [*der Politische Staat untergehe*]. This is correct inasmuch as *qua* political state, *qua* constitution it is no longer equivalent to the whole. In all states distinct from democracy the state, the law, the constitution is dominant without really governing, that is, materially permeating the content of the remaining non-political spheres. In democracy the constitution, the law, the state, so far as it is political constitution, is itself only a self-determination of the people, and a determinate content of the people.[30]

Thus, the Marxian vindication of democracy can be understood as the search to prevent the modern abstraction of the political from setting itself up over and against the human being as a separate and dominant element. In this way, Marx goes beyond the liberal-radical demands that characterized his period in the *Rheinische Zeitung* and begins to delineate his theoretical field.

27 See Dotti, *Dialéctica y derecho*, pp. 253–258.

28 See Ariel Eidelman, "El joven Marx y el debate del Estado moderno, 1842–1848," in *Hic Rhodus. Crisis capitalista, polémica y controversias*, no. 4, 2013, p. 5.

29 See Abensour, *La dèmocratie contre l'Ètat*, pp. 72–83.

30 Marx, *Critique*, p. 31.

6 On the Interpretations of the *Critique of Hegel's Philosophy of Right*

In addition to these two theoretical subjects (the separation between civil society and the political state, and the question of democracy), interpretations of the *Critique* have worked on two fundamental elements. These are, on the one hand, the epistemological break with the Hegelian dialectic and, on the other, the influence of Feuerbach on this break.

In the first place, following the reading of the Italian Marxist Della Volpe, we can find in the *Critique* of 1843 the first elements of what later become the specifically Marxian methodological development, starting from the general critique of Hegel's speculative dialectic. In effect, Marx's analysis leads to the "verification of the validity of the general materialist critique of the *a priori* and with it the demonstrated necessity of substituting every philosophical-speculative conception by a philosophical-historical or sociological-materialist conception."[31] This is the famous "inversion" of the dialectic, which in Hegel is found in a mystified form, and which Marx puts on its real material basis. In the same sense, Jorge Dotti summarizes the Marxian task:

> To recover the (supposed) "rational core" of dialectic in a scientific exposition of reality, Marx rehearses in 1843 a complicated salvage operation, the results of which are as uncertain as they are lasting, articulating it as follows: (a) he rejects the idealistic framework of Hegelian mediation; (b) he re-inverts the opposites, i.e., "straightens" the opposition..., (c) he welcomes the figure of "contradiction" because he understands that it represents the real reflexive movement between the foundation and the phenomenal.... Finally, (d) he elaborates a critical discourse on the state and politics.[32]

That is to say, in both a defense of Marxism (Della Volpe) and a critical perspective (Dotti), it is emphasized that in the 1843 text we find, centrally, the moment of Marx's theoretical break with Hegel and the first modulations of dialectical thought that will inform his later intellectual development. In other words, in this line of interpretation, it is in the 1843 text that can find the point of no return in Marx's critique of Hegel. At the same time, there is considerable literature that proposes the idea that the instrument with which this

---

31 Galvano Della Volpe, *Rousseau e Marx, e altri saggi di critica materialistica*, Rome: Riunitini 1997, p. 145.

32 Dotti, *Dialéctica y derecho*, pp. 233–234.

theoretical rupture was carried out was taken by Marx from Feuerbach's philosophy. Rocca summarizes this idea as follows:

> Marx would finally prove the insufficiency of the Hegelian dialectic, its mysticism, its hypostasis, its panlogism, and its transformation of real oppositions into ideal oppositions that can then be resolved in a speculative synthesis, which is evidenced as abstract and formal and, therefore, unreal. It would also be here that we would find the Marxian search for a real subject—no longer the Idea or the Spirit—of this movement of oppositions, which Marx would try to achieve by applying Feuerbach's transformative method.[33]

Thus, the Feuerbachian influence can be summarized as the adoption of the transformative method:

> The method of the reforming critique of *speculative philosophy* as such does not differ from that already used in the *Philosophy of Religion*. We need only turn the *predicate* into a *subject* and thus as *subject* into object and *principle*, that is, only reverse speculative philosophy. In this way, we have unconcealed, pure, and untarnished truth.[34]

In the same way, Sanchez Vazquez affirms that "the young Marx extends Feuerbach's critique to Hegel's political philosophy and, as a fruit of his own critique, sees in this philosophy a speculation or mystification analogous to that denounced by Feuerbach."[35] For his part, Poulantzas shares the interpretation that would understand the Marx of 1843 as a Feuerbachian. Referring to the reception of this work, Poulantzas points out that the Italian Marxist school of Della Volpe

> has radically challenged the vulgarized conception of the state as the simple tool or instrument of the dominant class/subject. Certainly, it has also posed original problems related to the question of the specific autonomy of the structures and the class practices in the capitalist mode

33 Facundo Rocca, "El Manuscrito de Kreuznach 1843. Crítica de la filosofía del Estado de Hegel," *Hic rhodus. Crisis capitalista, polémica y controversia*, no. 16, 2019, p. 101.

34 Ludwig Feuerbach, "Preliminary Theses on the Reform of Philosophy," in *The Fiery Brook: Selected Writings. Ludwig Feuerbach*, trans. by Zawar Hanfi, London and New York: Verso 2012, p. 154.

35 Adolfo Sanchez Vazquez, "Economía y humanismo" in Marx's *Cuadernos de París* [*Notas de lectura de 1844*], Mexico City: Ediciones ERA 1974, p. 20.

> of production. However, it locates Marx's originality relative to Hegel in his critique (in the works on the Hegelian theory of the state) of the speculative empiricism which invariably characterizes Hegel's problematic. But this critique is in fact only Marx's revival of the critique which Feuerbach made of Hegel.[36]

For Poulantzas, influenced by Althusser, recognizing the "epistemological rupture" between the works of youth and maturity is a fundamental methodological premise for any approach to Marx's scientific work. In Poulantzas's view, the young Marx is still working within the framework of a historicist (because of his use of Hegelian language) and anthropological (for using Feuerbach's critical model) reflection. This blocks a scientific Marxist understanding of the state, which is only possible as a result of his passage from youth to maturity, where "Marx elaborates the scientific concepts of the mode of production, class, class struggle, base, and superstructure."[37] Complementing this vision, Jorge Dotti adds:

> Whether dealing with the state or with capital, the unchanged demand is that critical thought must go beyond the immediate phenomenal (formal law, prices) to the foundation (civil society, contained labor-value), of which the appearance cannot but be its realization, even if it seems to be denying it. Modern bourgeois conditions as a whole are—according to Marx—the contradictory realization, the "alienation" of an essential instance (the *Soziale Qualität* of man, production in general).[38]

From this perspective, the Marxian logic of investigation necessarily depends on an essence, the hidden content of the forms of manifestation which it adopts. The essence (man's social quality) would express itself, realizing itself, in an inverted (i.e., contradictory) way in the state, which is nothing other than the alienated and necessary expression of man's social quality, which is its fundament. The interpretations of Dotti and Poulantzas lead to overvaluing the concept of essence. This essence would be presented as an ontologically invariable fundament, which results in interpreting Marx within an idealist framework. In Poulantzas' view, this would be nothing more than the symptom of Marx's youthful problematic. According to Dotti, it would indelibly mark Marxian reflection as a whole, accompanying Marx throughout his intellectual

36 Poulantzas, *Political Power and Social Classes*, p. 136.

37 Poulantzas, "Estudio de la hegemonía en el Estado," p. 40.

38 Dotti, *Dialéctica y derecho*, p. 233.

biography ("Whether dealing with the state or with capital"). This interpretation is, however, open to debate.

Dotti's argument presents the following difficulty: it is not evident that Marx's central theoretical concern is to "discover the hidden essence" of phenomena. If this were the case, Marx would remain within the coordinates of the classical idealist thought of modernity. However, the Marxian quest is different.

Dotti points out that Marx's "critical demand" is found in both his critique of politics and his critique of capital. If we consider that the critique of politics lacks systematic treatment, we can turn to Marx's own remarks in *Capital*.

In the systematic investigation that Marx carries out in his critique of political economy, his central concern is not exclusively or primarily the attempt to discover the hidden content of phenomena. In the case of the critique of political economy, this would reduce its contribution to discovering the labor contained in the substance of the value of commodities, remaining within the limits of the Ricardian school. However, Marx's guiding question is different: "Political economy has indeed analyzed value and its magnitude, however incompletely, and has uncovered the content concealed within these forms. But it has never once asked the question why this content has assumed that particular form."[39] That is to say, the distinctive feature of Marxian research is not to identify the content hidden behind the form but to explain why that content adopts that form and not another. Transferring that reasoning to politics, the question becomes *why civil society adopts the form of a representative state in modernity.*

In the Postface to the second edition of *Capital,* Marx quotes approvingly a review describing his method: "The one thing which is important for Marx is to find the law of the phenomena with whose investigation he is concerned; and it is not only the law which governs these phenomena, in so far as they have a definite form and mutual connection within a given historical period."[40] Again, this search is not limited to identifying the hidden content in those phenomena, but looks for the logic and rationality that makes those phenomena the necessary form of expression of the contents manifested in their connection with a historical period. That is, it seeks to discover the law that governs them. In this quotation, if we were to follow Dotti, the "law" would consist of the hidden content, as if it were a foundation. In Marx's thought, to the contrary, the search to identify the relationship (in this case, between con-

39 Karl Marx, *Capital: A Critique of Political Economy*, trans. by Ben Fowkes, London and New York: Penguin Books in association with New Left Review 1982, pp. 173–174.

40 Ibid., p. 100.

tent and form), expressed through the "law" that critical thinking must identify, takes precedence. When one transfers the reflection to the field of politics, it is a question of determining what makes the state in bourgeois society present itself as something separate from society, denying the social determinations of individuals and abstracting from them.

In addition, some readings propose to moderate Feuerbach's influence on the *Critique*. In this way, while Antoine Artous does not deny Feuerbach's influence on Marx, he insists on not overestimating it.[41] Artous warns that subordinating the Marxian approach to the Feuerbachian framework prevents us from identifying the particular twist that Marx gives to the problematic of alienation in its application to politics. He points out that Marx had already begun to distance himself from Feuerbach when criticizing him for not applying his method to politics. According to Artous, the attempt to apply the method to Hegel's political work implies a transformation of the method itself, which leads Marx to pose a different problematic from that maintained by Feuerbach.

Artous' argument holds that Marx, contrary to Feuerbach, no longer refers to "abstract man" but to concrete man as historically situated. In this way, one can differentiate the Feuerbachian critique of religion (which has its origin in the individual consciousness) from the critique of politics (which has its origin in the social structure). Thus, reading Marx through Feuerbach runs the risk that "the critique of politics as alienation then becomes an ethical-political critique or a critique of critical psycho-sociology, but not a work on an objective social form."[42]

Artous, for his part, polemicizes against Poulantzas by pointing out that the latter mistakenly considers that the notions of "generic man" and "concrete individual" are identical in Marx's text. He argues that political alienation is not a problem related to "concrete individuals" but rather to the generic man as a social quality of the human being. Whereas the former would lead to a humanist-empiricist problematic, the latter leads to an understanding of alienation as social and structural.[43] That is to say, for most of the literature on the subject, political alienation would be nothing more than a simple illusion of the alienated consciousness and would not constitute an objective form proper to modern society. However, Artous correctly insists on considering alienation in the young Marx as an objective social process. Moreover, he

41 See Antoine Artous, *Marx, el Estado y la política*, trans. by Tomás Callegari and Jonathan Rocca Funes, Barcelona: Sylone 2016, pp. 58–60.

42 Ibid., p. 46.

43 See ibid., p. 61; see Poulantzas, *Political Power and Social Classes*, pp. 124–125; and also see Poulantzas, "Estudio de la hegemonía en el estado," pp. 40–41.

appropriately suggests also that the *Critique* of 1843 does not coincide exactly with the framework of analysis of *On the Jewish Question*, written in the fall of 1843 and published in 1844, or with the *Economic and Philosophic Manuscripts* of 1844. Whereas in *On the Jewish Question* alienation operates in the individual (through the opposition between *bourgeois* and *citoyenne*), in the *Critique* the opposition is between social forms: civil society and the state. At the same time, although the process of alienation described in the *Economic and Philosophic Manuscripts* describes a socially objective process, the permanent allusion to the "species-being" of man brings Marxian reflection closer to an anthropological and essentialist problematic with Feuerbachian roots. By contrast, Artous' reading of the *Critique* can be articulated with the purpose of this article: to read the problematic of abstraction and separation of the state as an objective and characteristic process of modern society.[44]

7 Abstraction as a Form of the Political in Modernity

Marx refers to the "abstract state" as the independence of state and politics from other orders. Political abstraction is understood in the light of the separation between civil society and the state but not reduced to their simple separation: it also implies the necessary division between a sphere that will function with the logic of politics, where freedom and equality are central concepts, and a non-political sphere, where different mechanisms of the lack of freedom will operate, and there will be objectively structured social inequality.

While in the medieval world the human being was linked to society by the estate to which he belonged, in modern society the human being appears as a free individual who pursues his own interests. This appearance of the selfish individual, the atom of bourgeois society, only becomes possible through the overcoming of personal relations of dependence and by abstracting from social determinations. Political representation implies a process of universalization, homogenization, and abstraction of civil society, which presents itself as a "crowd" and a "mass" of selfish individualities.

The generalization of society is achieved only through its transformation into a sum of individuals, equal in their egoism and their juridical freedom: abstractly equal before the law and abstractly free as citizens with political freedom. The only way to establish political ties in such a society is through the "abstraction" of the state, in a double sense: by postulating a juridical equality

44 Artous also identifies Marx's treatment of bureaucracy as a distinctive element of modern statehood. See Artous, *Marx, el Estado y la política*, pp. 70–72.

that abstracts from the inequalities present in civil society, and insofar as the state is "abstracted," separated from the civil society it represents.

Thus, the modern process of disembedding social, economic, and political relations is not only a condition of the possibility of the state, but the emergence of the state is itself the very expression of this process. The social rise of the bourgeoisie implies the separation of economic domination from social and political ties, a process which produces the abstraction of political domination from social and economic relations. In this way, Marx finds that in modernity political power is necessarily presented as something "indifferent" to social and economic relations, as something abstracted and separated from them. This is not a casual occurrence but constitutes an essential aspect of modern sociability. What emerges as a distinctive element of modern political relations is the existence of a separate state, as a "split" expression of civil society. To the extent that the very logic of the modern state consists in representation, it implies that society, as such, is not present.

Thus, the concept of the "abstraction" of the state should not be confused with a kind of "illusion," a "delusion of consciousness," confronted with the "concrete and real" character of civil society. As analyzed previously, this type of reasoning is closer to the Feuerbachian theme of alienation. At most, perhaps it could be found later in the notion of the state as an "illusory community" in *The German Ideology*, which reinforces the importance of the *Critique*.

By contrast, the political abstraction proper to the state that Marx thematizes in this early text is inherent to the emergence of the social relations characteristic of capitalist modernity and not a mere mirage of consciousness. Indeed, in this point lies both Marx's recognition of the Hegelian approach and his signaling of its limit: the impossibility of overcoming the split lies in the fact that it is a real separation and not a mere speculative problem.

8 Political Abstraction and Real Abstraction

"Political abstraction" is a concept that makes it possible to theoretically capture the specific configuration that political domination acquires in modern societies: it necessarily implies the separation between a sphere of political domination and the economic relations present in what Hegel called "civil society." This separation allows the universal political equality of citizens and the constituent elements of the modern state that emerged from the French Revolution to coexist with the inequalities inherent in civil society. The sphere of the state is, therefore, an objectively autonomous space separated from the field of the social; this separation is the form of its real functioning, and, from our perspective, it is what generates the condition of the possibility of a specific theoretical treatment of modern statehood.

Consequently, abstraction refers to objective social forms, characteristic of modernity, because "abstraction of private life belongs only to modern times."[45] Political abstraction is not a mere effect in consciousness but resembles what Sohn Rethel calls "real abstraction." Referring to the abstraction of the value form, this author states:

> While the concepts of natural science are thought abstractions, the economic concept of value is a real one. It exists nowhere other than in the human mind, but it does not spring from it. Rather it is purely social in character, arising in the spatio-temporal sphere of human interrelations. It is not people who originate these abstractions but their actions.[46]

In the same way, political abstraction has no empirical existence: social and economic differences between individuals do not cease to exist at any time. However, political abstraction operates as the objectivity of social functioning: equality as citizens in the representation of the state.

Deepening this line of interpretation, authors such as Artous propose to draw a parallel between the *Critique* and the mature works.[47] He points out, for example, that in the *Grundrisse*, the treatment of modernity, in contrast to pre-capitalist relations, can be read in the logic of the domain of abstraction:

> These *objective* dependency relations also appear, in antithesis to those of *personal* dependence (the objective dependency relation is nothing more than social relations which have become independent and now enter into opposition to the seemingly independent individuals, i.e. the reciprocal relations of production separated from and autonomous of individuals) in such a way that individuals are now ruled by *abstractions*, whereas earlier they depended on one another.[48]

In turn, in considering the analysis of the fetishism of the commodity present in *Capital*, Artous advances in the same way in the theoretical configuration

45 Marx, *Critique*, p. 32.

46 Alfred Sohn Rethel, *Intellectual and Manual Labor*, trans. by Martin Sohn Rethel, London and Basingstoke: Macmillan Press 1978, p. 20.

47 See Artous, *Marx, el Estado y la política*, pp. 91–127.

48 Karl Marx, *Grundrisse*, trans. by Martin Nicolaus, New York: Random House 1973, p. 164.

of objective forms of capitalist sociability.[49] For him, the fetishism of the commodity is a theory that seeks to conceptualize the forms of social opacity constitutive of capitalism. In this, the role of abstraction (as the concealment of social relations, and as the separation of abstract labor and value from concrete labor and use value) is analogous to the objective functioning of political abstraction (as the concealment of social differences, and as the separation of the political state of citizens from the civil society of bourgeois man).

On the other hand, we can add that the problem of political abstraction, as it founds the modern political juridical subject in its formal freedom and equality, will appear later in the mature economic studies. In effect, the juridical freedom of workers as free men constitutes the premise for the formation of a labor market, in which the abstraction of their concrete differences is produced insofar as they are bearers of an "equal" substance (labor power). In the same way, the sphere of commodity exchange necessarily presupposes that the subjects are formally equal before the law. The free worker as a possessor of labor power and the capitalist, despite all their differences, find themselves as two abstractly equal subjects within the exchange relation: they are equals as commodities owners.[50] Thus, there is an intimate connection between the characteristics of political abstraction and the logic of capitalist social relationships.

That does not imply a new form of "subsumption" of the understanding of the political under the economic. Instead, it contributes towards reconfiguring the two fields of problems within a shared and broader framework: that of the social forms proper to modernity.

However, beyond these approximations, no hasty conclusions should be drawn in this regard. There is undoubtedly an affinity between the different treatments of the concept of abstraction in the various stages of Marx's thought, but it does not follow that the notion of "political abstraction" formulated in the *Critique* is equivalent to the "abstraction of the value form" present in *Capital*. Despite these reservations, we can conclude by addressing the implications of the concept of "political abstraction" for the Marxist theory of the state.

49 See Marx, "The Fetichismus of the Commoditie and Its Secret," in *Capital*, pp. 163–177.

50 See Marx, *Capital*, p. 280.

9 From Political Abstraction to the Marxist Theory of the State

The Soviet jurist Evgene Pashukanis summarizes the central question for a Marxist theory of the state as follows:

> Why does class rule not remain what it is, the factual subjugation of one section of the population by the other? Why does it assume the form of official state rule, or—which is the same thing—why does the machinery of state coercion not come into being as the private machinery of the ruling class: why does it detach itself from the ruling class and take on the form of an impersonal apparatus of public power, separate from society?[51]

For the reasons mentioned at the beginning of this article, it is evident that Marx's youthful reflections contained in the *Critique* cannot give a systematic answer to this question. However, it is relevant to note that in his critique of Hegel, Marx identifies the process of abstraction as a process inherent to modern politics. Thus, the separation between society and state does not respond to a phenomenon of "alienation" of consciousness but expresses the objective forms of the structuring of the political in modern society. Insofar as the political is "abstracted" from society, it generates an autonomous dimension that allows for its specific level of analysis.

Therefore, this concept of political abstraction can be linked to the more elaborate contributions that, within later Marxist thought, attempted to develop the elements for a theorization of the state. In the following paragraphs, we will limit ourselves to presenting some possible avenues of research on these links, which are not without their difficulties.

First, we can emphasize that abstraction implies the development of a universality that dispenses with the particular elements from which it is abstracted. The abstraction of the state as a modern mode of political domination implies the subsumption of the particularities of civil society. Analogously, the Gramscian concept of hegemony supposes a logic of abstraction as its critique of the instrumental conception requires the construction of a hegemonic gaze. In turn, this involves the articulation of heterogeneous aspirations and wills, which could not develop without a process of universalization. A group, to become hegemonic, must be abstracted from its social particularity to offer a political universality to the whole.

51 Evgeny Pashukanis, *The General Theory of Law and Marxism*, trans. by Barbara Einhorn, New Brunswick and London: Transaction Publishers 2003, p. 139.

This family relationship between "abstraction" in Marx and "hegemony" in Gramsci does not, however, preclude there being other theoretical tensions to resolve. For example, where Marx emphasizes the separate character of state and society, Gramsci proposes a concept of the "extended state," which synthesizes society and the state apparatus.

Secondly, the concept of "political abstraction" can be related to the Poulantzian notion of "autonomy of politics." Indeed, the whole of Poulantzas' argument rests on the autonomization of the instances of politics and economics as the distinctive mark of domination in modern society, an autonomization that rests on the process Marx conceptualizes as the "abstraction of state." For his part, Poulantzas considers that the separation between civil society and state presented in the *Critique* are not homologous to the separation between the instances that he proposes. However, as we have seen, his argument rests on a mistaken interpretation of the influence of Feuerbach's ideas on Marx. Therefore, it is possible to explore a connection between both concepts: the Marxian idea of "abstraction of the state" may be functioning as the condition for the Poulantzian notion of "autonomy of the political."

Finally, the arguments about the state "derivation," which consider political domination and economic exploitation as two modes of expression of the same set of social relations specific to modernity, can also be articulated with the notion of "political abstraction." Joam Hirsch, the main exponent of this current, maintains,

> The social character of human beings is externalized, on the other hand, in social forms separate from them.... The two basic social forms in which social interrelation in capitalism is objectified are value, which is expressed in money, and the political form, which is expressed in the existence of a state separate from society.[52]

The contributions made in the framework of the discussion of state derivation are probably those that can be most directly articulated with Marx's argument about the "abstraction of the state." The separation of a proper field of political domination within capitalism not only supposes separation with respect to economic relations but also the abstraction of legal equality and political freedom of citizenship with respect to the relations of economic exploitation and subjection of individuals.

52 Joam Hirsch, *El Estado nacional de competencia. Estado, democracia y política en el capitalismo global*, Mexico City: Universidad Autónoma Metropolitana 2001, p. 34.

These are only hints of possible lines of research in this direction. Thus, whether by linking with the notion of hegemony or problematizing the concept of the extended state, illuminating the separation of economics and politics, or connecting with the idea of state derivation, the concept of political abstraction can be connected with these current lines of research within the field of Marxist reflection.

This article began by affirming that it is possible to develop a theoretical reflection on the state from the coordinates of Marxist thought. For our part, we maintain that this task is key to fresh development in the social sciences and political philosophy. Thus, despite the limitations of the early text in which the concept appears, it is possible to affirm that the concept of political abstraction can contribute to Marxist reflection on the state. At the same time, it is possible to articulate this concept with the most elaborate developments within this field of research. Furthermore, it is reasonable to consider that this is not the case of an isolated concept. On the contrary, we can suppose that there is in Marx's less visited works a source of concepts that can be articulated with the theoretical demands of the present, opening new spaces for reflection. Thus, the possible articulations presented here are briefly suggested in such a way as to lay the groundwork for future research.

Bibliography

Abensour, Miguel, *La dèmocratie contre l'Ètat. Marx et le moment machiavélien*, Paris: Presses Universitaires de France 1997.

Althusser, Louis and Balibar, Étienne, *Lire le capital*, Paris: Maspero 1967.

Althusser, Louis, *On the Reproduction of Capitalism: Ideology and Ideological State Apparatuses*, trans. by G.M. Goshgarian, London: Verso 2014.

Althusser, Louis, *Pour Marx*, Paris: Maspero 1965.

Althusser, Louis, *Marx dentro de sus límites*, ed. by García del Campo, trans. by Beñat Baltza Álvarez, Sánchez Cedillo and García del Campo, Madrid: Akal 2003.

Artous, Antoine, *Marx, el Estado y la política*, trans. by Tomás Callegary and Jonathan Rocca Funes, Barcelona: Sylone 2016.

Balibar, Étienne, "The Notion of Class Politics in Marx," *Rethinking Marxism*, vol. 1, no. 2, 1988, pp. 18–51.

Bobbio, Norberto, "Esiste una dottrina marxista dello Stato?" *Mondoperaio*, no. 8–9, 1976, pp. 24–31.

Bobio, Norberto, *Ni con Marx ni contra Marx*, trans by. L.C. Levi and I.R. Alvarado, Mexico City: Fondo de Cultura Económica 1999.

Bonnet, Alberto and Piva, Adrián (eds.), *Estado y capital. El debate alemán sobre la derivación del Estado*, Buenos Aires: Herramienta 2017.

Borón, Atilio, Amadeo, Javier and Gonzalez, Sabrina (eds.), *La teoría marxista hoy. Problemas y perspectivas*, Buenos Aires: CLACSO 2006.

Della Volpe, Galvano, *Rousseau e Marx, e altri saggi di critica materialistica*, Rome: Riunitini 1997.

Dotti, Jorge, *Dialéctica y derecho*, Buenos Aires: Hachette 1983.

Eidelman, Ariel, "El joven Marx y el debate del Estado moderno, 1842–1848," *Hic Rhodus. Crisis capitalista, polémica y controversias*, no. 4, 2013, pp. 1–11.

Feuerbach, Ludwig, "Preliminary Theses on the Reform of Philosophy," in *The Fiery Brook: Selected Writings. Ludwig Feuerbach*, trans. by Zawar Hanfi, London and New York: Verso 2012, pp. 153–176.

Gramsci, Antonio, *El Risorgimiento*, Buenos Aires: Las Cuarenta 2008.

Gramsci, Antonio, *Cuadernos de la cárcel*, vol. 3, México City: ERA 1984.

Gramsci, Antonio, *Cuadernos de la cárcel*, vol. 5, Mexico City and Puebla: ERA 1999.

Hirsch, Joam, *El Estado nacional de competencia. Estado, democracia y política en el capitalismo global*, Mexico City: Universidad Autónoma Metropolitana 2001.

Holloway, John and Picciotto, Sol (eds.), *State and Capital: A Marxist Debate*, London: Edward Arnold 1978.

Lefort, Claude, *L'invention démocratique*, Paris: Fayard 1981.

Marx, Karl, *A Contribution to the Critique of Political Economy*, Beijing: Foreign Languages Press 1976.

Marx, Karl, *Capital: A Critique of Political Economy*, trans. by Ben Fowkes, London and New York: Penguin Books in association with New Left Review 1982.

Marx, Karl, *Critique of Hegel's Philosophy of Right*, trans. by Annette Jolin and Joseph O'Malley, New York: Cambridge University Press 1982.

Marx, Karl, *Cuadernos de París [Notas de lectura de 1844]*, trans. by Bolivar Echeverría, Mexico City: Ediciones ERA 1974.

Marx, Karl, *Grundrisse*, trans. by Martin Nicolaus, New York: Random House 1973.

Miliband, Ralph, *The State in Capitalist Society*, London: Weidenfeld & Nicolson 1969.

Moreno Tonda, Daniel, "El Manuscrito De Kreuznach," *Antítesis. Revista Iberoamericana De Estudios Hegelianos*, no. 1, 2021, pp. 111–138.

Pashukanis, Evgeny, *The General Theory of Law and Marxism*, trans. by Barbara Einhorn, New Brunswick and London: Transaction Publishers 2003.

Poulantzas, Nicos, "Estudio de la hegemonía en el Estado" and "Marx y el derecho moderno" in Poulantzas, Nicos, *Hegemonía y dominación en el Estado Moderno*, trans. by María T. Poyrazán, México: Ediciones Pasado y Presente 1986, pp. 36–86 and 109–130.

Poulantzas, Nicos, *State, Power, Socialism*, London and New York: Verso 2000.

Poulantzas, Nicos, *Political Power and Social Classes*, trans. by Timothy O'Hagan, London: NLB 1975.

Rocca, Facundo, "El Manuscrito de Kreuznach 1843. Crítica de la filosofía del Estado de Hegel," *Hic Rhodus. Crisis capitalista, polémica y controversia*, no. 16, 2019, pp. 99–107.

Rubel, Maximilien, *Karl Marx, ensayo de biografía intelectual*, trans. by Saul Karsz, Buenos Aires: Paidos 1970.

Sanchez Vazquez, Adolfo, *Filosofía de la praxis*, Mexico City: Siglo XXI 2003.

Sohn Rethel, Alfred, *Intellectual and Manual Labor*, trans. by Martin Sohn Rethel, London and Basingstoke: Macmillan Press 1978.

Stewart, Jon, *Hegel's Century: Alienation and Recognition in a Time of Revolution*, Cambridge: Cambridge University Press 2021.

Tarcus, Horacio (ed.), *Debates sobre el estado capitalista 1*, Buenos Aires: Imago mundo 1991.

Index of Names

Index of Subjects

Printed in the United States
by Baker & Taylor Publisher Services